MORE [illegible] FOR THIS SERIES

"If any American doesn't already own a good, comprehensive work on World War II, this is the book he or she should buy."

—*St. Petersburg Times*

"Oral history at its very best."

—*BookPage*

"Vivid, frank eyewitness accounts . . . a most impressive tribute."

—*World War II* magazine

"**A sweeping, imaginative oral history** . . . succeeds by the thoughtful coupling of a narrative that touches on most of the war's most important engagements with the reminiscences of hundreds of participants. . . . Astor offers the most salient facts in what otherwise could have been an overwhelming mass of detail. He also turns up some surprises. Invaluable to historians, with much to interest general readers as well."

—*Kirkus Reviews* (starred review)

"Will make you feel as though you were there in the midst of the fighting. A moving account . . . remarkable."

—*West Orange Times*

more . . .

"Strong, effective, absorbing . . . a genuine tour de force . . . brilliant text and breathless pace . . . stimulating and down-to-earth. . . . My compliments and congratulations go, with great admiration, to Gerald Astor."

—Martin Blumenson, author of *The Battle of the Generals*, from his review in *Parameters* magazine

"Astor succeeds admirably, creating the finest . . . oral history available of the American soldier in World War II. . . . Well-chosen entries . . . fast-paced, smoothly flowing narrative. . . . Astor has written the first oral history to include all of the services and theaters of the war. Highly recommended."

—*Library Journal* (starred review)

"A remarkable job of weaving together an extraordinary amount of oral evidence with more traditional narrative, turning out a quite readable seamless treatment of the war . . . a valuable addition to the literature of the war."

—*New York Military Affairs Symposium (NYMAS) Newsletter*

"If you want to buy your grandchildren a gift they will remember, spend the money for this living reference book."

—*Veterans Voice of Austin*

THE GREATEST WAR

VOLUME III

THE BATTLE OF THE BULGE TO HIROSHIMA

GERALD ASTOR

An AOL Time Warner Company

WARNER BOOKS EDITION

This Warner books edition is published by arrangement with Presidio Press.

Cover design by Jerry Pfiefer
Cover flag photo by Philip James Corwin/Corbis
Cover inset by U.S. Army Signal Core

Warner Books, Inc.
1271 Avenue of the Americas
New York, NY 10020

Visit our Web site at
www.twbookmark.com.

For information on Time Warner Trade Publishing's online publishing program, visit www.ipublish.com.

 An AOL Time Warner Company

Printed in the United States of America

First Warner Books Printing: November 2001

10 9 8 7 6 5 4 3 2 1

For the late Donald I. Fine

Contents

PREFACE

When I told Gen. George Ruhlen that I intended to write a book covering the battles fought by Americans during World War II, he wrote to me, "How many pages are you projecting, 5,000 or squeeze it into 3,000?" His comment was well taken, for an encyclopedic account of what happened to Americans in World War II would require many volumes and in fact the historian Samuel Eliot Morison produced something on the nature of twenty books covering just the engagements of the Navy and the Marines.

However, my intention was not to cover the war from objective to objective nor was it to describe the details of strategy and tactics. I freely confess that, even in an oversize manuscript, I have omitted many hard-fought battles, units, and individuals who underwent the same hardships, terror, and sorrow, and who, in spite of their ordeals, overcame. Instead I hope to present a sense of what the American fighting man (women in World War II were restricted to clerical and service positions although as the book indicates, some nurses underwent much of what the men did) experienced in terms of what he thought, felt, saw, heard, and tried to do. Words on a page cannot match those moments under fire but by their own voices the soldiers, sailors, and airmen reveal the nature of that war well beyond anything shown in films or TV, except perhaps for *Saving Private Ryan.* (Even here one might quibble about the premise upon which the story unfolds.)

Having written six books on World War II, I am well aware that eyewitness accounts or oral histories have their weaknesses due to faulty memories, skewed perspectives, and the common human resort to self-service. On the other hand, these same deficiencies also afflict official reports. In his letter to me, George Ruhlen remarked that a friend of his named Brewster commanded a task force whose mission was to regain possession of a crossroads during the Battle of the Bulge. "Some 20 accounts were written by 'historians' who were never there, most inaccurate, but only one writer ever contacted Colonel Brewster for his recollection of that action."

I expect there will be some who will dispute an individual's version of some events in this book, but I believe that by relying on as many sources and veterans as I have the essential truth of the experiences is correct. Although many of the sensations and the reactions of those on the scenes seem similar—the most replicated comment was "Suddenly, all hell broke loose" there were significant differences from year to year, from campaign to campaign, from area to area.

It was the biggest of all wars and those who fought the battles deserve to be heard.

ACKNOWLEDGMENTS

So many people have shared their memories and experiences with me that I cannot cite them individually. Their words are credited to them in the text and to some extent through Roll Call.

I received special help from Paul Stillwell of the United States Naval Institute in Annapolis; Joseph Caver of the United States Air Force Historical Research Center at Maxwell Field, Alabama; Dr. David Keough at the United States Army History Library at Carlisle Barracks, Pennsylvania; the United States Naval Historical Center; Debbie Pogue at the United States Military Academy Library; Jim Altieri; William Cain; Tracy Derks; Len Lomell; Benjamin Mabry; Jason Poston.

Small portions of this book appeared in some of my previous writings on World War II.

1

Silent Service, Peleliu, Mars

ALTHOUGH THE JAPANESE ATTACK AT PEARL HARBOR SHATtered most of the Pacific fleet, no bombs blasted the U.S. submarine fleet. Admiral Stark ordered the submarines, along with other naval units, to execute unrestricted warfare upon enemy shipping. The early, swift Japanese conquests wiped out precious fuel depots and torpedo stores, but the main problem lay in the quality of the American sub fleet, its armament, and the thinking of the day. A substantial number of the undersea vessels on duty in 1941 were obsolete. Defective torpedo mechanisms plagued the undersea warriors for two years. Although a modernized building program had begun late in the 1930s, some pigboats dated from another era. S-class boats lacked air conditioning and sailors sweated out a stifling atmosphere during patrols in tropical zones. The elderly subs fired a World War I–vintage Mark X torpedo that swam at a maximum thirty-six knots, slow enough for enemy ships to evade them. The newer model submarines used the faster, longer-range Mark XIV which, to save money, and perhaps for security purposes, had never been test-fired with its detonator set to explode a warhead. During the first two years the torpedoes frequently failed to explode, even as exasperated submariners heard them clunk against an enemy hull or saw them run deeper than directed. Not until 1943 did the Navy correct the problems of depth mechanisms and detonators.

Pre–Pearl Harbor tactics called for submarines to hug the bottom, out of earshot of the the sound-detecting sonar, and out of sight of air patrols able to spot objects 125 feet deep in the clear Pacific waters. The concern for safety canceled out effective attacks, which were based upon the submarine's less exact sonar rather than its eye, the periscope. Too little periscope experience and a lack of night surface practice, plus an absence of tactical intelligence and aerial reconnaissance, seriously handicapped U.S. submarines during the early war years.

Naval Academy graduate Slade Cutter, after observing the destruction at Pearl Harbor, was the navigation officer aboard the *Pompano* as it carried the war to Japan. On the first cruise toward Wake Island, a PBY spotted the sub. There were no recognition signals and, Cutter explained, "You were on your own and you expected to be attacked by any aircraft." The PBY relayed information about the unidentified submarine and planes from the *Enterprise* actually bombed and slightly damaged the *Pompano*. It continued its patrol until it saw a big transport, a former luxury liner, *Kamakuru Maru*. "We reported sinking it, because we heard the hits, and saw the splash of water. Lew Parks [his skipper] assumed it was going to be sunk. When we came up there was no *Kamakura Maru* around. She had just bailed out, hadn't been hurt at all. Two duds bounced against her and caused the splashes which Parks took to be hits."

Unlike a number of the American submarine commanders early in the war, Parks was anything but timid. He insisted on driving the *Pompano* dangerously close to breakwaters for enemy-controlled harbors. But as navigator, Cutter said he was handicapped by turn-of-the-century charts that could be in error plus or minus five miles. At one point, a pair of Japanese destroyers started to prowl the waters, possibly suspecting the presence of the *Pompano*. "Parks maneuvered all day long, trying to get in position to hit them, but they never settled down to get a good firing position. Finally, in desperation, he decided to shoot. He took a sixty-degree gyro angle, which was much too much for those torpedoes at that time. I was on the TDC [torpedo data computer] and got from Parks,' Range 1,200 yards, speed 25 . . . 'I put on the solution light, 'Fire!' We fired both torpedoes and both of them prematured. About this time Parks said, 'Slade, did you ever have so much fun before with your clothes on?' Over the loudspeaker system.

"I wasn't worrying about having fun with clothes on or off at that stage of the game. Looking at this thing on the torpedo data computer, this target at 1,200 yards would be over [us] in a minute or so. He came and that's the first depth charge we ever heard. We had never had one fired in practice. I didn't know what they sounded like. A barrage came over and I knew what it was like to face death right then because we heard the water rushing through the superstructure. We learned later that is normal but we thought we had been holed. I figured that's the end and you don't feel anything. We realized very shortly that we hadn't been holed. Lew Parks maneuvered the submarine around, all ahead full, starboard back full and port ahead full, to evade those guys up above dropping their depth charges. Then he shifted to hand steering to reduce our ship's noise and had two men turning the steering wheel by hand. That was our baptism of depth charges. Parks thoroughly enjoyed it. He was having a hell of a time. After that, every time we went out on patrol, one of the prepatrol training exercises was to have a destroyer drop one or two depth charges 100 yards away so everybody could hear what they sounded like."

On the *Pompano*'s second voyage, it ventured into the China Sea. "We were on the surface one night," said Cutter, "and we picked up a contact. We shut off our engines and put our stern toward it. We didn't want to be picked up but the contact saw us and turned toward us. Parks sent for me to man the .50-caliber machine gun that we had aft and I got the thing ready.

" 'Put it on them,' he said. We made another course change and the guy turned toward us again. Parks said, 'Let him have it.' That's what he would say instead of 'commence fire.' I pulled the trigger. They had tracers on and were going right into it; I guess he was about 300 yards. It was a fishing boat, good size, probably twenty men aboard. After the first burst of probably fifty rounds, a guy held up a lantern to show the rising sun on their flag. He thought we were the Japs. The captain said, 'Let them have it,' so I opened up again and we just kept firing. Finally the thing caught fire. I guess the tracers set off the fuel and it burned. We got out of there. It was a fisherman. I think about it lots of times. That's one of the terrible things of war. He was harmless."

Parks left the *Pompano* and Lt. Comdr. Willis Thomas succeeded him. On 9 August 1942, the sub sneaked near the entrance to Tokyo Bay. An intercept of Japanese naval transmissions indicated ships would be coming through their area. "It was after sunset and I looked through the periscope and thought it looked dark," remembered Cutter. "You can't tell because you don't get much light transmission through a periscope, not as much as through binoculars. We got on the surface and, my God, we thought we were naked. It was daylight. Since we were on the surface and nobody was around, we thought we would wait it out because it was going to be dark in a little while.

"All of a sudden, on the starboard quarter, searchlights illuminated us and six shells came out from two 8-inch turrets. A cruiser fired at us. They went over. We didn't stay to see the next salvo. We got under, and the destroyers came and they worked us over. The battery was down because we had been bucking the current all day, all we could do was dive, go down there and hope to God they weren't lucky. We couldn't take much evasive action. We didn't have enough battery for it. We couldn't run our pumps for fear the Japs would hear them because they made a hell of a lot of noise. Water was coming in aft through the inboard exhaust valve, leaking from the engine room, and flooding the engine room bilges. The main generators were attached to the engines so water got up into the generators. The *Pompano* was 252 feet test-depth. We got down to 407 feet and there were all these crackling sounds. The cork started to buckle loose on the bulkheads.

"All of a sudden they left us, lost contact, I guess, and they were gone. I was navigator and had no idea at all where we were. The captain blew all main ballast in order to come to the surface. I was the first one out; I don't know what I was looking for [as navigator] but I was the first out of the hatch. I looked up and Jesus, here was what I thought was a searchlight right on us. I said, 'Oh, shit!' which is a good expression under the circumstances. I thought it was a cruiser with that searchlight high above us. It was the Mikomoto Light [a Japanese lighthouse]." The submarine slowly limped away;

only two of its four engines started and with the fuel pumps grounded out by the water leaks the *Pompano* could not afford to dive. The crew improvised, taking a working motor from one device to drive the fuel pumps, slowly building a battery charge, and repairing damage with the mechanical ingenuity that came from years of submarine duty.

Promoted to executive officer on the *Seahorse,* now under Lt. Commander Donald McGregor, Cutter left Pearl Harbor for a patrol around the Palau Islands. A frustrated Cutter recalled, "One night off Toagel Mlungui Pass in Palau, we picked up a convoy coming out. They had a big, three-stack transport, about 15,000 tons. It was heavily escorted and they were heading toward the Philippines. They went past us. We could have attacked but we didn't. That was all right with me. The captain said, 'We'll get more of them on the surface at night. If we attack now, they will hold us down and we'll lose them.' So we surfaced and got way ahead of them. The captain went into the wardroom and there he stayed. He let me maneuver and stay ahead.

"I kept going down to tell him, 'Captain, we are in position to dive.' He delayed it. There was a quarter moon. Finally, I said, 'Captain, it's getting toward daylight, we'd better dive now. The moon is going down.' He hadn't even dark adapted, didn't have on red goggles, which you were supposed to wear at night. He was just sitting there in a lighted room. [Ultimately] I said, 'The moon is set, Captain. It's two hours before sunrise. We've got to go now.'

"He said, 'All right, dive.' We dove and he came to the conning tower, not dark adapted, put up the periscope, and said, 'I can't see anything. Take her down.' We went to 300 feet and the convoy went right over us and we didn't do a thing about it. It was terrible. We let them get away. I was sick. We surfaced and again he went below." For several more hours, the *Seahorse* tracked the enemy ships, maintaining visual contact through the periscope. Having been on duty for twenty-four hours without sleep, Cutter yielded his post to another deck officer who awakened him with the news that they had lost contact. The skipper had changed course, sending a message to Pacific submarine command reporting the breakoff from the quarry being pursued. A curt response ordered the *Seahorse* to resume its stalking at the Toagel Mlungui Pass.

According to Cutter, "We ran into an unescorted tanker coming out of Palau. He was 150 to 200 miles off the coast, no escorts, no planes. We picked it up at about 10,000 yards. The officer at the periscope sent for me instead of the captain. I took a look and said, 'Right full rudder, all ahead two-thirds. I took another look and we were about 2,500 yards off the track, range 10,000 yards. We were in a beautiful spot. All we had to do was keep coming around, get ourselves on a 90-degree track, go dead slow speed, and wait for him to come on. We were going to fire at about 800 yards, like shooting fish in a barrel. This guy wasn't zigging, a big ship. I sent for the captain and told him the situation. After we had steadied course for a 90-degree track shot, he said, 'Right full rudder, all ahead two-thirds.' I said 'Captain, what are you doing?'

" 'I'm coming around for a stern tube shot. I want to give the after room some practice.' We hadn't given the forward room any practice yet. I couldn't believe it. By God, we opened out and fired four stern torpedoes at a range of 4,500 yards instead of 800. They were steam torpedoes. The guy saw the wakes and he maneuvered to avoid. I couldn't believe my ears again. [McGregor] said, 'Make ready the bow tubes, set all torpedoes on low power.' That gave about a 9,000-yard run at twenty-seven knots as opposed to forty-seven knots at 6,500 yards. By God, he came around again and here is this tanker going with a 180-degree angle on the bow—in other words we were looking up his rear end and we fired six torpedoes. They were smoking along and this guy was making about 15 knots and the torpedoes could never catch him. There went six more torpedoes down the tube. I couldn't believe it. We had wasted ten precious torpedoes."

The disastrously nonproductive excursion of the *Seahorse* required explanation to the sub command. While the *Seahorse* sailed back to Midway after fifty-five days at sea with zero results, McGregor drafted a patrol account to exonerate his performance, politely relieved Cutter of his duties, and filed an unsatisfactory fitness report on him. Cutter for his part wrote a letter putting his superior on report for his behavior. The submarine command identified McGregor as the real culprit for the *Seahorse*'s failures. McGregor was only one of a number of overage sub commanders unsuitable for their posts. Another skipper adamantly refused to rise to periscope depth to attack enemy destroyers that were oblivious to the sub's presence. A third, during an engagement, locked himself in his stateroom and told his second in command to take charge.

When the *Seahorse* tied up at Midway, a radio dispatch sacked McGregor, elevating Cutter to the top position. With Cutter in command the *Seahorse* put to sea. Unknown to him, on the trip back to Midway, McGregor had disparaged him to the crew who, as a result, had zero confidence in him. "He [McGregor] said words like, 'He isn't in his right mind.' That I was nuts. I never found that out until much later. Those kids were loyal. They didn't say anything about the captain." The chief of the boat, the top enlisted man in a submarine, who is sort of an assistant executive officer, informed Cutter that if they had been anywhere else but Midway, half of the crew would have gone AWOL. But since there was no place to go, they remained with the sub."

The *Seahorse*, led by a skipper desperate to prove himself to his people, entered enemy waters. "The first thing we ran into were some fishing boats, trawlers. They had about fifteen to twenty men aboard, pretty good-size ships. We were told to knock them off because they were supposed to serve dual purposes, fishing and outpost. This was after the Jimmy Doolittle 1942 raid; supposedly they had all these boats out there with radios. I didn't like the idea of attacking what I thought was an unarmed ship." Whatever Cutter's preferences, as the commander, he felt obliged to obey an imperative that declared, "You shall attack all enemy ships encountered with either gunfire or torpedoes." Dutifully, the *Seahorse* knocked off three such vessels.

"There were no survivors," remembered Cutter. "I said, 'Goddamn it! I'm not going to do this anymore.' We moved into the area where we were firing torpedoes and it was sort of forgotten." With his boat now lurking off the Japanese-controlled Tsushima Strait, Cutter said, "We got desperate—we had to sink some ships. I was chicken about going in there until I just had to. I figured if we picked up a convoy and followed it in, it wouldn't go through mineable waters. We decided to go at night on the surface so we would not have to dive where the mines might be at about 150 feet. We'd follow them in, and after we made the attack, come out the way we went in. We sank a tanker that disintegrated in a tremendous explosion. They were carrying gasoline."

The submarine also blasted a second tanker, and then as they sailed back toward the open sea a destroyer noticed them. "He started signaling us, sending a recognition signal. All we had left were the torpedoes aft, so I made a 180-

degree turn and fired as soon as we steadied up. I had to fire at long range, a torpedo run of 4,200 yards. We bailed out of there at full speed and I called for a cameraman to come up and take a picture. If this thing went, I wanted to see it. I was starting to swear because so much time had gone by. It seemed forever. At 47 knots, for 4,000 yards it took about two or three minutes. Finally, the kids below heard it, which you always did through the water—an explosion hit. I heard the cheering from below so I knew we hit him and then fingers of flame ran the whole length of that ship. Red flames came out. All of a sudden it went up just like a huge mushroom, sort of a dark beige, lighted from beneath, I guess. That thing hung there in the air and in the end turned into a brilliant blue white. You could read a newspaper. We saw pieces of this ship falling into the ocean. We were then more than two miles away."

When the *Seahorse* came back to Pearl Harbor, Cutter raised the subject of the fishing boats with Adm. Charles Lockwood, commander of all submarines in the Pacific. "I said, 'Admiral, I sank three of these things with gunfire. Jeez, it was just murder. We went aboard one before we sank it and there were fifteen- and sixteen-year-old kids aboard. What would you do?'

"He said, 'Slade, let your conscience be your guide,' a hell of an answer. I said, 'I'm not going to attack any more.' " While at Pearl Harbor, Cutter was asked by Comdr. Richard Voge, Pacific submarine operations officer, where he would like to go on his next voyage. Mindful of the missed opportunities with the convoy at Toagel Mlungui, Cutter answered, "The *Seahorse* has unfinished business down in Palau. I want to go back there." He noted, "[Voge] held the area open for six days to let us get in. It was another hot area [where they] wanted a submarine there all the time. We never got there. We picked up a convoy before we got there and messed around with it, got a couple of ships."

Still bent on revenge at Palau, Cutter, as the result of intelligence intercepts on Japanese naval traffic, sought out another convoy and the encounter evolved into a prolonged epic. "I was in the conning tower 82 hours and 33 minutes except for when I went down to the toilet, never changed clothes. I was in pajamas when I was called to the conning tower and I was in pajamas when it was all over 82 hours later. It was a terrible strain. I lived on benzedrine. You get along on benzedrine. We couldn't get in good position until the last day and we sank two of them on the final attack. Our torpedoes were gone and we headed for home. We sank only three ships—should have done better than that but it was pretty heavily escorted. I was exhausted. The crew was wiped out, too. We dove, leveled off, and everybody was secured except the bare watch just to keep the submarine going." Cutter, however, could not fall asleep, even though he downed a pint of whiskey and swallowed sleeping pills. He gradually wound down while the *Seahorse*, empty of torpedoes, combed the ocean near Wake Island to act as a lifeguard for downed bombers.

He took the *Seahorse* out for one more patrol. It was while on this voyage that Cutter observed a portion of the Japanese fleet bearing down on the Marianas. After five tours, Cutter was rotated back to the States. Upon completion of leave he waited out the construction and commission of a new submarine, *Requin.* Submarines skippered by Cutter accounted for nineteen confirmed vessels sunk, making him tied with Dudley "Mush" Morton of the *Wahoo*, who disappeared with his sub, and second only to Richard O'Kane's twenty-four on the *Tang*. O'Kane became a POW after an errant torpedo ran in a circle, blasting the sub, while it was on station in the Formosa Strait.

The gathering momentum of the march toward the Japanese homeland at sea, in the air, and on land induced one of more egregious errors of the campaign, the invasion of Peleliu, a six-mile-long, two-mile-wide island in the Palau group. Nimitz disregarded Halsey's advice and insisted his command using the 1st Marine Division would invade Peleliu, site of an enemy airfield. Not only was Peleliu of dubious strategic importance but the intelligence gathered on its terrain and garrison proved appallingly wrong. Thick scrub hid the tortuous surface from aerial observation and photos. Major General William Rupertus of the 1st Marine Division confidently predicted conquest within four days. He apparently had no inkling of the resolve of the 15,000 defenders hunkered down in the usual honeycomb of caves dug into the soft coral of the atoll.

In December 1942, E. B. Sledge, an Alabamian who chose to drop out of the Marine Corps V-12 officer-training program, attended boot camp before assignment as a replacement to Company K, 3d Battalion, 5th Marines, 1st Marine Division. On the island of Pavuvu he studied the trade of a 60mm mortar man while gaining insights into the attitudes of his fellows. "A passionate hatred for the Japanese burned through all Marines I knew. The fate of the Goettge patrol was the sort of thing that spawned such hatred." (The Guadalcanal patrol was led into ambush by a Japanese prisoner.) Sledge also said the enemy tactic of feigning death or injury and then attacking a medic, along with memories of the raid on Pearl Harbor, inflamed Marines.

According to Sledge, "We had been told that the 1st Marine Division would be reinforced to about 28,000 men for the assault on Peleliu. As every man in the ranks knew, however, a lot of these people included in the term *reinforced* were neither trained nor equipped as combat troops. They were specialists attached to the division. . . . They would not be doing the fighting." In addition to the leathernecks, the Army's 81st Division would be involved.

From his place in the amtrac bouncing on the water, a nauseated Sledge saw an inferno envelop the beach as the fleet offshore bombarded the strand. Around him great gouts of water spouted from missiles fired by Japanese guns. Then the American shells moved deeper into the island as the landing craft's moment arrived. Sledge wrote in *With the Old Breed*, "My heart pounded. Our amtrac came out of the water and moved a few yards up the gently sloping sand. 'Hit the beach!' yelled an NCO moments before the machine lurched to a stop. The men piled over the sides as fast as they could. I followed Snafu (a fellow leatherneck), climbed up, and planted both feet firmly on the left side so as to leap as far away from it as possible. At that instant a burst of machine-gun fire with white-hot tracers snapped through the air at eye level, almost grazing my face. I pulled my head back like a turtle, lost my balance, and fell awkwardly forward down onto the sand in a tangle of ammo bag, pack, helmet, carbine, gas mask, cartridge belt, and flopping canteens. 'Get off the beach! Get off the beach!' raced through my mind.' "

After falling in the sand, Sledge regained his feet, then scuttled across the strand while enemy guns scoured the beach. The entrenched defenders had recovered from the shock of the preinvasion barrages. When the young Marine glanced back, he saw a DUKW disintegrate into pieces of metal from a direct hit. No men left the shattered amphibian. "I caught a fleeting glimpse of a group of Marines leaving a smoking amtrac on the reef. Some fell as bullets and fragments splashed among them. Their buddies tried to help them as they struggled in the knee-deep water.

"I shuddered and choked. A wild desperate feeling of anger, frustration, and pity gripped me. It was an emotion that always would torture my mind when I saw men trapped and was unable to do anything but watch as they were hit. My own plight forgotten momentarily, I felt sickened to the depths of my soul. I asked God, 'Why, why, why?' I turned my face away and wished that I was imagining it all. I had tasted the bitterest essence of war, the sight of helpless comrades being slaughtered, and it filled me with disgust."

Crouching low, Sledge ran across the sand; one foot barely missed a pressure plate set to trigger a huge mine. He joined men from his company as they were pinned down by a torrent of mortars and machine-gun fire. Haplessly, the Marines burrowed into craters where they sweated, prayed, and cursed the enemy. "Under my first barrage since the fast-moving events of hitting the beach, I learned a new sensation; utter and absolute helplessness." When the shelling waned he saw walking wounded making their way back to the beach. A friend with a bloody dressing on his arm paused to brag, " 'I got the million-dollar wound. It's all over for me.' We waved as he hurried on out of the war."

He soon saw his first dead enemy, stared in horror at the glistening viscera of a ripped-open stomach. Almost in a trance he watched veterans come along and strip the corpses of souvenirs, spectacles, a flag, a pistol, and other items. He later became inured to the sight of Marines routinely, methodically looting bodies, extracting gold teeth—in one instance, from a badly wounded but still living soldier. A few yards from his introduction to that behavior Sledge noticed a medic beside a dead leatherneck. "The corpsman held the dead Marine's chin tenderly between the thumb and fingers of his left hand and made the sign of the cross with his right hand. Tears streamed down his dusty, tanned, grief-contorted face while he sobbed quietly."

The attacking forces slowly overwhelmed the defenders closest to the shoreline. Japanese soldiers tried to flee and riflemen cut them down as they bolted from a mangrove swamp or from behind rocks. As a mortar man, armed with a carbine which was ineffective at the distance from the foe, Sledge did not fire. "We headed into the thick scrub. . . . I completely lost my bearings and had no idea where we were going." The dense vegetation concealed trails, hid snipers, and denied contact among units. In contrast with previous engagements, the Japanese on Peleliu abandoned the usual concentration of forces at water's edge to build a formidable defense in depth.

Ed Andrusko, recovered from his New Britain wound, said, "Our company was in the first wave landing on Peleliu. During the amphibious landing, enemy shells burst near our tractor. We received incoming shells starting at the reef, across the harbor, and on the beach. We were pinned down on the beach for some time. When we finally advanced inland, I stepped on a land mine. While others were killed, I was wounded in the legs and back and evacuated to a hospital ship." His was not quite a million-dollar wound; he would recover and return. But he escaped the carnage that followed in the days immediately after the initial landings.

A former drill instructor, Jim Moll, early in 1944, as a buck sergeant, joined A/1/7, Able Company, 1st Battalion, 7th Marine Regiment. Moll recalled, "My first taste of combat was Peleliu. We went in on a Higgins boat, which meant we had to climb over the sides—later models of landing craft had ramps that were lowered. Nobody was talking because there was so much noise, you couldn't hear. As you passed between all the big battlewagons, cruisers, etc, they were all blasting away with all their big guns. As you looked toward the island, all you could see was explosions, smoke, fire, and overhead planes were diving to drop bombs, fire rockets. You wondered how the hell anybody could be alive on the island when you hit the beach.

"You looked at the men on the landing craft and everyone was solemn. Some were staring in awe at all the fireworks. Some had their eyes closed. Some were talking to themselves; you could see their lips moving, probably praying. I said a few prayers myself. As we got closer to the beach, we could see the enemy's shells dropping and some of our landing craft being hit. I could hear machine-gun bullets hitting the armor plate in front of me. As we got closer, my heart was beating like a jackhammer. I was sweating profusely and I was waiting for the boat to hit the beach, as I was to be the first one out on the right side. There was so much anxiety, anticipation, hope, and other things whirling around in my brain, I don't think there was room for fear. One of my thoughts that consoled me was that this is what I had asked for and if I died, I wanted to go like a good Marine. I knew every guy in that boat felt the same way.

"Fortunately, most of the men in my craft made the beach. Other boats carrying men from our platoon weren't so lucky. When we hit the beach, my legging caught on something as I was climbing over the side. I fell headfirst into the water. I quickly got up and waded onto the beach. About fifteen feet off to my right a Jap machine gunner located in a shallow pilbox was firing on some Marines wading through the water. I crawled over to the pillbox and aimed my Tommy gun into it. The damn thing wouldn't fire because sand got into the mechanism when I fell into the water. I pushed a hand grenade in the hole and eliminated him.

"About two minutes later, I was hit in the upper arm by shrapnel, about one inch square. It went through my sleeve and lodged an inch from where it punctured the skin. It didn't even hit the bone as it traveled almost parallel to it. The shrapnel was red hot and burned like the devil, so maybe it cauterized itself. I was able to dig the piece out with my Ka-Bar knife, so I never turned into sickbay with it. My only regret is that I never will receive a Purple Heart for being wounded.

Another A/1/7 replacement, Philadelphian Earl "Rags" Rice, said, "The night before we left for Peleliu we had a big drinking party, home-brewed stuff. Everybody got drunk. A fellow named Boland, a big, good-looking sergeant, talked to me about what I was going to do after the war. I said I thought I'd travel and just see the rest of the world. He couldn't believe that I wasn't going to get more education. He'd already been to college and was a very smart guy.

"When we went in to the beach at Peleliu, it was terrible. I had never seen dead bodies like this, lying on the beach, floating in the water, mangled. Cat Allen was in a hole with another marine who saw a Jap soldier but froze and couldn't fire. He told Cat there was one out there. Cat stuck up his head to look and took a bullet right through his skull. They called me as a stretcher bearer to get him. I carried him back and dropped him off at a collection place. There wasn't anything to do for him."

After depositing Allen's body, Rice returned to the outfit's position and, as night fell, was directed to occupy a vacant foxhole. Only after he settled in did Rice realize that he was alone. There would be no one who would stand watch if he slept. "It was a most terrifying night. I was dead tired from the day and I couldn't stay awake. I started to doze off and then I could hear them out there crawling toward me on my right and left. I tried to peek out but I couldn't see a thing; all I knew is that they were coming toward me. Around 5:00 A.M. it finally became light enough to see and when I looked out what I had heard were land crabs, crawling all over the place.

"It became very hot, and not having slept, and with all that heat while I carried men on stretchers, around midday I just went down. That hurt my pride. They took me to the hospital ship, stayed overnight. [I decided] my days as a stretcher-bearer were over. I was going back to my outfit as a rifleman, come what may. I missed two days, the only two days I missed combat while I was in the war. When I got back, a guy told me I had missed the biggest day there, when a lot of guys got killed. Boland, who talked to me about getting educated, had been sick and they told him to get behind some trees until he felt better But he wouldn't do it. He came forward and was killed. MacDonald, a weight lifter, who wrote letters to his wife regularly and who'd been so good to me, had his whole chest blown out. My squad leader, Joe Gallant, stood on top of a tank blasting away with his submachine gun when he was killed. They were both brave men who will live in my memory until I die."

Shaken but unhurt, by late afternoon, E. B. Sledge had reached the edge of the Peleliu airfield. Japanese tanks stirred up fear of a counterattack just as some American Shermans arrived to take them under fire. Sledge and Snafu set up their 60mm mortar. He and his fellows prepared for the usual Banzai suicide counterattack. Instead, the enemy countered with a well-coordinated tank-infantry thrust eventually driven off by leathernecks on the left flank of Sledge's outfit. Although the Japanese had been repulsed, their actions indicated they would not necessarily rely on futile gestures but instead could defend with careful calculation.

Orders directed Sledge's 3d Battalion to charge across the fire-swept airfield, while on an elevation known as Bloody Nose Ridge, Japanese gunners poured devastation from their well-emplaced weapons. Sledge said he mumbled the first verse of the twenty-first Psalm as he scurried across the open area. Bullets snapped past him, explosions hurled bits of coral that stung his face and hands, shell fragments spattered about on the rock like hail. "Through the haze I saw Marines stumble and pitch forward as they got hit. I then looked neither right nor left but just straight to my front. The farther we went, the worse it got. The noise and concussion pressed in on my ears like a vise. I gritted my teeth and braced myself in anticipation of the shock of being struck at any moment. It seemed impossible that any of us could make it across. We passed several craters that offered shelter but I remembered the order to keep moving. Because of the superb discipline and excellent esprit of the Marines, it had never occurred to us that the attack might fail."

Four days after a mine wounded him just beyond the beach, Ed Andrusko returned to duty with his company, some of whom huddled in a steep ravine, while above them Japanese troops occupied entrenched positions. Andrusko said, "It was high noon, 110 degrees, no shade, and a merciless tropical sun. The hostile defenders were now firing down on us from all sides. The cross-fire was deadly and we were trapped.

"As the message runner, I returned to the command post and reported our new losses and serious situation to the top sergeant. He radioed for reinforcements, for medical corpsmen, water, and as many stretcher-bearers as he could get. The word came back negative. No reinforcements. No stretcher-bearers. All reserve units were committed in an all-out battle throughout the island with heavy casualties. There was no help available."

Desperate for aid, the sergeant ordered Andrusko and one other marine, nicknamed "Ski," to accompany him on a dash to the beach area to recruit anyone available. Under covering fire they sprinted to the rear and vainly sought succor from other unit commands. "Exhausted from the heat, we rested near the beach in the shade of a damaged supply truck. A young black sergeant who had overheard our plight walked up and said, 'I heard you all were looking for some troop replacements.'

"Our top sergeant looked a little stunned and speechless at the black, uniformed sergeant. The Top cleared his throat and asked, 'Who are you? What unit or company are you with? Are you Army, Navy, Seabees, or what?'

" 'I am a U.S. Marine platoon sergeant. My men and I are all U.S. Marines.' I remembered seeing and talking to the black troops on the beach when I first returned to battle weeks before. He continued, 'My men have all finished their work on the beach. We are cleared with the division headquarters to volunteer where needed. We are Marines from an ammunition depot and have had some infantry training.' Our top sergeant appeared very puzzled. How could he bring in an all-black unit to rescue members of a line company that was part of the famous, all-white 1st Marine Division? It was heavily complemented with Southern officers and men, home-based at New River, North Carolina, and 'the pride of the South.' He tried to discourage the volunteers, stating they were not trained nor qualified for the terror of battle. But by now the black marines had armed themselves heavily and lined up behind their platoon sergeant, who insisted we lead the way to the front lines. Our top sergeant said, 'Well, don't say I didn't warn you people.' When we reached our mauled company area, it looked like Custer's last stand. The top sergeant came upon our new replacement officer in command of the company and said, 'Sir, I have a platoon of black—I mean a platoon of Marine volunteers who came to help.'

"The young, new commanding officer said, 'Thank God. Thank you, men. Sergeant, take over. Get our wounded and dead out.' We gave covering fire and watched in awe as our new, gallant volunteers did their job. Some of these new men held a casualty stretcher gently in one hand as true angels of mercy. Then, when necessary, they would fire an automatic weapon with the other hand, while breaking through the surrounding enemy. The grateful wounded thanked the volunteers as each was brought to the rear aid station and safety. One badly wounded Southerner said, 'I felt like I was saved by Black Angels sent by God. Thank you. Thank you all!'

"The platoon of black Marines made many courageous trips to our area for the wounded. With each return from the rear they brought back badly needed ammunition, food, and water. It was nightfall when the evacuation of all the wounded was completed. The volunteers moved into our empty foxholes and helped fight off a small, nighttime enemy counterattack.

"The next morning, our company commander ordered us to take the hill. After several bloody hours of fighting, Item Company survivors and our black volunteers did just that. We were relieved from the gruesome mountain by a U.S. Army infantry company. As the soldiers passed, they asked sarcastically, 'Who are the black guys in your outfit?' Our top sergeant bellowed, 'Why, some of our company's best damn Marines, that's who!' "

On several other occasions, African American leathernecks participated in combat, but the Corps never assigned them to such duty. The Marine Corps, dominated by a Southern-bred hierarchy, stoutly resisted even admitting blacks to its ranks until 1943. Forced to accept them, the Marines consigned them to service, supply, and labor units, with the exception of a provisional combat group toward the end of the war and which never went into the field.

The treatment of dark-skinned Americans by the Navy was hardly better. At the start of World War II they were restricted to food handling and valet service. Later, they also performed as laborers and on supply duty. To appease critics a handful graduated from officer training programs, and a destroyer escort, the USS *Mason*, and a subchaser were the only seagoing vessels with deck ratings and officers drawn from men of color.

The Army enrolled the most blacks but it, too, limited the opportunities to engage in the fighting. The Tuskegee Airmen struggled mightily to overcome discrimination and flew with the Fifteenth Air Force in Italy. The segregated 92d and 93d Infantry Divisions, with a fair number of African Americans as junior officers under white superiors, were trained for combat. But when the latter reached the Pacific theater, after its first few engagements, it was broken up for use in base maintenance, stevedore work, and similar menial duties. The 92d, under an openly racist commander, shipped to Italy to replace one of the outfits taken away from Mark Clark's Fifth Army for Dragoon. Although individual soldiers and small units performed creditably, the 92d achieved mixed success in combat and white enlisted personnel and officers lynched its reputation. The Army also fielded a few smaller combat units such as tank destroyer, tank battalions, field artillery battalions, under white commanders. Some of these won recognition for valor while others were tagged as ineffective or worse.

General Rupertus, so cocksure of a swift victory on Peleliu, brought in the 81st Division's 321st Infantry Regiment to relieve the badly chewed-up 1st Marine Regiment after the first week cost the leathernecks just under 4,000 casualties. The 5th Marine Regiment, with Sledge, carried on, and he learned just how nearly impregnable enemy pillboxes were. With several mates, Sledge advanced on an enemy bunker. The Nipponese inside tossed out their own grenades and any lobbed through openings by the Americans. Not even explosives dropped down a ventilator pipe neutralized the inhabitants because their engineers cleverly installed concrete baffles that shielded the occupants. The Marines sent a runner to the beach for a flamethrower and an amtrac with a 75mm cannon. Some of the Japanese began to flee their stronghold while the Marines cut them down with rifle and machine-gun fire from the amtrac. "They tumbled onto the coral in a forlorn tangle of bare legs, falling rifles, and rolling helmets. We felt no pity for them but exulted over their fate. We had been shot at and shelled too much and had lost too many friends to have compassion for the enemy when we had him cornered."

After the 75mm piece whammed three armor-piercing shells into the target, occupants emerged. "Even before the dust settled," wrote Sledge, "I saw a Japanese soldier appear at the blasted opening. He was grim determination personified as he drew back his arm to throw a grenade at us. My carbine was already up. When he appeared, I lined my sights on his chest and began squeezing off shots. As the first bullet hit him, his face contorted in agony. His knees buckled. The grenade slipped from his grasp. All the men near me, including the amtrac machine gunner, had seen him and began firing. The soldier collapsed in the fusillade, and the grenade went off at his feet.

"Even in the midst of these fast-moving events, I looked down at my carbine with sober reflection. I had just killed a man at close range. That I had seen clearly the pain on his face when my bullets hit him came as a jolt. It suddenly made the war a very personal affair. The expression on that man's face filled me with shame and then disgust for the war and all the misery it was causing." Sledge quickly rejected what he called "maudlin meditations of a fool" for feeling ashamed because he had killed someone about to kill him with a grenade.

"Near the end of the battle for Peleliu, I had my 'bells rung' pretty good. Late on one afternoon, Baker Company attacked up a hill but got pinned down with very intense fire. They sent our company (Able) up so Baker could withdraw. By the time Baker left and we started back, it was getting dark. The Japs were laying down some of their big mortar shells. As I was coming down the slope, one of these came down near me. All I can remember is that I was airborne. When I came to it was pitch dark. Fortunately, I wound up in our own lines. My whole brain seemed numb and everything ached, from my toenails to the hair on top of my head. I wasn't able to shake off some of the effects of that concussion until we got back to Pavuvu. To add to the misery, the few of us left from our platoon all had bad cases of dysentery."

On 13 October, nearly a month after the first Marines hit the Peleliu beaches, Ed Andrusko said, "Our company was battling in caves, valleys, and the limestone hills of a moon-looking mountain range. After the capture of a large treeless mountaintop, there was an ominous quiet, a lull that comes in battle. It was time for a well-needed rest in 115 degrees heat. I unslung my rifle, removed combat equipment, and a sweaty shirt, laid my helmet down next to me, and nestled down near some large boulders to read my mail. This would be a real happy moment, a cherished personal one. Suddenly there was a loud sharp crack from a nearby sniper's rifle. The calm had been broken as a bullet pierced the air. The bright streak of a tracer bullet burned across my right forearm, hit my holy religious cross on a rosary I was wearing around my neck, tore across my left forearm, continued, and ricocheted off a large boulder only to come at me again—this time across my back. This same bullet incredibly hit me for the third time. It expended itself by landing in my helmet which was lying on the ground next to me. Three days later, I was evacuated aboard the hospital ship USS *Solace* for home."

E. B. Sledge and his fellows were delighted to greet GIs from the 321st Infantry Regiment as their relief. Two weeks later, Sledge boarded a transport that carried him back to Pavuvu. But it would be another six weeks before elimination of the last vestiges of enemy resistance on Peleliu. Between the Marines and the Army, American casualties amounted to almost 1,800 dead and more than 8,500 wounded. The Japanese lost approximately 11,000. Peleliu was a useless acquisition; its airfield of no consequence. In contrast, elsewhere in the Palaus, Ulithi, occupied with no resistance to the 81st Division six days after the assault upon Peleliu, supplied an excellent base for staging operations against the Philippines and Okinawa.

In the European and Mediterranean theaters many GIs whose ethnic backgrounds provided fluency or at least a smattering of the local tongues helped gain intelligence. In Pacific operations, fear that anyone with a Japanese background was untrustworthy deprived American forces of the talents of Nisei—Americans born of Japanese ancestry—a prime source for interrogations of prisoners and translation of captured documents. To compensate for the shortage of Japanese language experts, the Army ran a crash program to train its own linguists.

Gerald Widoff, as a nineteen-year-old graduate of the City University of New York in 1942, had studied elementary Japanese and, with additional instruction at an Army language school, received a commission. As head of a small team of enlisted Nisei he reported to CBI headquarters in New Delhi. "CBI was primarily a British operation [Stilwell was in China] and the Americans were decidedly in the minority. Someone decided that more token American presence was needed in the Allied effort and I was selected—I know not why—to work in the war room every morning. Very early each day I would meet with a British lieutenant and we would go over all the dispatches that had come in overnight, and climbing on ladders would move pins on a huge map of the theater. About 9:00 A.M. some British generals and some Colonel Blimp-types would show up, along with a few American colonels. Shortly after, two large doors would swing open and in would stride Lord Louis Mountbatten, the supreme allied commander, resplendent in a white admiral's uniform glittering with honors and decorations. Never in my years growing up in the Bronx would I have imagined that laundry could ever come out so blindingly white! Mountbatten was movie-star handsome, had enormous presence, and most impressive of all, actually seemed highly able. He spoke for ten or fifteen minutes, reviewing the situation, without referring to any notes and without any hesitations, in perfectly formed sentences."

Although no one ever officially told Widoff that his duties included checking the honesty of the work done by his subordinates, Widoff understood this to be a basic demand upon him. "I always assumed that most of the Nisei, but not all, knew more Japanese than I did. Many however were not particularly fluent in English. Once I got to know the members of my team I never doubted their integrity. I checked every translation before passing it up the line and almost all of my input was an effort to put it into intelligible English, which required going back to the original document. Any alteration of meaning or insertion of extraneous material would have been easily spotted. There never was any. It was foolish of the Army not to have granted commissions to the capable ones, although that was rectified toward the end of the war. Most of the work we did consisted of translating captured documents."

Widoff replaced a Caucasian officer, KIA, assigned to vet the work of the intelligence Nisei with Merrill's Marauders. "The most difficult part of the early weeks of the Burma campaign for me was merely to fend off total exhaustion and keep up with the unit. There were no roads. The Burma Road was being built behind us as we advanced. The one time I saw it, it was an impenetrable cloud of red dust. There was no transport. We had mules but they were only used as pack animals. We would walk up a trail to a mountaintop and then go down a trail on the other side. Everyone from the general on down walked. For the first few weeks I thought I would not make it, that I would reach a point where I could no longer place one foot in front of the other. I would fall by the side of the trail and either die or somehow become a Kachin tribesman. I frequently started the day at the head of the column and ended it with a group of stragglers at the tail. Some of the guys who were having difficulty would tie their hands to the harness of one of the mules and the poor beast, in addition to carrying a heavy load of artillery shells, would also be dragging a GI. I thought that was too humiliating to even contemplate and struggled on. By the end of the week, I was only halfway back in the column and by the end of the second week I was enjoying the hike each day. Sometimes we walked through fields of elephant grass taller than I. [He was more than six feet tall.] The blades of grass had razor-sharp edges and we used our machetes all day but still wound up with lots of little cuts and nicks. Sometimes we slept in little clearings surrounded by rather sweet-smelling mounds, which we later learned were elephant turds.

"There was a fever, common in Burma, which was known to everyone by its Japanese name, tsutsugamushi fever, and it took quite a heavy toll. Malaria was quite common and many guys in my outfit had severe cases, in spite of the fact we all took atabrine tablets. These were supposed to prevent it but just seemed to turn us all yellow. Amebic dysentery was quite widespread and there was a fear of cholera and smallpox, for which we seemed to receive an excessive number of vaccinations, but which must have worked because I never heard of a case of either."

In the company of 4,000 Chinese soldiers and several hundred Kachin Rangers, the Americans, with Widoff as a member of the headquarters staff, crossed a 6,000-foot mountain to outflank the enemy. The expedition caught the garrison dozing and the principal goal at Myitkyina yielded with modest resistance. "Prisoners were hard to come by," said Widoff. "When I first joined the Marauders I went around to many patrols and gave a little talk on the importance of prisoners, the lives that could be saved by what could be learned, etc. Frequently, someone in the back would say, 'Hey, Lieutenant! Ya wanna prisoner? Go get him yourself!' " The campaign in Burma went through another reorganization and Widoff became a member of the Mars Task Force, a piece of an elaborate plan to trap the main body of Japanese troops. "The war in Burma was a very small-time affair compared to Europe, North Africa, or the South Pacific," said Widoff. There were no large masses of troops and no great sustained battles. My impression is that most of the action occurred when small groups on patrol stumbled into one another, unawares. There was no heavy artillery and no heavy barrages. We (HQ) sometimes heard small-arms fire nearby but it never seemed directed at us, although most of the time we were never quite sure where we were in relation to everyone else.

"During the entire six months of the campaign we were supplied exclusively by air drops. Cargo planes would fly low over us and boxes of supplies would be pushed out of the plane with small parachutes attached and would more or less float down to a prearranged field. Sometimes they would float a bit too much and wind up supplying the Japanese. Sometimes they drifted into areas where it was too dangerous to retrieve them. Most of the time we got them and there was always plenty for our basic needs. We lined our foxholes with the parachutes."

2

Paris, Brest, and Market Garden

THE BREAKOUT BY THE THIRD ARMY AND THE ADVANCES ALONG the entire Allied front swept northeast in a fashion that obliged the Germans to retreat to lines that left Paris vulnerable. Wary of the high costs of a block-by-block, house-to-house ordeal that would destroy a jewel of civilization, Eisenhower intended to bypass Paris and enter it at a propitious moment. Once the war swept beyond Paris, the enemy trapped there might be induced to surrender without a fight.

Hitler had hurriedly dispatched a new commander to Paris, Gen. Dietrich von Choltitz, and typically called upon von Choltitz to defend to the ultimate. "Paris must not fall into the hands of the enemy except as a field of ruins." For the task, the *Wehrmacht* mustered about 25,000 soldiers, most of whom deployed outside the city. No armor and scant artillery supported these troops. Emboldened by the proximity of the Allies, citizens of Paris walked off their private and public jobs. Roaming bands of FFI seized police stations, newspapers, and even city hall. Von Choltitz prepared to deal forcibly with the weakly armed insurrectionists. After a truce collapsed, resistance factions fanned out for a full-scale fight with the occupiers.

Alarmed that Paris, packed with unarmed civilians, might now become enveloped in a conflagration of shot and shell, Charles de Gaulle threatened to send his own Free French units into the city. Indeed, the French 2d Armored Division, acting on its own, moved a reconnaissance group of 150 to the outskirts of the capital. Although some American outfits had been closer to Paris, Eisenhower with his customary diplomatic discernment authorized the French armor to enter the city. With the aid of the local resistance, after a day of hard fighting, the soldiers, on 25 August, drove out the main body of enemy forces, capturing von Choltitz. For his part, the defeated German general had refrained from the scorched-city policy ordered by *der Führer*.

Motorized units from the 4th Division were the first Americans inside Paris, while de Gaulle staged a parade to celebrate liberation and his Free French operations. Three days later, on 29 August, the population enjoyed an opportunity to cheer Eisenhower and a march down the Champs-Élysée by the 28th Infantry Division, which had not fired a single shot on behalf of the liberation. Originally destined to make the D day invasion, the 28th had been spared that dreadful experience and on 22 July arrived, dry-footed, in Normandy. Although baptized by enemy fire, the 28th was still a relatively unblooded outfit. Ralph Johnson, in a service company with the 110th Regiment, said, "It was a nine-hour parade with bands playing and all colors flying and the men had the time of their lives—wine, women, song (and bicycles by the hundreds) was the unofficial order of the day. Late that afternoon our point ran into the rear guard of the German Army evacuating the city and a firefight broke out causing many casualties. My feelings as we marched along in the parade were that surely the war must be nearly over, as how can we have a parade like this. . . . I could not have been more wrong. So many of my friends and comrades were to be killed before that happy moment would arrive. Hitler just would not give up."

Although Dragoon struck along the Mediterranean coast, the Brittany ports remained attractive, particularly Brest. The assignment to oust the Germans fell to a portion of Patton's Third Army, the VIII Corps under Gen. Troy Middleton. One of Middleton's assets was the 83d Infantry Division. After bouncing about storm-tossed seas in the Channel for six stomach-churning days, the "Thunderbolts" finally debarked 21–24 June at Omaha. Within less than a week the organization relieved the hard-hit 101st Airborne around Carentan. Subsequently, it was assigned the objective of St.-Malo, a small Brittany seacoast town.

Tony Vaccaro served in the intelligence section for the division's 331st Regiment. Born in Pennsylvania, Vaccaro had lived in Italy from 1925 to 1939, until the advent of war forced Americans to return to the States. Schooled as a rifleman, his knowledge of French, German, and Italian qualified him for intelligence work. Before leaving for Europe he attended a course in techniques to capture prisoners and interrogate them. The instructions emphasized not to fire a weapon but if necessary use a knife. "We would go out at night, in a group of four, try to capture one of the enemy, talk to the farmers or members of the underground. It was from a Frenchman who had been in hiding that I first learned that the Nazis were killing the Jews. Until then it was all rumors, but this man said he had seen what they were doing. I already had a great hatred for the fascists but this increased my dislike for the Germans. One night, we went out to try and find a route for our regiment to cross the Rance River, where all the bridges had been blown. Another regiment needed our help because they were trapped. We were in a jeep when suddenly we saw a truck full of German soldiers drive by. We quickly headed down a road away from where the truck was going. Suddenly the roadway ended and our jeep was bumping along railroad tracks on an embankment. We stopped and then we heard noises. I had learned to tell the differences between Americans and Germans. American shoes didn't make sounds but the Germans had nails in their boots and you could hear them on pavement or stones.

"We got out of the jeep and we could see in the moonlight the clear outline of a German soldier's helmet coming toward us. We jumped him; somebody grabbed his hands, another man put a hand over his mouth and I took the bandanna I carried and tied it over his mouth. One of our guys, George Goodman, was Jewish. He had heard how the Germans were killing Jews and he really hated them. He took out his pistol and said, 'I'm going to kill him.' I said, 'No, no, we have to take him back. If you fire that pistol they'll know it is a .45 and they'll be after us.' But Goodman was acting crazy, making a lot of noise. The sergeant who was in charge did nothing. I took my bayonet and put the point against his neck. I said if you shoot him, I will kill you.' Back at headquarters I tried to question the prisoner. He didn't respond to French, Italian, or Spanish. Finally, I mumbled the few Polish words I knew. His face brightened and I yelled for someone who spoke Polish. He gave us everything we needed to know."

In his knapsack, Vaccaro packed an Argus C-3 camera, a modest 35mm impersonation of a Leica. "I shot ten rolls in Normandy that I tried to send home but the censor destroyed them. Other rolls were ruined by the contaminated water.

Because I went out mainly on night missions I had time to shoot pictures during the daylight hours." To procure film and chemicals for processing, Vaccaro would ask French civilians if the Boche were still in a village or town. When they answered in the negative he would hurry ahead of his comrades, who thought him daft for entering an area that might contain the enemy. "I would find the local drugstore or chemist and buy the materials. Many of the Germans we captured carried cameras and film and the guys would give me the film. I had no scales to weigh chemicals but I remembered the size of the mounds my high school teacher, Mr. Lewis, used. To process the pictures I borrowed some steel helmets."

His odd linguistic background saved the life of an ancient Frenchman accused as a saboteur who cut the division telephone lines. "The division interpreter, who was born in France, could not communicate with the man, who was illiterate in French. They called me in and I tried but nothing seemed to work until I made a sign that I remembered from the period when I lived in a small village that had once been occupied by the Normans. He responded and I started to talk to him in the dialect of that town. That was the only language he knew. He had come across wires lying in the mud alongside a stream. Having lost a cow to mines, he cut the wire and used it to tie up his cattle to prevent them from wandering. I showed our officers what he had done and they let him go. In a one-in-a-million shot, I, who happened to have lived in that one village, gone to America, and come back as a soldier, had been on hand when he could have been executed."

Robert Edlin, the Ranger struck in both legs on the beach and evacuated to England during the evening of D day, although not fully recovered, talked his way back to his outfit.

Shortly after he rejoined his company, he and his associates opened fire on an enemy antitank crew. "Afterward, I rolled over the man I had shot. I see his face at night, even after almost fifty years. I wondered then and now what happened to the beautiful little boy and girl in the picture that the proud father carried to show his friends."

Rudder nominated Edlin to take a reconnaissance patrol, locate minefields, and bag a prisoner or two for intelligence about those manning a fortress at Lochristi. "Along about dawn, September 10, we came down to within 200 yards of one of the largest pillboxes I had ever seen. The fort itself stood above us like a ten-story building. The big guns had been largely silenced and we were in so close that not even the 88s or mortars could fire on us. Only machine guns and rifles could get at us. We paused at a high stone wall. I told my platoon sergeant, William Klaus, to hold the rest of the platoon there and cover us. Sergeant Bill Courtney, Sgt. Bill Dreher, and my runner, Warren Burmaster, and I came within fifteen or twenty yards of the pillbox. There was an open doorway and we could hear Germans talking inside. I motioned to Burmaster to cover our rear. An excellent man, he would report back to the company if something happened to us. We entered the pillbox with no opposition. They were surprised to see American soldiers. They were unaware any of us were within several miles. We captured the emplacement with forty men, some machine guns, and the radio equipment before they could use it. There was no firefight at all.

"There I was, a twenty-two-year-old lieutenant, sitting with prisoners in the shadow of the strongest emplacement on the peninsula. I called in Burmaster and told him to have the radio man notify Colonel Rudder and Captain Arman that we had captured the pillbox and were within 200 yards of the fort itself. I knew if I asked Colonel Rudder if we should go ahead and try to enter the fort, he would likely say no. It would just be too much of a risk. I also thought, if I wait for permission and don't get it, there will be an all-out assault and a lot of men will be killed. There were only four of us and we had a chance to prevent it.

"I decided to go into the fort. Courtney had been speaking to a lieutenant we captured and who spoke fluent English. He said he could take me directly in to the fort commander. The German lieutenant guided us through a minefield and to the fort entrance. We came through a tunnel like in a football stadium and when we opened the door, the German was in front with me directly behind him, a Tommy gun in his back. We walked into a hospital room, a large ward. There was an operating room and a lot of white-clad doctors, nurses, and patients everywhere. When we showed up in American uniforms with guns in our hands it was just turmoil.

"Courtney, who spoke pretty good high school German, yelled, *'Hände Hoch!'* All hands went in the air. The German lieutenant asked if he could speak to them in German and I agreed as long as he spoke slowly enough for Courtney to translate. He told the Germans to remain calm, to sit down. He would lead us to the battery commander to try to negotiate a surrender and avoid more casualties. Everybody quietly went about their business and we passed through the hospital section, the German in front, my gun in his back, and Courtney behind me. As we passed several German soldiers on guard at the cross corridors, the lieutenant would speak to them and they would immediately lower their weapons. Courtney explained to me he was telling them I was being taken to their commander and not to cause problems or trouble.

"We came to a doorway and the German started to open it. I stopped him when he told Courtney it was the commander's office. I instructed him to step aside. I turned the knob and stepped into the office with Courtney right behind me, both of us with Tommy guns. A middle-aged colonel sat behind a large ornate desk with carpet on the floor. He was apparently surprised that anyone would enter without knocking. I immediately said, *'Hände Hoch!'* He raised his hands and we closed the door behind us. I told Courtney to talk to him in German but he answered that wouldn't be necessary. He spoke English well. I said the fort was completely surrounded by American soldiers. The air force attacks and artillery had lifted to give him a chance to surrender. He should immediately use the P.A. system and announce that the whole fort should give up.

"He reached for his telephone and I said for him to leave it alone. He told me he just wanted to check how many Americans were there. About the only alternative I had was to shoot him and that wouldn't gain anything. So we let him call. He asked if we would care to have a drink. I couldn't have taken a drink or anything else. My stomach was so upset, my heart up in my throat. I don't know who was the scaredest, me or Courtney. We were in a position which we couldn't back out of. If he surrendered, we'd have done a great job. If he didn't, then we obviously would become prisoners. The two of us with Tommy guns could hardly defeat the whole garrison.

"The phone rang after a couple of minutes and he spoke in German. Courtney looked over at me and shook his head. The officer hung up and said he'd found out there were only four Americans, two at the pillbox and us two and we were his prisoners. For half a minute Courtney and I were prisoners but we were very dangerous ones. I had made up my mind we would shoot him, barricade the office with desks, and wait until either the Germans got us out or until our guys attacked the next day and when they came in, we'd still be alive.

"Something struck my mind. I don't know where the idea came from or why I did it. But I told Courtney to give me a hand grenade. I took the grenade, pulled the pin, walked around the desk and shoved it into the colonel's stomach. I told him either surrender or he was going to die right there. He said I was bluffing. I said, 'I'll show you how much I am bluffing. I'll count to three, turn loose the lever.' It would flip off and the grenade would splatter his stomach and backbone all over the wall. He just sat there. I counted, 'One, two,' and he said, 'All right, all right. I believe you.' I told him to get on the phone, use the P.A. system to announce to his men he had surrendered the fort, given up, and the combat was over. We would immediately get word to our battalion commander and stop any action coming in.

"Over the P.A. system he spoke in German. Courtney understood him and it was plain and clear that he had ordered his people to lower their arms and not take any hostile action against the American forces. He said he would prefer to surrender to a higher-ranking officer than a lieutenant. I didn't give a rat's ass who he surrendered to. I said I'd take him to my battalion commander and he could handle it." By radio, Edlin informed Rudder what had happened and the Ranger CO assured him there would be no artillery or air action.

"We went back to the pillbox and took out the prisoners we had obtained there while Rudder entered the fort to deal with the colonel. When I looked back, the sight was unbelievable. There were 850 men coming out. I had figured may-be 150 or even 250, but 850 lined up in military formation, stacked their arms, and there was sort of an old-time formal surrender ceremony. While we were inside, Courtney had talked the German into calling the Brest commander, General Ramke, and advising him he had surrendered the fort and, on Courtney's suggestion, telling him he, too, might as well give up. That didn't work. After the ceremony, and we started to march off the prisoners, Colonel Rudder congratulated the four of us and told us we had done a wonderful job. Then he called me aside and proceeded to tear me a new butthole. He was nearly crying about the tremendous risk we had taken. I asked him what he would have done and Rudder answered he hoped he would have done the same as I did."

There was talk of a Medal of Honor for Edlin, who insisted that, while he appreciated the tale of four Rangers capturing 850 men and four artillery pieces, the men of the 29th Infantry Division, the other Rangers, the artillery, the engineers, and air corps were what achieved the results. The recommendation for the nation's highest military honor was knocked back to a Distinguished Service Cross, with Edlin's three associates receiving Silver Stars.

While the defenders in Brittany were effectively cut off from any reinforcements or resupply, they nevertheless fought "fanatically," according to Eisenhower. To maintain a solid front, the commander of the enemy garrison spread through the ranks a contingent of SS soldiers. "At any sign of weakening," said Eisenhower, "an SS trooper would execute the offender on the spot." The draconian discipline may have been due to an infusion of Italian, Russian, and Polish men, like Vaccaro's captive, whose enthusiasm for the fighting probably was less than wholehearted. Manning the fortifications and barricades were as many as 50,000 soldiers from portions of three divisions, a motley collection of naval and marine units, all backed by considerable field artillery, as well as big coastal guns swiveled about to fire inland.

George Duckworth's company, in the 2d Infantry Division, which occupied a strategic hill, could testify to the tenacity of the foe after repulsing a bloody, two-day counterattack. Given a few days to recuperate, his unit assaulted through the hedgerows toward the city. "The strength of the company at this time was about 170 enlisted men and 7 officers [about 20 percent below the normal complement]. Approximately 30 percent were veterans who had landed at Omaha Beach on D plus 1. The others were replacements but had seen considerable combat in Normandy and Northern France. I was the only officer who had landed with the company on D plus 1. Besides being individually well equipped, the men had extra allowances of special weapons consisting of two Thompson submachine guns and two Browning automatic rifles for each squad. This additional firepower was necessary in hedgerow fighting." Throughout the war, experienced soldiers toted extra automatic weapons, bazookas, and other items not specified in the table of organization and equipment.

Duckworth and his people worked their way through barbed-wire entanglements mangled by artillery blasts. They entered the town of St.-Marc fairly easily, only to meet concentrated enemy fire from a large château. In a coordinated attack, F Company of the 23d Infantry Regiment overran the site, killing a number of defenders and capturing two dozen prisoners. The full battalion followed and 200 of the enemy, mostly Italians, Poles, and Russians, surrendered. Although the fighting had been intense, when the 2d Division GIs settled down for the night, a hot meal was served.

Further progress entailed house-to-house combat. Duckworth recalled, "It was sudden death to step into the streets and the bodies of several civilians lay in the streets where they had been shot down by the Germans. The only way the streets could be crossed was by throwing a smoke grenade and dashing quickly from one covered position to another." To knock out a pillbox surrounded by trenches, tank destroyers and heavy machine guns hammered the emplacement hard enough for assault platoons to rush forward and clear the pillbox and the trenches.

Throughout the campaign for Brest the big guns on both sides relentlessly banged away. The fury of the American artillery gradually reduced everything to a shambles and the foot soldiers scrambled through the ruins of shattered, burning buildings until the fires at one point became so hot that the attackers were forced to wait until they burned themselves out. When the GIs resumed their efforts, Duckworth noted, "The buildings were still hot and smouldering in many places but some areas were passable and the walls that were still standing provided protection for the men as they advanced. The hot ruins burned the soles of the men's shoes but no casualties from burns were reported." After five days of this operation, another company relieved Duckworth's unit. Four more days would pass before the battle of Brest ended.

Despite the impressive capture of Paris and the rollback of the enemy forces, the Allied armies racing east, crossing the Seine, Meuse, and Moselle Rivers, were literally running out of gas. The Red Ball Express, an operation in which 60 percent of the drivers were African Americans, labored mightily to maintain a river of trucks containing fuel, food, and ammunition, but the advance began to grind to a halt short of the German border. Ahead lay some formidable obstacles, the defense in depth of the Siegfried line, a thickly infested chain of interlocking fortifications chock-full of weapons and troop bunkers fronted by "dragon's teeth," the man-made concrete tank barriers. However, the Siegfried line had been neglected and seemed more menacing than real. Natural barriers included the mountainous terrain of the Vosges, the steep hills and deep ravines of the Ardennes, the thickets of the Hurtgen Forest, and the approaching winter that would render roads and fields inhospitable to enemy armor.

Bernard Montgomery had always presented a prickly problem for the American generals. He was as strongly convinced of his own theories of warfare and his superiority in putting these into practice as Patton or any other of the hubris-infected top ranks. Unlike Patton, the British general ordinarily refused to commit to battle until he believed his forces achieved a total readiness in manpower, armor, and logistics. To Americans he seemed agonizingly slow to act and they complained frequently of the Briton's pace. He had lost some of the reputation gained in North Africa by the inability of the British forces to march inland following their gaining of the Normandy shore. Having captured Antwerp, a major port whose Scheldt Estuary to the North Sea stretched sixty miles, the British squandered a great opportunity to occupy the lightly held turf around the Scheldt. When enemy forces recovered, they quickly brought in sufficient forces to control passage through the estuary, making Antwerp all but useless.

In September, as the Allied drive stalled, Montgomery proposed to jump-start the advance. He sketched a plan for combined Allied airborne forces to drop along a narrow corridor some fifty miles behind the enemy in the Netherlands. The parachutists and glidermen placed in the rear of the

Germans could seal off the region through the capture of vital water crossings, and the British Second Army would outflank the Siegfried line and punch into the Ruhr industrial centers. Montgomery astounded Eisenhower, Bradley, and the others with this bold, imaginative adventure that displayed none of the caution associated with him. Aside from an opportunity for Montgomery to reclaim his prestige with a stunning victory, the scheme offered attractive strategic and political rewards. A surprise thrust of this nature had the potential for a great military victory. If successful, the maneuver would enable the Allies to free up Antwerp. Eisenhower had also been urged by Washington to use his airborne forces, now unemployed at bases in England. Furthermore, the contested area contained sites for V-2 rockets launched at London, and there was pressure to put an end to this terror.

Code named Market for the airborne element and Garden for the ground portion, the operation went from proposal on 10 September, to reality on 17 September, only one week later. During the frantic preparations, disquieting intelligence from the Dutch underground reported the presence of two panzer divisions being outfitted with new tanks. Montgomery waved off fears of heavier resistance. The 82d and 101st Airborne Divisions along with their British counterparts geared up to drop on three principal places, Eindhoven, closest to the foot soldiers, Nijmegen, some miles north, and Arnhem, across the Rhine, the farthest intrusion. Americans were assigned to the first two areas. A lack of aircraft reduced the size of the airlift, with only half of the totals scheduled for the first day. Because of fears of severe losses in planes and gliders in the initial efforts, the Air Corps granted the transport carrier request for only one flight per day. Unlike previous airborne operations, Market would occur during daylight.

The troopers of the 101st Airborne looking out the doors of their C-47s could see the massed columns of tanks, half-tracks, armored cars, and personnel carriers of the British XXX Corps, poised on the Belgium-Holland border, awaiting the moment to rumble toward the objective of Eindhoven. Heartening as the vast deployment of Allied might may have been, any euphoria quickly dissipated as they approached their drop zone north of Eindhoven. Enemy gunners opened up on the aerial armada. The usual saturation of bombs, rockets, and strafing had preceded the 101st troop carriers. While many antiaircraft weapons were destroyed, great quantities of them, some well camouflaged in haystacks, devastated the C-47s. In *A Bridge Too Far*, Cornelius Ryan recorded the words of Pfc. John Cipolla, awakened by "the sharp crack of antiaircraft guns, and shrapnel ripping through our plane." The GI, draped with ammunition belts, bearing a rifle, knapsack, raincoat, blanket, grenades, rations, plus his two parachutes, also toted a land mine. He could barely move and as he watched, "A C-47 on our left flank burst into flames, then another, and I thought 'My God, we are next! How will I ever get out of this plane!' After Cipolla jumped he glanced back at his plane. It was afire and heading toward the ground.

All about the drop zone, the transports, their pilots desperately attempting to keep them on course, shuddered and lurched from hits. Engines burned, fuel tanks flamed up. On one ship only three troopers, severely burned, and the two-man crew, escaped. Out-of-control planes chewed through those dangling from the silk and the propellers chopped into the hapless troopers. Although a staggering 16 of the 424 C-47s crashed and many more were damaged, almost the entire complement of 6,700 troopers landed close to the appointed locations. When glider forces arrived later, clusters of ground fire also battered them hard but they added their forces and vehicles to the 101st's forces.

As the last of the serials bearing airborne passed overhead, Gen. Brian Horrocks, the XXX Corps commander, signaled his Garden to grow. A tremendous bombardment preceded the tanks cracking into the enemy lines. Behind strong fortifications, the Germans waited out the barrages and then zeroed in on the lead tanks. The entire advance halted as disabled armor blocked the road to Eindhoven. The 101st leader, Gen. Maxwell Taylor, expecting the XXX Corps to supply the heavy firepower, brought no artillery in his gliders and soon engaged in fighting without the aid of British tanks or big guns. Fierce firefights inflicted heavy casualties upon both sides. Lieutenant Colonel Robert Cole, recipient of a Medal of Honor for valor at the Carentan causeways, was among those killed. The inability of the ground troops to reach Eindhoven enabled the Germans to hold out against the paratroopers long enough to blow a pair of critical bridges at Son and Best, guaranteeing further delays in establishing the alley north through Nijmegen and Arnhem. The advance was well behind schedule before the first elements from the XXX Corps linked up with the Screaming Eagles in Eindhoven.

Bill Dunfee, now an 82d Airborne veteran of three drops, Sicily, Italy, and Normandy, said, "I looked forward to this as perhaps the last airborne operation. I had mixed emotions about a daylight jump. It would certainly expedite assembly when we hit the ground. However, we would make pretty good targets in the air. Then again, the Air Force might get us on the right DZ. My feeling was two out of three were positive for the daytime drop. The Army used reverse psychology on this one. They allowed us to go to town the night of the fourteenth, telling us we would move to the airports the next day for a combat jump. From that we assumed it would be another 'dry run' but it wasn't. When we got to the airports in England on September 15, we were briefed and confined to the area around the hangars. It was the most thorough briefing I had been exposed to. On the sand tables they showed the town of Groesbeek, the German border, the forest and fire towers, all of which I noticed while descending in Holland.

"After taking off from England, and formed up over the English Channel, we could look out the door—C-47 doors were removed for combat operations—and as far back as we could see there were C-47s. At the very end of the formation, gliders carried personnel and equipment for a field hospital. There were P-51s flying cover for us and about halfway to our destination, we passed a group of B-24s returning from a bombing raid, we hoped in Holland. It is impossible to convey how impressed I was with this display of power. As we crossed over the Netherlands, we picked up a little AA fire. However, the farther we went inland, and the closer to our drop zone, the more intense it became. At 1305 hours, we jumped near Groesbeek. I noticed quite a bit of antiaircraft fire on our DZ from the direction of Nijmegen. After hitting the ground, we assembled rapidly. Due to the intensity of the AA fire, everyone was very anxious to clear the DZ.

"While moving on Groesbeek, I watched a C-47 heading back. It had been hit and was burning from the tail forward. As the fuselage burned up to the wing, only one parachute came out of the plane. At that point the wing and cockpit started fluttering down. I quit watching. My thought was, 'You poor bastards.' Two if not three men perished. We secured and outposted Groesbeek. We occupied the area without incident, other than receiving 88 and artillery fire from the direction of Nijmegen and the Reichswald. The Dutch people welcomed us with open arms. I knew from past experience that the honeymoon would not last long. Usually, within a few hours of our landing, the enemy would bring everything he could muster against us.

"A Dutch man told me there was a German soldier hiding in his barn. Taking a Thompson submachine gun, I entered the barn very cautiously. Inside there was a loft with a stairway leading up to a tack room. I figure, if he were still in there, that's where he would be. I went to the bottom of the stairway and sprayed the doors and sidewalls of the room with the Thompson. Then I called out in my best German, *'Deutsch Soldaten, Komen sie here, Hände Ho!'* There was no response, only the noise of harness and wooden shoes falling around me. I yelled again and punctuated it with another burst from the Thompson. Shouting at him again, I could see movement through the door I had shot away. My concern was he would roll a potato masher—grenade—down the stairs. He exposed an arm waving a handkerchief. I told him to come on down and took him outside. Turned him over to Jim Beavers to take to regiment for interrogation. I told Jim, 'If he as much as blinks, blow his fucking head off.' The German understood English. When Jim returned, he told me the poor bastard had shit himself."

After being wounded at the Anzio beachhead, Ed Sims missed the Normandy jump but had returned to duty in time to make his second combat leap during Market Garden. "Over the Scheldt Estuary, German antiaircraft opened fire on our formation. Our fighter planes were on them immediately and able to neutralize most of them. One plane in my formation was hit and the men forced to make an emergency jump from the crippled aircraft. All but two who jumped were taken prisoner. The pilot and copilot went down with the plane.

"The remainder of Company H [504th Parachute Infantry] jumped at about 1305 hours on the designated area near Grave. Initially we supported other units in securing the Grave Bridge over the Maas [Meues] River and bridges over the Maas Waal Canal. Intelligence reports placed some 4,000 SS troops and a German tank park in the Grave/Nijmegen area but resistance near Grave was light. All of our initial objectives were secured by 1800 hours that first day. Upon landing, I had reinjured my back but did not go for treatment because I felt nothing could be done. I carried on in less than top physical condition. We set up a company command post near a small cluster of homes. There I met a Dutch family and their fifteen children. The mother made room for me to stay with them and in the evening she prepared a delicious stew, using beef she had previously preserved. They wanted to celebrate our arrival and their liberation from the Nazis."

With the enemy seeking to close down the route from Eindhoven back to the border, Maxwell Taylor directed the 101st in a mammoth attack that deployed the 502d Regiment and the 327th Glider Infantry, backed by British armor. They swept the defenders from the area, killing some 300, capturing another 1,000 along with artillery pieces and smaller arms. Even as that victory was being concluded, the Germans struck in another area. Taylor mobilized his headquarters troops—ordinarily dedicated to staff and administration—who knocked out several tanks to preserve a route over the newly installed bridge at Son.

"On 19 September," said Sims, "we moved to an area west of Nijmegen and received a briefing on a new mission that included crossing the Waal River in assault boats and seizing the north ends of the railroad and road bridges spanning the river at Nijmegen. The south end of each bridge had not yet been taken as the Germans were fiercely defending them. We heard that the British parachute units (Red Devils) who had the mission to seize the bridge over the Neder Rijn [Rhine] River at Arnhem were unable to accomplish this. Elements of the German 9th and 10th Panzer Divsions were mauling them. Because of this tense situation, before the Germans destroyed both of the bridges over the Waal, it was imperative that at least one be taken. This would allow British armor coming up from the south to cross and rescue what was left of the Red Devils.

"For our crossing the British provided twenty-six assault boats. My company was on the right nearest to the railroad bridge. Company I [506th Parachute Infantry] was to our left. The remainder of the 3d Battalion would cross in subsequent waves. Our first objective was the north end of the railroad bridge. The plan included support from artillery and a smoke screen, neither of which helped. We did get good supporting overhead fire from our own 2d Battalion and a few British tanks that had arrived early from positions along the south bank of the river.

"The time for crossing had to be moved to 1500 hours on 20 September, because the boats arrived late. We were all amazed at these flimsy assault craft that had folding canvas sides and wooden bottoms. Each had a capacity for sixteen and each had eight paddles." According to Cornelius Ryan in *A Bridge Too Far*, in some cases there were not enough paddles and the troopers improvised by using rifle butts to stroke through the water. Said Sims, "It took us a few minutes to adjust and secure the canvas sides and then move to the river's edge for launching. Within minutes we were receiving incoming enemy fire from the north side of the river and the railroad bridge. As we progressed, it became more intense. Many boats received direct hits and sank. A number of boats had trouble navigating, but the men with me, including two engineers who had to return the boat, were calm and rowed in unison. (Only eleven of the twenty-six made it back to the south bank.) It seemed like eternity before my boat landed on the north bank but it was only ten minutes. My group landed some distance west of the railroad bridge and disembarked rapidly into a skirmish line. Another boat that landed nearby had many casualties. I ordered those who hadn't been wounded to join my group. I led this combined bunch, eighteen men, in a frontal assault on the dike that was several hundred yards farther north. I carried an M1 rifle and directed an assault forward by bounds with rapid fire from all, including myself. Enemy fire was heavy but the men did not falter. Because of these few soldiers, the dike was seized within a short time and those German defenders still alive were routed or taken prisoner. I later learned there were numerous enemy dead on this part of the dike."

Safely across, Sims said, "I was joined by other members of Company H. Lt. [James] Megellas took his platoon [half of whom had been lost when their boat sank] and moved out to seize a nearby old fort. I took my eighteen men and headed for the north end of the bridge. Lt. [Richard] La Riviere, with a few soldiers, moved east to flush out a sniper who had shot and killed one of his people. Resistance at the north end of the bridge was light and it quickly fell into our hands. I directed a few men to look for explosives and to cut all wires. We set up a defense around our end of the bridge. Lieutenant La Riviere and the few with him joined us, not a moment too soon, because German troops, en masse, were coming across the bridge toward us." They apparently were fleeing an attack by the British at Nijmegen. "We let them come within range, then opened fire and continued to do so until all enemy movement stopped. After we ceased firing, we allowed those still alive to either withdraw or surrender. We held the advantage because the Germans on the bridge had nowhere to deploy. They suffered a large number of casualties. I was told that the bodies of 267 were removed from the bridge and the number that jumped or fell from the bridge into the river will never be known. We had little concern about destroying the large enemy force opposing us. My men and I were tense and angry because of the strenuous fighting and the loss of our own men during the crossing. Often, in my mind, I relive this particular action and always conclude that this terrible slaughter of humans is not something to be proud of or to brag about. It continues to bother me that I had to make the hasty decision that led to the death of so many young men, our own and those opposing us."

The bloodshed inflamed anger to a murderous level. Ryan's book quoted Cpl. Jack Bommer, who, when he climbed over the crest of the embankment, saw "dead bodies everywhere, and Germans—some no more than fifteen years old, others in their sixties—who a few minutes before had been slaughtering us in the boats were now begging for mercy, trying to surrender." Bommer said that some of these "were shot out of hand at point-blank range."

Bud Warneke, of the 508th Parachute Infantry Regiment, having weathered the D day drop and the succeeding weeks in Normandy, accepted a battlefield commission as the unit added replacements and refurbished its equipment in England. On 17 September, about two weeks after he pinned on his gold bars, Warneke acted as jumpmaster for half his platoon destined for Market Garden. "It was a nice Sunday afternoon, no problem seeing all the landmarks. The whole company jumped right on our objective. My platoon was in battalion reserve when the British linked up with us. My platoon received an order to join a British tank platoon with the mission of going into Nijmegen. We were to capture a German headquarters and post office where intelligence thought switchboxes to blow the main bridge over the Maas Waal River were located. We took the buildings without any resistance. The Germans had vacated before we got there. A search found no switchbox and we returned to our unit that night. This had been the first time I worked with British troops. They were good soldiers, but compared to us I thought they had a nonchalant attitude about the war. They would stop whatever they were doing, brew some tea with crumpets, but then again I did not work with them much."

A column of British tanks waddled across one of the bridges secured by Ed Sims and associates with the 504th Regiment. However, the armor paused on the road to Arnhem for a day before advancing forward. Seething over the ferocious losses his outfit absorbed, Col. Ruben Tucker, the CO of the 504th, confronted an officer from the British armored division. Tucker was overheard to snarl, "Your boys [the British paratroopers] are hurting up there at Arnhem. You'd better go. It's only eleven miles." The Briton demurred on the grounds he could not proceed until his infantry arrived to accompany his tanks. Tucker voiced the frequent criticism of the ally. "They were fighting the war by the book. They had 'harbored' for the night."

Sims commented, "By then the Red Devils at Arnhem had many more dead and wounded. As usual they stopped for tea. I will never understand why the British did not take advantage of the turmoil we created and immediately push north. Company H had fifteen men killed in action and thirty-eight wounded. In my opinion, this specific operation was poorly planned [many paratroopers had never trained in river crossings with boats of this nature] and lacked adequate support. It was accomplished only because of the courage and determination of the junior officers and the fine men they led. For my part I was awarded a Silver Star."

American leaders also came in for criticism from their troops. Bill Dunfee reported, "If the Army operated on the democratic principle of consensus, the orders we received would have been dismissed for being so stupid that no rational person should comply. But being good soldiers, there was no question that we would obey. I was ordered to lead a daylight patrol into a town we could see from our vantage point in Groesbeek. It was on the German border, approximately two miles from our outposts. We were to check it out for enemy presence and report back. I took Roy McDaniels, Bill Curley and five others with me. It was about 2:00 P.M. when we started out. I decided to go straight down the road and into the town. There seemed no point in attempting to sneak there. The sun was high in the sky; there was no natural cover, and the area was flat as a pool table. There was just no place to hide. My reasoning was, if we boldly walk down the road, a column spread out on each side, the enemy might fire prematurely and we could get the hell out of there.

"We made it to within a quarter mile of the town, McDaniels leading one column and me the other. I observed three Germans with a light machine gun walk out on the road at the edge of town. I called McDaniels's attention to them. He replied, 'Hell, that's nothing. Look to the field on your left (his side).' There was a company-strength group of Germans spread out as skirmishers moving toward Groesbeek. I told my patrol to do an aboutface and head back to our lines. I told them, begged them, to 'walk as fast as you can but PLEASE don't run.' I prayed to myself, 'Please, Dear Lord, don't let anyone panic and start running.' I didn't want to draw fire any sooner than we had to. I was hoping the Germans would think we were the point of their attacking force, and ignore us, or at least not shoot us. I kept looking over my shoulder, checking on the MG squad that was about a city block distance behind us. Should they stop and set up that damned MG, I intended to tell my guys to hit the side of the road (no ditch). We were able to move back toward Groesbeek about a quarter of a mile before the riflemen on McDaniels's side of the road wised up and popped a few rounds at us. It was not necessary to tell our guys to haul ass out of there. We ran, zigzagged, fell down, got up, and ran again. We all made it back in one piece. I dove through a hedgerow into our position. I lay there, exhausted and scared. When we were within our defensive perimeter, the company opened up and stopped the German attack. At that point, a spontaneous phenomenon occurred, something that happens rarely in a combat situation. Without orders from anyone, we charged out of our foxholes and drove the enemy back through the town they had occupied. We then withdrew to our original positions."

Glider pilot Vic Warriner went along as observer in a C-47 paratrooper drop on the first day of Market Garden. He had been assigned to bring in Anthony McAuliffe, the deputy commander of the 101st Airborne, the following day and he seized an opportunity to study landmarks. The target was the area just north of Eindhoven. Because of a shortage of qualified glider pilots, there would be no copilots. Instead, Warriner and the other aviators gave a ten-minute course to a trooper so that if the pilot were incapacitated the GI could land the ship. Because of what had happened to the unfortunate General Pratt on the Normandy trip, there was a sense of urgency about delivering McAuliffe safely and at the targeted spot. His glider was to be landed as close as possible to a schoolhouse selected as a command post. On the return from that first trip, the troopers had just exited the transport when ground fire intensified. Warriner said, "Several planes went down in flames around us. Tears came to my eyes as I saw one plane with smoke pouring from it dive toward the ground and land on its belly in the soft dirt. The hatch over the pilot's compartment opened and I saw a man start to climb out when the whole plane went up in a ball of fire. I recognized the ID letters on the nose and tail. It was the plane and flown by the pilot that had so steadfastly towed me to France. The troop compartment of a C-47 was so big and empty after everyone has jumped. The straps and buckles on the static line flap and slap with the wind and bang on the sides of the plane. You wonder how many of the young men who just left are going to live to jump again. It's a sad and lonely place.

"My sleep that night was especially restless. I learned from Troop Carrier Command that our losses had been so heavy during the day's drop that we would go in from the opposite direction. I had made that hair-raising trip for nothing. I wasn't looking forward to going through that fire again in a glider. But you can't pass. The next morning we met at my glider with General McAuliffe, his staff. An exception was made for a copilot. In the skytrain when we assembled it was an awesome sight. There were gliders and planes as far back as you could see. It was the largest airborne operation to date. From time to time Allied fighters would buzz over our column, then pull on above us to act as guardians for our slow-moving armada. It gave us comfort. However, as we approached the coast of Holland, the fighters couldn't help. The Germans opened up with flak guns, and only the fact that they didn't have our altitude figured correctly enabled us to fly under those puffs of smoke, nasty blocks of death that burst just over our formation.

"What I saw was discouraging. The Germans had blown the dikes and water covered nearly everything, including the towns that dotted the area. We were low enough to see people. The ones who were waving were Dutch citizens. The others, who fired pistols at us, I presume were not. My VIP passenger had never uttered a word to me once we boarded but was in deep discussion with his staff. When the copilot was flying, I would turn in my seat to glance at him, he always gave me a wink or a thumbs-up. He seemed completely unconcerned. I don't think he realized how serious the situation was. When we first encountered the flak and the ride became bumpy, I looked back and he was sound asleep. As we started the run to the LZ we were encountering heavy ground fire. Some ricocheted off the metal tubing of the glider and some would pass on through the fabric with a loud pop as they entered and left. Now the general was wide awake. He wanted to know if there wasn't some way we could shoot back at those 'bastards.'

"He even suggested knocking off the entry door so he could lie on the floor and fire at them. The general was a great advocate of the Thompson submachine gun. It was rumored that two nights before the Normandy invasion, after a prolonged night at the officers' club, he had returned to his BOQ, sat on his bunk, and created a plate-size hole in the roof with his beloved Tommy gun. It was also rumored that Gen. Maxwell Taylor had personally taken his Tommy gun away from him and made him go into Normandy without it. Through conversations with his troopers I learned they personally idolized him and would follow 'Old Crock' anywhere.

"We were now close to our LZ, getting down in speed and altitude, but to our dismay, smoke started pouring from our tow plane's right engine. We could see licks of flame around the cowling. I was certain that Colonel Whittaker [the tow ship's pilot] was aware of this trouble and would take appropriate measures. I knew we would have to release if he couldn't get us to the LZ and start looking around for a spot to land. I knew the colonel well enough that he would get us to the LZ if he had to get out and push. I was right between two of the toughest men I had ever known. The general suggested I call Whittaker and tell him about the engine fire. I hesitated because Whittaker had his hands full trying to douse the fire and keeping us in line to the LZ. Also the ships behind us were following his lead. The general insisted so I finally called Whittaker. I got the exact reply I expected: 'Goddamn it, Warriner! You fly your glider and I'll fly this goddamn airplane!' Click! I turned to the general and said, 'He knows.'

"We were going slower and slower with one engine and the ground fire was becoming even more intense. We could see the Germans as they fired on us and the flashes made you tend to try to get your whole body perched on the flak jacket that we all sat on instead of wearing. Then suddenly, silence, as we had crossed over the German lines and the LZ was dead ahead. Whittaker got on us there and I glanced at some smoke on the ground to get the wind direction and prepared to land. We had been briefed on the soft sandy soil in the LZ that could stop a glider too quickly and flip the glider on its back. We landed softly and after a short run stopped Everyone started jumping out.

"I prepared myself for a bit of critical comment from the general, for I hadn't the least idea of where that schoolhouse that he had circled on a map was. To my amazement, the general slapped me on the back and remarked that was the best bit of flying he had ever seen. I looked in the direction he was pointing and there was that schoolhouse about 100 yards away. I didn't disabuse the general of the notion that I had the least idea of what in the hell I was doing. He insisted I accompany him to meet General Taylor. I tried to explain that I had a bunch of glider pilots landing that I needed to contact and gather into one group. He answered they weren't going anywhere for a while. His jeep had arrived. We rode over to the schoolhouse and McAuliffe informed Taylor that Whittaker and I had done a great job. I saluted and shook hands with Taylor, who muttered something like 'well done' and went back to more important matters. McAuliffe thanked me again, told his jeep driver to return me to the LZ. I saluted and went back to deal with the common man. Later I got a letter from McAuliffe thanking me and commenting on the great job by the glider pilots. He asked me for a statement on Whittaker's skill with a one-engine airplane. I complied and Whittaker was awarded a richly deserved Legion of Merit.

Glider pilot Pete Buckley reported to the flight line on D plus 2 to fly three soldiers from a field artillery unit with a jeep and equipment. "Little did we know that this day would turn out to be 'Bloody Tuesday.' Before the morning was over, seventeen of the gliders were forced to ditch in dense fog over the Channel. Five others crashed over land because of bad weather. Dozens of others were cut loose or broke away over Belgium, and seventeen of the C-47s were shot down by enemy flak over Holland. Of the 385 gliders that left England carrying the 101st Airborne Division, only 209 made it to the LZ.

"Shortly after we crossed the English coast, the entire formation flew straight into a heavy fog bank. If there's one thing that really upsets a glider pilot, and I'm sure the tow pilots, it's flying into a dense fog in tight formation with 700 planes and gliders. You have no way of knowing who's going where, when, or how and the possibility of a midair collision or accidental release is enough to make your hair stand on end. I could see only about three feet of the tow rope and had to fly blind for what seemed an eternity. Fortunately, I had the glider in perfect trim, so it practically flew by itself. Even so, I had no way of knowing what the tow plane would do. If he made a sudden change in any direction, we'd be in big trouble. Luckily, he did not. When we emerged on the other side of the fog bank there was not another plane or glider in sight in any direction. It was the biggest vanishing act I have ever seen.

"Our course brought us in the landing zone between the town of Best on our left and Eindhoven on our right, less than one minute away from our objective on the outskirts of Son. At Best, a battle was still raging between the Germans and our paratroopers for control of a key bridge near the town. Eindhoven was not fully secured and some fighting was still going on in the streets between the 506th Parachute Infantry and the Krauts. As we flew past Best at roughly 600 feet, a mobile flak wagon which I could see out of the corner of my eye on the left, opened up on our tow plane. I watched, fascinated, as shells went up through the left wing and into the left side of the fuselage and exited out the top right side where the radio compartment is. Small bits of aluminum from the plane and spent pieces of flak flew back and peppered the front of our glider. Just when I thought the enemy fire would move back along the rope and knock hell out of our glider, it stopped. Throughout the whole time we were under fire, our two ships never wavered, changed course, or took evasive action. I found out later that on the way back out, after we had cut loose, the plane was hit quite badly but managed to get back to England with no casualties.

"In a matter of seconds the landing zone appeared directly in front of us, strewn with hundreds of parachutes and gliders. Some of the latter were in one piece, others had crashed badly and their cargo lay scattered around the wreckage. The remains of two C-47s that had been shot down moments before were still burning in the craters they made when they crashed in the center of the LZ. I cut loose and made an approach well into the center of the area just in case the Germans were in the dense wood around the edge. I found out after we landed that indeed they were there but some of the 506th paratroopers held their attention while we landed.

"We came to an abrupt stop in the soft dirt of a potato field, which partially buried the nose of the glider. The first thing I did when I got out was bend down and run my fingers through the dirt. It was so nice to be down in one piece. After about fifteen minutes of digging, we managed to get the front section of the glider opened up and unloaded the jeep and equipment. Lieutenant Linz and the other two took off in the general direction of Best where the firing seemed to be the heaviest. I went alone on foot across the landing zone to find the road to Eindhoven. On the way I stopped at the 326th Medical Tent set up on the edge of the LZ. Inside, a surgical team of airborne medics, flown in by glider, were performing operations on the wounded and victims of glider crashes. Some of the medics were the same who had flown into Normandy on D day.

"I stuck my head in to see if any glider pilots were being treated there. Some had been and some of the crews of the C-47s, who had been terribly burned on the face, head, and hands before they bailed out, were still there. Within sight of the tent you could see what was left of their planes still burning on the LZ, and in the wreckage were crewmen unable to get out in time. While the medics and surgeons worked on casualties, the Germans outside the perimeter were shelling the LZ at random. These courageous medics never batted an eye; they kept right on working."

Warriner remembered, "Our next few days were spent as perimeter guards for the command post and feeding and guarding German prisoners who had been accumulating at a rapid rate. Using the glider pilots in this manner freed many airborne troopers to join their units on the front lines. Our area began to get smaller and smaller due to German counterattacks and the lack of reinforcements because bad weather in England grounded planned resupply missions. On D plus 2, some got through despite deplorable conditions over the Channel. On that day, it seemed we on the ground were more in danger of being killed by falling C-47s than German bullets. At least a dozen of them were shot down that day. Each went through the same fatal routine. As they were hit, the nose rose to almost a vertical attitude, then over it would tumble and roar straight down into the ground with a tremendous fireball. Several times we were close enough to feel the concussion and heat. We watched intently to see chutes appear as the plane reached the high point before starting down. But very seldom did we see even an attempt at jumping. Soon after this we were very short of ammunition and food. We were reduced to digging up potatoes and other roots to make soup. The free milk we were offered began to look better and better. Before the mission we had been warned against fresh milk because of the possibility of getting tuberculosis. After a while we figured, what the hell, they'll probably come up with a cure for TB."

"We were being probed on a continual basis by patrols and artillery harassment," said Bill Dunfee, on the outskirts of Nijmegen. "My platoon had taken over the point of a small orchard that included a hedgerow perimeter facing the West Wall. There was a farmhouse with a rather large garage in the rear that held the platoon CP. We were receiving rather severe artillery fire. Suddenly mortars came in. I knew they had to be close by but the sun hadn't completely burned off the fog of the night so visibility was poor. Artillery I could live with, but the mortars, having a much shorter range, indicate nearby enemy infantry.

"I saw a haystack to our right front. I thought I detected movement from its backside. I suspected muzzle blast from a mortar. [Did] not want to open fire and give our position away without being sure. I ran to the CP to get binoculars. Because of the intensity of the artillery and mortar fire, I anticipated an infantry attack. I picked up Lieutenant Carter's binoculars and headed back. Between the garage and house, Sergeant Sutherland was down. He didn't appear seriously wounded. Lupoli was with him and asked me to help carry Sutherland to the CP. I told Lupoli to put him in a wheelbarrow from behind the house or get someone from the CP to help.

"I ran around the house and back toward my squad. They were dug in about 100 yards to the front of the house. When I was within twenty feet of my foxhole, I heard the swishing sound of an incoming mortar round. I thought I could make it to my foxhole, but didn't. The concussion knocked me down. A piece of shrapnel sent my helmet flying. I crawled like hell to my foxhole and went in headfirst. I yelled to my machine gunner to open up on the haystack and set it afire. Then I started to check my vital parts—spectacles, testicles, wallet, cigars. I knew if I were hit, it wasn't serious. I called out to DiGiralamo to give me a hand. He asked if I were hit. I said I thought so. He yelled for a medic. To me, combat medics had a very special brand of courage. Their duty required them to expose themselves to enemy fire at the cry, 'Medic!' The one that showed up was very young and this was his first combat exposure. I asked him how it looked. He said, 'You've got three big holes in your back and you're bleeding like hell.' He insisted on giving me a shot of morphine. I didn't want any medication that would slow me down, in case I needed to get out of there. I finally lost patience and ran him off. DiGiralamo came over and administered first aid. I stayed in my foxhole until things cooled down a bit, then walked back to the battalion aid station. They were storing the wounded in a small building. It was hot in there and didn't smell good. I sat outside until an ambulance came for us. I still had my rifle and grenades. They wouldn't let me in the ambulance with them. We were taken to Brussels, where I spent one night in a hospital. They did preliminary and emergency surgery. The following day, we who were ambulatory were flown to a general hospital near Bristol, England."

A paratrooper remarked, "The command was aware of our dire need of supplies so they enlisted the aid of a group flying B-24s to make a drop. Why B-24s I don't know, except perhaps they figured they were fast enough to get in and out without the casualties of the slower C-47s. Late in the afternoon we heard them coming. Everyone stood out there waving, thinking how good even K rations would taste. They dove to a very low altitude at full throttle. But they waited too long in dumping the bundles. We watched everything sail over our heads and behind the German lines. Fortunately, Dempsey's armor [Lt. Gen. Miles Dempsey commanded the British Second Army] broke through and we got our stomachs full."

From day one, the Market Garden campaign teetered on the edge of disaster. All of the airborne endured a terrible pasting. While the 20,000 who arrived that first day for the most part secured their objectives, the Germans rallied swiftly and effectively and Allied forces soon retreated. The British and Polish contingents lost nearly 80 percent of their 10,000-strong who dropped near Arnhem. The figures for the nine days of the operation show more than 7,500 casualties among the 82d and 101st Airbornes, with air crew losses of 424. There was no road to the Ruhr, no coup that opened up a pathway across the Rhine and straight to Berlin. Instead, the Allied forces pulled back to consolidate small gains across the Belgium-Holland border.

3

Winter Comes to Europe

CLOSURE OF THE BRITTANY CAMPAIGN AND THE COLLAPSE OF Market Garden opened up the gasoline taps for the American armies halted because of fuel shortages. The armor rumbled forward but the delay had allowed the Third Reich to reorganize its legions. The defenders drew further advantage from the ability to concentrate their war machine within a shrunken territory. But they no longer had the luxury of fighting on someone else's property since the Allies began to crowd the borders of Germany itself. Eisenhower ordered the offensive to grind on throughout autumn, as the weather worsened.

At the start of October, on the northern shoulder of the U.S. lines—British and Canadian forces occupied the left flank—the First Army struck at Aachen, a sacred city in the Nazi pantheon because it housed the tomb of the revered Charlemagne, and the garrison stuck by its guns and emplacements. The bombs, shells, and bullets resonated symbolism beyond the historic. For the first time, ground battles ripped into German turf. Tanks, self-propelled artillery, and flamethrowers blasted and burned pathways through the Westwall to make gaps for infantrymen who fought from the jumble of wrecked buildings against the stubborn defenders. After little more than two weeks, the GIs occupied block upon block of rubble, all that remained of Aachen.

Bitter fighting erupted in the sodden Vosges Mountains of Southern France where the American Sixth Army Group advanced after Dragoon. Patton's Third Army struck across the Marne and then the Meuse into the province of Lorraine. The struggle to feed the armor and keep it rolling continued. Specially modified B-24s, transformed into flying tank cars, flew gasoline from England to airstrips abandoned by the Germans, but the juggernaut needed more. Robert Johnson, the erstwhile B-17 crew chief now driving a tank for the 4th Armored, said, "We were just north of Metz, approaching the Moselle River. Supplies were slow coming. General Patton had sent a message to General Ike about the problem. He had told Ike that soldiers could eat their belts but the tanks had to have gas."

According to Johnson, the enemy forces were even worse off when it came to the necessities for tank warfare. "The day after the shooting, we engaged in a battle with tanks of the German 2d Panzers. They were dead out of supplies and could not move. We walked through them like plowing new ground." But outside of Metz, the Third Army, to the dismay of its leader, instead of charging east settled into a grim siege. Patton now admitted frustration with "too little gas and too many Germans, not enough ammo and more than enough rain." Casualties without significant results piled up. Carlo D'Este noted, "Patton had fallen victim to the very tactics he scorned in infantry generals. He had failed to concentrates his forces for a decisive attack that might have taken Metz, then refused to accept that he had anything to do with that setback. . . . Lorraine became Patton's bloodiest and least successful campaign."

During the stalemate outside of Metz, the Third Army added the 95th Infantry Division to its complement. Carl Ulsaker was the son of a career army officer and a 1942 graduate of the USMA. As a commander of a heavy weapons company in the 378th Regiment, Ulsaker remembered that prior to the outfit's first mission officers and a representative number of noncoms assembled to hear a speech by Patton. "Because it was a chilly, overcast fall day, 'Old Blood and Guts' wore an overcoat that concealed his normally resplendent uniform and his ivory-handled pistols. He was taller than the other two generals and wore a helmet with three silver stars prominently displayed. Erect in bearing and wearing his famous scowl he made an impressive enough figure for us in the absence of his normal accouterments.

"When Patton began to talk I was surprised at his high-pitched, squeaky voice. From such a big aggressive person one expected to hear the words roll off his tongue in deep, resonant tones. Once the general swung into action, however, what he had to say captured our undivided attention and the timbre of his voice became inconsequential. After an opening statement of welcome, he launched into a litany of how he wished us to fight and behave in the Third Army. Much of what he told us seemed very practical and, to our surprise, often ran contrary to what we had been taught was army doctrine. He spiced his talk with considerable profanity and colorful figures of speech. I understand he did this on purpose because such was the general practice of soldiers and the general wanted to communicate clearly with them."

Recalling as best he could that oration forty-three years later, Ulsaker quoted, "You men were all taught to assault the enemy using fire and maneuver; that is, some of you take cover and fire, while others advance in short rushes. Well, in practice, that doesn't work. First of all, when you get close enough to the enemy to get shot at, you'll find that half your men won't get up and rush when they're supposed to. They feel too secure hugging the ground. Second, you won't see the German son of a bitch until you're right on top of him. Therefore, I want you to use marching fire to attack from the last point of cover. Close with the Hun, get as many rifles, BARs, and machine guns as possible in a line of skirmishers and put a hail of fire in front of you. Shoot at every bush, tree, house—anywhere an enemy might be. Hell, we may be short on artillery rounds but we've got plenty of small-arms ammunition. The old Bunker Hill crap of 'don't shoot till you see the whites of their eyes' doesn't work here. Besides, the Germans don't have any whites to their eyes; the bastards have God damned little yellow pig eyes!

"On maneuvers in the States you were all taught to dig in whenever you halted for any appreciable time. I believe the slogan was 'dig or die.' My motto is 'dig *and* die.' Troops who spend all their time digging are too exhausted to fight when they finally close with the enemy. I want my troops to save their energy for our principal purpose, to kill as many of the bastards as we can. Anyhow, where we're going, the Germans have already been; and they've dug enough foxholes for all of us. I don't want you to walk if there's any way you can ride. Overload the vehicles. If you squeeze hard, you can get a dozen men on a jeep and trailer. The ordnance people would have you think that the truck would break down if you put more than a quarter ton on it. Don't you believe it; those sons of bitches have been putting overload safety factors in the vehicle specs ever since we relied on escort wagons for supply. Why wear yourself out walking when you can ride? If the damn thing breaks down, we can get another. It's a damn sight easier to replace a truck than a combat-trained soldier.

"When you were children I'll bet your mother would make you go inside when it rained. You know the expression, 'He doesn't have sense enough to come in out of the rain.' I don't want that said of anyone in the Third Army. It so happens that in Europe everywhere you look the people have built houses. I want you to take advantage of this shelter to the maximum. Now, in France we are allies and liberators, so just say politely, 'Move over.' But soon we'll be in Germany; there you tell the Nazi bastards, 'Get out!'

"If you believe what you read in the papers, you'd think that generals win wars. Hell, generals don't win wars; you are the people who do that. You junior leaders—sergeants, lieutenants, captains—do things that win wars. An army in combat is nothing more than a whole bunch of small unit actions where the issue is decided by how those small unit leaders behave. Jesus Christ, any old fart can be a general. Look at [Walton H.] Walker [XX Corps commander] here."

"With that Patton slapped the shorter General Walker across his rather expansive stomach and let out a loud guffaw. Walker looked slightly pained but endured his leader's jibe in stoic silence. I noticed that our general, [Harry L.] Twaddle, whom we knew to abhor the use of profanity, also looked somewhat pained. But Patton was in the saddle; he talked the language of the troops. Furthermore, he talked common sense. I made a mental note of the fact that much of the guidance he gave us wiped out a lot of the Mickey Mouse stuff that we had been forced to digest on maneuvers in the U.S. Here was a leader of men worth following into battle."

The 95th made its debut with some success, according to

Ulsaker, obliterating a series of forts that denied access to Metz. Nevertheless, the foe retained a terrifying capacity to retaliate. When his battalion set up an observation site upon a hilltop, the Germans reacted swiftly. "Shells began to rain down on the command group and on my mortar platoon and the battalion reserves in the Bois de Woippy. Volley after volley fell in our area, about twenty to thirty shells per volley. They appeared to come from the German equivalent of our 105mm howitzer. One could hear a sound like a giant ripping a sheet of paper in the distance; it would grow louder and louder, finally rising to a piercing shriek, then dissolving into a series of loud explosions as the shells burst all around us. We of course would flatten out on the ground to minimize our chances of getting hit, taking advantage of small depressions and the smoking craters left by previous shellbursts.

"Not one of us was hit (the command group of about fifteen people) although in the reserve companies one man was killed and a few more wounded. The effect on one's nerves was intense. I literally tingled from head to foot from nervous tension and when a volley would explode all around me, I mentally willed myself to roll up in a little ball inside my steel helmet. If the firing had not slacked off when it did, I don't know how much more we could have endured. What saved us from being hit by flying fragments was that the shells would dig into the ground softened by several days of wet weather and burst after burying themselves a short ways in dirt."

Not everyone regained his equilibrium. A subordinate reported to Ulsaker that one of his mortar-section leaders had been evacuated by medics for combat fatigue. "He was a young fireball who I thought would hold up better in combat than most of my men. In West Virginia he had scaled rocks like a spider, seemingly unafraid where the rest of us had hung on to our pitons and ropes for dear life. In the most rugged training he had always been exemplary and an enthusiastic inspiration for those who tended to lag behind. It showed me that you can't predict how a man will react in combat."

Ulsaker's 3d Battalion focused on a bridge over the Moselle River in the village of Longeville. The line companies achieved good gains. From the observation post, the command could see the general flow of the fight but buildings obscured the bridge objective. A radio message reported I Company GIs in hot pursuit of enemy soldiers retreating along a riverfront boulevard that led to the bridge. Lieutenant Crawford, the company commander, then advised that the Germans now were in full flight across the span and asked for permission to chase them. The battalion commander okayed the advance, cautioning Crawford to have his point men immediately find the enemy soldier manning the exploder habitually installed on bridges.

"A few minutes passed," said Ulsaker, "and Crawford reported his first platoon on the bridge with the lead scouts having gained the far side. Suddenly, we heard a tremendous explosion; it was apparent the bridge had been blown up. Kelly [the battalion commander] called Crawford for a report. All that stunned officer could say was that the American soldiers were still on the bridge when it blew and that he had spent the next couple of minutes dodging large chunks of concrete that rained down everywhere in the general vicinity. Kelly turned pale, sank down on a bench in the room where we had all gathered, and said, 'My God, I sent those men to their death.'

"The radio operator announced that Crawford was calling for orders, but Kelly sat in a kind of daze, shocked by the traumatic turn of events. Lundberg and I looked at each other, then I commented to Kelly, 'I know it's rough, Colonel, but we still have a war to fight, so let's get on with it.' He did not respond, apparently in such a state of shock he didn't hear me."

With the battalion leader temporarily out of action, as the senior officer, Ulsaker radioed Crawford to consolidate his position and ascertain a way to retrieve the handful of GIs on the far side of the Meuse. Kelly gradually emerged from his funk. The entire command moved into Longeville where they learned that five soldiers actually had crossed the bridge, while eight still on it vanished in the massive explosion. One man somehow survived after being hurled into the river. Platoon leader Bill Harrigan located a rowboat and under covering machine-gun and mortar smoke stroked his way across. He picked up three soldiers; two others had been killed by enemy fire. Subsequently, Ulsaker wrote up all fourteen of those who had either been on the bridge or gotten to the other side for a Silver Star. He was told to resubmit for Bronze Stars. Disappointed, Ulsaker complied. However, four months later when he read in *Stars and Stripes* that engineers who unsuccessfully sought to defuse explosives on a Rhine bridge received the higher award, he clipped the item and with a copy of his original recommendations sent it to the awards board with the comment, "My men crossed in the face of enemy fire and ten of them died in the effort!" Their Bronze Stars were upgraded to the Silver.

Ulsaker, coming up behind attacking rifle companies, noticed prisoners of war being led to the rear. "As I approached, I saw to my horror one of our noncoms plucking Germans at random from the POW column and sticking them in the belly with his bayonet. Several of the wounded

Krauts lay groaning in the ditch. I accosted the man and instructed him in no uncertain terms to stop this mayhem, warning him that as soon as I saw his company commander, I would see that he was placed in arrest and charges preferred for court-martial."

Ulsaker met with the GI's superior and first consulted with him on the tactics for the next move. He then reported the atrocity to the company commander, who agreed the misconduct warranted prosecution. "As I returned the way I had come, I passed the L Company weapons platoon, now moving forward. Not seeing the noncom who had been stabbing prisoners, I inquired about him. The platoon leader informed me that a few minutes earlier they had been shelled and that the noncom in question had been seriously wounded and probably would lose a leg. Apparently, a higher court had seen fit to pass sentence!"

On 22 November, Metz finally passed into American hands. Ulsaker accompanied a squad of riflemen to the front entry of the railroad station, a massive door that was closed and barred. "One of the soldiers banged on the door with his rifle butt and commanded in German to open up. Someone inside peered through a small window in the center of this door and asked by what authority we demanded entrance. Another soldier pointed the business end of a bazooka at the window and said, 'By this authority.' The door opened immediately and a number of German soldiers filed out with hands in the air. By this time the streets were filling with hundreds of surrendering enemy and it was apparent that the battle of Metz was over. Civilians began streaming out of the houses where they had taken refuge from the occasional shots and shells fired earlier. They greeted us with great joy, shaking hands and hugging the American troops."

Like the other organizations committed since D day, the

90th Division refilled its platoons with men processed through replacement centers. Private first class Noel Robison stepped onto Omaha Beach on an October morning after a tractor pushed sand right onto the gangplank of his LCI. Robison loaded onto a truck that carried him to a last repple depple before he reached the combat zone across the Moselle. "We twenty infantry riflemen replacements of L Company [358th Regiment, 90th Division] stood around a horse-drawn farm wagon in the barn. Captain Charles B. Bryan, in ODs, with a new-style field jacket on, stepped to the head of the wagon and said in a clear firm voice, 'You may think all American GIs are brave and disciplined but that is not so. Some Americans are yellow cowards and run when faced with enemy fire. I don't want any of you to run. We're all here to finish this job and you have to do your share.' "

Bryan inquired if anyone had medical experience and when a pair raised their hands he assigned them as medics. He asked about Signal School backgrounds. "Private first class Harry Cooley, a streetwise Brooklynite, and I had gone three days for Signal School training. Cooley put up his hand. I had always heard never volunteer in the Army. I decided to make an exception and follow Cooley's decision. It probably saved my life. It certainly made my combat days more pleasant." Posted to the headquarters platoon as a runner to the rifle units, Robison noted, "I carried messages, mail, and supplies. We generally were billeted in houses rather than enduring cold nights in foxholes as did the rifle platoons."

Beyond Metz, the defense remained stalwart and the Third Army struggled to plow through deepening mud and fanatic holdouts. In the mind of the Allied high command, the war would be won once the troops crossed the Rhine

River, opening up broad flat terrain with a few serious natural obstacles. They believed it highly desirable to attain that objective before the Germans refitted their shattered phalanxes of armor and replaced the fallen infantry. But ahead of the Rhine lay a lesser stream, the Roer. To forestall the possibility the Germans might blow up a pair of dams on the Roer, creating an impassable lake, the First Army kicked off an attack through a wooded zone known as the Hurtgen Forest, a fifty-square-mile area packed with tall fir and hardwood trees. Heavily overgrown hills and deep ravines created a natural redoubt. Roads were practically nonexistent except for small trails. The Germans had established solidly protected gun and troop emplacements. In the open ground they sowed deadly Schuh mines.

The Air Corps delivered an enormous volume of ordnance, with as many as 3,000 Allied planes dumping 10,000 tons of bombs. But because no clearly defined front line could be established, as happened on D day, the explosive tonnage left the enemy positions closest to the assaulting troops untouched. In a follow-up, American artillery blasted the Hurtgen until, said George Mabry, "The forest was literally being chewed to pieces by the exploding shells. Trees were shot off and fell across each other making large areas absolutely impenetrable. However, the Germans were so well dug in that they suffered only slight casualties."

The first units to cross the line of departure from Mabry's 2d Battalion of the 8th Infantry hemorrhaged from a wicked amount of artillery tree bursts and mortars. The advance brought the GIs into a minefield garlanded with barbed wire that rose higher than a man's head. The German small-arms fire enveloped those trapped among the mines. Mabry reported, "Men trying to dig in were blown to pieces where they lay. If a man rose from the ground he was almost certain to be hit by the machine-gun fire even if he escaped the artillery and mortars."

By the end of the first day, he reported the area of contention "literally covered with the dead and wounded of the battalion as only limited evacuation had been possible due to the heavy enemy fire. The outfit had lost all rifle company commanders and a large proportion of platoon leaders and noncoms. However, permission to withdraw was denied and regiment ordered the attack renewed the following day. The night became miserably cold and wet but blanket rolls for the men were out of the question. Everything had to be hand carried up the steep slope of the ravine and too many things took priority over the rolls. The night was pitch black and the casualties could only be found by their cries of pain. A roundtrip for a litter team required one and a half to two hours. Many of the wounded died from exposure before they could be evacuated."The killed and wounded added up to about 135. The two other battalions of the regiment remained in reserve, while Mabry's badly mauled unit attacked again.

Although supported by tanks, the outfit, hewing to the plot of the previous day, advanced only as far as a barbed-wire fence. Bangalore torpedoes, inserted at substantial loss of life to those bearing them, declined to explode because of mud and water damage to fuses. Lieutenant Bernard Ray sacrificed his life to blow one gap, earning a posthumous Medal of Honor. But individual heroics meant little against the wall of resistance. The failure to achieve the objectives brought relief of the battalion leader and Mabry assumed the top spot.

To his dismay he learned that after a single day to reorganize and refit, the disheartened GIs, supplemented by 200 untested replacements, would attack in conjunction with brother battalions. Even with another fifty newcomers, the battalion's strength fell to less than 50 percent of its authorized complement. When one company encountered a deadly minefield, Mabry at great risk personally reconnoitered the area and located a pathway. His unit pushed forward and warded off counterattacks for three more agonizing days. Mabry's own efforts earned him a Medal of Honor. After the war he wrote a paper for the Advanced Infantry Officers Course in which his objective tone does not hide devastating criticism of the planning and intelligence of the Hurtgen operation. "To attack a position a second time from the same direction with the same scheme of maneuver after the first attack has failed, unless unavoidable, is unsound." He noted the upper echelons ignored the need for rest and rehabilitation of hard-hit soldiers and the lack of training for replacements. He insisted, "Higher commanders must recognize when a unit has reached the point when it is no longer capable of making a successful attack." He concluded that while the enemy paid dearly for his defense, "The Battle of the Hurtgen Forest, as bloody and bitter a fight as any of the war, brought no glorious victory. No major breakthrough was made nor large area overrun by our troops."

The same terrible consequences befell the 28th, 1st, 8th and 9th Divisions. Bereft of their usual advantages of aerial support and armor, the GIs fought the Germans on an equal footing, using basically standard infantry weapons. At the same time, while American artillery now used the proximity fuses, the Germans improvised by relying on the tree branches to detonate their shells, with deadly consequences even for those who burrowed into the earth.

John Marshall, a tanker in the 707th Tank Battalion, attached to the 110th Infantry, remembered pulling into the

Hurtgen early in November. "We had just dug a trench wide enough for two men to sleep in, side by side. We would then drive our tank so that the tracks would straddle it—giving protection to whoever may be in it. All of us then would get a chance to stretch our legs as we rotated sleeping under the tank. However, we decided to leave the tank where it was and spent the night in the tank. Two soldiers asked us if they could have the trench, which we gladly said they could. About 2300 hours the Germans saturated the area with heavy shelling. One shell landed directly in the trench, killing the two men. None of us slept that night.

"It wasn't quite daylight yet and we traveled several hundred feet when Mike Kosowitz leaned out of the turret to ask two infantrymen from the 110th a question. With my hatch closed I watched the men's expressions through my periscope. They were less than two feet away. They were dirty, tired, scared—I did not realize that they had been there for over a week before we arrived, clean and fed. At this moment there was a tremendous explosion as a heavy mortar hit our tank between the two front hatches. I was crushed with a strange numbness from the concussion. Although I had blood in my mouth, my nose was bleeding, and I was temporarily deaf, I was not wounded. I was alive. I looked over at our driver, John Alyea, and he was staring straight ahead as if in a trance but I concluded that he was not 'hurt' either. I removed the shattered periscope and replaced it with a spare and peered out. All that remained of the two soldiers was a leg with the shoe still on, a head bared to the skull, and a shredded overcoat. I tried to believe this was a bad dream until I heard someone faintly calling me as though he were miles away in a cave. It was Mac, Leonard McKnight, our gunner, telling me, 'Mike got it and needs help.' I crawled back in the turret. As I tried to make him comfortable I could see that his chest was torn from his body. His last words to me were, 'Don't kid me, how bad am I?' I answered, 'You won't be able to write for a while but you will be okay.' He died before I finished the sentence.

"The shelling continued, exploding so close that mud came into the tank like rain, but no direct hits. We turned the tank around and went back to the aid station and turned Mike over to the medics. They processed him and placed him with the others. The bodies were stacked four high and sixty feet long—there may have been many more but I saw two such 'stacks.' "

The tank, now operating with a four-man crew, rolled toward a church in the village of Vossenack. "We received a direct hit in the rear of the tank," reported Marshall. "It went forward for fifteen or twenty feet down a swale and into a tremendous burst of exploding mortars. The now trackless side of the tank dropped into some of these craters, rendering it immobile. We discovered the turret could not traverse; the 75mm gun was useless but we were alive and for the moment 'safe,' because the tank now was lower than the grassy mound on our left.

"The Germans, knowing we were there, kept shooting at us many times with heavy guns. The shells would slam into the mound, tear through the earth like a giant mole, and then glance upward with a sickening 'whirring' sound, raining dirt, rocks, and grass into our tank. It seemed like forever, but the shelling directed at us finally stopped. The tank was a mess with blood mixed with mud and debris. Because the gun was not working, we decided to abandon the tank. I was for jumping out while it was still daylight but John and Mac thought it would be unwise; we should wait until dark. John then suggested we set up a machine gun outside the tank and take turns on guard. We decided against that move. John often wished he had an M1 of his own. The field to our right was littered with dead Americans lying near M1 rifles. Just to hear myself talk I said to John, 'There's your chance to pick up an M1 rifle for yourself.' John thought a moment and then opened his hatch, unseen by the Krauts because it was much lower than the turret. Nothing happened until he ventured a short distance from the tank to pick up the rifle and was now in view of the Krauts. Again all hell broke loose, prompting John to throw the rifle down and run like mad back to the tank.

"Darkness comes early at this time of the year but there was still daylight left when we decided our evacuation procedure. One man at a time would exit the tank and run, diving from shell hole to shell hole for forty or fifty yards, then run again when the second man exited. We were to repeat this procedure so that we would all be heading toward the command post forty or fifty yards apart." The quartet reached safety and accepted an offer from the cooks to use their tents. As Marshall tried to relax on a cot, he realized, "We had lost all our possessions. We had lost our tank with thousands of rounds of ammunition. I nudged John [Alyea]. 'Do you realize we never fired a shot?' Exhausted, sleep came quickly. So ended our first day in the Hurtgen Forest."

Antitank crewman John Chernitsky said, "I had never seen such destruction to forest land. The German artillery kept firing at the tops of trees and artillery bursts hit the trees—the shrapnel fell just like rain and the artillery was constant—day and night. The casualties in the 110th were heavy. The movement of medics and ambulances was noticeable in the Hurtgen Forest. When they had a chance they picked up the dead. The German losses were heavy also, but we never could figure out what happened to the Germans who were wounded or dead. We would hear screaming and cries for help but the next morning, we couldn't see any wounded or dead."

The horrendous bloodshed in the thickets of the Hurtgen—6,000 casualties—all but destroyed the 28th Division. Survivors took to calling the red keystone shoulder patch "the bloody bucket." GIs from the 8th Division took over some of the 28th's responsibilities and the 4th Division moved up to bolster the left flank on the edge of the forest. The 500-man 2d Ranger Battalion relieved elements of the badly mauled division. Sid Salomon, the Ranger captain who participated in the capture of Pointe et Raz de la Percée overlooking Omaha Beach, noted, "Cold weather and a driving rain did not help the morale of the inexperienced American troops. Trench foot and casualties helped to add to the confusion that was rampant. After one month of fighting, the Americans had barely advanced twelve miles into Germany. The Rangers of Baker Company were amazed to see the GI equipment, clothing, and even weapons that had been discarded by the division troops who had previously held this area."

After Brest, Bob Edlin and A Company of the Rangers relished a month-long sojourn at a rest camp before trucking to the Hurtgen area. "You could always tell when it was getting time to go into combat. Good things started happening. We were visited by General Eisenhower. The whole battalion gathered around and he just flat-out asked if anybody could tell him why we didn't have the new boot packs. One of the men yelled out, 'Hell, everybody back at headquarters has got them,' which was true. Back in army headquarters and corps headquarters and division headquarters, everyone was wearing boot packs, parkas, and warm clothes. Up in the front lines [that gear] never leaked down. We were still wearing summer clothing and the temperature was now down in the low thirties, high twenties. General Eisenhower said that will be taken care of and God rest his soul it was. A few days later we received boot packs and even wristwatches. He must have raided the whole damn headquarters to get enough for one Ranger battalion."

Edlin's A Company exchanged places with units from the 28th Division's 112th Infantry. He encountered a friend from OCS who said, "'Bob, this is the meanest son of a bitch that you've ever seen in your life up there. I wish you wouldn't go. I wish you'd just flat tell them you're not going any farther.' He told me that there were men up there that you wouldn't believe would ever lose their nerve but have gone completely blank. They absolutely can't hold out any longer. I thought—you know how you are as a Ranger—we'll calm things down. How in the hell I thought 500 men could do what four infantry divisions couldn't, I don't know. When I left Jack he was actually crying and told me not to do any more than I had to."

Amid drifting snow, the platoon climbed a trail up a steep hill to the village of Germeter. As the Rangers appeared, men from the 112th Infantry emptied from the houses. Advised they would only be there a few days, warmed by a charcoal fire, and with a roof overhead, Edlin decided that maybe it was not such a bad situation. "Suddenly, the artillery starts coming. It's the purest hell I've ever been through. It was just round after round of crashing and smashing, beating on your head till you think there is no way you can stand it. I was lying on my back on the floor and the only way I can keep my sanity was by joking with the men on the floor around me. Most of them didn't take it as a joke and got pretty upset that I was calling directions for artillery fire on the house, hollering 'up 100,' 'right 100,' 'up.' In several hours, they literally shot the house down around us."

Colonel Rudder requested a patrol into the town of Schmidt to find out if it were infested with Germans. Edlin led the same band that had accompanied him in the capture of the fort guarding Brest. The Ranger leader suspected that the same sort of trap that had destroyed the Ranger battalions at Cisterna might lie in wait. Edlin and his crew crept into Schmidt and he became highly suspicious at the absence of any visible German presence. When he informed Rudder of what he did not see, Rudder was convinced the open town was a snare. Back in the basement of the house, Edlin with only about twenty left to his platoon endured "another hellacious shelling," including one round that penetrated the cellar. "I heard Sergeant Fronzek moan. When I got to him it was the most terrible-looking wound I had ever seen. Shrapnel had torn across his chest. I think his lungs were exposed. He had a pack of cigarettes in his pocket. I could see the tobacco shreds being sucked into his body as he struggled to breathe. I yelled at Sgt. Bill Klaus to get a jeep in here and get him out. In minutes we had a medic. They carried him to the jeep and he was gone. We heard from Dr. Block he would make it and he did."

Headquarters now summoned Edlin, who assumed his paltry few were about to be relieved. "I went down that son of a bitch fire trail, past Purple Heart Corner, artillery fire on our [his runner accompanied him] asses all the way. The trail was frozen. New snow lay ass-deep to a tall Indian. We were slipping and sliding; hell, they could have heard us in Berlin. It was early evening but darker than the inside of a black cat. At headquarters someone told me Rudder wanted to see me. I knew we're not being relieved. I don't need to see the colonel for that.

"Rudder was billeted in a small building, like a hunting shelter about the size of a small bathroom. There was a little kerosene stove, a table, a couple of chairs, a double bunk bed. Colonel Rudder was huddled by the stove. Big Jim, as we called him. He was only thirty-five years old but he looked like a tired, worn-out old man. I had never seen him that way." The Rangers CO dispensed with military formality and invited Edlin to sit. "He handed me a cup of hot coffee, looked at me for a minute, and said, 'Arman [Company A commander] is here to make arrangements to relieve B Company. But we've got a problem. I heard from Sid Salomon. A short time ago, B Company was pinned down in a minefield. They were under heavy artillery and machine-gun fire with a lot of casualties. I need a volunteer to take a patrol in, find a way to get to them, arrange to relieve them, and try and bring out some of the wounded. The patrol needs to go in now. A will relieve B tomorrow night. I'm not going to ask you to go, but that's the situation.'

"The picture runs through my mind like a kaleidoscope. I can't stand to take any more of this. I'm tired and scared. This will be pure hell and I can't stand any more of my platoon getting slaughtered. But then I can see B Company suffering up there. We've been through a lot together. Shit, I've got to go. I looked at Arman and back to Jim. There's no rank here, just Rangers. 'God, Jim, I hate to ask my guys to go, they're pretty beat up, and I don't know if they'll make it or not.' The colonel just nodded and said, 'Yeah, I know.' 'Okay, we'll be on the way. It'll take me an hour to get back to the platoon. We should be in B's position in a couple of hours.' Rudder said, 'There will be a medical jeep at your CP when you get back. Good luck.' The son of a gun knew I would go."

After another but uneventful trek up the snowy trail, navigating the always dangerous Purple Heart Corner, Edlin asked for volunteers. He chose Courtney and Dreher. They would travel without helmets, packs, or even weapons. Accompanied by a driver and medic from battalion headquarters, they passed slowly along a hardtop road, aware that at any moment shells might fall upon them. At the point where the remainder of the trip would be on foot, Edlin told the driver, whom he did not know, to stay with the jeep. He said, 'Lieutenant, they ain't nobody gonna steal it. Let me go with you. I can help carry the wounded out. The medic handed the driver a litter, took another on his shoulder and said they were ready. I said, 'Let's spread out in single file. Keep as much interval as you can without getting lost. We don't want one round to get us all.' "

The would-be rescuers slid through ice and snow, aware of a potential mine at every step. "It was so dark it was almost impossible to move. The trees are down as if a mad woodcutter had been through with a giant buzzsaw. 'Shit, I forgot the marking tape.' Courtney sensed the problem and said I've got it and we're marking the path. I prayed Lord just give me the strength and guts to make a few more yards then we can rest a minute. A shell landed thirty yards off; damn, that was close. A few more yards I could hear German machine-gun fire; a German flare lights up the scene. The snow is almost blizzard conditions. The flare shows trees uprooted, dead American and German soldiers, twisted bushes. No satanistic artist could dream up such a sight."

Edlin faltered, feeling he could not continue. Dreher's hand clutched his shoulder and the sergeant said, "I'll get it [lead] for a while." Courtney, ten yards behind, called out, "What's the matter, Lieutenant, you volunteered for the Rangers, didn't you?"

Bullets rustled through the underbrush from unseen gunmen and then a quiet voice challenged the patrol. Nobody knew the password, but when questioned on the first name of Lieutenant Fitzsimmons, Courtney answers "Bob," and they are welcomed.

"I'm led to Captain Salomon's CP," recalled Edlin. "It's under a small bridge by a woodcutter's trail. I talk with Sid a few minutes and he tells me to go to Fitzsimmons who's got the worst wounded. I inform Sid we've marked the path and A Company will be in at 8:00 P.M. tomorrow night, November 23. He thanked us for coming and said the B Company medic would meet us at Fitszimmons's position. Artillery was still coming in and there was occasional machine-gun fire.

"We found Fitzsimmons and decided we would carry out two wounded at a time. The jeep driver and Courtney started back with the first litter. The two medics loaded another litter. I took the front end and told the battalion medic to stay with B Company. He was at the other end of the litter. As he stepped back to let Dreher replace him, he stepped on a mine. It went off. I learned later this heroic man lost a foot. Fitzsimmons was hit in the face. I saw the Ranger on the litter bounce into the air. The blast of shrapnel knocked me into a tree. I must have been unconscious. For a moment I'm completely blind and deaf. My left hand hurts. I reach over and can't feel my hand. It must be gone at the wrist. I'm going to die right here in this damn German woods. Strong arms picked me up, Dreher throws me over his shoulder. I can't see or hear. They were carrying me through the woods to the jeep.

"I woke up, lying on a stretcher. I'm not blind; there is a dim light. I heard Doc Block's voice, 'Wash his eyes with boric acid [to remove dirt and mud].' I have some hearing in one ear. I hear Doc say, 'Take him back to a hospital.' 'Wait a minute, Doc. How bad is it?' 'You ain't hurt, you goldbrick, a little shrapnel in your hand and face. They'll fix you up back at a field hospital. It's mostly shock and mud.' I asked someone else about the others and all they tell me is that everyone will be okay." Loaded into an ambulance, he lay next to the medic whose foot had been destroyed. "I don't know what route we took, but German artillery chased us a good ways. It ought to be against the rules to shoot at you when you're leaving."

At a field hospital Edlin quickly recovered his aplomb and his temper. He demanded an audience with the head doctor, pleading for quick repairs, explaining, "Major, there's about fifty men from B Company still in that woods. About the same number of A Company are going in to relieve them. I know the path into that death trap. If you'll clean up my eyes and hearing I'll take them up there." The surgeon argued that Edlin risked severe infection but eventually agreed to debride and stitch the wound. The doctor and several oversized aid men showed up to perform the work. Edlin learned that if he received an anesthetic it would require an overnight stay. Having abjured unconsciousness, he watched the surgeon remove the crusty, bloody bandage. "Shit, that hurt. Then I found out what the big aidmen were for. One held my legs, one grabbed my right arm, the nurse had my left arm. He took a pan of hot soapy water and a scrub brush and went to work, cleaning my hand. I'm raising hell, it hurt so bad. The hell with B Company and the rest of the Rangers, ain't nothing ever hurt so much. After this short period of torture, he took a knife and some tweezers. I remember he said, 'This is really going to hurt.' Right, Doc, it did. They counted forty-eight pieces of shrapnel, plus whatever is still in there. They put a bandage and sling on my arm, patched up my face, and the surgeon said, 'You're on your own.' I knew he would catch hell about the paperwork but he just answered, 'Get a couple of Krauts for us.' I gave him some real German marks one of the Krauts had loaned me. He was quite a man and one hell of a doctor.

"I knew if I went back to battalion headquarters, Block would kick my ass so I took off up that damn Germeter trail again. It hadn't changed, slick, slippery, slimy. It's one dark, cold, snowy night. My ass is dragging when I get past Purple Heart Corner. I go into our beat-up old house and it's empty. The charcoal fires are out and the platoon is gone. I realize they have gone to relieve B Company without me. It's twenty-four hours since I left. My hand and face hurt and I still can't hear. I've had about all of this bullshit I need."

Edlin staggered back to battalion headquarters, where he learned Rudder had left for a meeting with higher-ups. Someone took pity on the exhausted platoon leader and told him to take the colonel's bunk for the night. Another samaritan brought some hot food from the mess, even cutting bite-size pieces, and offered to feed him. Surgeon Block checked his hand and face, then chewed him out for not remaining in the rear. When Edlin asked for a painkiller that would enable him to rejoin his men, Block ordered him to remain in the bunk, where he drifted off to sleep.

"When I woke it was still dark but it was twenty-four hours later. Colonel Rudder was dozing in a chair while I was using his bunk. They just don't make colonels like that."

The enemy meanwhile occupied dominant positions on high ground around the towns of Schmidt and Bergstein, from which it poured abundant artillery and mortars upon anyone who sought to advance through the minefields and withering small-arms fire. The locale provided the defenders with a commanding view of any movement of U.S.

troops. The general in charge of the task force specifically asked Gen. Leonard Gerow, corps commander, for Rangers to assist the 8th Division's assault on Bergstein and Castle Hill or, officially, Hill 400.

Len Lomell, now commissioned, and George Kerchner, with D Company, started for Bergstein on 6 December. Morale dropped as word passed that their revered commander, Colonel Rudder, was departing to lead the shattered 28th Division's 109th Regiment. In the early morning hours of 7 December Rangers sifted through Bergstein and rousted those Germans who resisted. At 0730, amidst a fearsome artillery duel, the Rangers jumped off for Hill 400.

According to Sid Salomon, "The CO at the appropriate time gave the word 'Go!' With a whooping and hollering as loud as possible, firing a clip of ammo at random from their weapons in the direction of the hill, the Rangers ran as fast as they could across the approximately 100 yards of open, cleared field into the machine-gun and small-arms fire of the German defenders. Crossing the field, and before reaching the base of the hill, the company commander and his runner became casualties, but still the remaining D Company Rangers continued their forward charge up the hill.

"The enemy defenders immediately became alert. A red flare shot in the air from an enemy outpost, apparently a signal to their higher headquarters. Shortly thereafter a heavy mortar and artillery barrage came down on the assaulting Rangers. Heavy small-arms and machine-gun fire was directed on the rushing Rangers. Casualties on both sides now began to mount, but still the charge continued. Some Germans were giving ground. Others of the enemy forces were seemingly safe in well-prepared holes or behind log emplacements. Rifle and automatic fire filled the air. A creeping German artillery barrage behind the assaulting Rangers produced more Ranger casualties. The enemy continued to offer stiff resistance. Ultimately the fast, unceasing, and determined forward momentum of the assaulting D Company Rangers stunned the German defenders, some of whom quickly moved away from the steadily advancing assaulting troops."

Within an hour, the enemy had fled, but it was an onerous victory. Well aware of the importance of the highland, the foe now rained down a murderous assortment of explosives upon the new kings of the hill. The rocky, tree-rooted ground defied the best efforts of entrenching tools. The only shelter lay beneath toppled trees or in shell holes. The battered able-bodied Rangers of D Company drew some comfort from the support of F Company that had secured the left flank. Lomell, now the sole officer of D Company still on his feet, reached a concealed troop shelter at the top of the hill. He threw in a grenade while another Ranger sprayed the interior with automatic fire. According to Lomell, "Survival was a matter of luck. We were under constant bombardment. Guys were lying all over the hill. We couldn't even give first aid. We were told we would be relieved and just to hold on. How long can you tell a guy bleeding to death to hold on? My God, he knew I was lying to him.

"I had tears in my eyes. We stopped another counterattack, but if the Germans had known how many men, or really how few we had up there, they would have kept coming." Bleeding from wounds of his hand and arm, Lomell offered a proposal to his noncoms. " 'If we retreat, they'll take care of our wounded. We can come back and take the hill later.' They adamantly refused to consider the idea." An explosion near him caused a concussion. "I was bleeding from the anus and the mouth as a result." Under cover of darkness, he was evacuated.

Originally informed they would need to control Castle Hill for no more than twenty-four hours before infantrymen of the 8th Division would take over, the beleaguered Rangers endured more than forty hours on the heights. Of the sixty-five Rangers who started the charge, only fifteen could come down under their own power. On the morning after Lomell came off Hill 400, German artillery slammed into the Ranger positions just as battalion surgeon Walter Block left his dugout to supervise evacuation of the seriously wounded. A shell fragment killed him instantly.

As one his last acts, Block spared his medical technician Frank South the worst of the battering around Hill 400. "The day before the battalion was sent into action at Bergstein, I passed out due to dehydration and a severe gastrointestinal problem. Not knowing we were about to be committed, Block insisted that I get to a hospital. I was unaware we were in action until wounded Rangers began to arrive. I immediately went AWOL from the hospital and hitchhiked back to the battalion, only to find the Battle of Hill 400 was over, the battalion decimated, and Block dead. He was the first and last medical officer we had that deserved the name of a Ranger. I still feel both guilty and somehow cheated that I was not part of that battle."

Sid Salomon, CO of Baker Company, 2d Ranger Battalion, who saw his GIs chewed up during the first exploratory thrusts into the Hurtgen forest, considered his people cruelly used. "After the invasion, there was no need for a 2d Ranger Battalion. We were used as an infantry company, attached to maybe ten different divisions. The people in command did not know what the Rangers were. They would put the Rangers first and keep their own casualties down. A Combat Command of the 5th Armored Division [ordinarily about 3,000 men with tanks and other armored vehicles] failed to take Bergstein. Three companies of Rangers [little more than 200 foot soldiers] captured it, going past burned-out tanks with GIs hanging over the sides." Salomon himself collected his second Purple Heart on Thanksgiving Day 1944, as an explosion lacerated his eyebrows and chin.

4

"I Have Returned"

FOLLOWING THE GAINS IN THE MARIANAS AND NEW GUINEA, the strategists debated the next major step. Prior to the most recent successes, the blueprints called for an orderly progression up the island stepping-stones, starting with the Palau group and then climbing up the Philippine Archipelago via the southernmost outpost, Mindanao. Buoyed by their successes, Admirals King and Nimitz argued for a giant leap that bypassed Luzon, the main Philippine island, in favor of Formosa, less than 1,000 miles from the enemy homeland. Adding to King's taste for Formosa was that it lay within the Navy's sphere of control. The proposal outraged MacArthur because it condemned the Filipinos to remain under the harsh boots of the Japanese. From a military standpoint, the grandiose notion to mount a successful invasion of Formosa in mid-to-late 1944 required manpower and supplies far beyond those available.

MacArthur drew support from an unexpected quarter. Admiral "Bull" Halsey reported that his ships and planes had seen little evidence of any strong enemy forces on the islands below Luzon. Although Halsey badly underestimated the strength of the Japanese, MacArthur persuaded Nimitz to accept an invasion of the Philippine Archipelago. Actually, through the campaigns that involved the Solomons, Marshalls, Marianas, and New Guinea, MacArthur and Nimitz, while occasionally squabbling over allocation of resources, had cooperated well.

Without committing themselves to taking back Luzon, the Navy honchos agreed that for a start it would be necessary to capture the southern and central Philippine areas. Mindanao, vulnerable since the conquest of Wakde, Biak, and Noemfoor, seemed ripe for the opening thrust, and then Leyte, strategically sited in the middle of the islands. A tentative schedule set 1 November as the date for landings on Mindanao. During the first two weeks of September, carriers from Halsey's fleet launched a series of preparatory strikes on Mindanao and the central islands. Halsey now reported to Nimitz that his pilots had destroyed the Japanese fuel supplies, sunk almost all vessels visible, and encountered few aircraft. Moreover, a downed flier rescued by Filipinos brought back the startling intelligence from the natives that there were no Japanese soldiers on Leyte. Halsey recommended that instead of Mindanao, the combined forces attack Leyte. Although MacArthur's staff correctly pointed out that the Filipino report of no enemy troops on Leyte was dead wrong, the Joint Chiefs, MacArthur, and Nimitz concurred on an invasion of Leyte rather than Mindanao and scheduled amphibious operations to open 20 October.

To reduce the capacity of the Nipponese to interfere with operations around Leyte, a component of the U.S. Navy's Fast Carrier Force, Task Force 38, steamed into the China

Sea and hammered the Formosa airfields and installations. Planes on the island engaged the carrier-based Americans in a furious, three-day affair. The attackers wrecked more than 500 aircraft, sank about forty cargo vessels, and blasted ammunition dumps, hangars, barracks, maintenance shops, and manufacturing sites. The naval air arm also rampaged across Luzon, targeting fields and fortifications around Manila. Simultaneously with these raids, the U.S. Army's Far Eastern Air Forces, taking off from Morotai, Biak, New Guinea, and other locales, pummeled enemy airdromes in the Philippines and laid waste to installations in the occupied Netherlands East Indies

During the Formosa engagement, the defenders crippled the cruisers *Houston* and *Canberra*, bounced a bomb off the carrier *Franklin*, and a flaming enemy bomber skidded across that ship's flight deck. Antiaircraft and dogfights cost the Americans seventy-six planes. While casualties among personnel aboard the three vessels saddened shipmates—the disabled cruisers reduced Task Force 38's power minimally—the *Franklin* remained fully serviceable. The losses of air crews and their machines hurt most but the overall impact upon the state of the fleet was negligible.

However, the Japanese Navy enthusiastically accepted the extravagantly false claims of success from their fliers and issued a communiqué triumphantly listing 11 carriers, 2 battleships, 3 cruisers, one destroyer or light cruiser sunk, another 8 carriers, 2 battleships and as many as 15 other ships severely damaged or set afire. The emperor issued a special decree to commemorate the great victory, while civilians and military plunged into a mass celebration of the fictitious triumph. A roseate view victimized the Imperial High Command. It eagerly sought this moment when it could swing the combined, full weight of the Army, Navy, and Air Forces against the now staggering Americans. A jesting Admiral Halsey radioed Admiral Nimitz on 19 October that he was "now retiring toward the enemy following the salvage of all the Third Fleet ships recently reported sunk by radio Tokyo," but the Japanese persisted in the belief America was about to fall.

U.S. intelligence on Leyte estimated a garrison of 20,000 one month before the scheduled invasion. But with more than 400,000 Japanese stationed throughout the archipelago, no one doubted that sizable reinforcements could be rushed to areas under siege. The battle order started with the 1st Cavalry, 7th, 96th, and 24th Infantry Divisions, plus the 77th and 32d as reserves. With the auxiliaries and service personnel, a total of more than 200,000 men headed for Leyte. Because the nearest strips for fighter cover lay 500 miles off, much of the air support lay with the Navy carriers. Also hurling its weight through the sky, the Army Air Corps would hit the Japanese with its bombers and be ready to blast ships carrying reinforcements for the island defenders.

The opening salvos from the U.S. fleet crashed down upon Leyte two days before A-day. (With D day now so firmly associated with the Normandy invasion, the planners had abandoned the tradition that dated to World War I and started to use other initials and codes to mark operations.) Planes from carriers concentrated upon neutralizing enemy airfields while the 6th Ranger Battalion eliminated installations on four tiny islands in Leyte Gulf. In the armada of 700 ships, MacArthur himself sailed on the cruiser *Nashville*.

At 0600 on A-day, battleships along an eighteen-mile line from San Jose down to Dulag on the northeast coast of Leyte shelled the beaches. From two miles offshore, MacArthur witnessed the start of the action. "I could clearly see sandstrips with the pounding surf beating down upon the shore and in the morning sunlight, the jungle-clad hills rising behind the town. Landings are explosive once the shooting begins, and now thousands of guns were throwing their shells with a roar that was incessant and deafening. Rocket vapor trails crisscrossed the sky, and black, ugly pillars of smoke began to rise. High overhead, swarms of airplanes darted into the maelstrom. And across what would ordinarily have been a glinting, untroubled blue sea, the black dots of the landing craft churned toward the beaches."

As his F Company from the 34th Regiment, 24th Division, approached Leyte, Paul Austin, the company commander, remembered, "We were awakened about 4:00 A.M., had the usual prelanding breakfast, steak and eggs. This was the only time we ever got that kind of food. The 24th Division landed on Red Beach with the 34th on the right and the 19th Regiment to the left. The 1st Cavalry Division landed three or four miles north of us in the vicinity of Tacloban and near the Leyte commercial airfield. Their objective was that airfield and Tacloban, the capital city.

"My company landed about 10:05, in the second wave. As we came off the boats, we ran across some shallow water and hit the sand. The first wave was still lying there. I asked what company is this and was informed K Company. I said, 'You're supposed to be about fifty yards in. What's the holdup?' They told me there were snipers and a machine gun that pinned them down. Shells were falling all over the place. I looked out to sea and saw a landing boat take a direct hit, probably an artillery shell. That boat literally disappeared, nothing left except a few pieces of scrap and steel helmets. The entire boatload, maybe twenty-five soldiers, lost along with the coxswain. Other boats were on fire, two LSTs and LCIs.

"Rifle fire was coming in pretty heavy. Our Captain Wye

from regimental headquarters was killed a minute after he set foot on the beach. Another company commander from the 1st Battalion was killed very near Col. [Aubrey] "Red" Newman [regimental CO]. I looked back and couldn't see anybody moving forward. Snipers, machine guns, mortars, artillery, had everyone pinned down on the beach sand. The beach was covered with palm limbs, fronds; the bombardment had stripped the coconut trees by the thousands. It was pretty hard to walk because of the heavy layers of limbs while the trunks of the coconut trees stuck up in the air like telephone poles. Very few had any branches."

As a telephone lineman with the 2d Battalion's Headquarters Company, Han Rants recalled a seven-day voyage to the shores of Leyte. "It was a time of great anxiety among the troops. There was much meditating, cardplaying, talking through the night. We liked going by ship because we felt the Navy food was really something compared to what we got in base camp or wherever we happened to be. While down in the hold our thinking all the time was that a torpedo hit would come right into the hold. That doesn't give you any real peace of mind.

"During the card playing, few of the fellows really had any money and they would play on the basis of IOUs. As that gambling went on, there was a fellow from Gardena, California, Pfc. Harold Moon, who won lots of money. He was a real rascal as far as a garrison soldier was concerned. He would have been in the stockade all the time because he wasn't a real spit-and-polish soldier. Within the first day of our trip from Hollandia, Moon showed up with a set of Navy fatigues, their blue work clothes. On occasion, he would slip on that outfit and could go through off-limits areas to get ice water or whatever he needed. He even showed up with a first lieutenant's bar for his Army fatigue hat. Moon was quite a poker player and he won big. I think he had around $1,200 in cash on him as we hit the beach at Leyte.

"The tension builds in any beachhead convoy and the nearer the island, the more tension. The day and night before a landing are wide-awake times with more knife sharpening and gun cleaning. Some of the Tommy gunners file or cut plus [+] or x marks on the cartridge heads. If properly done, this causes the slug to split four ways when it hits the body so that a large hole and much damage results. Many GIs stand at the rail all night, some weeping, some meditating, some cursing, but all weighing their chances of getting through another campaign. It gets to be pretty emotional. Some buddies sit quietly after having lived together day and night, never more than an arm's length away. You know the other guy's family; you know his sweetheart, you know everything about everyone. I remember so vividly the last few nights with fellows saying, 'If I don't make it, will you do this for me?'

"When the people are loaded in the landing craft (LCVP) they go away from the ships and circle until everyone is loaded. As we got into our circling position, our planes had gone in to do some bombing of the beach, and our battleships who were out deep behind us were throwing shells over our heads. The beach seemed to be one big explosion. We got to feeling confident that there couldn't be anything alive in there with all of this. The LCIs were going in closer and firing with heavy machine guns. They also had some multiple-launch rockets fired at close range. The destroyers in shallower waters would blast away with five-inch guns.

"Just before 10:00 A.M. we were circling in those boats, with people getting really sick in them. They pop around the ocean like corks and the smoke from the motors is somewhat like following a city bus, just breathing in the fumes, a horrible smell that you breathe continuously. After riding around a length of time, many of the troops would just as soon die if they could reach the beach. Right at 10:00 A.M. the shelling stopped and all of these boats spread out and started in. It was deathly quiet as there was no firing while were going in because they didn't want to take a chance on shells falling short, hitting us. As we got within 200 yards, enemy shells started coming out. Mortars sometimes hit a barge but usually missed. They turned artillery and antiaircraft guns on us. Everybody was scared. The Navy men driving these barges were on raised platforms like sitting ducks. They stood up high with a very small shield and wanted to dump us and get out. They smacked the beach and yelled at us to get out. Sometimes, some started back before the last guy got out of the barge. They had to go back and get another load and come in later.

"We were supposed to be the fourth or fifth wave but we got there second or third. As our barge hit the beach and the door flopped open, we jumped out, scared as can be. There is no pain or hurt as bad as being scared to death, and scared to death we were. There was no combat group in front of us, no troops to gain some ground and make a place for us to set up a headquarters. As wiremen we had no rifles, only our switchboard and rolls of wire for telephone communications. Our weapons were .45s, meant to defend ourselves close range. We tried to hang at the beach but as we came off that landing barge, within ten feet of us was a fellow who had been cut in half by an artillery shell. There was no bottom half of him and he was stretched out, guts pouring from the bottom half, which was half in the water, and half out. Everybody just stopped, looked at some of the dead people hit in the first wave and then looked at each other. We knew we couldn't run back into the water because there was no place there. People seemed stunned. The Navy had to stop shelling but the landing barges had .50-caliber machine guns firing over our heads.

"About this time," Rants continued, "Colonel Newman, a big redheaded man and a real tough guy with a lot of guts, jumped up on the beach twenty or thirty feet from me and said, 'Get the hell off the beach! Get up and get moving! Follow me!' It was just enough to get everybody awake. GIs started moving, crawling, jumping, running combat-style. You run a little, roll over and try to take cover before moving again. We thought we would get some sort of position before they saw us but they apparently knew we were coming because they had managed to build some pillboxes. They had coconut logs covered with dirt and machine guns shooting from narrow slits in these mounds of dirt and logs. The only way you can get people out of these places is to be close enough with a flamethrower or get in closer under the machine-gun fire and toss a grenade in.

"A hero came forth but we knew he had come to this battle to die. He was a big Hawaiian captain, one of the most popular officers. Before we left Hollandia he had received word his wife just had a baby although he'd been away for twelve months. This really shook him and we knew he was going to fight with everything he had, even if he got killed in the process. Word passed that he was really ripping and had knocked out three pillboxes. With real luck, he was jumping, running, dodging, and crawling under machine-gun fire to get hand grenades in the fortresses. At about the fifth one they got him, laced him with fire and he was hit ten times through the chest. He was the one who really broke the spell enough for our people to start moving in."

Austin's memory of the morning action was slightly different. "For all of that heavy bombardment, the enemy fire was very heavy. I heard someone yell, I'm pretty sure an officer from K Company, yelled, 'Let's go!' [Newman was about 150 yards away from Austin] and K Company jumped up and ran into the jungle off the beach. I let them move about fifty yards ahead and then shouted for F Company to move. Our two platoons on the beach started forward. My instructions were to follow the 3d Battalion, K Company, as it turned out, to a certain point and then we would pass through them to take up the attack. F Company would lead under the theory that by the time we covered 300 yards, the 3d Battalion would have suffered so many casualties, the second wave would have to take over the advance. Luckily it didn't turn out that bad, although K Company had taken some casualties. I had my men get on their bellies and crawl, trying to make harder targets for the snipers. I kept them on their bellies for at least seventy-five yards.

"A light tank came roaring down the beach and he turned into our area and drove the tank right up to the 3d Battalion line to our front. Colonel Postelwaite, the battalion CO, walked up behind the tank, took the telephone in his hand and talked to the gunner and driver. He started directing fire from that tank. They put a 75mm shell into everything that even looked like it might contain a Jap or a machine gun. He'd fire at two or three targets, then move the tank forward twenty or thirty yards and repeat the process. I knew he destroyed two log pillboxes with shells right into the apertures of them. Colonel Postelwaite moved his front line right up to the edge of a big rice paddie full of water. I saw him talking to the tank and then the gun swung around, to line up on a building across the rice paddie. It put a shell into a small building a few yards away from a house and blew it to pieces. I could see chickens and chicken feathers flying."

Joe Hofrichter, formerly with an engineer unit, had been

transferred to the 24th Division after a misunderstanding about returning from a leave. As an outsider and buck private, Hofrichter had worked the worst details during his first weeks with the 24th until a sergeant took him to a supply tent. "He emerged holding a flamethrower, which he threw at me. 'This is a flamethrower,' I protested. 'Right, and it's all yours,' the sergeant replied. I said, 'Sergeant, I just got into the infantry. I don't know the first thing about a flamethrower.' Starting with almost a whisper and progressively getting louder and louder he repeated, 'I know you don't know anything about a flamethrower, but by the time we hit the beach in the Philippines, you're going to be the best damn flamethrower operator in the entire Army.' "

Hofrichter underwent a two-day crash course in the operation and care of his new weapon. He was assigned to an LST that carried M8s, self-propelled artillery pieces resembling tanks. Hofrichter and four riflemen were assigned to support an M8 bent on destruction of enemy bunkers. "If fire from the M8 failed to silence a bunker," says Hofrichter, "I was to move forward under protective fire. I was to find an opening in the bunker and, at close range, hit the opening with several bursts from the flamethrower. After the briefing I felt as though I had been hit in the stomach with a sledgehammer. I kept thinking how inexperienced I was and why I had been chosen to wield such an awesome weapon. It made no sense but that was not unusual in the Army. You didn't need a Ph.D. from MIT to operate a flamethrower. Privates, especially replacements, were considered expendable, referred to as 'cannon fodder.' "

On 19 October, after a final rundown on the specific missions, Hofrichter noticed that all the joking had ceased. Few slept and, as a newcomer, Hofrichter was excluded from small groups who spoke quietly to one another. The novice flamethrower operator says he spent the night thinking of his "beautiful young wife, parents, kid brothers and sisters, and a role model from high school, a football coach." At the Mass conducted by a chaplain, Hofrichter prayed not so much that he be spared but that God grant him the strength and courage to face what lay ahead. He could not stomach the steak and eggs and munched on a piece of roll with his coffee.

Scheduled for the third wave, Hofrichter and his group donned their gear at 9:30 A.M. "A fellow by the name of Johnny Lomko helped me get into the harness of my flamethrower. As he did, he said, 'There, you lucky bastard. No Jap will dare get close to you.' Indeed I was the lucky bastard . . . Johnny would die shortly after we landed. At 10:30 or thereabouts, the twelve LSTs headed for shore at full speed and soon attracted Japanese artillery fire. Before reaching shore, four had been hit and one was burning. The one I was on came to a grinding halt long before reaching the beach. We had hit a sand bar. Engines were reversed and the commander of the ship swung the rear of it back and forth for what seemed an eternity. We became a sitting target. Japanese artillery shells kept falling to the left and to the right, closer and closer. Suddenly they also started dropping to the front and back of the ship as they tried to zero in on us. I had never experienced such a feeling of despair and hopelessness.

"We all took cover under vehicles on deck. Some men fought for places of safety. Others prayed, out loud. I did so inwardly, as I lay with the upper part of my body under a truck, my feet beneath a jeep. The rest of me was exposed. Fortunately, a destroyer saw we were in serious trouble. They shot a line to our LST and in no time we were freed and headed out into the bay. Our second run was successful and we poured onto the beach."

Like the others, Hofrichter was astonished to find the troops from the earlier waves still burrowing into the sand of the beach. The words, orders, and leadership of Newman galvanized the men around Hofrichter. "A fellow dug into the sand not far from me looked at me, got up, moved forward, and said, 'Give 'em hell, Buddy!' " A tank trap temporarily blocked passage for the M8 with Hofrichter, but a bulldozer filled the pit. "The bunkers were well concealed, hard to see. But the concentration of firepower coming from them gave us an idea of where they were located. The first three were silenced by fire from the 75mm cannon of the M8. The fourth, despite countless 75mm shells, was not completely silenced.

"Once we moved off the beach, things were happening so fast the adrenaline kicked in and helped ease my initial fears. Now it went into high gear. I was so focused on what I was supposed to do I didn't have time to think as I moved under protective fire toward the bunker. I reached the dirt-and-log emplacement miraculously without drawing fire. Two machine guns were still firing. I could not find an opening to use the flamethrower although the shells from the M8 had caused part of the bunker to cave in. As I leaned forward against the logs of the bunker, about four feet in front of me, I suddenly began to see dirt between the logs start crumbling. A few seconds later I saw the shaft of a sabre push through, creating the opening I needed.

"As soon as the sabre was drawn back inside, I placed the nozzle in the hole and shot three bursts into the bunker. The screams I heard were of intense agony. The machine guns were silenced and the stench of burning flesh drifted through the openings where the guns were. I vomited on the spot. Four more times on A-day I used the flamethrower and I vomited each time. After the third time there was nothing left to bring up. The last two bunkers left me with the dry heaves." By midafternoon, the team with Hofrichter had accounted for sixteen bunkers.

"At Red Beach," said his supreme commander, Douglas MacArthur, "our troops secured a landing and began moving inland. I decided to go in with the third assault wave." Actually, the moment chosen to carry out the promise to return occurred about four hours after the third wave reached the shore and establishment of a beachhead. The general's account of the trip on his barge noted, "The coxswain dropped the ramp about fifty yards from shore, and we waded in."

In his biography of MacArthur, William Manchester reported the wet landing was unexpected after the vessel with the supreme commander ran aground. "MacArthur had counted on tying up to a pier and stepping majestically ashore, immaculate and dry. Most of the docks had been destroyed in the naval bombardment, however, and while a few were still intact . . . the beachmaster had no time to show them where they were. Like all beachmasters, he was as autonomous as the captain of a ship. When he growled, 'Let 'em walk,' they had no choice."

In the famous photograph of the event, as MacArthur strides through the shallow water, he wears a grim scowl on his face. Manchester attributed the look to a "wrathful glare" at the offending beachmaster, rather than a sign of determination. Red Beach at the moment was shakily secured. Japanese snipers occasionally harassed the invaders. Close by, automatic and small-arms weapons ripped through nearby groves as GIs pressed forward. American planes from carriers passed overhead on the way to bomb targets and naval vessels hammered at distant targets. Those responsible for MacArthur's safety sweated out his tour as he inspected the 24th Division command post, kicked a couple of enemy corpses, drafted a brief message to President Roosevelt, and then spoke over a microphone hooked to a mobile communications truck.

He declared, "People of the Philippines: I have returned. By the grace of Almighty God, our forces stand again on Philippine soil—soil consecrated in the blood of our two peoples. . . . The hour of your redemption is here . . . I now call upon your supreme effort that the enemy may know, from the temper of an aroused people within, that he has a force there to contend with no less violent than is the force committed from without. . . . Rally to me. Let the indomitable spirit of Bataan and Corregidor lead on. . . ."

Han Rants held a ringside seat for the appearance of the general and had his own interpretation of the event. "It had been quiet on the beach perhaps an hour or so when some ceremony or commotion seemed to be coming from out on the water. About three landing barges were coming in, and from the flags we could see it had to be MacArthur. We really didn't have a lot of love for MacArthur because as a general he wanted to win wars fast. He wanted to push as many people as fast as he could to get it done, so he had spoken out against rotation of troops so old ones would get a leave home. He wanted to keep the veterans until the war was won.

"We had only about 1,200 yards of beach but here came the landing barge with the tide right for a good, flat, dry landing. I have an idea it was kind of staged, too, as it stopped a little short, the gate flopped down, and MacArthur, with fifty aides of his, officers of various levels, waded about knee-deep through the water [a different appraisal than Manchester]. Cameras were grinding to film the triumphant return. Later, after the war was over, we saw the very same picture with the caption in *Collier's* magazine reading 'MacArthur leads the troops ashore.' It was quite some time later than H hour and it just hadn't been safe any sooner.

"I happened to be hanging in a coconut tree close enough to hear the speech loud and clear. He mentioned that three years ago he told the people of the Philippines that he would return and now, 'I have returned.' While seeming to be a kind of grandstand thing for a show, it really took some kind of courage for a man of that level to be there. Much as we disliked the guy [because] of his wanting to use veteran troops to win wars, we knew there was no one who knew the Philippine Islands better, and we knew that had we landed somewhere else, we probably would have had a lot more people killed than we did."

At his Collecting Company station on Red Beach, battle surgeon Phil Hostetter learned from wandering GIs of the imminent arrival of MacArthur. Hostetter elected to remain at his post for orders. A second report confirmed the general's appearance and that he wet his trousers to the knees. Casualties grabbed Hostetter's attention and he administered plasma to an infantryman with a compound fracture of his arm from a bayonet fight. "After a while, someone asked," recalled Hostetter, "'Do you know who was just here? General MacArthur and some admiral! They watched you for quite a while.' No one told me we had visitors so the general watched me but I was too busy to see him. We thought the presence of our highest officers on the beach at that time was foolhardy. We did not understand the significance our Filipino allies saw in his coming. The general said he would return and he did. The next day some guerrilla soldiers came to the beach. One said, 'I am delighted to see you here but where is General MacArthur?'

" 'He was here yesterday, we all saw him,' I replied, lying a little.

" 'Oh, I cannot believe it,' he answered with joy. 'This means you are here to stay. It is no commando raid.' The General understood well the Oriental regard for personal leadership."

As darkness enveloped them, the 2d Battalion of the 24th, wary of the Japanese propensity for night assaults, prepared for the possibility. "Colonel Newman," said Paul Austin, "ordered G Company to set up a roadblock a quarter of a mile down the road toward Pawing [a Leyte village]. Approximately thirty men dug in astride the highway. I felt in my bones we'd be attacked that night. They had boasted they would throw us back into the ocean if we landed there.

"About 1:00 A.M. rifle and machine-gun fire erupted down at the roadblock position. That woke everyone up. Almost immediately a Japanese mortar shell hit the roof of a building right near our foxhole. I became pretty frightened and worried about our situation as the gunfire got hotter and hotter down the road. Presently my two machine guns, set up to support each other with cross fire, opened up."

Han Rants, in the communications section, remembered, "Telephone lines were kept open so those men out on points to spot trouble could kind of whisper, 'We've got people coming in.' On this particular night, Private Moon, the guy who won all the money on the ship, was holding one of the point positions with a couple of buddies. He called in and said, 'This is the big one, they're really coming and they seem to be all around.' They used a rice paddie and not only had machine guns but mortars mounted on rafts in the water. They could move the raft quickly, and they'd fire a burst then move real quickly so when we returned fire, it wasn't there.

"They came near Moon's point and he would kill three or four of them who tried to take it. The enemy determined they would try to take that point before anything else. It was kind of fortunate they did because it bought us a whole lot of time until daylight came. The Japanese started to maneuver to get the three guys in that hole and finally killed two of them. Moon was there alone but well supplied with a Tommy gun and clip after clip of ammunition plus grenades.

"We could hear exchanges; some of the Japanese spoke English and would yell at him. He knew he should be quiet so they couldn't really zero in on him but he really meant business and called them all the names in the world. He kept yelling 'Come and get me! If you want me, come and get me!' Moon called back coordinates of enemy positions, and mortars hit these targets.

Joe Hofrichter, having completed his assignment in support of the M8, located his unit, Company F under Paul Austin. Hofrichter shared a foxhole with Troy Stoneburner, who awakened him from a sound sleep as gunfire shattered the silence in the G Company sector. "It went on for hours," said Hofrichter. "Suddenly the firing stopped. We could hear clearly an American GI cussing and taunting the Japanese to come and get him. There would be a short burst of fire, then more cussing at the Japanese. At one point Troy said it looked like the fellow doing the cussing was out of his foxhole, firing bursts from an automatic gun. 'No way,' I said. Soon Troy poked me and told me to look toward the beach between two clumps of trees. I located the spot and silhouetted against the open background, a man was standing, firing a gun in rapid bursts. We were both convinced this was the nut doing all the cussing and shouting. About 4:00 A.M.

a major shootout took place in G Company's area and then it grew silent. Early the next morning, we learned that they had repulsed a night attack and that a kid named Pvt. Harold Moon had killed countless Japanese within a few feet of his foxhole before he was overrun and killed. [Remnants of Moon's platoon broke the enemy line with a fixed-bayonet charge.]

"As we moved up the road at daybreak, I saw a lot of dead Japanese and one dead American soldier. Before they covered his body with a poncho, I saw his face. It was the kid who winked at me on the beach and said, 'Give 'em hell, Buddy,' and it was Pvt. Harold Moon!"

"Moon had fought by himself at the roadblock for an hour or hour and a half," remarked Austin. "He took all the ammunition his buddies had left lying around and, with his Thompson machine gun and a box of grenades, he had fought those Japs until they finally gathered in a large group, knocked him down and killed him. That morning there were fifty-five Jap bodies all lying in front of his foxhole. Across the entire front of our battalion, we estimated some 600 to 700 Jap bodies. Part of them were from an air strike called in from a carrier. We marked the ends of our lines with red panels and the pilots coming over the area after daylight could see the area. Their bombs fell right in the midst of the Japanese soldiers. I saw one bomb go off and two or three bodies flying in the air, mixed with debris, mud, and water."

"One of the first details, after the first night on Leyte," said Han Rants, "was to go out and get Moon. One of the lieutenants headed that detail and the guys all knew Moon had 1,200 bucks on him. The lieutenant took charge of the money and as far as we know, he sent it back to the family. Moon had been shot many times, and they had cut him up with a saber or knives, even after they killed him, out of extreme anger at the number he had killed. Even in their hurry to try and take us, they took time to take out some frustration on him." Harold Moon, for his extraordinary performance, was awarded a posthumous Medal of Honor.

On A-day, after the customary pounding of the shore defenses from the air and sea, the 1st Cavalry Division using amphibian tanks raced toward White Beach, a 2,000-yard-long strand of coral sand that began almost a mile north of Red Beach. Rifleman Sal DeGaetano, newly acquired from antiaircraft duty by B Troop, 12th Cavalry Regiment, rode the first wave ashore.

"As we neared Leyte," says DeGaetano, "the Navy was all around us. As the first wave formed, I looked at some of my buddies to see if they were as nervous as I was. I was fascinated by the big smoke rings the big guns made as they pounded the beach, and then walked the bombardment inland while we prepared to land. I was amazed at the little resistance we encountered that first day. But in spite of that, in my foxhole that night, my buddy Ray York and I were shaking like leaves with apprehension until we fired at some noise and then settled down."

Compared to what the 24th Division endured, passage to White Beach and immediately beyond proved relatively easy. The pounding administered by aircraft and ships drove the defenders to abandon most of their fortifications. The most difficult task that first day seemed to be crossing a deep swamp. By nightfall, the division had achieved its objectives.

The 24th and 1st Cavalry Divisions, grouped as the X Corps, formed the right flank for the assault, with the 1st Cavalry responsible for the northernmost zone. Some fourteen miles south of the edge of the 24th's Red Beach, the 600-ship convoy bearing the the XXIV Corps, composed of the 96th and 7th Divisions, zeroed in on a series of beaches designated as Orange, Blue, Violet, and Yellow. Unlike the other divisions, the 96th came to Leyte unblooded. Its GIs were also a mix of extremes in education and background. Bob Jackson, a platoon leader in the 382d Regiment, recalled, "Many of the noncoms were not draftees or even early volunteers, but men who, in the severe Depression of the late thirties found a home in the Army. While not highly sophisticated, they had learned 'the Army.' We draftee officers [he graduated from OCS] were a different lot. Most of us were recent college graduates."

The need for replacements for outfits already overseas drained the 96th of some of its people. To fill the ranks of the 96th, large numbers of men from the recently closed-down Army Specialized Training Program [ASTP], an operation that sent GIs to college, entered the 96th's ranks. "It was a sad situation," said Jackson, "they had no military training to speak of. A barracks was set aside and we were charged with making soldiers of these men. They were very bright—they must have had very high IQs because they'd been accepted at prestigious universities, but they knew nothing about soldiering. We were given about six weeks to bring them up to speed. Discipline was the greatest problem. They were not used to the restraints on their individuality that the Army required. Most turned out to be superior soldiers in combat."

Dick Thom, a lawyer in civilian life and older than most at his level, was a regimental staff officer. He, too, fretted over the infusion of these raw newcomers. "They turned out to be smart kids, quick to learn, good riflemen, good shooters, solid killers, and thoroughly reliable."

The preliminaries off Orange 1 and 2, Blue 1 and 2, featured a barrage led by the battleship *Tennessee*. Within thirty-nine minutes, the ships methodically painted the area with 2,720 rounds of high explosives. Carrier planes swept over the sector, unloading more bombs and strafing targets of opportunity. As the amphibious tanks and landing craft rendezvoused for the final swing to the beaches, LCIs added a barrage of rockets and mortars to the cacophony of shells.

Bob Seiler, a former ASTP enrollee, said, "It was like a hundred fourth of Julys, all at once. The rockets were the most impressive. They looked awesome. How anything could live through that was hard to believe." George Brooks, from the same program as Seiler, recalled tense early moments. "There was very little conversation while we were loading into the amtracs and then heading for shore. On the way in, one of the guys sitting opposite me in the amtrac was very nervous, as we all were, and fiddling with the safety on his rifle. He had the rifle butt down on the deck with the barrel up alongside his cheek. All of a sudden we heard a loud bang and when we looked at this guy, his eyes were bulging way out with a startled expression on his face. There was a black powder mark up the side of his face and a hole through his helmet. Nobody laughed.

"The amtracs were supposed to carry us on shore for a hundred yards or more, but when we got to the beach there were coconut logs driven into the sand at the water's edge like pilings. There were three or four logs cabled together and spaced so closely an amtrac could not get between. So we stepped out into the water from the rear of the amtrac and raced across the beach as fast as possible. It was 10:00 A.M. when we hit the beach and 98 degrees Fahrenheit. I found one of our guys passed out from heat exhaustion. His canteen was empty. I called a medic over and went inland. That very first day our battalion commander flipped his lid and had to be taken back. We continued inland through a swamp, waist-high or more. Of course one thinks of snakes in this environment but I didn't see any. Late in the afternoon, we got orders to dig in."

"The immediate reaction when coming under fire for the first time is self-preservation," noted ASTP alumnus Norman Fiedler. "The ingrained training received through basic training caused one to immediately react as a combat man—hit the ground, seek protection behind rocks, trees, etc., and move forward. Some men lagged behind but no one stayed behind, the noncoms incessantly urging, 'move forward, move ahead.' " Fiedler's outfit apparently bumped into a more determined band of defenders. "Our company was pinned down just beyond the beach, in what appeared to be rice fields. We dug foxholes by nightfall but because of the water table, they filled up with water. Because we could not leave the foxholes, we remained in water up to our necks all night. In the morning, our entire bodies, hands etc., were wrinkled from being soaked."

"Of course no one slept that first night," said Brooks. "Off our left flank we heard a lot of shooting and noise. We heard that Japs had made a banzai charge in the 7th Division area. One of our guys, whom I knew very well, got out of his foxhole and crawled toward the company CP. Someone shot him in the head. We had been told over and over not to get out of our foxholes at night. They thought he may have heard something on the radio and was trying to crawl over to tell the company commander."

A-day called for the 32d, 184th, and 17th Regiments of the 7th Division to penetrate the one mile of coastline denoted as Violet 1 and 2 and Yellow 1 and 2. A swamp separated the Yellows. The strategists earmarked Dulag, a barrio beside Highway 1, and its airfield, as the principal objectives. The 32d at Violet 1 and 2 encountered fierce opposition from well-emplaced defenders, who temporarily held up an advance spearheaded by tanks. Intensive fire silenced the foe. Elsewhere the GIs pressed ahead with a minimum of interference. By nightfall, the invaders held Dulag, occupied the turf at the edge of the air strip, and straddled Highway 1.

Douglas MacArthur now paid a second visit to Leyte, splashing through shallow water to observe the 1st Cavalry at work. His annoyance over the first day's wet steps to the beach had vanished once the dramatic photographs of the event appeared. Neither broadsides issued by the Japanese authorities nor the sonorities of MacArthur meant a spent cartridge to the GIs now struggling inland. The 7th Cavalry Regiment [descendant of the ill-fated outfit commanded by George Armstrong Custer] battled its way into the island capital of Tacloban. The Japanese, embedded in the 1,500-foot hills that overlooked the town, hiding in buildings and sniping from foxholes, fought tenaciously. Tanks, artillery, mortars, and dismounted cavalrymen routed them. The citizens of Tacloban showered the GIs with gifts of eggs and fruit and vigorously waved the Stars and Stripes.

All along its front, the 1st Cavalry expanded the American-controlled territory. Squadrons from the 8th Regiment drove northward near the shoreline to combine efforts with men from the 7th Cavalry ferried up the coast. Together they secured approaches from across the San Juanico Strait, which lies between Leyte and neighboring Samar, where a large garrison of enemy soldiers might seek to reinforce their comrades on Leyte. Some of the 24th Division infantrymen to the south struggled against large numbers of determined defenders and unfriendly terrain.

After his first night on Leyte, Paul Austin had left the safety of his foxhole for a quick look down the road to where Harold Moon took his stand when an enemy machine gun sent him scrambling back to safety. "I got behind a tree trunk and he just kept pouring bullets into it. I waited until he gave up and then dashed for the foxhole. When I got in there I looked at Cuffney [a replacement lieutenant sharing the space with Austin] and realized there was something wrong with him. 'I'm hit,' he said, 'in my hip here.' He pulled his trousers down and below his hip joint I could see the point of a bullet sticking out of his skin. It seemed to have come all the way through his thigh and ended up on the other side.

" 'We'll get a medic, Cuff, and get you out of here as soon as we can,' I told him. He lay there, not saying anything and he wasn't bleeding. He'd evidently been struck by a ricochet as plenty of them had come off the trees and ground. Medics came and took him away. I laughed as he was leaving and said, 'It's been good knowing you, Cuff.' And he was gone, having been with F Company only a month, and after his first night on Leyte. Other fellows went all the way through the war without ever being hit."

Han Rants, who had inspected Moon's remains, observed the results of GIs' experiences with the enemy. "From our very first contact with Japanese soldiers in New Guinea we saw and felt them violate every rule of war and of humane treatment of civilians and soldiers. The great majority of enemy soldiers we faced were worse than uncivilized savages or wild beasts seeking to kill. A savage or an animal has some sense of self-preservation or desire to stay alive. To the Japanese soldiers we faced, honor and life-ever-after came only from being killed in battle for their Godlike emperor. They said they would be forever disgraced and disowned if they returned home without victory. A wounded Japanese soldier would fake death, sneak a chance to use a grenade or shoot someone before killing himself. We learned quickly after each battle to make sure all bodies left were really dead. The best way was to put one more bullet through the head if not sure, or to kick them in the testicles."

"Their barbaric torture of civilians and my buddies triggered an anger and hatred in me that resulted in my doing things that are unacceptable in the civilized world. Each of us had to cope with their butchery in our own way but for me vengeance was the answer. It took many years for me to share some of the deeds that I regret so deeply and some will go to my grave with me except for dear war buddies who respected my fighting ability. Absolutely no one can make judgment on a combat soldier's behavior until he/she has lived like a hunted animal in a hole for a year or more.

"Some of us were gold-tooth collectors, and it was helpful to be in the wire section with a good pair of pliers to collect the gold. From the minute when you knew you were going to be killed yourself to the time that it had gone the other way, the GIs were out picking up what they could find." Rants recalled, "We were all so close to being wiped out. Not much longer than ten seconds later the cleanup that happens in war, which is barbaric but releases anger, began. The live enemy were gone and our guys jumped up, ran out, and started picking up sabres, guns, watches, rings, whatever souvenirs were available."

"I thought the Japs were good soldiers. I never had the good luck to run up against one who was not," says platoon leader Bruce Price, of the 19th Infantry Regiment. "We were told that if we took prisoners, we would have to feed them out of our rations, which were not too plentiful in combat. I did not consider them to be inferior humans. They could kill me as well as I could kill them. Headquarters also said, 'If we want prisoners, we will send out units to get them.' "

"The mosquitoes and other animals were awful," remembered Bob Jackson, the heavy weapons platoon leader of the 382d Infantry, 96th Division. "This swampy country was home to leeches and we had all been frightened by the medicos about the liver fluke for which this animal was the host. Our feet were a mess because we dared not take off our boots; we might not get them on again. Most of us had developed fungus—about which the medicos had warned us—but we were unable to take the correct precautions of changing socks. I took off my boots about the fourth day and was shocked at the huge ringworm-type lesions all over my feet and up my legs. The carefully husbanded foot powder was about as useful as an invocation to the gods."

Bob Seiler spoke of extreme shortage amid a hostile environment. "Supplies of food and water were nonexistent the few first days because nothing could move through the swamp we were passing through. Water was always in short supply. We got it about once a day but it was always close to 100 degrees every day and water didn't last long enough. One day we passed through some very high cogon grass and I passed out because there was no air to breathe. When I came to, my old buddy Horowitz was using his water to revive me. And water was scarce. I used my Halazone tablets [for water purification] every day. We would shoot holes in coconuts and drink the juice. Chewing on a piece of sugarcane helped. It seemed as if it rained every night and one night we had a typhoon. That time you had to bail our your foxhole to keep from drowning. You took for granted you were going to be wet all night. Some nights it felt rather cold and your teeth would chatter.

"At first we went without food for days. The first thing we got came from a small observation plane dropping something like dog biscuits and salt tablets. We had to take atabrine tablets [antimalarial drug] every day and we were all yellow and had dysentery. Looking back, I think the Japs were more afraid of me than I of them. Either that, or their plans were just to slow us down. Very few times did they stand up and fight. Once or twice we had banzai attacks but they lasted only a short time. We were asked to try to get some prisoners but we all felt the only good Japs were dead Japs. I was always fearful that the wounded or dead were boobytrapped and would rather put another round in them to be sure. Because I was cautious about booby traps, I never picked up any souvenirs."

5

The Battle of Leyte Gulf and the Kamikazes

ATOP HILL 331 ON LEYTE, PAUL AUSTIN SAID, "WE COULD turn around and see the entire Leyte Gulf, the San Pedro Beach, all of the shoreline practically from the Tacloban airfield way down to Hill 522 [held by the 19th Regiment] near Palo. We could see all the ships in the armada that brought us there, all the supply ships, sitting out there, hundreds of them. On the morning of the third day, we were standing up eating breakfast. I heard a noise overhead and looked up. There were nine Japanese Betty bombers coming directly over us and headed straight for the bay and all of our ships. They were at a pretty low altitude and we could see the rising sun on their wings. Just as I thought they're going to bomb our fleet and there is no way they can be stopped, I heard what sounded like a giant string of firecrackers going off. It came from way up in the air, above the bombers. All of a sudden, each one of those Bettys began to smoke, began to burn. As they glided on toward the beach, one by one they turned belly up, plunged into the ground within the beach-head. Some hit the highways, one went into a long glide after which he guided that plane right into the side of a Liberty ship and exploded."

What Austin and his comrades observed was the overture to the full-scale involvement of the Japanese air and sea forces in Gen. Tomoyuki Yamashita's proclaimed *Sho Ichi Go*, the victory operation. The focus of the action around Leyte shifted from the efforts by GIs to widen their patch of the island to Leyte Gulf to primarily a titanic battle between the opposing navies with land-based Japanese aircraft and the limited U.S. Army air resources in the area. On 24 October, from bases on Luzon, the defenders aired massive raids directed at the American Leyte lodgement on land and at sea. As an estimated 150 to 200 mostly twin-engined bombers approached, antiaircraft gunners peppered the skies, while U.S. combat air patrols from the carriers and land-based Army fighters pounced on the slower-moving, poorly protected foe.

Among the huge armada of American ships participating in the Leyte venture was the USS *Suwannee*, one of four escort aircraft carriers (CVE) converted out of fleet oilers. With a combat history dating back to the landings in North Africa in 1942, and a dozen island campaigns, the *Suwannee* was home for Air Group 60 with both torpedo/bombers and Grumman Hellcat fighters. Tex Garner, who flew one of the latter, said, "*Suwannee* was much smaller than the *Hornet* [his previous base] and we were mostly catapult shots off it, maybe 99 percent were cat shots because of the extreme loads we carried and the very low wind condition over the deck. But it was an excellent ship. We started supporting the troops; first for me was Tarawa, then Enewetak, Kwajalein,

Guam. We would come in and work an island over for about a week before a landing, become familiar with the terrain, know how to lay our ordnance in to do the most good, destroy as much of the gun emplacements as we could, and then keep the air clean of planes.

"The Japanese pilots, as far as I am concerned, when we first saw them were very good. They were seasoned, had been in China. As the war went along, those men were thinned out and the quality of Japanese pilots deteriorated fast. By the same token, ours were getting stronger all the time. Every carrier and air group had some fantastic people in it. But our being together for thirteen months was an opportunity for camaraderie most carrier pilots never get."

Garner, who knocked down his first enemy, a twin-engine "Lilly" a month before the *Suwannee* came to Leyte, was a member of a predawn patrol with three others, on 24 October. He recalled, "We had been on station about four hours and ready to return to the *Suwannee*. A radio reported, 'Tally Ho. Eight bombers at ten o'clock heading toward Leyte.' I swept the sky and spotted a formation of Lilly bombers [fast, twin-engine aircraft]. I Tally Ho'd them. We dropped our empty belly tanks and climbed to intercept them.

"Lip Singleton and I set up one line of the formation while Edgar Barber and Ralph Kalal set up on the other wing of the Vee. We all rolled in at the same time. It was perfectly coordinated and four Lillies were knocked down on the first pass. Each pilot had a bull's-eye. After that run we whipped the Hellcats around for another target and for an instant all four fighters had the same bomber and fired at him—so long Lilly. All four scrambled for another bomber. Lip burned one, Kal exploded one, and the last bomber pushed over, hellbent for our landing ships. I called on my Hellcat to give her all, closing very slowly. I was trying to get to him before he got to the fleet because there was no way he would miss 'em. I began to realize some of our AA were trying for him, too. I either had to break off or go for him into our ships' AA.

"I bore in firing all six .50-caliber guns. He began to smoke. I noticed the bomb-bay doors open. There was no way he should have done that because that slowed him down enough for me to catch him. I closed to within four feet. I thought I'd ram him. I came across from his left engine, left wing spar, cockpit, right spar, right engine. On the sweep back as I crossed the cockpit area, I saw like an accordion door open and the pilot appeared. The six guns cut him in half. The plane exploded with the bombs still on board.

"I knew I was in a tight spot with all those ships still firing and if I pulled up I was a dead man. I pushed over, leveled off at about eighteen inches off the water and went zigging through the ships like a scared rabbit, hunkered down behind the armor plating and praying. I was amazed when I reached the other side, wringing wet but still alive, with 18 holes and nothing serious."

For the Japanese air arm, the first day of the Battle of Leyte Gulf was catastrophic. Sixty-six planes were definitely shot down with eighteen probable kills. Three U.S. aircraft crash-landed—two on the Tacloban strip and one in the water. The ability of the Imperial High Command to threaten the U.S. fleet from the air was seriously impaired. Notwithstanding this weakness, elements of the Japanese Navy hastened toward the area, threatening to sever the lifelines of those ashore on Leyte and provide easy access for tens of thousands of reinforcements from elsewhere in the islands. Short on seaborne aircraft, the Imperial Navy mustered massive firepower with seven battleships, including two that were bigger, faster, and mounted larger guns than anything in the U.S. Navy arsenal, and thirteen heavy cruisers as well as destroyers.

The grand strategy devised by the Imperial Navy split its resources into three fleets. Vice Adm. Jisaburo Ozawa, head of the Northern Force, commanded a convoy dominated by a pair of old carriers half-converted for flight operations, several legitimate carriers for whom few planes or pilots were available, a batch of cruisers, and destroyers. The Ozawa group, approaching from the north, would be a decoy to lure the strongest of the U.S. elements, Adm. William Halsey's Third Fleet, most notable for its mighty carriers and concentration of air operations.

Meanwhile, VAdm. Takeo Kurita, in charge of the First Striking Force, led the principal armada toward Leyte Gulf. All of the battleships and most of the heavy cruisers sailed under Kurita's banner and followed a circuitous route to avoid submarines. A smaller aggregation under VAdm. Kiyohide Shima, comprised of three cruisers and nine destroyers, departed from Formosa to add its weight to the offensive planned for Leyte Gulf.

The Japanese also brought a new tactic. By autumn 1944, the Japanese admirals charged with waging the naval air war against the onrushing Allies accepted what Tex Garner had noticed; they were no longer a match for their adversaries in either pilots or machines. Desperate to reverse the tide or inflict severe losses, VAdm. Takajiro Onishi of the First Air Fleet called for volunteers to act as suicide pilots. By crashing their bomb-laden planes into ships they could do far more certain damage than through conventional raids. The first kamikaze corps had entered a training phase on 19 October, a few days prior to the start of the great victory operation.

The American admirals did not expect an onslaught in the vicinity of Leyte. Once again, the division of command created possibly serious consequences. The Leyte campaign involved the Seventh and Third Fleets, two separate organizations. Vice Admiral Thomas Kinkaid bossed the Seventh Fleet, the organization responsible for landing and supporting the invasion force, and reported to MacArthur. Flotillas of troop and supply ships, dozens of destroyers, a handful of battleships, escort carriers like Garner's *Suwannee*, and support vessels comprised the Seventh Fleet.

The air-oriented Third Fleet of Bull Halsey consisted of the Fast Carrier Force deploying most of the Navy's big carriers, under VAdm. Marc Mitscher, plus cruisers, destroyer screens, and support ships. Halsey came under the command of Admiral Nimitz and felt little obligation toward the Seventh Fleet. "Its mission was defensive," said Halsey. "It had bombarded the beaches, convoyed the transports to the landing area, and stood by to guard them while they unloaded and it was to protect them during their retirement.

"My mission was offensive. When I received orders to cover the Leyte landings my mission did not change. It was still offensive. The tasks assigned my force were to gain air supremacy over the Philippines, to protect the landings, and to maintain unremitting pressure against Japan, and to apply maximum attrition by all means in all areas. Finally, should opportunity for destruction of a major portion of the enemy fleet offer, such destruction would become the primary task of my forces." Indeed, severe criticism had lashed Adm. Raymond Spruance for hanging about the Marianas to protect invading marines rather than aggressively pursuing enemy naval forces. Submarines attached to both fleets prowled the sea lanes searching for any enemy naval reaction to the invasion. Following a series of voyages aboard other subs, David McClintock assumed the con of *Darter* for her final two patrols. On 10 October 1944, the USS *Dace* under Comdr. Bladen Clagget formed a two-ship wolfpack with *Darter*. Alerted to the invasion on 20 October, the pair roamed the Balabac Strait, the shortest route from Singapore to Leyte. Radar signals indicated possible enemy ships but these had vanished from the screens.

A few minutes into 23 October, after a rendezvous with *Dace*, McClintock received word from his conning tower, "Radar contact—30,000 yards—contact doubtful—probably rain." McClintock said, "*The Jap Fleet* was what flashed through my mind. Almost immediately the radar operator stated the contact was ships. *Dace* was given the range and bearing by megaphone. The answer came back, 'Let's go get them.' By twenty minutes after midnight both *Darter* and *Dace* were chasing the contact at full power. The ships were in Palawan Passage, headed north.

"It was now apparent that we had not a convoy, but a large task force, which we assumed was headed for Leyte to interfere with our landing. Three contact reports were sent—the final one estimating that the force included at least eleven heavy ships. I decided we should not attack before dawn, considering it vital to see and identify the force. The left-flank column, nearest us, consisted of five heavy ships. The last gave by far the largest radar pip. Probably a battleship. There may have been more ships in this column, but at the long range at which we were tracking, and the probably close formation, this is all that showed up on the radar screen. I picked this column for *Darter*'s target, hoping for a crack at what we thought was a battleship. *Dace*, trailing us very closely, was assigned to the starboard column. We planned a periscope attack at dawn.

"At about 0430 all hands were called for coffee before the expected attack. At about ten minutes before five we manned battle stations, and ten minutes after five we reversed course, headed down the throat of the column. It was getting faintly light in the east. There wasn't a cloud in the sky. In twenty minutes we wanted to shoot. The first periscope look showed a huge gray shape. It was the whole column seen bows on. A look to the southeast where the light was better showed battleships, cruisers, and destroyers. The gray ships kept getting larger. We would pass on almost parallel courses. At 5:25 the first ships in the column could be identified as heavy cruisers, with huge bow waves. There were sighs of disappointment that the targets weren't all battleships. A beautiful sight, anyway. I hoped the lead ship would be the flagship. It was! At 5:27 the range to the leading cruiser was under 3,000 yards. All tubes were ready.

"Then the column zigged west to give a perfect torpedo range of just under 1,000 yards. Their profiles could be seen clearly, *Atago* [class] cruisers. I had the 'scope up for what seemed like several minutes, watching. The leading cruiser looked huge now. She had a bone in her teeth. The forward slant of her bridge seemed to accentuate her speed. [It was] the *Atago* [with Admiral Kurita aboard] my favorite target on the attack teacher. Estimating the angles on the bow off her flat bridge face was easy; I had done that many times before on models."

The range dropped further and McClintock called out instructions with a final, "FIRE ONE!" He unloosed five more forward fish as a searchlight on the cruiser flickered signals. "Did she see our torpedoes?" wondered McClintock. "She was going by now. No, she wasn't zigging! 'Shift targets to second cruiser' . . . 'bearing mark' . . . 'Give me a range . . . give me a range,' yelled the torpedo officer." Finally accommodated with the requisite data, the stern torpedoes left the *Darter*. As they did, the sub rocked from heavy explosions.

"Depth charges!" exclaimed the exec officer. "Depth charges, hell . . . torpedoes!" McClintock responded. Another officer, jumping up and down with each explosion shouted, "Christ, we're hitting 'em, we're hitting 'em!"

Recalled McClintock, "After the tenth torpedo was on its way, I swung the periscope back to the first target, which had been hit with five of the bow torpedoes. She was belching flame from the base of the forward turret to the stern; the dense black smoke of burning oil covered her from forward turret to stern. She was still plowing ahead, but she was also going down by the bow. Number-one turret was cutting the water. She was finished."

McClintock knew for certain he had sunk one vessel and probably another. The crew of *Darter* had little time to exult as the enemy destroyers attacked with depth charges. But the sub escaped damage. *Atago* went down within eighteen minutes carrying 360 of the crew to their deaths. A Japanese destroyer plucked survivors, including Admiral Kurita, from the water. While *Darter* fled to avoid depth charges from destroyers, its companion *Dace* stalked the flotilla and slammed four torpedoes into another cruiser. Unfortunately, *Darter* ran aground on a reef. When efforts to free the vessel failed, *Dace* removed the crew. Most important, Halsey now had firm intelligence on the approach of the enemy armada.

On the morning of 24 October, planes combing the area west of Luzon and Leyte spied the Japanese on a presumed course for the Leyte vicinity. The Third Fleet commander directed three of his fast carrier groups into positions for attack. Limited as their resources were, the Japanese threw the first punches, even as Halsey's subordinates maneuvered their carriers. From Luzon, bombers and torpedo planes went after Task Group 3, which included the big carriers *Essex* and *Lexington*, and *Princeton* and *Langley*, lighter flattops. Hellcats from the quartet met the enemy and splashed most of them; one pilot, Comdr. David McCampbell of the *Essex*, alone knocked down nine, an all-time record for carrierborne fighters. However, a lone bomber, hidden by cloud cover, suddenly emerged in perfect position to plant a 550-pounder on the *Princeton* flight deck. The bomb crashed through the thin skin of the deck before exploding deep in the ship's innards. The blast ignited gasoline stores, then set off a series of torpedoes on planes sitting in the hangar deck. Damage-control crews on the *Princeton*, and from other ships that lent assistance, fought valiantly to squelch the inferno. A further series of detonations from munitions not only doomed the *Princeton* but wrought heavy casualties aboard the *Birmingham*, a cruiser trying to serve as a tugboat. A useless hulk, the *Princeton* stubbornly refused to founder. American torpedoes finally scuttled the ship.

Lieutenant Bill Anderson Jr., a torpedo/bomber pilot assigned to the USS *Cabot*, a light carrier with Air Group 29, a composite unit that included nine torpedo/bombers and twenty-one fighters, was one of five from the torpedo squadron who took off on 24 October. Also on the mission was exec John Williams and two good friends of Anderson's, Howard Skidmore and John Ballantine. "Somehow we became separated from McPherson and Williams and we never saw them when we reached the Japanese fleet or on the way back. Williams was shot down and rescued. The three of us came over the Japanese fleet at about 15,000 feet. We circled looking for a target and we started down. I automatically adjusted speed and altitude. The ideal was at about 270 knots and an altitude between 150 and 300 feet. The only way you could get that kind of speed in a TBM was through a steep dive at full power and when you leveled off you might be at about 315 mph. You would rapidly slow down, but if you could pick up your aiming point and drop the torpedo from 300 feet up, chances were for a good torpedo entrance. It was a fairly restricted envelope in which to work. You also had to have wings level, not nose up or down, when you released, or else the torpedo might not have the proper attitude when it hit the water."

At Leyte Gulf Anderson picked out a battleship and started his attack. "There were bursts of antiaircraft fire all around but not close enough to rattle anything in the aircraft. We lost sight of our other planes. The Japanese fleet started evasive maneuvers and it was necessary for me to pass over the battleship and pick up a cruiser target on the other side. They were shooting at us with their major-caliber weapons. A 16-inch shell is not a proper weapon against aircraft; the chances of being hit are like those of being struck by a lightning bolt. They did throw up geysers of water and you'd turn so as not to be hit with falling water. The water would be full of color; the Japanese did this in order to tell how close they came.

"We got in pretty close, straight and low, opened the bomb-bay doors and pickled off the torpedo. Any torpedo pilot who says he saw where it went after he dropped it is probably dreaming, because after you fire it you're so busy making a hard turn to get out of there you can't stop to look over your shoulder. My gunner, Richard Hanlon, said he saw it drop and head for the cruiser before he lost sight of it. Radioman Joe Haggerty said it hit the cruiser. I was credited with having hit the cruiser and got a Navy Cross, but I'd be hard pressed to swear to the fact." Anderson and the others from Air Group 29 were part of wave after wave of Hellcats, Helldivers, and Avengers from Task Group 38.2, who sortied across Leyte against a fleet bereft of air cover. Shot and shell from every gun on the Japanese ships including the main batteries of the battleships ripped the air but splashed just eighteen of the several hundred swarming over the targets.

Still puissant with a galaxy of battleships, cruisers, and destroyers, Admiral Kurita temporarily halted his voyage toward Leyte in hopes that sorties of land-based aircraft might drive off the American carriers or else protect him from their deadly stings. Unfortunately, there were no planes available to support Kurita. He resumed his course, urged by his superior that he had "divine guidance." He steamed toward the San Bernardino Strait, which would swing his massive firepower around the northern tip of Samar and then into the Leyte Gulf, to confront the less heavily gunned U.S. Seventh Fleet. The hours wasted while Kurita's fleet dallied eliminated any hope the Center and Southern Forces could rendezvous at the appointed hour in Leyte Gulf, to form a kind of nutcracker enveloping the U.S. Seventh Fleet. Admiral Shoji Nishimura, in command of the Southern Forces, wavered momentarily but shook off the minor destruction and plowed ahead.

Meanwhile, Admiral Ozawa, to the north, artfully coaxed Halsey to chase him. He issued radio messages, hoping American intelligence would intercept them. He wandered around the Pacific Ocean off Luzon, his ships seductively languishing, visible to any prying spy plane. He even mounted a seventy-six-plane strike on a group of Third Fleet ships. Desperate to lure the Americans, Ozawa directed his pair of half-battleship, half-carriers, *Ise* and *Hyuga,* to run south. American planes scouring the area finally spotted the pair around 4:00 P.M. on 24 October. Other searchers located the main carriers an hour later; the fish had gone for the hook.

Halsey was an eager candidate for the bait. He knew the enemy retained a significant number of aircraft carriers and he salivated for an opportunity to attack them. While Halsey always insisted the Seventh Fleet possessed ample weapons to handle an enemy fleet like Kurita's, he seemingly took steps to ensure that if the Third Fleet left the area, adequate reinforcements for the Seventh Fleet would be on hand if needed. He had created Task Force 34, replete with battleships and cruisers. But it was a paper organization and not specifically charged with responsibility for guarding the San Bernardino Strait. Critical intelligence errors added to Halsey's misperception. The aviators returning from their missions against Kurita's Center Force, like the Japanese at Formosa, exaggerated their success. Halsey claimed he was told, "At least four and probably five battleships torpedoed and bombed, one probably sunk; a minimum of three heavy cruisers torpedoed and others bombed; one light cruiser sunk, one destroyer probably sunk and four damaged . . . reports indicated beyond doubt that the Center Force had been badly mauled with all of its battleships and most of its heavy cruisers tremendously reduced in fighting power and life." The first information from returning pilots indicated Kurita's fleet moving west, away from Leyte Gulf.

Halsey's information on Ozawa's armada was erroneous. The pilots who flew over the *Ise* and *Hyuga* mistakenly identified them as full-scale battleships when, in fact, refitted as carriers, the ships lost four of their twelve big guns. Instead of a fleet with a quartet of dangerous battleships, Ozawa packed much less weight. The faulty evidence, however, persuaded Halsey to sprint after the retreating Ozawa. Task Force 34 remained a figment so far as the Gulf of Leyte was concerned, for all of its vessels sped north, where the Third Fleet planned to blaze away with all its big guns in conjunction with the carrier-launched bombers and torpedo planes. Even after intelligence advised that, contrary to early reports, the Central Force of the Japanese instead of retreating now seemed embarked on a course toward Leyte, the Third Fleet command refused to release Task Force 34 to guard the San Bernardino Strait, the avenue open to the Japanese.

Admiral Nishimura's Southern Force, in two sections, picked its way through the archipelago via Mindoro and then toward the Surigao Strait between southern Leyte and Mindinao. The Seventh Fleet strategists, alerted to the movement, but unaware of the gaping hole of the San Bernardino Strait in their Leyte Gulf line, plotted a devastating reception. Kinkaid, having correctly interpreted the approach of Nishimura's fleet, ordered VAdm. Jesse Oldendorf to deploy the U.S. ships in preparation for a night engagement. At his disposal Oldendorf counted six battleships, four heavy cruisers, four light ones, and almost thirty destroyers. They far outnumbered and outgunned the opponents. The grand assortment of ships of the line formed a stately procession, steaming back and forth across the Surigao Strait mouth, a scant twelve miles in width. At the southern end of the strait, where the enemy would enter, Oldendorf stationed a flotilla of forty-five PT boats that would detect the arrival of the enemy and then harass them with torpedo runs.

As a gunnery officer, James L. Holloway III was aboard the USS *Bennion*, a destroyer attached to the left flank of the American screen. "At sunset, we had set Condition 1, and we could overhear on the TBS [Talk Between Ships, a voice radio] the tactical commands and reports among our own ships as we waited tensely for the enemy during this dark and squally evening. By midnight we began to think that the

Japanese would disappoint us and a general relaxing was perceptible. Suddenly, at about 0200, over the TBS [official accounts place the contact with the enemy fleet several hours earlier] we heard one of the PT boats reconnoitering in the southern strait call out excitedly, 'I've got a big one in sight!' then a pause, and 'My God, there are two more big ones, and maybe another.' Suddenly the TBS became alive as the 'Martinis'—that was the call sign for the PT boats—got ready for their torpedo attacks."

In the hit-and-run melees that lit up the strait with gunfire, searchlights (from the Japanese ships), and exploding shells, the PTs unloosed thirty-four fish. Only one struck home, wounding the cruiser *Abukuma*. Nishimura kept coming while the gun crews under Oldendorf readied their weapons. Gunnery officer Holloway, fearful for a moment the foe would depart after the Martinis struck, was reassured as the Japanese force showed up on the ship's radar, advancing at twenty-five-knot speed. The American destroyers responded, charging toward the enemy ships as they emerged from the strait, pouring out black smoke as they cut through the water at thirty knots. "From my battle station [in the fire-control director] I had a view of the whole scene: from the panorama of the two fleets to a close-up of the Japanese ships through the high-powered lenses of the MK37 [fire] director. As our destroyers started the run to the south, we were immediately taken under fire. It was an eerie experience to be rushing through the dark toward the enemy at a relative speed of fifty knots, not firing our guns, or hearing the enemy fall of shot around us. The awesome evidence of the Japanese gunfire was the towering columns of water from the splashes of their 14- and 16-inch shells, some close enough to wet our weather decks. Star shells hung overhead and the gun flashes from the Japanese battle line illuminated the horizon ahead.

"Oldendorf's battleships and cruisers opened up with their main batteries. Directly over our heads stretched a procession of tracers from our battle line converging on the head of the Japanese column. I recall being surprised at the apparent slowness of the projectiles. They almost hung in the sky, taking fifteen to twenty seconds in their trajectory before reaching their targets. It was a spectacular display. Through the director optics, I could clearly see the bursting explosions of our battleships' and cruisers' shells as they hit the Japanese ships that were enveloped in flames.

"Our column was headed directly for the lead battleship, the *Yamashiro*, so the division had to turn in a sequential movement for a clear shot, each destroyer launching successively as it executed the turn. As *Bennion* was the second ship in the last element, at a fifty-knot relative speed, our firing point closed rapidly with the Japanese battle line. We started launching our five torpedoes at a range of about 7,000 yards. At this distance, the silhouette of the *Yamashiro* completely filled the viewing glass of the rangefinder optics. [I thought,] that looks exactly like a Japanese battleship with its pagoda foremast and then realizing that it was a Japanese battleship."

As the tin cans closed the distance, Oldendorf inquired the range from his flagship [the heavy cruiser *Louisville*] and upon the answer of 17,000 yards, the admiral ordered his biggest ships to open fire. "It seemed as if every ship on the flank forces and the battle line opened at once, and there was a semicircle of fire that landed squarely on one point, the leading battleship. Explosions and fires were immediately noticed. The semicircle of fire evidently so confused the Japanese that they did not seem to know what target to shoot at. I remembered seeing one or two salvos start in the direction of my flagship, but in the excitement of the occasion I forgot to look to see where they landed."

Aboard the *Bennion*, Holloway observed the turmoil. "As we retired to the north in formation at thirty knots, still making max black smoke, explosions erupted close off our port beam. It was one of our destroyers, the *A. W. Grant*, being hit by large-caliber shells. The scene of the action was becoming confused and Oldendorf ordered his battle line to cease fire for concern of hitting our retiring destroyers in the melee." In fact, Oldendorf noted that after some of his destroyers launched their torpedoes and came under heavy fire, they quickly fled directly up the Surigao Strait. Some of the U.S. fleet mistook these friendlies for the foe. "The *Grant* was hit by some of our own six-inch shells from the light cruisers, as well as shells from the Japanese ships."

With his smaller ships racing out of harm's way, Oldendorf brought his five cruisers to bear upon some battered, burning Japanese ships. Salvos dispatched a pair of destroyers. At about 4:30 A.M., as dawn approached, Oldendorf directed the units that included the *Bennion* to race south and engage any surviving Japanese ships. "In the pale, predawn twilight," said Holloway, "the scene in Surigao Strait was appalling. I counted eight distinct fires, and the oily surface of the gulf was littered with debris and groups of Japanese sailors who were clinging to bits of wreckage and calling out to us as we raced past.

"*Bennion* did not pause to pick up survivors, as we had sighted the Japanese destroyer *Asaguma*, badly damaged, on fire, and limping south. *Asaguma* was still afloat, and if she still had torpedoes aboard, she constituted a definite threat to our ships. With orders to destroy the Japanese ship, we changed course to close the *Asaguma* and opened fire with five-inch salvos at about 10,000 yards. We shifted to rapid, continuous fire at 6,000 and she blew apart and slipped beneath the waves as we passed close aboard. On the *Bennion*," remembered Holloway, "the crew was dogtired, but spirits were elated. As we listened to the reports come in from the TBS and witnessed the hundreds of survivors clinging to the smoking wreckage of the Japanese fleet, we all sensed that a great victory had been won." The final tally for the battle of Surigao Strait showed 2 Japanese battleships and 3 destroyers sunk with only a cruiser and a destroyer, both badly damaged, able to escape. The losses to the Americans added up to 39 killed, 119 wounded, mostly on the *A. W. Grant,* struck by its sister ships.

The celebration on the *Bennion* and the other vessels in Oldendorf's command halted abruptly. According to Holloway, "Suddenly—and the transformation of spirits was dramatic—elation turned to real alarm, when over the TBS we heard that the Taffy groups [the smaller flattops left behind to protect other entrances of Leyte Gulf] were under attack at close range by Japanese battleships and cruisers. We couldn't believe it. We thought all of the capital ships of the Japanese reaction force had been destroyed in the night battle in Surigao Strait."

When Admiral Kincaid sent Oldendorf to block the Surigao Strait in an anticipated night action, he kept sixteen escort carriers—"baby flattops" or "jeep" carriers—steaming back and forth across Leyte Gulf to the north off Samar. These slower, smaller ships, accompanied by a screen of nine destroyers and twelve destroyer escorts, were organized as Task Group 77.4 and divided into Taffy 1, 2, and 3. On the morning of 25 October, the Taffies began to catapult their planes for antisubmarine searches and combat air patrols. A few minutes before 7:00 A.M., lookouts aboard the ships noticed antiaircraft shells in the distance and radios picked up Japanese voices over the interfighter net. But no enemy ships were believed within 100 to 150 miles.

Suddenly, one of the antisubmarine patrol pilots reported sighting four Japanese battleships, eight cruisers, and a flock of destroyers. A skeptical RAdm. Thomas L. Sprague, chief for Taffy 1, demanded a check on the identification, believing the airman had spotted part of Task Force 38 from Halsey's Third Fleet. The answer came promptly from a source close to home. Not only did the lookouts on Sprague's ships see the unique, pagoda-shaped superstructure of Japanese battleships poking over the horizon, but brightly colored splashes signaled hostile shells.

Without Task Force 34 on the scene, no one had watched the San Bernardino Strait, and Admiral Kurita, with the Center Force intact, passed into the waters off Samar without detection. Kurita packed a tremendous potential wallop in his battlewagons but he had no carriers to provide air cover. The Taffies could muster several hundred planes but their surface weapons in the destroyer screen amounted to popguns compared to the huge rifles pointed at them from Kurita's battleships and cruisers. The lineups presented a near-classic encounter between an armada of seagoing Japanese behemoths and the lighter, aircraft-dominated U.S. forces.

The unexpected appearance of the Japanese so close at hand exposed Task Force 77.4 to disaster. The Center Force had an opportunity to blast the carriers and their screens before they could assume any defensive posture. Apparently, the Japanese believed they might face battleships and full-size carriers. Admiral Kurita, still fearful of another series of air attacks, and an eyewitness to the ineffectiveness of his AA gunnery, erred tactically, ordering a general attack instead of directing his ships into position for more effective, coordinated firing.

About twenty miles separated Taffy 3 from Taffy 2 to the southeast, with Taffy 1 as much as 100 miles off. The Center Force began the action of Samar blasting away at Taffy 3, commanded by RAdm. Clifton "Ziggy" Sprague—no kin to the CO of Taffy 1. Caught in the sights of enemy cruisers and battleships, Ziggy Sprague circled his wagons, the six carriers operating around a diameter of 2,500 yards while the destroyer screen steamed in parallel, 6,000 yards from the center. All ships ran at flank speed, made smoke to hide themselves, while the carriers emptied their flight decks. Nature smiled faintly upon the Americans, adding a rain squall to help obliterate them as targets, and poorly functioning Japanese radar further hampered the enemy gunnery.

Temporarily shrouded, Sprague signaled his three destroyers to counterattack the big enemy ships, boys sent to perform men's jobs. The *Johnston* ran a gauntlet through the heavier vessels of the foe and scored a few hits from her main battery on the cruiser *Kumano*, and then let fly all ten of her torpedoes at the *Kumano*. At least one, perhaps more, exploded on target and eliminated the cruiser from further combat. Japanese gunners pinpointed the destroyer. A fusillade of shells ripped into the *Johnston*. Huge holes opened up in the deck; one explosion knocked off pieces of the radar on the mast, the falling debris killed three officers. Many died below deck as projectiles pierced the thin hull and then blew up. Still, the destroyer persevered.

Others from the Taffy 3 screen, destroyers *Hoel* and *Heermann*, plus the "Little Wolves"—destroyer escorts—charged at their oversize foe. They dashed through the roiling, explosion-riven water, threw their much smaller-size shells at their antagonists and launched torpedoes, with little if any success. The Japanese registered hits upon the little boys. Abandon ship had sounded for the *Hoel* and a DE, the *Roberts*, when the *Johnston* engaged in its finale, an exchange with the light cruiser *Yahagi* and a destroyer. The *Johnston* scored a number of hits before a firing squad of enemy ships surrounded it and hammered away until it went dead in the water, then rolled over on the way to the bottom.

Taffy 3's screen inflicted little material damage upon its much larger adversaries, but the torpedoes and five-inch guns required the Center Force to take evasive action and deal with the interlopers. While the disarray would buy time for the planes of Taffy 2 to enter the fray, four heavy cruisers with murderous intent stalked Taffy 3's six carriers. As his ships desperately attempted to steam away from the ever closer shell splashes, Ziggy Sprague advised them to use their puny, single-deck gun: "Open fire with the peashooters when range is clear." The longer-range weapons of the attackers began to find their marks. Some of the armorpiercing shells tore through the thin skins of the converted oilers and passed out the opposite sides of the ships. But multiple hits killed, wounded, and damaged. Crews immersed in as much as five feet of seawater plugged holes, repaired engines, sealed ruptured pipes, while helmsmen hand-wrestled with controls designed for mechanical operation.

The first casualty among the flattops was the *Gambier Bay*. The Japanese cruisers narrowed the gap to the American vessel and at 10,000 yards put a shell into her that ignited fires. *Gambier Bay*, slowed by her wounds, staggered as the enemy gunners peppered her. The carrier capsized and sank. A sister ship, the *White Plains*, insists its "pea-shooter" vanquished the heavy cruiser *Chokai*. The 5-inch 38 gun on the fantail claimed six hits upon the *Chokai* that knocked out both the forward turret and her engines. Whatever the *White Plains* achieved, torpedo bombers executed the *Chokai* with fatal blows amidships. It blew up and sank within five minutes.

In support of Taffy 3, Taffy 2 mounted three strikes that included both fighters and torpedo bombers. They started their raids about ninety minutes after Kurita's Center Force hove into view. The planes from the two Taffies, using torpedoes, bombs, and incessant strafing, rattled the commander of the enemy fleet. Fighter planes, including some that had expended their ammunition, dove on the enemy vessels repeatedly, forcing them to use up their shells and bedeviling the crews. Taffy 1, which included the *Suwannee*, also scrambled planes to meet Admiral Nishimura's group. Tex Garner said, "They were shooting at us before we even got to them. They shot at us in every color there was. The whole sky was just full of different color bursts. [As they did in surface gunnery, the Japanese employed color as a means of zeroing in on targets.] I said to myself, 'There's no way you're going to get through that kind of barrage.' But we did. We went in and hurt 'em as much as we could. I took my four planes in and I got my four out. We had holes in us, but we were still flying. We dropped our bombs and strafed. It was amazing how we got in and out, how they could miss. All our air groups from *Suwannee*, *Sangamon*, *Chenango*, and *Santee* were jumping on them as they came through the straits. The sky was full of planes, Technicolor puffs, and tracer shells." The furious action and the extended flight time from the carriers to the combat area drove some of the American pilots to land on the Tacloban airstrip, secured only five days before.

Well out of range of the Japanese ships, Taffy 1 staved off land-based Japanese raids. The task group recoiled from the first successful kamikaze attacks. In the days preceding the Leyte Gulf sea battles, rumors of pilots committed to crashing into American ships circulated among American sailors. One alleged source was a deciphered Japanese message to a pilot that read: "It is absolutely out of the question for you to return alive. Your mission involves certain death. . . ."

About twenty minutes or so before 8:00 A.M., on 25 October, spotters among the Taffy 1 ships saw four enemy planes breaking out of the clouds about 10,000 feet up. Gunner's Mate 3d class John B. Mitchell, son of a World War I wounded vet, and a shipyard worker before he enlisted in 1943, captained a gun mount on the *Santee*. The 40mms were not loaded, because, according to Mitchell, "On several invasion landings, men got kind of jumpy and there were occasions when guns were fired by accident, error, or stupidity. I was wearing the combat headphone set and it was reported that we had some bogeys in the area. Almost immediately the gunnery officer, Lieutenant Commander Mills, yelled that a bogey was diving on us, dead astern. I ordered my 'pointer and trainer' to bear on the target. Both used gunsights. One man had responsibility for the horizontal and the other for the vertical position of the gun. It took a great deal of practice for the two of them to act in unison. We did have a Mark 14 sight and there were fire-control men who could automatically fire our guns, but you always needed a pointer and trainer in case the electrical system failed.

"I ordered the crew to load and cock both guns. Before we were able to bear on the target, the bogey was in a dive and strafing the stern deck. I watched it come in all the way. I could not believe that the plane was not coming out of its dive. I was screaming, 'Pull out, you bastard! Pull out!' It came in so fast and with such surprise we didn't get off a single round. The plane used our aft elevator as a target and crashed just a few feet forward and to port of the elevator."

Some seven minutes after the *Santee* won the dubious honor of first ship to be a kamikaze victim it took a blow from a more conventional enemy, as Japanese submarine I-56 executed a successful torpedo run. "It hit directly below my gun mount," remembers Mitchell. "The first sensation I had was that of the deck suddenly being pulled out from under my feet. I don't know how high in the air I went but I was told later that I was tossed above the gun mount.

"When I came down I thought I had been pitched overboard and immediately started to swim. I was attached to the mount by my combat phone and for some reason my helmet was still on my head. And there I was, flailing my arms, thinking I had gone into the drink, and all I was doing was swimming back to the spot in my gun tub where I normally would be. The gun tub was filled with wet debris and several dead bodies."

On the ships in the area, the spotters had seen three of the original four planes dive toward the carriers. Gunners had thrown up a wall of metal but, as Mitchell saw, one aircraft penetrated the curtain of fire and, blazing away with machine guns until the final moment, crashed onto the forward deck of the *Santee*. A Zero making for the *Sangamon* exploded in midair when a five-incher from *Suwannee* struck home. A third kamikaze dropped into the water after concentrated AA fire shattered its controls or else killed the pilot. Suddenly, from 4,000 feet up, the last of the quartet of kamikazes dropped almost straight down. It seemed as if every weapon in Taffy 1 were shooting at the Zero [some say it was a Judy, a navy dive-bomber], which trailed a thin stream of smoke, as though afire. The concentration upon him notwithstanding, the pilot held his course and drilled into the *Suwannee* flight deck, to explode into pieces, the Zero's nose penetrating three decks below, just shy of reaching the aviation fuel stores. The suicide plane carved into the flight deck an impression of its front silhouette, a round hole for the engine and slits from the wings.

Petty Officer 2d class Erich Kitzmann, a native of Detroit, bossed crews that prepared planes for operations on the *Suwannee*. When the "Flight Quarters" signal was blown at 0300 on 25 October, because of blackout conditions, Kitzmann and hands worked in the dark getting the TBF Avengers topside. Hours later, Kitzmann and half of his plane handlers were at breakfast, eating beans, the standard Wednesday fare, when general quarters sounded. He tossed aside his mess tray, carelessly slung his life jacket over one shoulder, and strapped his helmet under his chin.

He checked his hangar deck for fire hazards, saw that auxiliary fuel tanks were removed from aircraft and jettisoned. Then he headed forward to a hatch where he could look out. "I could see the *Santee* burning and listing to port. A Japanese Zero was coming in from the starboard at mast level and strafing us. I drew back behind a stanchion to get out of the line of fire when I heard this crash, which was the kamikaze hitting the flight deck. I never heard the bomb go off."

Kitzmann found himself in the sea. "I saw my helmet turning over and over under the clear blue water of the Mindanao Trench as I surfaced. I discovered that my dungarees were no longer on my body except my belt and shorts, no shoes or socks. Yet my life jacket was still on my shoulder. Trying to gain my composure, I looked around and saw smoke billowing from the stern of the *Suwannee*. It was a big blur as I was bleeding from my eyes and began struggling to put my other arm into my life jacket. My face felt like someone had hit me with a baseball bat. I regained my senses; it became apparent I was not alone. Mournful cries of help and despair were all around. A body came up near me without a head and it did not shock me at the time. It did make me aware of my situation. As my ankle began to pain, I was afraid to look down to see if my foot was still with me. I realized I was going to make it; panic and fear left me.

"The next thing I remember is the bow of the USS *Bull* [a destroyer escort] plowing through the water and her Skeeter (as they call the commander of destroyers) calling on her speaker horns, 'Rendezvous in the rafts we are going to drop and we'll pick you up later.' I don't know how many men in the water understood the message but I did. I began to swim for the rafts and when I reached one I discovered it had flipped upside down into the water. It was no small thing as I dove under it to reach the paddles and began paddling around to find shipmates.

"I don't recall how long it took but I picked up Frank Yeomans and H. O. Olson, Aviation Machinist Mates, 3d Class. Olson was holding up Yeomans as I pulled them onto the raft. Yeomans was hit hard by the blast and did not become coherent until later that night aboard the *Bull*. I picked up two black men who were burned badly. Their skin was hanging from their bodies. One had lost half of one leg and the other had a hole in his neck. I put my belt around the man who had his leg half gone to stop the bleeding. I administered morphine to both men.

"To get the morphine I had to dive under the raft to bring up the five-inch shell can that contained medical supplies. I could not open the can and asked Yeomans for a knife. I'll never know how I was able to open that container with a Navy jack knife. About that time the man with a hole in his throat asked for water. The water keg I brought up from the bottom of the raft had no cup so I opened the spigot and let the water run into his mouth. It came right out his throat.

"Later in the afternoon, it seemed like years, the *Bull* returned and sent out her whale boat to pick up our survivors. As I climbed the cargo net of the *Bull*, the little pains began to ache. But I was alive and that was all that mattered at the time. In the wardroom of the *Bull*, a pharmacist mate told me I was bleeding from my shoulder, ankle, and groin. I told him to take care of the man lying on the table whose ankle was blown away. The pharmacist mate offered me a glass that contained some liquid medicine. After I drank it I walked out on the afterdeck to identify the bodies of some shipmates. Sneed, from Redding, California, was lying there without a mark on his body. Anglin was still alive with a hole through his stomach, begging me to put a .45 to his head and end his pain. At this point, the world seemed to spin and I dropped to the deck, out cold."

While other vessels plucked men like Kitzmann from the sea and tended to their injuries, Phil Phillips, one of the three flight surgeons on the *Suwannee*, narrowly missed injury or death himself. "I had no particular instruction about handling the sick before we went to sea. There was no specific educational process to prepare except to familiarize ourselves with the ship and the potentials for dealing with sick people. The medical department on the *Suwannee* was adequate in a rustic sort of way. It had an eight-bed sick bay and a little room for holding sick call. We had about ten first-rate hospital corpsmen; most had training ashore but some didn't and they were eager learners." The medical team included three doctors and a dentist.

Phillips remembered standing in the parachute loft when the kamikaze struck. "The stretcher-bearer assigned to my battle station was wounded. The explosion was so horribly loud and the sheet of metal on the inside surface of the parachute loft where I stood was riddled with shell fragments.

There were so many dead and wounded on the hangar deck that I scrambled out of the parachute loft headed for the hangar deck to do what I could. Going by the main sick bay, I could see that our little ward had quickly overflowed with patients. Stretchers lay in the passageway and on the deck of the operating room. Others were being carried into the pharmacy and the clerical office. Quickly the wardroom became an emergency aid station.

"The hangar deck was still filled with smoke. Through the eerie light streaming in from the hole in the flight deck it was easy to see that here lay our worst casualties. Mangled bodies and portions of bodies lay about the deck, where they had been blown from the explosion. Steel decks were slippery with blood. Men followed with stretchers, and one by one we gathered the wounded from their ghastly surroundings, applied temporary dressings, and sent them to the wardroom.

"In the wardroom were six to eight long tables on which we could put patients who needed immediate care. It was a helluva bad day and we lost fifty-five dead that morning and more than that were wounded. Most of the men were doing their best under the difficult circumstances. Through the night gun crews stayed at their guns while scores of volunteers assisted the doctors and hospital corpsmen in caring for the wounded. But one senior person hid himself in an ensign's room and with a bottle, trying to intoxicate himself."

On the following day, shortly before noon, the flattop's guns began to fire amid the sound of general quarters. A few TBMs, having finished their morning's work, were being taken aboard and one was in the process of taxiing to the forward elevator. The suicide plane crashed the *Suwannee* atop the taxiing TBM, annihilating the plane, and killing all three crew members. The blast wrecked the elevator and gasoline leaked from the aircraft on the deck to spread fires. The second explosion probably resulted from rupture of the compressed air tank of the ship's catapult.

Many of the ship's crew engaged in handling planes and ordnance died outright. Others received terrible burns, some fatal. Rounds from .50-caliber machine guns cooked off in burning airplanes. The bridge had been severely damaged, sailors stationed there killed. The detonations blew some men into the water. Others jumped into the sea to avoid the flames. The skipper, bleeding from shrapnel wounds, continued to direct damage control. The inferno created molten metal out of bulkheads and fittings.

Bill Dacus had begun his navy career as a deckhand but once assigned to quartermaster duties demonstrated such aptitude that he climbed to the exalted title of chief quartermaster. Dacus recalled that after the initial explosion, "A group of us were laying on the passageway deck in front of the chief's quarters, when someone wanted to get up and run into the hangar deck. Other sailors laying there told him to stay down. He kept getting up, wanting to run to the hangar deck where the explosion occurred. I finally said in a very authoritative voice, 'Get down and stay down!' He did and it was then we heard a second explosion, from the catapult.

"It was a good thing the man hadn't moved because that explosion killed everyone in the hangar deck. The blast went through all passageways fore and aft. They actually had to scrape a sailor off a passageway bulkhead. Shortly after, Chief Shipfitter William Brooks came up the passageway with a hose on his shoulders. He told me to grab a hose on the bulkhead nearby. I did and followed him up the passageway to the hangar deck. As we went, we both looked out a porthole. We saw our sister ships quite a distance from us and a lot of sailors in the water with 40mm-shell containers [for flotation] spotting the ocean. I asked him if we should jump out. Brooks, who was a very chubby guy, said very emphatically, 'I don't know about you but I'll never make it.' I just followed him up the stairs with the hose."

As Dacus struggled to connect the hose to a valve, another explosion rocked the ship, knocking Brooks unconscious for a few seconds. When he regained his wits, Brooks crawled under the planes on the hangar deck and opened valves from a sprinkler system. The heavy spray prevented the fire from spreading to the gassed planes. Dacus managed to keep his poise and, following Brooks's lead, started pushing the high-octane gas on the hangar deck into the elevator well, as if cleaning the sidewalk.

The conflagration heated the metal in some areas until it was too hot to touch, forcing some sailors to abandon ship. But with everyone, including the flight personnel, tending the fire lines, the *Suwannee* remained afloat, albeit she was down four to six feet at the bow. Unable to function, with at least half of the 1,000 of the complement killed or wounded, the *Suwannee* received orders to transfer her most seriously injured to hospital ships, bury her dead, and steam for the Palaus to repair the damage. Bill Dacus recalled dealing with dead shipmates. "They brought up Robert Wilding, a good friend of mine, on a stretcher. I tried to tell him something of encouragement. One of the stretcher-bearers told me he was dead. A sailor came up to us and said we should come with him to the forward, starboard 40mm gun turret. There he pointed to three bodies in the fetus position, hugging one another and burned so badly that we could not recognize them."

Word of the Japanese thrust went to Halsey with the Third Fleet and to Nimitz as the Pacific commander. The former, upon receipt of the message, replied he was already involved with the enemy but did order a carrier group under Adm. John McCain to come to the aid of the Taffies. Unfortunately, the carriers commanded by McCain were well over 300 miles from the scene. It would be noon before their planes could hope to get over the targets.

Greatly concerned, Nimitz radioed Halsey a coded question: "Where is Task Force 34?" The yeoman assigned to transmit the query thought he detected a note of emphasis in the admiral's voice. He added a repeat of the first two words, "Where is." And when actually sent, padding was inserted on both ends of the question to mislead eavesdropping Japanese. As a consequence, the complete transmission read: TURKEY TROTS TO WATER RR FROM CINCPAC ACTION COM THIRD FLEET INFO COMINCH CTF SEVENTY-SEVEN X WHERE IS RPT WHERE IS TASK FORCE THIRTY FOUR RR THE WORLD WONDERS.

The communications people on Halsey's flagship, *New Jersey,* recognized the TURKEY TROTS TO WATER as intended to fool the enemy and deleted that from what was handed to Halsey. Unfortunately, the staff believed the final three words purposely included and an irate Halsey read, WHERE IS, REPEAT, WHERE IS, TASK FORCE 34, THE WORLD WONDERS. He interpreted the final phrase as a rocket from Nimitz. Months would pass before he accepted an explanation for what he regarded as a deliberate insult.

The postmortem investigation became an argument about language. The dispatch from Halsey on 24 October that described a "Battle Plan" named the specific ships that "will be formed as Task Force 34." The seabag lawyers now debated whether a "Battle Plan" can be extrapolated to mean a battle or operation order. Critics of Halsey insisted "will be formed" meant this would now happen rather than indicating that the creation of Task Force 34 was a conditional future.

MacArthur refused to criticize any individual. Instead he reiterated his disapproval of divided commands. "The near disaster can be placed squarely at the door of Washington. In the naval action, two key American commanders were independent of each other, one under me, and the other under Admiral Nimitz, 5,000 miles away, both operating in the same waters and in the same battle." He ignored his own attempt to create a divided command when he left Corregidor.

The issue, however, became moot, due to timidity by the aggressors. Convinced of imminent defeat by superior forces, Kurita withdrew, although, had he persisted, his outfit could have thoroughly whipped the Taffies. To the north, Halsey, in spite of the distractions concerning the plight of the Seventh Fleet, destroyed what he believed were the main elements of the Japanese Navy still afloat. Admiral Ozawa now reaped the bitter rewards of his scheme. With a paltry dozen or so planes for a combat air patrol from his carriers, the Japanese admiral's seventeen ships depended upon antiaircraft to defend themselves. The torpedo-bombers and fighter-bombers from the *Essex*, *Lexington*, *San Jacinto*, *Intrepid*, *Langley*, *Belleau Wood*, and *Franklin* overwhelmed the enemy. When the sixth and final air strike of the day, a total of 527 sorties, landed on the flight decks, the U.S. airmen had wiped out four carriers and a destroyer. American cruisers and submarines disposed of two more destroyers and a cruiser.

The Japanese could no longer fight from flattops. However, large numbers of navy and army planes stationed at bases in the Philippines, where intelligence located between eighty and a hundred airstrips, and other islands, menaced American ground and seagoing forces. On 30 October 1944,

William "Pappy" Turner and a flight of P-38s from the Air Corps' 36th Fighter Squadron traveled from Morotai some 750 miles over water to strafe the harbor and airfield at Sandakan on Borneo. "We arrived over the target without incident and evidently without warning—who would expect a fighter strike when the enemy was so far away? I saw no Jap fighters in the air, but it didn't take those Japs down below very long to contest our intentions. Ack-ack was everywhere. We made our strafing runs from all different approaches and at airspeeds of 400 miles per hour. The .50-caliber ground fire was intense.

"On a high-speed run a target is picked and that's it. You don't have time to change targets, but probably you will see another one that you wish you had chosen. So, most of us gained altitude again and made another high-speed pass. How the smoke rose from those Jap gun pits as they burned their barrels up, trying to hit those 400-mile-per-hour planes. On both my runs I picked out a plane on the runway. A fighter on the first and a bomber the second.

"As I finished and streaked off out over the harbor, I saw a camouflaged ship, a good-size one, covered with camouflage netting. As long as I was here, why not? This ship was anchored between the main shore and a small island with a rocky, perpendicular cliff on its east side. I figured I would go out to sea, out of sight behind the island, gain some altitude to convert into a high-speed run around that cliff, and hit them broadside. My strategy was good, I gained the altitude, my wingman, Lieutenant Maynard, who'd been with us only three weeks, was still beside me, and two or three others had joined up. In one big string we snaked down and around the cliff.

"We were close to the top of the cliff as we cut by. How those gun emplacements sent up the smoke as we went by!

You could see the men on those guns, we were that close, but they got no hits. Now I had passed the cliff, brought my plane out of its steep banked turn, and leveled off for my firing run. I squeezed off a few rounds to make them nervous as I closed in, saving the rest for a turning run where I could stitch them the full length of the ship.

"They had other plans. They were ready for us and as I closed in I was hit by their gunfire. It threw my plane out of control and somewhat spoiled my run. I leveled her up and fired my guns, just missing the mast with the crow's nest. Here a gunner was firing as I came in, passed over. I could see men in white uniforms running about; this ship was no freighter. As I went away from them, the water below was being churned up with their fire and it was rapidly going out ahead of me as they were getting a better lead on me. I pulled back on the wheel, gaining altitude sharply, and with much effort made a turn to the right. Seconds later I was out of range.

"They had concentrated on me and those behind me all got their runs in without being hit. The third or fourth man's fire apparently hit some high explosives on the deck. There was an explosion that cleared the decks and left the ship helpless in the water. No one could stick around to find out its fate. We had overstayed our anticipated time; now it was time for a three-hour-plus ride for home. I limped along, slowly gaining altitude. How bad I was hit, I couldn't tell. My instruments checked out okay—engines were running, gas gauges were stable. But my controls were messed up—the plane wanted to turn to the left. It took about all the strength in my right leg to keep it leveled up and on course. Soon I had both feet on that right rudder pedal. I knew they would tire before long. Then I saw a nice long new pencil that the crew chief had missed when he had strapped me in or had shook loose from somewhere. Very carefully I experimented until I got that pencil at right angles to that right rudder and wedged in so the force was straight on it. I slowly removed my two feet and, glory be, it held." Turner fluttered toward Morotai while Maynard remained on his wing. Just short of seven hours after he took off he landed safely.

Although MacArthur and Nimitz had parceled out responsibilities in the South Pacific, jurisdictional squabbles and tactical differences ignited ugly confrontations. While army troops grappled with Japanese defenders on Leyte, according to Jimmy Thach, who directed air operations for the navy units supporting the landings, MacArthur drew across an east-west line that ran just north of Legazpi on the southern leg of Luzon that stretches toward Leyte. Thach described the gist of MacArthur's order to his seagoing partners, "The carriers will take care of the enemy air north of the line and the Army Air Corps everything south of the line. So don't attack anything south of the line and the Air Corps won't attack anything north of the line."

When a kamikaze blasted one of the carriers, knocking out the flight deck, the ship's planes were instructed to land at an Air Corps base. Enroute, the navy fliers noticed an enemy field near Legazpi within the territory reserved for the army. The pilots reported to the Air Corps operations officers the malignant presence. According to Thach, they responded that they did not believe the Japanese base was a threat. The navy men protested that the attack on their carrier probably originated at this field. The Air Corps relented and, in Thach's words, said, "All right, we'll take off tomorrow morning and we'll give you some bombs and you can go with us. You lead us up there and show us these airplanes."

Said Thach, "[The Army] flew pretty high but the Navy airplanes always liked to fly lower. They [the Air Corps] said 'We don't see any.' Of course you couldn't see them from that altitude. The torpedo planes were going in, winding around the trees, picking out an airplane and dropping a little bomb on it. One of the strike leaders of the Army planes said, 'We'd better get up higher. There's a lot of antiaircraft going off down there.' They couldn't even see our torpedo planes either."

The carrier pilots persuaded their counterparts to make their bomb runs, and between the two forces they wreaked considerable devastation. When the navy aircrews returned to carriers that made room for them, they reported what happened. "We sent a blistering message," said Thach. "We argued against this line in the first place. Halsey immediately saw the problem and he argued with MacArthur against the line, too. He finally told MacArthur that when his carriers were called in to do a job they had the right to protect themselves and to hit any airfield that was within range because the kamikazes were undoubtedly coming from airfields that had not been properly attacked, such as the one at Legazpi. He just told [MacArthur] and we didn't hear any more about the line."

The Legazpi boundary was another instance in which MacArthur had practiced what he had preached against.

6

The Ardennes

AS OMAR BRADLEY WROTE IN HIS AUTOBIOGRAPHY, OF THE four paths to France open to the Nazi armies in 1940, that of the Ardennes, a harsh, craggy, ravine-gouged, heavily timbered region inhospitable to armored warfare, seemed least appetizing as a route of attack. But just as they had in World War I, the Germans had surprised the French and the Belgians with their blitzkrieg through that sparsely populated area, avoiding the Maginot Line and the best defensive positions. With winter on hand in 1944, Bradley claimed awareness of history, but insisted he believed that with 70,000 GIs plus the armor stationed on the shoulders of the Ardennes, the risk of penetration there was acceptable. Furthermore, he had the impression that if anything untoward occurred, reinforcements could rapidly plug any holes.

On 16 December, the enemy, under a plan devised by Hitler, who considered himself both a student of history and a military strategist, struck for a third time in the Ardennes. On that day, newly promoted to the rank of five-star general of the armies, Dwight Eisenhower attended the wedding of his valet, Mickey McKeogh, and Women's Army Corps sergeant Pearlie Hargrave, in the Louis XIV Chapel at Versailles, near Paris. General Elwood (Pete) Quesada, the chief of the tactical air forces in Europe, Bradley, and Gen. Courtney Hodges, head of the U.S. First Army, which faced the Germans on the Siegfried line, visited with a Belgian manufacturer to arrange for custom-made shotguns. For the past few days, Bradley, in a chauffeured staff car, had escorted actress Marlene Dietrich, who was performing morale-building shows for American troops. He had been somewhat bemused by her complaints about the food and accommodations. She also dallied with various senior officers, most notably the 82d Airborne's James M. Gavin. Hodges had devoted some of the previous day to welcoming a contingent of major-league baseball stars, Frank Frisch, Bucky Walters, Dutch Leonard, and Mel Ott, building morale with visits to the troops. Maxwell Taylor of the 101st had flown to England for a conference.

The top brass acted according to the evaluations of their intelligence experts. These groped through thickets of information—intercepts of enemy communications via the code-breaking medium of ULTRA, photos and observations produced by the Air Corps, gobbets of gossip and facts coaxed from prisoners, tales from civilians who crossed the lines, and accounts of troops up on the line. The fodder fed to the decision makers also reflected a certain amount of competition and ego among the analysts. While the American Office of Strategic Services (OSS), precursor to the Central Intelligence Agency, was available to supply data, there was a distinct antipathy of some military men toward civilian input to the military hopper. And to this point, the armed forces had little reason to call on the OSS. During the drive across France, Belgium, and Holland, local civilians gladly informed on the hated occupation troops. But now, on the border of Germany, that resource dried up.

A desire to get the job over with, by the start of the New Year if possible, a sentiment heartily endorsed by the civilians and those in uniform, seemed to affect evaluations of conditions for both the civilian leaders of the Allied governments and their brass-hat subordinates. There had been, according to Gen. Edwin Sibert, the Twelfth Army Group's G-2, and a rival intelligencier to his inferior Col. Benjamin "Monk" Dickson, G-2 for the First Army, complaints concerning the dullness of the reports from Sibert's realm. Officers allegedly failed to study them because the files read so dully. To remedy the situation, Sibert ordered Col. Ralph Ingersoll, a former newspaperman, in effect to jazz up the memos. In retrospect, Sibert remarked, the result was to deliver overoptimistic accounts, the kind of stuff the warriors enjoyed reading. Some of the happy talk undoubtedly also owed its origins to the air corps' penchant for overestimation of its results. Its top management insisted no one could possibly continue to work and produce with all the high-explosive tonnage dumped on the enemy. But as post–World War II statistical analyses and debriefing of Nazi officials revealed, the Germans with their slave laborers kept right on manufacturing the tools of war in spite of all the bombing.

At the Twelfth Army Group, the summary issued on 12 December followed the victory-is-imminent line. "It is now certain that attrition is steadily sapping the strength of German forces on the Western Front and that the crust of defenses is thinner, more brittle, and more vulnerable than it appears on our G-2 map or to the troops in the line." The allegedly rosy view of the "troops in the line" was made before GIs of the 2d and 99th Divisions confronted strenuous resistance to advances toward the Roer.

Over the next few days, qualms ruffled some military intelligence specialists. ULTRA, the code-breaking system, flagged down messages that roused suspicions about the German intentions. On 9 December the U.S. 83d Division had seized a prisoner who said there were strong rumors of an all-out attack within the next few days. A couple of deserters as well as two men captured by the 4th and 106th Infantry Divisions claimed they were told of an imminent big push. The G-2 office sounded a vague alarm but at most divined a strengthening of the enemy defenses in the plains before the Rhine rather than indicating an assault. On 15 December, an officer from the 28th Division scrawled a smudged pencil report detailing his interrogation of a Luxembourg woman, Elise Dele-Dunkel. She spoke of many horsedrawn vehicles, pontoons, small boats, and other river-crossing equipment coming from the direction of Bitburg and moving west through Geichlingen. In Bitburg she overheard some military personnel saying that it had taken three weeks to get them from Italy. She described the presence of men whose uniforms belonged to the Waffen SS, the most fanatical Nazi soldiers, and she saw many artillery pieces. The intelligence officer interpreted her information as indications of an offensive operation. However, a day went by before this report passed on to higher authorities.

While some of the Americans on the front lines, like Lt. Alan Jones of the 106th Division, which had just come to the combat zone, were watchful, the complaisant attitude that pervaded the uppermost echelons seemed to filter down. There was no general order insisting upon a high state of alert. General Hasso von Manteuffel, commander of the Fifth Panzer Army, personally observed the front and from what he could see the "Amis" (Americans) stayed on guard one hour after dark, then returned to their huts to sleep, reappearing one hour before dawn. Dick Byers, as part of a field artillery observation team with the 106th Division, confirmed Manteuffel. "Before the Bulge, we were a nine-to-five army in the Ardennes."

Originally, said Manteuffel, Hitler scheduled the onslaught to begin at 11:00 A.M. However, the general persuaded his leader that with darkness coming by 4:00 P.M. the Germans would have too little daylight to achieve maximum success. Accordingly, the first salvos were to boom at 5:30 A.M. Furthermore, on the grounds of preventing the Americans from becoming fully alert, instead of a lengthy artillery preparation, Manteuffel planned for less than an hour of the big guns before sending his infantry forward. His armor, relying on searchlights bouncing illumination off the clouds, would pass through the infantry at night and be ready to break out the following day.

While Manteuffel controlled the tactics of the Fifth Panzer Army, Sepp Dietrich, in charge of the Sixth Panzer Army, insisted upon a full-scale softening up through artillery. In both instances, the two German generals thought in terms of foot soldiers creating wedges for the armor, unlike Patton and Rommel who used their tanks to crash through. Before the targeted hour for the attack, paratroopers were scheduled to drop. However, the requisite number of trucks needed to carry the troops to the airdromes failed to show because no one had authorized fuel for the vehicles. The entire operation was scrubbed, to be reinstated twenty-four hours later.

The Nazi armies also put into play a carefully crafted plot to hoodwink the Americans. In the train of the advance group for Dietrich's legions marched the 150 Brigade, a unit led by Otto Skorzeny, a Hitler favorite who plotted the rescue of Mussolini when Italy had surrendered. Operation Greif, Skorzeny's assignment, traveled in tanks disguised to look like Shermans, genuine U.S. jeeps, and trucks. Their assignment was to race forward and seize Meuse bridges after Peiper carved a wedge through to the river. While the bulk of Skorzeny's 150 Brigade awaited their opportunity behind a task force under Col. Jochen Peiper, a veteran panzer officer, forty-four advance men from Greif garbed in American uniforms infiltrated the Allied lines. Demolition teams sought to blow up bridges and munitions and gas dumps. Several small squads were to reconnoiter as far west as the Meuse River to gather intelligence. These men reversed road signs, switched mine markers, and performed similar acts to mislead Americans. Others disrupted communications, cut telephone wires, blew up transmitter stations and issued false commands.

Private First Class Nolan Williams, on patrol for Company K of the 99th Division's 394th Regiment, discovered the massing of enemy forces on the night of 15 December. "Shortly after dark, we made our way around enemy outposts and bumped into an enemy patrol. There were some small-arms shots but I don't remember that we returned fire. We did skirt around the patrol and move deeper into enemy territory. Soon, we were hearing mass movements of tanks, tracks, and men. The sergeant tried to contact our headquarters with his hand radio but could not get a response. He believed the troop movement important enough to cut short our mission and return to report. We flopped down on the first floor of the Bucholz farmhouse. Very early in the morning [16 December] a shell or grenade exploded in the courtyard, throwing glass on us. Someone said, 'Let's go down in the basement to get out of this shelling.' I put on my belt, hung my rifle over my chest, tucked a box of K rations inside my shirt and carefully picked up my new overshoes—I had only been issued them the day before.

"In the dark, I went down the hall and started down the steps. I heard someone speaking German, very rapidly. I assumed it was one of our interpreters. But then there were several voices, all German. In the dark, I placed my hand on the head of the person just in front of me on the steps, pulled his head over to me and whispered, 'There are Jerries in this basement.' All of our helmets had netting on them and suddenly I realized that the one I was holding had no net! At that moment, a German officer in the basement pointed a flashlight on us and said in perfect English, 'Hands up, boys. The war is over.' I'll never forget the saucer-sized eyes of the young German into whose ears I had just whispered. He must have been as frightened as I.

"But I responded, 'Like hell it is!' And I shoved the young soldier down the steps on top of the officer. Up the stairs, down the hall, out toward the courtyard I practically flew, meanwhile clutching my new overshoes in my right hand. In the doorway, silhouetted by the white snow, stood a German with a burp gun in ready position. I hit him with my overshoes, ran over him from toe to head like a freight train, and on to the barn. But I dropped the overshoes. To show how important they seemed to me, I seriously considered going back to the yard to retrieve them."

"I went into the barn and began to get control of myself. I unwound myself from the rifle straps and had the butt ready to defend myself. Someone else began to enter the barn and just as I was about to smack him with the butt, I recognized the sergeant. We decided we would try to get some help. We made a dash for the road and I noticed a German halftrack parked by the house. Now I saw the road was bumper to bumper with tanks, troop carriers, and infantrymen. We hid a long time in a ditch, then dashed between the tanks. Eventually, we were reunited with nine of the others from our original thirteen-man patrol. We became part of the general withdrawal."

About the time Nolan Williams stumbled into the enemy, the big guns of the Sixth Panzer Army opened up all along their front. A murderous downpour of everything from 14-inch railway pieces to mortars crashed down upon the men of the 99th Division. In their log-and-dirt-covered burrows, casualties were few, but the cascade of high explosives tore up the network of wire lines necessary for communications. The Fifth Panzer Army, in spite of Manteuffel's fear of waking up the Americans, blasted away, and the Seventh Army contributed long-range shelling.

Sergeant Ben Nawrocki, with a brother regiment to Williams's, noted, "At 4:00 A.M. on December 16, it seemed all hell broke loose with artillery shells landing all over. The ground shook. We had a wool sock in a bottle of gasoline for a light but the artillery kept blowing it out. We could not stick our heads up. Trees and branches fell all over, and shrapnel whined around. The tree bursts were very dangerous. We found it better to squat, rather than spread-eagle; squatting made a smaller target.

"When the artillery started to let up around 6:00 A.M. and we stuck our heads out of our holes, an eerie sight greeted us. There were lights of all descriptions, lighting the sky and ground. The lights pointed up into the sky and into our positions. They beamed from tanks, trucks, pillboxes, everywhere. This was to help the Germans see the terrain and us. The snow was hip-deep with a heavy fog. If the lights were intended to throw fear into our troops it didn't succeed with us. The enemy were between us, and the lights made them a good target. Some wore American uniforms, throwing grenades, a few were seen on skis. Some wore white snow-suits. We kept cutting them down. In many places the Germans piled up on top of one another like cord wood."

An entire regiment of the 277th Volksgrenadier Division had hurled itself at Company B. "On the left flank of the 3d platoon, a rifleman with a BAR was firing at the oncoming Germans, who piled up three or four feet high in front of his foxhole. I don't know his name but he was bucktoothed and when he looked down at his feet, I heard him yell, 'God-damn, I'm barefoot.' He had been so busy for six hours he never had time to put on his shoes." The embattled GIs in Nawrocki's sector, aided by artillery fire from the big guns to the rear, inflicted heavy casualties, The resistance stalled the enemy infantrymen, jamming up the armor behind.

Along the Luxembourg border, on the right flank and to the south, the impact and the immediate problems varied. George Ruhlen, then a lieutenant colonel commanding the 3d Field Artillery of the 9th Armored Division, recalled, "At 0615 on the sixteenth of December, shells of 105mm, 150mm and 170mm came whistling into Haller [a town on the Sauer River below its junction with the Our]. The fire increased and as all ran for cover, the rumble of enemy guns could be heard echoing up and down the Sauer Valley. It was soon apparent that this was not a local raid nor a retaliation for harassing fire delivered the previous night. Bells in the Haller church struck three high notes, then three low notes, and then incessantly for half an hour until the bell ringer was evicted. An estimated 800 to 900 rounds fell in and near the town between 0615 and 0715. Columns of smoke and dust from tremendous explosions were seen in the vicinity of Beaufort. Nebelwerfer rockets fell near gun positions with their characteristically terrifying shriek.

"An observer reported sixty Germans crossing the river on a small pontoon bridge near Dillingen, but they were not carrying weapons and it was believed they were coming over to surrender. A minute later came the report that these Germans were carrying machine guns and frantic calls for normal barrages came from all observers almost instantaneously. All wire lines were shot out except the liaison line to the 60th Infantry Command Post. A heavy ground mist made observation very difficult, let alone making close air support impossible. In the forward areas, vague figures appeared in the fog, unidentifiable even a hundred yards away."

In the area occupied by the 106th Division, the huge shells launched from railway guns thundered into St.-Vith, division headquarters. Up front the amazed troops watched the searchlight beams carom off the low-hanging clouds to illuminate roads and open fields. More ominously, they spotted white-clad figures in the distance advancing toward them, the clatter of tracked vehicles reached their ears.

From a snow-encrusted emplacement for a light machine gun, the 423d Regiment's Pvt. Frank Raila watched the searchlights bounce off the cloud cover. "It was a pretty sight." Sightseeing ended with the dawn. "We saw a Tiger tank in the trees to our front. Our machine gun fired tracers to point out the tank to the tank destroyer unit nearby. Two or three of them went out to get it. Then 88 shells started coming, landing in the woods behind us where we put on our backpacks. Small-arms fire was directed at us and we fired back, with machine guns, mortars. The tank destroyers came back. One had been hit. Its .50-caliber machine gun was at a twisted tangle. A dead crewman was strapped in front. He was the first dead American I saw.

"I could barely make out figures, far ahead of us, 500 to

1,000 yards, with dark, flapping greatcoats. As soon as people began to shoot, they disappeared. The place we were in apparently had become untenable. I had gone back to get ammo twice for the machine gun and the sergeant said we were going on the march. We all hit the road, passing U.S. trucks burning, with ammo exploding, an occasional shell shooting into the air, pyrotechnics! It got very confusing. We were not much of a company anymore. There were different platoons and companies. We were told to walk down a field in front of us to the right of a road. Everything was quiet. I think the Germans let the point keep walking. Then when we reached an area of a few acres, all hell broke loose. It was very surprising. There had been no sound of incoming; mortars may make a sound but I didn't hear anything until the explosions started to rock the ground. Dirt flew up everywhere, pelting you in the chest and back. We all dropped down, paralyzed. People were hollering and screaming until the sergeant said, 'Get out of here!' We crawled back until the explosions didn't follow and then we ran like crazy. We straggled back to the 'front lines,' a miserably thin line of GIs, including my own machine-gun platoon."

Initially, there was little to even hint at a cataclysm for Phil Hannon and the others from Company A of the 81st Combat Engineer Battalion. "We were roused by 'calling cards' mailed by 88s on Saturday morning. We were 'green' and so, shrugging our shoulders, said, 'What the hell, this happens every so often. And off to chow we went. Chow was good as chow always is to guys who are in good shape, and the gang was full of laughs about the close calls that had dropped in on us. The heavy firing in the east didn't register, so the talk was about Christmas and the mail that was starting to come in. We didn't think it strange that all the

German civilians were up and in their basements long before the shelling started.

"The third platoon had a couple of jobs to finish up front, so we loaded up and moved out. The same old horseplay went on. The KPs got the everyday razzing as we rode by the kitchen. We dropped off the second and third squads and mine went up farther to finish the corduroy road we had begun the day before. The front was quiet. The shells were going over and beyond, and we felt safer than in our little village. We felt safer until we noticed the worried looks on the faces of the officers. A major walked by with a .45 in his fist, so we woke up. No work on the road this day and we headed for home. We never got there."

John Collins, a member of A Company of the 81st Engineers, was less blasé about the first salvos. "We were literally knocked out of our beds by artillery shells landing in and around our company area. We dressed quickly and went downstairs to find the German family crouched in a rear room, fully dressed. It looked as though they knew it was coming. We crouched with them until we could collect our wits and the shelling slacked off. But not much. We now knew what it feels like to be under fire and we were scared. Really scared. Maybe a better word would be frustrated. If someone is shooting at you, you can retaliate, but this shelling was for the birds.

"At about 0600 we left for the mess hall to find most of the company in line for chow. When a shell would come in, everyone hit the ground. Immediately afterward they were back in line." As Phil Hannon noted, the three platoons left the area after breakfast to perform routine chores. John Collins was temporarily left behind, assigned to bring up the outfit's equipment. He had almost finished the task when the shelling increased. The company commander decided to recall the three platoons and dispatched Collins with a Lieutenant Coughlin to retrieve the men. They reached the first and second platoons without trouble and passed the word.

"We headed to the 422d Regiment to round up my 3d platoon. As we neared a guard shack about 800 yards behind the lines, Lieutenant Coughlin very nonchalantly said, 'Sergeant, turn around real easy and let's get the hell out of here.' I swung the jeep around and slowly retraced our way back. It was then that I saw the white-clad enemy in a field about 800 yards to our left. At this point we were only about seventy-five yards from the guard shack and I really poured the juice to the jeep. We heard some rifle fire but with my sliding on the snow and the lieutenant yelling 'Faster!' we made it without any hits if they were shooting at us. The lieutenant told me that the guard at the shack had on white boots and his rifle did not look like ours."

Collins's company commander ordered everyone to pull back to the village of Heuem. Lieutenant Coughlin organized a defense from buildings behind the retreat. Accompanied by foot soldiers, a quartet of German Tiger tanks trundled up the road and blew away the houses, scattering Coughlin and his men. The remnants of the 81st Engineers assembled briefly at Heuem, but the pressure from the enemy continued. Collins and the others retreated toward St.-Vith, where Gen. Alan Jones [father of Lt. Alan Jones Jr.], as CG of the 106th, sought to restore control. From a hillside, the general's namesake son watched with dismay as the enemy battered the town of Bleialf, inhabited by a brother regiment, the 424th. The junior Jones himself was not in imminent danger. "There was very little shelling on our positions the first day, and not much on the second, either."

On the night of 15 December, the observation section for

C Battery of the 371st Field Artillery, which included Dick Byers, slept in a house located at the center of Murringen. According to Byers, his bedroom shared the back wall and roof in common with the barn. "Just before dawn, on the morning of the sixteenth, we were awakened by a muffled explosion and a slight tremor of the house. None of us thought enough of the occurrence to get out of a warm sleeping bag to investigate. But so far as our group was concerned this was the start of the Battle of the Bulge.

"One of the guys finally went downstairs and out to the latrine. By the early light he saw that a delayed-fuse artillery shell had gone through the roof of the barn, just two feet from the wall of our bedroom. The round had buried itself in the haymow before exploding. Throughout the morning, shells struck at seeming random around the village. One exploded among a group of artillerymen lined up for breakfast and killed several. By midmorning, we realized there was a pattern to the explosions. They fell close to houses occupied by American troops. Later, we heard that a captured German artillery observer had a map marked with all of the occupied houses. The information must have been given to him by someone planted in the area by the Germans.

"In the afternoon I drove an officer to a command post for a conference. I stayed with the jeep and was caught in the first and worst barrage I've ever been in. I was caught flat-footed in a pine forest without any adequate cover. The shells were hitting treetops and spraying the ground all around us with steel fragments. I believe I actually pressed a slit trench into the snow and frozen ground with my body, trying in my terror to become as small and flat as possible. The noise was so incredibly loud it could not be heard. It rang in my ears and vibrated my body. Imagine putting your head up inside an enormous bell while giants pounded it with sledgehammers. Most young soldiers felt invulnerable even when their comrades were dropping all around them. When they lost that sense of invulnerability and suddenly realized the truth of their situation, terror replaced it, shortness of breath, and a pounding heart. I had a terrible feeling of my back being so vulnerable."

The quietest sector for the 106th defenses until 16 December had been that held by elements of the 424th Regiment just inside the German border above Luxembourg. Shortly before dawn on the sixteenth, a noncom burst into the cabin where Harry F. Martin Jr. bunked and yelled, "The Germans are coming! The Germans are coming! We'll be killed!" Martin and Bill Williams snatched up their rifles and steel helmets. They ran to their position, a two-man foxhole on the extreme left flank. The remainder of the platoon took their stations in log bunkers. Said Martin, "Seconds later I could see hundreds of shadowy heads bobbing up and down, coming over the crest of the hill just before dawn. They acted as though they were drunk or on drugs, screaming, shrieking. I was absolutely terrified. They had already outflanked our company and now they were coming to finish us off. With nothing on our left and out of sight of our platoon on the right, it felt almost as if we were against the entire German Army. I was horror-stricken. There was no thought of running away or surrendering. I had an absolute conviction to fight to the death, while being certain we would be killed. Bill tugged on my leg. I was vaguely aware he asked me to let him know when the Germans were close enough. Neither of us had ever fired a rifle grenade before and we did not have the slightest idea of the effective range. There were so many of them storming down the hill coming right for us. There was no way of stopping all of them. I had a feeling of utter hopelessness; I was panic-stricken. I felt my entire life force had left my body. I was already dead and fighting like a zombie. Sheer panic caused me to fire without thinking or aiming. I was unaware of my body, just terror, firing as fast as my finger could pull the trigger.

"They kept coming as though immune to death. Apparently I was not hitting a thing. I was so transfixed with fear and terror my eyes did not focus on the individual enemy. I was firing blindly, without thinking or looking through the sights. In my terror-stricken seizure I continued to fire in the general direction of the swarming sea of terror, the huge mass of bodies charging toward me. It was as though the entire hillside was alive, moving with huge tentacles to devour me. Bill tugged on my leg again and yelled, 'Are they close enough?' I can remember telling him no, but my brain didn't register distance. I could not even think about what he was saying. He must have tugged my leg half a dozen times during the battle and I kept telling him no. In the middle of this terrifying battle I heard a very confident, calm voice inside my head say, 'Squeeze the trigger.' I calmed down instantly, took careful aim at one of the charging Germans through my gunsight and squeezed the trigger. He flung his arms up over his head and fell down dead, shot through the head. I felt a sensation surge through my whole body. I was no longer a zombie. My life force had come surging back. I was alive and for the first time I felt that I had a chance to come out of this battle.

"At this very moment I was a veteran combat soldier. I continued to shoot the attacking Germans until they finally stopped coming. The battle was over. After such intense fighting it was very strange how suddenly the battle ended. How quiet everything had become. A feeling of disbelief it was over. At the time it seemed as if it would never end. Later I thought about the voice I heard telling me to squeeze the trigger. I failed to qualify with the rifle in basic training. I had to go back and do everything by the numbers without live ammunition, again. For the next five weeks after supper and on Sundays the practice continued. Over and over they drummed the procedure into my head, always ending with 'Squeeze the trigger, do not jerk the trigger, slowly squeeze the trigger, sque-e-e-ze the trigger.' After awhile, at night I dreamt about squeezing the trigger. We had made fun of doing things by the numbers but it had saved my life."

In support of the 106th Division's 422d Regiment and the men of A Company from the 81st Combat Engineers—Phil Hannon and John Collins—was the 589th Field Artillery. The executive officer of Battery A was Eric Fisher Wood Jr. Within the first few hours of 16 December Lt. Eric Wood became the acting battery commander as the advancing Germans captured Battery A's nominal leader, the boyishly exuberant Capt. Aloysius J. Mencke, in a forward observation post. The 2d Division artillerymen had earlier dug sufficient foxholes for all of the gun crews. But Eric Wood was unhappy to discover that there was no cover over the foxholes. He ordered his cannoneers to roof over every position. By 14 December, the troops were protected from overhead bursts by pine logs. In addition, he arranged to build some flexibility into the emplacement for his number-four gun. By this alteration, he gave the battery not only the capacity to fire in support of ground troops but also means to defend against an enemy advance along the only paved road.

The spearhead for the Sixth Panzer Army under Sepp Dietrich belonged to SS Lt. Col. Jochen Peiper, a veteran of the eastern front, where his harsh reprisals against villages suspected of aiding the Red Army brought him the nickname of "Blowtorch Peiper." *Kampfgruppe Peiper* (Task

Force Peiper) and its 4,000 men expected to advance in a fifteen-mile-long column that would reach the Meuse River. Tactically, the extended line of soldiers, tanks, half-tracks, artillery, trucks, and other vehicles weakened the task force's striking power. But the narrow, sinuous roads of the Ardennes prohibited broader movement. To compensate, Peiper sought to equip his armor component with the lighter Panther tanks rather than the heavy, underpowered, and sluggish big Tigers. The task force toted enough ammunition for four or five days, fuel for an even shorter period because two entire trainloads of gasoline never reached the assembly point. Additional supplies of fuel would have to be captured, taken from Allied dumps.

While *Kampfgruppe Peiper* with its impatient commander idled its engines awaiting the clearance of mines and repair of an overpass, twenty-year-old 1st Lt. Lyle Bouck and the handful of others in the Intelligence and Reconnaissance platoon of the 3d Battalion, 394th Infantry Regiment, 99th Division, remained in place on the outskirts of Lanzerath, directly in the path of the spearhead. "We had made contact with the task force from the 14th Cav," said Bouck "and knew they had some machine guns and antitank guns on our right flank and in Lanzerath in front of us. But they were in a different corps so the communication between us was limited.

"Sometime before dawn, the artillery fire began. I don't know how long it lasted but it seemed like a long time. At first it went over our heads. Then they started to hit in front of Lanzerath. There was a short lull before quite a bit began to drop on our positions. I had the impression we had been bracketed. It was intermittent for more than an hour, a lot of tree bursts. Initially, we were in a shocked, stunned state. I kept wondering when we'd start taking casualties but the log coverings over the foxholes shielded us. I called regiment when it began and they'd been half-asleep when it started. But the word was artillery fire was hitting the entire regiment. The only instructions I got were to be doubly alert.

"After about two hours, the firing lifted. I went to every foxhole to make contact. To my surprise, nobody had been hurt. But we were all scared. I told everyone that somebody would attack us soon. Maybe an hour later, we suddenly heard motors, American vehicles moving. The tank destroyers pulled out, traveling toward Bucholz Station. I took Slape, my platoon sergeant, Tsak [Bill Tsakanikas], and a fellow named John Creger and we ran down the hill and into the house. Inside the place we found a civilian, using a telephone. Tsak was ready to shoot him but I said let him go. We couldn't handle prisoners and I was not going to shoot an unarmed man. From the second floor we could see where the road dipped, then crested about 600 yards away. Through my field glasses I saw German soldiers wearing the helmets of paratroopers. We had taken along a field wire and I told Slape and Creger to stay there and keep me posted. I tried to get artillery fire from regiment but they said they couldn't give us any. Just about then, a jeep pulled up. It carried Lt. Warren Springer and three enlisted men from a field artillery observation unit."

Indeed, Springer, Sgt. Peter Gacki, Cpl. Billy Queen, and T4 Willard Wibben belonged to C Battery of the 371st Field Artillery, the outfit in which Dick Byers served. Byers remembered, "We had all been worried about them. They had reported on the night of December 15 that Losheim [behind the German lines] was lit up like a Christmas tree." Springer volunteered to join his tiny band with the I&R Platoon. Bouck accepted and urged Springer to see if he could raise some artillery fire upon the oncoming enemy host. The field artillery observer, using a radio in his jeep, contacted the

371st gunners. Springer watched the results: "Some rounds came in on Lanzerath. I sent corrections, and there were more rounds. Then something hit the jeep, either mortar or artillery fire, and halted all communications."

Bouck was advised of an emergency. "Slape called to tell me that Germans were in the house. I promised help. I ran to the front of the platoon and picked three men. Aubrey McGehee was a strong, rugged man who'd played football. McGehee knew the layout of the house, and he'd knock the crap out of anybody. Jordan "Pop" Robinson was thirty-seven and he'd shoot anything he saw. I could count on Jim Sivola from Florida to back up McGehee. Slape and Creger decided not to wait. They made a break for it, ducking through a door to an adjoining barn where they hid themselves under some cows. Meanwhile, my three guys arrived at the house and quickly got into a firefight with the Germans. Slape and Creger bolted from the barn, circled into the woods, and then came back across the road, which ran north-south. A machine gun opened up and shot off the heel of Slape's left shoe. He fell hard on the road, breaking a rib and his chest bone. But he and Creger made it back to our place. McGehee, Robinson, and Sivola were cut off by the machine gun and isolated on the east side of the road.

"While all of this was going on, here comes a German column up the road, walking toward us, single file on both sides of the road, their weapons slung. They were singing as they marched. I ordered don't fire until I give the word or I start shooting. There was an advance party of maybe thirty and then the main body of troops with the command group. That's whom I wanted to hit. I was also wondering whether they would turn left and cut us off but they kept on straight ahead.

"Just as I was running all this through my head and about

to open fire, a little girl of about thirteen ran up to three officers in a jeep at the front. She pointed up the road, in our direction. I still think she was showing them which way the tank destroyers went. I don't believe she knew we were even there. But the paratroopers suddenly dispersed. As they did, Tsak opened fire and so did the rest of us. McGehee, Robinson, and Sivola saw no way to get back to us. They took off from the east side of the road and tried to reach the 1st Battalion. When they came to a deep railroad cut, they went down and then up the other side. German soldiers in camouflage caught them. Sivola was badly wounded in the shoulder, a bullet tore off most of the calf in Robinson's right leg, and seeing the situation was hopeless, McGehee and the other two surrendered.

"For us, the shooting stopped as the Germans retreated. We could see people crawling around to reorganize. Then after maybe an hour and a half they came screaming and yelling, in a direct frontal attack up the snow-covered hill. They were firing at us but they had no targets. And there was a typical farm fence that bisected the hill. The paratroopers had to climb over this fence. For us it was like target practice. We had a couple of BARs and a .30-caliber machine gun manned by Risto Milosevich. Tsak and Slape took turns on the .50 caliber machine gun of the jeep, until it was hit in the breech and blew up. The other guys had M1s, while I had a carbine. I could see blood all over the snow, I heard screaming, hollering.

"Then they stopped coming. Someone waved a red flag and in poor English yelled 'Medics! Medics!' It was approaching noon. For forty-five minutes, except for the sounds of wounded men in pain, the field and woods were quiet. They tended their injured, dragged them backward. We had our own casualties. A rifle grenade had smashed into

Lou Kahlil's face. It didn't detonate but it broke his jaw in four places, and hammered five teeth into the rest of his mouth. Someone stuffed sulfa powder in the wound, then rubbed snow on his face. Lou got back on his feet."

When the third attack came, Kahlil again was firing at the enemy. Risto Milosevich operated a machine gun by himself. "It was like shooting clay ducks at the amusement park. But while I was concentrating hard on a German, I didn't notice another one about fifteen yards from my hole. He had a potato masher in his hand, cocked and ready to swing it forward. He was looking right at me. I had the machine gun in my hand and fired point-blank. He scared me so badly that I think I kept firing so long I cut him in half. But by myself I couldn't keep the gun from jamming.

"Slape came into the hole with me. He took over the machine gun while I fed the belt. He kept firing and firing and I was harping at him to shoot in bursts of three." The weapon became so hot that it cooked off [fired] rounds even when Slape released the trigger. He could only shut it down by raising the cover. The barrel finally bowed from the heat and became inoperable. We had to use my M1 since Slape hadn't brought his to the foxhole. It worked out well though I kept shouting at Slape to save one bullet until I loaded the next clip. I saw a German medic about thirty yards from our hole. He was working on a soldier whom I thought was dead. That made me very suspicious. The medic kept looking at us and his lips moved constantly. After the medic had appeared, mortar fire was landing right on us. I was sure he was directing it. And then as I watched him, he turned. I noticed a pistol in his belt. I asked Slape for the rifle so I could shoot him. He refused, saying there were too many other Germans in front of us. When I explained about the medic, Slape shot him." During a lull, the platoon sergeant discovered two bullet holes in his jacket. Springer and his companions also poured small-arms fire on the enemy. An enemy slug struck Cpl. Billy Queen in the stomach. There was nothing his companions could do for him.

Enemy fire had destroyed the platoon radio. Bouck detailed Cpl. Sam Jenkins and Pfc. Robert Preston to carry word of the I&R Platoon's plight back to headquarters and either return with reinforcements or permission for the unit to withdraw. The two sneaked back through the woods. But the area behind the platoon was now a hive of enemy soldiers. For thirty-six hours, Jenkins and Preston hid out, trying to reach friendly forces. They were captured on 18 December

Bouck decided to pull out. "It was late in the day, but still light, somewhere between 3:30 and 4:30 in the afternoon. I sent word that when I blew a whistle three times, everyone would leave the foxholes with their weapons. We'd rendezvous at a point on the road. We would move by night through the woods. I told Slape and Tsak to remove the distributor caps from the jeeps. Tsak was with me in a foxhole as we prepared to take off. I heard the sound of boots and Germans hollering as they fired. I had one full magazine left in my carbine. I saw two figures running toward us. I had filed the sear [metal piece in firing mechanism] off my carbine so when I squeezed the trigger it operated like a machine gun. I emptied the clip at those two. I was satisfied that I had fired my last round.

"I saw the muzzle of a gun poke into our hole. I pushed Tsakanikas to get him out of the way and then someone yelled, 'How many of you? How many of you?' I didn't speak much German but I answered 'Zwei! Zwei!' With that came a burst of gunfire. The next thing I knew I am lifting Bill Tsakanikas, who was making a horrible gurgling noise, out of the foxhole. There was an arm helping me and whoever it was, he pulled Tsak out. Someone shone a flashlight on his face. 'Mein Gott! Mein Gott!!' I heard. When I saw what a bloody mess Tsak was I couldn't recognize him. Half his face had been shot away. His right eyeball hung in the gap where his cheek had been. There was still some small-arms fire going on. An officer who spoke very good English demanded, 'When are your men going to stop shooting?' I answered, 'Those must be your guys. We don't have any ammo left.' The firing ceased. I felt very hot. I had been hit in my boot."

Springer also surrendered. "I heard a mixture of German and English. We were told to throw our guns out and come out or they would throw hand grenades in. I expected that they would shoot us but I thought I would rather go that way than to be inside the enclosed space of the dugout when a grenade went off. So out we came and I was surprised when they didn't fire."

A soldier motioned for Bouck to pick up Tsak. "I don't know how I did it. There was a German helping me support him down the hill. We climbed over that fence past all of the bodies of the German dead. Another soldier was right behind us and he suddenly came around in front. He kept asking if we had been at St.-Lô. I answered 'Nein! Nein!' He started screaming about his comrades at St.-Lô. Shit, I didn't know what else to say. Then he stuck a gun in my back and pulled the trigger. I don't know whether it was a misfire or the gun was empty. But someone said, 'Raus! Raus!' He disappeared and we went into Lanzerath.

"They put us in a room with a bench. They sat me there with Tsak, who leaned on my left shoulder. He'd been bandaged and only one eye and his nose were visible. Blood seeped through my field jacket and I realized I had been grazed. I could walk okay, without pain or discomfort. The rest of the platoon showed up. Sergeant George Redmond carried in Lou Kahlil. You could only see a nose and eye on him also because of the bandaging. They brought in [Joe] McConnell. His field jacket had been cut away and he had a bad wound in the shoulder. There were German wounded all over the floor."

In the darkness, Peiper, following the road, never saw the hundreds of bodies still lying in the fields. Estimates of the German dead, almost entirely attributable to the small arms of Bouck and his platoon, range from 300 to 500. Although he claimed that except for occasional artillery rounds, he initially encountered no Americans, Peiper realized mines planted by both the Americans and left by his countrymen when they retreated threatened his column. With his timetable already badly disrupted he decided simply to roll over the mines as if they were no more than speed bumps. From Lanzerath he set his sights on Honsfeld as his first objective.

At the Café Scholzen, several hours after *Kampfgruppe Peiper* clanked away, and as dawn broke, his captors informed Bouck he would be taken outside. "I asked if I could speak with Tsak and Kahlil. Tsak was conscious. I told him they were taking him to a hospital and I'd see him after the war. I said 'I'm putting your Bible,' which he always carried, 'and that picture of your sweetheart in your pocket. I'll say a prayer for you.' He couldn't answer me but I'm sure he heard because he squeezed my hand. And as I stood there, they hauled Kahlil and Tsak to a flatbed truck and drove off with them." Herded by guards, Bouck, his leg still oozing blood from where he was hit at the top of his boot, started a series of long hikes that marked the lives of so many American POWs. German doctors operated upon Tsak and pulled him through.

Jochen Peiper's advance guard pushed toward Honsfeld. The route followed the road through Bucholz Station, a tiny cluster of houses. Earlier, Dick Byers from the 371st Field Artillery, which had already lost one forward observation quartet with Bouck's I&R Platoon, was dispatched to replace the captured team. The new party amounted to three men, a lieutenant, Sgt. Curtis Fletcher, and Byers. "We pulled our jeep off the road into a barn attached to a farmhouse. It was across the road from Bucholz Station. Some GIs from the 1st and 2d platoons of K Company, 394th, were dug in on the side of the woods away from the road. From their holes they could see Bucholz Station and the road from Lanzerath. A few K Company men and the aid station were in the farmhouse basement. From midnight to one o'clock, I stood guard with an infantryman on the porch of the house. We took turns ducking into the house to warm up with a cigarette. It was a quiet, cold night. We could clearly hear the SS Panzer troops shouting back and forth, the racing of tank engines, the squeal of bogie wheels as *Kampfgruppe Peiper* worked its way from Losheim, over to Lanzerath, and then on towards us. I commented that their noise sounded like a bunch of quartermaster troops on maneuvers in Louisiana."

When Peiper's column, guided by men on foot, clattered up the road hard by the farmhouse, Byers was asleep. A departing GI rifleman paused long enough to shake Byers and whisper urgently, " 'Get up! There's tanks outside!' I mumbled something, rolled over and went back to sleep. Sergeant Fletcher, also asleep, never stirred. But as our lieutenant started to leave, a wounded GI called out and attracted his attention. He shone his flashlight and saw Fletcher and me, still lying there, sound asleep. He really woke us up! We grabbed our coats and helmets, buckled on our pistol belts and headed outside. There we pulled on our galoshes and ran for the barn, thinking we'd use the radio stashed there to call in artillery fire.

"As we opened the back door of the barn, we saw three German paratroopers silhouetted against the white snow, but they couldn't see us with the black courtyard behind us. Since they appeared armed with Schmeissers [burp guns] and had the backing of an entire panzer battle group, we decided not to argue over possession of the radio. We took off through the side gate into a patch of pine woods parallel to the road. I recall a feeling of exhilaration. We could hear them, thus we knew where they were and where to go to avoid them. And we knew where they were to kill them, if we had to. I thought, it's funny but the closer you get to the Krauts, the less scared you get. That is, when you see them, you can kill them. But when you don't know where they are and what they are up to, you fear the unknown. Fletcher had not taken time to buckle his galoshes before going out of the gate and they were clinking. He knelt down to fasten them while we went on. He was captured from behind before he finished.

"We wandered through the woods between the road and infantry foxholes and dugouts. A couple of times we approached a hole and the lieutenant said in a tense, still voice, 'Don't shoot, men. This is Lieutenant——of C Battery, 371st. Don't shoot!' Then he would remember to use the password, 'Shining.' Only then would we see the two gun barrels aimed between our eyes and hear the countersign, 'Knight.'

"Eventually, I realized this wasn't getting us anywhere. We couldn't function as artillery observers without our radio and with .45-caliber pistols we weren't going to be much help against paratroopers and tanks. In fact, my pistol hand felt paralyzed from gripping the weapon so tightly that I must have permanently embossed my fingerprints on the butt. I suggested to the lieutenant that I knew the way back to our gun positions via trails. He accepted the idea and we headed north. There was still a steady stream of tanks, half-tracks, and paratroopers on the road, which was lined with big, low-limbed pines. We ducked under one into a roadside ditch and waited for a break in the convoy. Enemy soldiers trudged by, just above our heads. When an opening finally came, we dashed across the road, dove into a ditch on the other side, then made our way toward Hunningen. Now my deer-hunting expedition paid off because I knew the route from that earlier trek through the woods and fields.

"Behind us, we suddenly heard gunfire. Apparently, some GI in K Co. had opened fire. The flak panzers with their 20mm cannons and quad machine guns mowed down the woods, knocking out most of what was left of the company. Then we looked over our left shoulders and saw a tank firing. We heard small arms from Honsfeld. When we reached the edge of Hünningen we were challenged by the 1st Battalion, 23d Infantry Regiment of the 2d Division. We told the men digging in what we had seen and they answered that they were oldtimers sent down to save our inexperienced asses. It was dawn by the time we reached our gun positions. The 'march order' had been given and we were just in time to jump on the back of a truck and leave for our next position near the twin villages of Krinkelt and Rocherath. I managed to grab some cold pancakes from the mess truck and ate them on the way."

Kampfgruppe Peiper now attacked Honsfeld. Occupied by a service unit of the 99th Division detailed to provide the amenities of a near-frontline rest camp—hot showers, hot food, entertainment—Honsfeld's U.S. garrison was ill prepared to host a confrontation with the brute power of *Kampfgruppe Peiper*. The captain in charge hastily formed a provisional rifle company out of his own men and some stragglers. A handful of antitank platoons arrived to confront the enemy and a small troop of men from the 14th Cavalry Group also had retreated to Honsfeld. Sentries were posted but the majority of the men bedded down to await a possible attack later.

In the darkness, perhaps an hour after leaving Lanzerath, the Germans rolled right past the Americans guarding the approaches to Honsfeld. Those on picket apparently failed to recognize the panzers that slyly joined the stream of U.S. vehicles traveling through the village by night. A belated discovery of the enemy on the outskirts generated brief and ineffective resistance. Peiper was pleasantly surprised by the ease with which he captured the village.

Peiper barely paused in Honsfeld before rolling onward. But as the echelons behind him followed, the murderous acts associated with SS forces erupted. An officer lined up eight prisoners rousted from their beds, barefoot and in their underwear, and sprayed them with a burp gun. A group of Germans disregarded a white flag displayed by five GIs and killed four, leaving one man alive. A tank then crushed the life out of his body. There were a series of similar incidents, and at the very least those prisoners not used for target practice endured blows from rifle butts. The Germans slaughtered civilians as well.

The worst offense occurred at a small Belgian village, Malmédy. There Battery B of the 285th Field Artillery Observation Battalion blundered into Peiper's spearhead. The Panzers quickly overwhelmed the lightly armed specialists and more than 100 Americans were captured and lined up in a field. Peiper rumbled off, leaving the prisoners in the hands of those trailing behind. Suddenly an orgy of murder erupted, first with pistols and then from machine guns on tanks or set up along a road that ran by the killing field. When it ended, eighty-six soldiers had been slaughtered, along with several civilians who sought to offer succor. A few escaped the massacre and reported what had happened. Word spread about the barbarity of the enemy, sharply lessening the willingness to give quarter.

Initially, protected by the fog of battle and American ignorance of the scheme, some teams from Greif passed themselves off as GIs quite successfully. They befuddled traffic and performed minor acts of sabotage. The advantage of American unawareness ended by midmorning, the very first day of the German attack. In the vicinity of where Harry Martin learned to "squeeze the trigger," Lt. William Shakespeare, who made sports page headlines a few years before while lugging a football for Notre Dame, captured a German captain from the 116th Panzer Division. Bagged along with the officer was a map case containing the plan of attack and papers outlining Operation Greif. The documents spelled out the recognition signals and the roads upon which the teams expected to operate. Within a few hours, the material circulated among the top echelons of U.S. intelligence. A number of the fake GIs were caught and executed.

7

Chaos

ON THE LEFT FLANK OF SEPP DIETRICH'S SIXTH PANZER Army, Hasso von Manteuffel's Fifth Panzer Army, which struck the 106th and 28th Divisions, applied increasing pressure. The initial impact of the shelling and advance of German infantry had halted the work crew with Phil Hannon from the 106th's engineer battalion. At regimental headquarters in Schönberg, Hannon and his mates learned they were cut off from the village they occupied. "The men in regimental headquarters had been taking a pasting from the German artillery. Some of their nervousness got to us. A buzz bomb clattered over, rather low. The boys bolted from the truck. We deployed by instinct on the outskirts of the town. No one had to yell 'Go here' or 'Do this,' We did the right thing automatically. A rock pile here, a depression, a ditch, a manure pile—we made use of them. My platoon of engineers was called on to unload ammunition for a platoon of tank destroyers that pulled in. The Heinies spotted us and threw 88s at us. Thank God, a number of them were duds!

After the first five or six shells landed we could judge where they were hitting. We were getting battlewise fast. The Heinies missed the boat when they didn't smack us that morning. Infantry companies fell back and set up a line on the outskirts of the village. Tank destroyers positioned themselves to cover the field and roads. We settled down to stick as long as possible. They asked for a bazooka man and since I had trained with a bazooka, I stepped out. Four of us went out on the road between the Heinies and regimental headquarters and dug in. We had one bazooka, seven rounds for it, and our rifles. By the time we finished digging in, it was pitch black, getting windier and colder by the minute. About midnight two of us decided we had enough of freezing. We were wearing field jackets, no overcoats. We left the other two as the bazooka team and returned to the village. While blankets were hunted up for us, we had a chance to clean our rifles. They were coated inside and out with mud. I doubt if they would have fired. The captain told us the mess hall was serving chow all the time. We got some stew and coffee and headed back.

"When daylight came we took a look around. We had been told the infantry was all around us when we went out the night before. Three hundred yards *behind* us we located them. We pulled back to the top of a little knoll where we could command the road and fields very well. The Heinies spotted a company of infantry that had moved into position on a hill behind us. Zing! I yanked in my head and did some worrying. Zap! Damn those 88s! The infantry on the hill behind was catching hell, but the shells sounded as if they were skinning my helmet on the way over."

Hannon gave up the bazooka slot to some infantrymen and rejoined his engineer colleagues. But the enemy artillery continued to bedevil the Americans in Schönberg. It became apparent that the small contingent in the village was trapped. "About two o'clock Monday afternoon, we got orders to abandon the town and try to break out. Two infantry battalions were supposed to be fighting to open the way and we all left the place expecting to get out. A protective barrage of smoke and time fire laid down by our artillery accompanied our pullout."

No longer a green replacement after his exposure to combat with the 28th Division's Company B of the 110th Infantry in the Hurtgen Forest, Ed Uzemack, along with his comrades, became uneasy toward 15 December after night patrols heard the ominous sounds of squeaking tank treads across no-man's-land. "The reports were dutifully transmitted to division headquarters where they were dismissed as unlikely because the terrain supposedly did not suit tanks.

"On the morning of the sixteenth we experienced an intense and longer bombardment. The quiet that followed was soon disrupted by shouts of alarm from GI lookout posts. German infantry in large numbers were moving up the hill toward our village of Clervaux, Luxembourg. The fighting that ensued was weird. It was like shooting ducks at a carnival. With a heavy blanket of snow on the hillside, the Germans wore no camouflage and the dark uniforms made inviting targets. Besides our M1 rifles, we had a couple of .50-caliber machine guns and perhaps a mortar or two. After encountering heavy fire from our vantage point, the enemy troops broke and ran for cover. The action was repeated several times during the day, in what were almost suicide missions. We retained control of our positions and retired to our quarters, in my case an inn at the intersection of three highways that served as platoon headquarters. There were about eight of us billeted at the inn, the platoon commander, a couple of noncoms, and us dogfaces.

"The next day we got our wakeup call, a barrage, a bit late but effective. As the almost one-sided infantry battle continued, the walkie-talkie crackled with requests for more rifle ammunition, casualty reports, and calls for a runner [Uzemack]. Running zigzag along the road between GI fire and that from the enemy, loaded with bandoliers of .30-caliber ammo, I turned onto an ice-covered walk where one of our squads was housed. A German machine gun opened fire to my right as I slipped and fell on my back, sliding toward an open door. A couple of GIs grabbed my legs and dragged me inside. After they found I was not wounded, they took the ammunition and questioned me on the status in other sectors. I knew as little as they did. I needed a cigarette badly after I realized how close I had come to cashing in my chips. Cigarettes were scarce and the guys suggested I get them from a guy in the next room 'who no longer needed them.' Enemy fire had killed the GI that morning. He had a nearly full pack of smokes in one of his pockets which, they felt, I was entitled to as a kind of reward for bringing the bandoliers.

"While with this squad I heard the cries of a wounded German soldier, lying a few yards away. The GIs said he'd been calling to his buddies for help for more than an hour. When the enemy retreated, though, they left the wounded man, whose cries would fade and then return, louder than ever. Finally one GI blurted, 'Why don't we put the bastard out of his misery!' He and a couple of other men slowly moved out toward the sound. We heard several bursts of fire and then no more cries from the wounded man.

"In the wake of some Sherman tanks, I returned to the platoon CP. It seemed we had successfully repulsed the enemy once more. At the inn, the platoon commander shared a bottle of scotch with those of us there to celebrate what we figured was a victory. We mixed the scotch with some canned grapefruit juice; why, I'll never know. I was in the kitchen preparing some hot chocolate when a GI sergeant burst through the main entrance to warn us of enemy tanks headed our way and only half a mile away. He left hurriedly, saying he had to warn others. We heard his jeep pull out and prepared to protect ourselves. Division HQ advised us to hold our positions.

"Our hastily formed strategy was to hide in the cellar, wait for the tanks to pass our post believing the darkened, shell-battered inn was deserted. We hoped then to join some other units and surprise the Germans from the rear. Obviously, it was both a brave and naive plan, because our heaviest weapon was a .50-caliber machine gun, not very effective against tanks. It wasn't long before we heard the tanks rumbling and squeaking outside our building. They moved around the perimeter of the inn, but to our dismay, several shut down their engines and parked. Moments later, the sound of heavy boots came tromping on the floor overhead, guttural voices and loud laughter followed as they found some of our personal stuff we hadn't been able to carry with us into the cellar. It dawned on us that the GI Paul Revere was probably a Jerry scout, disguised in a GI uniform and driving an American jeep. He was checking out where Americans were and at the same time encouraging them to take off.

"Around midnight, the noise upstairs quieted down to snores and barely audible talk. Sitting amid abandoned crockery, we hardly dared to move or even breathe. A muffled radio inquiry to division HQ brought the response, 'Hold your positions.' They claimed help would come but there would be no further radio contact. At dawn, the outside door of the cellar was kicked open by a heavily armed German. A sleeping GI awakened by the intruder yelled, 'Hey, guys. They found us!' We were herded out by a handful of Germans with burp guns. As we marched to the front of the inn, we saw at least two huge tanks facing the building with their awesome 88s pointed toward the cellar. They had played cat and mouse with us all night long."

John Chernitsky, from the antitank company of the 28th Division, had hardly arrived at Wiltz in Luxembourg to serve on the faculty instructing fledgling noncoms, when orders directed teachers and pupils to rejoin their respective units. Enemy fire, however, blocked some roads. Chernitsky and others returned to Wiltz. "I stayed in Wiltz with the organized riflemen who were made up of members of the band, clerks, cooks, bakers, and any men caught between Wiltz and Clervaux. After an artillery barrage, I was hit in the back with shrapnel. I covered the wound with sulfa powder from the packet on my cartridge belt and wrapped my undershirt around my back." Chernitsky and the improvised rifle troops dug in to resist the enemy advance.

When the attack began on 16 December most of the top brass regarded it as at most a retaliation for the attack by the 99th Division and elements of the 2d Infantry Division toward the Roer dams or perhaps a gambit to relieve the pressure generated by Patton's advance into the Saar Basin. After Eisenhower attended the wedding of his valet he presided over a reception at his house, dined with associates, and played several rubbers of bridge before retiring. However, he seemed to have been the first to have grasped the possible seriousness of the challenge. He began mobilizing troops to meet the growing Ardennes challenge.

In his diary of 16 December, Maj. Gen. Everett Hughes from the SHAEF staff wrote, "Brad [Omar Bradley] says Germans have started a big counterattack toward Hodges.

Very calm about it. Seemed routine from his lack of emphasis." His demeanor may have seemed unruffled but by midafternoon of that day, Bradley telephoned Patton and told him to send the 10th Armored Division, then in reserve near the Luxembourg-France border, into the Ardennes. The Third Army commander protested the loss of one of his outfits: "There's no major threat up there. Hell, it's probably nothing more than a spoiling attack to throw us off balance down here and make us stop this offensive." Bradley, however, was adamant. Furthermore, he arranged to shift the 7th Armored Division, which was also in reserve, to give Hodges more punch.

By 17 December, however, any doubts about the seriousness of the enemy attack vanished. The enemy forces quickly carved out a forty-mile-deep, sixty-mile-wide bulge in the American lines. On the third day of the German breakthrough, the 106th Division's 422d and 423d Infantry Regiments appeared to be encircled and the vital town of St.-Vith menaced. The latter regiment received orders to attack toward its rear. The strategy called for the enemy to be trapped between the infantrymen and the 7th Armored Division, summoned from reserve, in the rear. Colonel George Descheneaux, Jr., who led the 422d, supposedly mumbled, "My poor men—they'll be cut to pieces."

The maneuver required the foot soldiers to shift their positions in the dark. Lt. Alan Jones Jr. said, "As night fell, we trekked through the Alf Valley. It was very muddy, very dark, the woods heavy, just terribly tough going. The transportation bogged down. There was enormous confusion." The Germans complicated the movement with artillery salvos. The leader of Jones's battalion was killed by shrapnel. Jones recalled, "The other two battalions went on the attack but ours seemed to lose direction. No one seemed to know what to do; finally the exec moved them out. I gathered some loose ends, put them into a company formation for tactical purposes. We had tankers, artillery, crewmen, infantry.

"By the time we were organized and caught up to the 1st Battalion, the word was to surrender. 'Tear your weapons apart and throw the pieces about.' I couldn't believe it. My battalion just had not been in that much fighting." Jones remarked his outfit was low on information and while requests for supplies dropped by air began on 17 December, the layers of approvals required before the first props would spin delayed any efforts. Inexplicably, the Air Corps handled all such missions from airfields in Britain which added flight time and interposed the volatile cross-Channel weather. When C-47s finally took off and arrived in Belgium, the local airdrome said it was "too busy" to accommodate them. No fighter protection could be given and the transports with their cargo had no map coordinates for a drop. Col. George Descheneaux, commander of the 423d Regiment, convinced, like Cavender, that his people would be slaughtered if they continued to fight, also surrendered. By 19 December, the exultant Germans counted more than 7,000 American soldiers from the 106th Division as prisoners.

The 7th Armored Division which rushed to support the 106th Division also reeled under the onslaught and some units broke down into a disorganized retreat. Alan Jones Sr., the 106th commander, decided St.-Vith could not be defended and he abandoned it. Now fully aware of the seriousness of the German thrusts, Eisenhower and his staff immediately rushed whatever forces available to plug gaps. The 101st Airborne Division under its assistant commander, Gen. Anthony McAuliffe, occupied the major road hub to the south, the town of Bastogne. They barely beat a strong

German force to Bastogne which surrounded the place and began a dramatic siege. The 82d Airborne moved to block the foe at the Salm River, north of Bastogne and west of St.-Vith. A third airborne unit, the 517th Regiment, which had been resting from its labors in the south of France-joined the effort to shut down the enemy advance. The only good news lay on the northern shoulder of the Bulge where the American 1st, 2d, 8th, 9th and 99th Divisions, while in some cases absorbing considerable punishment, kept the enemy from widening his advance.

Frank South, the medic with the 2nd Ranger Battalion, recalled, "The woefully understrength battalion was attached to the 8th Division and placed in defensive positions in and around Simmerath on the Siegfried line. Headquarters and the Aid Station were located in a former German hospital that was under intermittent artillery fire. Of course the hospital's belfry was used as an OP from time to time. It was assumed that we were expected to hold our position should the push come to involve us. Most of our activity consisted of reconnoitering and combat patrolling to discomfit the enemy and take prisoners for intelligence purposes. We had some men killed and a few wounded but the level was relatively low."

When the center of the American front collapsed, Eisenhower on 19 December convened a council of top commanders and sought to set an upbeat tone to the session with an opening remark: "The present situation is to be regarded as an opportunity for us and not of disaster." Patton seemed to think similarly, saying, "Hell, let's have the guts to let the sons of bitches go all the way to Paris. Then we'll really cut 'em and chew 'em up." Some revisionist historians have suggested the Ardennes collapse was a shrewd piece of strategy that exposed the German armies to destruction.

That viewpoint does not square either with the panicky reaction to the penetration nor the awful casualties inflicted upon Americans caught in the maelstrom.

The best option for relief of Bastogne and a counterattack lay with Patton's Third Army. The supreme commander asked the man-of-the-hour, "When will you be able to attack?"

"The morning of December 21st," answered Patton, obviously relishing an opportunity for a heroic achievement.

"Don't be fatuous, George," reproved Eisenhower, concerned for Patton's cockiness. "If you try to go that early, you won't have all three divisions ready and you'll go piecemeal. You will start on the 22nd." Eisenhower even allowed that if necessary the Third Army might begin a day later. Patton had promised Eisenhower he could begin to lift the siege of Bastogne within two days. His genius for putting the armor and troops on the road achieved its zenith.

Carl Ulsaker recalled a moment when his 95th Division outfit was moving forward and a procession of vehicles came down the road. "Someone said, 'Look, there goes Lucky 6.' Lucky 6 was the radio code for General Patton. Sure enough his jeep was passing by with Old Blood and Guts sitting in the right front seat behind a machine gun mounted on the dash. Suddenly, the Jeep braked to a halt and backed up to a point opposite where we stood. 'My God,' I thought. 'We failed to salute and he's going to bawl us out.' We popped to attention and saluted tardily.

"Patton dismounted and approached us on foot, head thrust forward and face set in his famous scowl. Gesturing with his right hand, in his high-pitched voice he said, 'Men, Von Runstedt's nuts are in the meat grinder and I have the handle in my hand."

To the north, a motley force of German troops, some in

standard field gray, some wearing white snow camouflage garments, and still others dressed in pieces of American uniforms with boots stripped from prisoners or yanked from dead mens' feet, battered the GIs ensconced along Elsenborn Ridge on the northern shoulder of the German salient. The Germans brought to bear whatever armor and artillery they could muster. Victory here would open up a northern road route to the Meuse. The Americans enjoyed the advantage of favorable terrain to entrench the troops and an ever-increasing superiority of artillery. Ben Nawrocki with the handful of men left from B Company labored over his foxhole along the crest of the ridge. "We had only our rifles and the ammo we could carry. The ground was frozen hard, like rock. There weren't any entrenching tools. We used mess kits, mess knives, bayonets and helmets to dig in. It was frantic, hard work but with shells flying all the time, we had to have shelter.

"We could see them shelling and attacking to our right rear in the Malmédy, St.-Vith area. They were coming at us through the deep draws leading to Elsenborn Ridge. We kept beating them off. We had a good open field of fire and a lot of artillery to help us. A day or two after the 99th dug in on Elsenborn Ridge, two hundred Germans with tanks came toward our lines. The 394th Regiment was in front. The Germans carried their arms in sling position on their shoulders and waved white handkerchief flags as if to signal surrender. They were told to drop their arms. They refused and kept coming. Obviously they wanted to get closer and overrun us.

"Our officers readied all our firepower along with artillery. After they didn't respond to repeated demands to drop arms and surrender, all of the firepower on the front opened up. They tried to and did run over some of the foxholes with their tanks. But our firepower and artillery really chewed them up. There were pieces of bodies and tanks flying all over. When the fire lifted, nothing moved. They all died. The tanks and equipment destroyed."

The only surviving platoon sergeant from his company, Nawrocki became first sergeant. "I made my first morning report on a piece of toilet paper on Dec. 21. It accounted for one officer and 13 men of Co. B, 393rd Infantry. We had 210 men on the morning of December 16th. Later, we started to get back some of Co. B who had mixed in with other troops and fought. But there still weren't many left. We received replacements almost daily. One batch of about 50 arrived, flown to Europe from the States. Some had very little training. I told them to dig in and they just stood there in the open when a few rounds of 88s struck nearby, wounding six. The rest started to dig in, as we used sticks of dynamite to break through the frozen crust."

The U.S. big guns continued to exact a huge toll. On December 21, they dumped a cloudburst of 10,000 rounds. The German dead piled up in awesome numbers; an early count by a graves registration unit added up 782 corpses in the Elsenborn area. Furthermore, as the enemy backed off from its assault that day, it left behind the broken remains of 47 tanks and tank destroyers. The stalwart efforts of the 1st Division squelched a pivotal series of assaults around the village of Butgenbach. At Dom Butgenbach, two miles south of the town of Butgenbach, members of the division's 26th Infantry Antitank Company, wielding their underpowered, undersized 57 mm cannons, blew away a number of tanks.

To the immediate south of the stalled elements of Sepp Dietrich's Sixth SS Panzer Army, the situation threatened disaster for the Americans. The enemy rapidly exploited their breakthrough of the line manned by elements of the 106th and 28th Divisions. They swept on a west-northwest course that would both widen and deepen the salient. A ragtag jumble of GIs from the 589th FA, the 203d Antiaircraft Battalion and some soldiers from the 7th Armored attempted to set up a roadblock at a crossroads known as Baraque de Fraiture. They were no match for onrushing German armor. As the German tide flowed around St.-Vith and Bastogne, the desperate U.S. commanders tossed in more blue chips. General James Gavin typically made his own personal reconnaissance. He was concerned that the loss of the crossroads could allow the enemy armor that his 82nd Airborne held at bay at Trois Ponts to bypass the paratroopers and the soldiers pulling back from St.-Vith. As a result of his survey, Gavin dispatched the 2nd Battalion of the 82nd Airborne's 325th Glider Regiment to strengthen the defenses at Baraque de Fraiture. Company F, led by Captain Junior Woodruff, drew the major assignment for the defense. Since Woodruff commanded the only complete tactical unit on the scene, he assumed direction for the overall strategy. To the GIs from the 325th, the battlefield now became known as Woody's Crossroads. Woodruff's GIs took instant courses in weapons shared with nine other fragmented outfits. They learned to operate AA guns, 75mms on the tanks and 76mms of tank destroyers.

"Captain Woody was a fine officer in both garrison and combat," remembered Joe Colmer, an ex-navy man who found himself drafted into the army and a member of Company F. "He was a natural leader and the kind of guy you wanted to follow. His people had such faith in him that while we were in Holland, there was a fellow close to me who had his arm blown off. I gave him his shot of morphine but he asked me to tell Woody to come talk to him. Most guys in his shape would have been hollering for a medic instead. When we moved into the crossroads, around noon of

December 22, there were only a few troops around, a couple of Sherman tanks and some half tracks. The soldiers were mostly from the 106th and they struck me as really tired and beaten. My platoon dug foxholes in an arc around the farm houses from the northwest to southeast, about 50 yards out front. It was fairly quiet that night. The next morning, however, the Germans began dropping occasional mortar rounds, a few artillery shells, and stepped up their patrols."

Along with Woodruff's crew, Companies E and G also assumed responsibility for holding the crossroads, occupying a ridge three-quarters of a mile to the northeast. Leonard Weinstein was among G Company as it hiked down an almost impassable trail choked with rocks, thick roots and mud. "Our positions were basically two lines of foxholes. There were no hot meals and we rotated, taking turns to go back to a nearby small building where you could warm up before a small fire. I was in the second line of foxholes on slightly higher ground. One night the enemy slipped in close enough to the first line to kill two of our men with either a bayonet or knife. The victims were the oldest and youngest guys in the company who occupied a single hole."

Combat Command A of the 7th Armored Division, the outfit that included the 40th Tank Battalion with gunner Jerry Nelson, committed a platoon from the 643rd Tank Destroyer Battalion (Towed). The unit of four three-inch guns pulled by half tracks and 40 crewmen faced its combat debut. When some 3rd Armored Divsion Sherman tanks, headed in the opposite direction, passed the tank destroyers, ammunition handler Edgar Kreft heard one of the men on the Shermans holler there was "nobody between you and the Germans." The platoon reached its assigned spot and dug in. At dawn, the enemy blanketed the hapless antitank crews with mortars and artillery, killing and wounding a number of men. German grenadiers overran the Americans, who los 18 killed, wounded and missing. Kreft became a POW.

Actually, the Germans were poised to overwhelm th small garrison for two days. Only an acute shortage of fue for their half-tracks and other armor delayed the launch. Bu supplies arrived on the night of December 22, within hour after Colmear and Weinstein put in their appearances.

When the Germans struck the following day, the attac battered the thin ranks of GIs. The 589th artillerymen go the word to get out any way they could. Two assaults by foo soldiers were beaten off but the 2nd SS Panzer tanks, in fierce encounter, devastated the American armor.

"I think it was about five in the afternoon," says Colme "when they started the all-out drive. We were complete overrun in 30 minutes. They had our tanks on fire. I was i a barn with three or four others and we were firing out c windows when the place started to burn. We stepped o when the place started to cave in. Someone mentioned th idea of trying to surrender but from what we could see the were shooting at everyone. I told the guys they could eith try to give up or make a run for it. I headed across the roa and was hit in the leg. I dove under a blown-down pine tre Hiding next to me was a man from the 106th. His name w Cook. We lay there for about 20 minutes as the Germa walked all around us. By this time it was getting dark. It h been hazy every day and that decreased visibility also. T shooting died down and the Germans began taking the tanks across an open field towards a wooded area abo 1,000 yards off. Foot soldiers followed the tanks in sm groups of two or three and the tanks were spread out wi spaces of maybe 50 yards or so between each. After the la group passed, Cook and I took off our helmets, turned our overcoat collars and followed the Germans across t field. Some of the Germans were wearing GI overcoats so they paid no attention to us. We passed one of our tanks, still burning with its ammo exploding.

"I was limping badly but could still walk. Once we entered the woods, we angled off to our right in the direction of some artillery flashes we took to be friendly. After about two hours, we came upon one of our engineering outfits. They were occupying a barn and some houses. They bandaged my leg, gave us food. We stayed the night with them, then caught a jeep that took us right to the 82nd command post in Spa. I was sent to a hospital and then to England. I never learned what became of Cook." Only 44 men, from the original 116 in Company F at the crossroads, escaped. The rest were KIA or added to the bag of prisoners.

The GIs assembled at the crossroads, enjoined not to retreat, were committed to a hopeless mission. But their sacrifice, like that of Lyle Bouck with his I&R platoon in front of Lanzerath and a ragtag band led by Captain Tom Riggs atop the Prummerberg in front of St.-Vith, bought the time, hours or days, that saved tens of thousands of their fellow Americans. Baraque de Fraiture, like many similar engagements in the Ardennes, was a kind of Bunker Hill; the enemy conquered the turf but at an exorbitant cost.

The fall of Baraque de Fraiture opened Highway N 15 to the advance of the Germans. In the path of Nazi forces lay some tankers from the Seventh Armored Division, and a portion of the 3rd Armored Division led by Col. Sam Hogan. Arnold Albero, a rifleman with the unit, said, "We moved out on December 19 in three columns. I think it must have been the coldest winter in my life. The roads were icy, muddy, the weather foggy in spots and always numbing cold. We lost vehicles that became stuck in the mud and all we could do was just push them to the side. We kept bitching that the column didn't seem to know where it was going. We sure in hell didn't know. On the way we picked up stragglers from other outfits which had been overrun. We also heard rumors that Germans in American uniforms were trying to disrupt our operations. It was a wild and crazy night. When dawn came we were relieved to have daylight but still confused about where we were and what was happening.

"We were now told to head towards Houffalize [a crossroads town on the Ourthe River between Bastogne and Liege] and secure the roads leading to it. But we were beaten back by a good, strong defense and retreated as our gas and ammo ran low. We moved into the town of Beffe, further west. The enemy [the 116th Panzers] engaged us with tanks, infantry supported by artillery and mortars. Forced further to the west, Task Force Hogan settled in at Marcouray, an Ourthe River village on high ground. We could look out and see the Germans moving around us. Gradually, they enveloped us while we fought back attacks and beat off their patrols."

Task Force Hogan, with Arnold Albero, was completely surrounded once the Germans forded the Ourthe behind the Americans. A state of siege commenced, Bastogne in miniature. Instead of thwarting the enemy advance after the conquest of Baraque de Fraiture, Arnold Albero and his 3d Armored GIs faced their own destruction. Food, ammunition, and medical supplies dwindled. Task Force Hogan tightened its cartridge belts and waited for air resupply and a promise that division would try to relieve the beleaguered garrison. Two attempts to parachute supplies failed because of an inability to pinpoint the drop area.

There were, of course, far many more Americans encircled in the vital hub, Bastogne. The Germans strengthened their band of infantrymen, armor, and artillery around the

Belgian village, and on 22 December, two German officers from the 26th Volksgrenadier Division drove up with a white flag flying. Stopped at an outpost, they announced themselves as parlementaires—negotiators bearing a surrender demand.

While the Wehrmacht major and captain awaited a response, their formal paper inscribed with a call for capitulation was brought to Gen. Anthony McAuliffe at the CP. In the absence of Gen. Maxwell Taylor, McAuliffe commanded the Screaming Eagles. The document from the emissaries stated: "Unconditional surrender is the only method of avoiding complete annihilation of the surrounded American units. Two hours' grace is granted hereby. Should this offer be refused, an artillery corps and six groups of heavy antiaircraft guns stand ready to annihilate the American forces." The message also appealed to the American commander to avoid further suffering for the 3,500 civilians as well as his own troops."

McAuliffe's chief of staff, Col. Ned Moore, broke the news. "We have a surrender ultimatum from the Germans."

McAuliffe asked, "You mean they want us to surrender?" When Moore confirmed that was indeed the message, McAuliffe, with a number of pressing problems, matter-of-factly reacted, "Oh, nuts!" Subsequently, when McAuliffe initiated a discussion about an appropriate response no one suggested they acquiesce. Still, McAuliffe asked, "What should I say?"

Colonel Harry Kinnard, of the headquarters staff, claimed, "I piped up and said, 'Well, General, I think what you said when we first told you about the message would be hard to beat.' "

Seemingly puzzled, McAuliffe inquired, "What do you mean?"

"You said nuts." According to Kinnard the others smiled and agreed.

McAuliffe took a plain piece of paper and scrawled: "To the German Commander: Nuts!" and appended his signature, A. C. MCAULIFFE, AMERICAN COMMANDER.

The message confounded the emissaries. They asked whether "Nuts" meant an affirmative or negative reply. Col. Bud Harper, regimental commander, their escort from the outpost, informed them, "It's decidedly negative. It means go to hell."

When the men of Bastogne heard of their leader's response they were almost universally enthusiastic. As paratroopers, trained to drop behind enemy lines and fight their way out, the situation in Bastogne was not extraordinary. In addition to the full complement of the 101st, as Kinnard noted, the holders of Bastogne had recruited additional people passing through, whether in disorderly retreat or on the basis of orders. The terrain provided adequate defensive protection and there was an unusually heavy concentration of artillery available.

Word that Patton's Third Army hoped to break through in time to celebrate Christmas further boosted morale in Bastogne. The major problems for the Bastogne forces were shortages of supplies and the inability to evacuate a growing number of casualties from air raids, artillery fire, and assaults. Poor flying weather interfered with air drops and protection against Luftwaffe marauders. The skies began to clear, however. And on 23 December, Pathfinder Sergeant Jack Agnew parachuted into Bastogne to join his fellow Screaming Eagles. With several companions, Agnew had been sent back to England to participate in experimental techniques and equipment. "When we were first alerted to the problems in the Ardennes, it was nothing new to us.

Starting in the Normandy campaign, the 101st was surrounded every time it jumped. We happened to be training with a Pathfinder troop carrier group attached to the Air Corps. The living conditions were great, the food great, and we had passes to London.

"But on December 22, we drew chutes and all the armament we could get from the Air Corps people. We left on a jump mission to land in the Bastogne encirclement and guide in vital supplies. Just as we were ready to stand up, the mission was recalled. I was quite concerned about our friends in the 506th since we heard they had gone into Bastogne with no more than two or three clips of ammo, little clothing and food. We left England again on the following day and completed our combat jump into Bastogne. We started to set up our pathfinder headquarters and were blown out of the first two locations. We finally established ourselves and prepared to guide the first resupply planes in."

Although the hoped-for dash to the Meuse was far behind schedule, the German breakthrough continued to expand, inflicting massive casualties, swallowing up chunks of territory, and forcing the insertion of more defenders. GIs trapped by the enemy attack retreated through an avenue of escape temporarily secured by the 30th Infantry and 82d Airborne Divisions.

Among the units engaged in the fluid defense, designed to slow the Germans while preserving their own hides, was the 14th Tank Battalion from the 9th Armored Division. It had been at St.-Vith, then Ligneuville, and staved off significant gains for a day and a half before the elements of the 7th Armored replaced the 14th. Dee Paris, a tank platoon leader from the 14th, coped with a maelstrom of confusion. "We'd be told what unit was on our flanks but couldn't establish any contact with the alleged units there. At one point my tanks were at least 200 yards apart. You could have driven an army between them. We were told there were Germans in American uniforms. When members of the 106th, fleeing from the front, reached us, we invited them to eat with us. A Belgian civilian pointed out a man in our chow line and said he was a German in American uniform. They took him away but I don't know what happened to him. I didn't see any German prisoners killed. But there is a moment when they start to surrender and you keep firing. There are at least two reasons. You don't trust them and you are so hyped on killing someone before they kill you that you just keep firing. There is a fine line between killing prisoners and killing men who would become prisoners if they weren't shot down."

By 22 December, the enemy seemed on the verge of swallowing up Dee Paris and his platoon. "One night I heard a noise on a nearby road. I contacted Paul Fisher and we jointly investigated. We found a horse-drawn wagon with straw in the back, driven by a man dressed as a farmer. I was suspicious; why would anyone be there at midnight? When I pulled the straw aside, I found a large army thermos container used to take hot food to the troops. That was my first knowledge that there were German soldiers in our rear. We shot the driver."

They prepared for a sprint to a more secure area. Paris had parked his tank in a barnyard, alongside a manure pile, disguising its silhouette with poles, while the others from the platoon sat on the road, 100 to 150 yards apart. "During the night, we had to take care of the occupant of the house who had insisted on repeatedly going to the barn with a lantern. When daylight came, I gave the order to pull out. I then discovered that we had sunk into the ground; the tank was frozen in the earth. We couldn't move. I radioed one of my tanks to swing into the barnyard and knock us loose. I alerted the crew to hang on. It took two good hits to get us free.

"Out on the road I started to lead the platoon. Suddenly a round passed a yard behind my tank. I wondered how long it would take the antitank gunner to reload. I waited a few seconds, and then shouted on the intercom, 'Stop!' My driver, Ray Waelchi, immediately halted and the next round passed a yard in front of the tank. I waited briefly and shouted, 'Kick it in the ass—give her hell!' Another round missed us. I still don't know how an antitank gunner only about 200 yards away could miss hitting a tank broadside."

On the ground, Arnold Albero continued to live in a hole with some wreckage from a wall around him. "We made deeper and bigger pits for the tanks and artillery. But unlike the Hurtgen Forest, there was nothing to cover the foxholes. My fear occasionally made me nauseous. I drank a lot of water, ate the snow. The thing was there was no place to run and hide. The noncoms had a lot to do with keeping us going. But nobody pulled rank. There was no saluting. Everyone knew what had to be done. We knew that the Germans had sent a surrender ultimatum to Colonel Hogan and he rejected it. We didn't expect to surrender. We'd picked up rumors that the Germans were shooting their prisoners at random. The unspoken word was to go down fighting and take as many of the bastards as you can with you."

Rebuffed by Hogan, the opposition charged the defenders huddled in Marcouray. Said Albero, "The first time they came at us up a slope. I was working a .50 caliber machine gun mounted in a jeep. I had an open view and I saw them fall. Luckily, we fended them off. The most terrifying moment was an attack with armored vehicles that broke through a roadblock where our tank's gun was frozen and couldn't shoot. Once they passed that point, they started shooting like crazy while driving through the town. However, one of our other tanks knocked them out, scattering German soldiers all over the place. We captured the ones who weren't wounded.

"After that incident, they pounded us mainly with artillery fire, guns of all calibers. We couldn't understand why they did not continue to go all-out against us. We would have been overrun; our ammunition was running low; we were out of gasoline. It may be that they were being hit from other areas than ours. Also they may not have wanted to slow their advance, so they just rolled around us and waited for us to give up. The stalemate dragged on. Finally through radio contact the word came no help was on the way. We were on our own; we'd have to fight our way out, leave on foot. When they told us to destroy our vehicles and the weapons we couldn't take, rather than let the enemy use them, that's when I learned what it is to be really scared."

The XVIII Corps, commanded by Maj. Gen. Matthew B. Ridgway, had recognized that the loss of Baraque de Fraiture imperiled the vital crossroads town Manhay and then Liége itself. To plug the gap on Highway N 15 from the crossroads to the village, Ridgway arranged for a group of units from the 7th Armored's Combat Command A to assume responsibility for Manhay and its environs. The task force's most potent weapon was its 40th Tank Battalion. A bit more than a mile southeast of Manhay, the Shermans from C Company deployed along the critical road. Their view down the highway from which the enemy would come was blocked after a short distance by a curve that disappeared into the trees. In one of the C Company tanks, gunner Jerry Nelson, still grieving over the death of his tank commander, Truman Van Tine, felt the loss even more keenly as he developed an active dislike for the replacement. "Burris was friendly enough but that's all. For example, in a Sherman, two guys can lay on their sides in the loader's area and try to sleep. Against the wall there is a small gas engine that runs at night to charge the batteries. Somehow the gas leaked out on Burris who was sleeping there. Actually, it was probably because he moved a lever. But whatever, he woke me and made me take the wet spot while he took my dry one. I could live with that but he showed himself to be an asshole later.

"At dusk, Sergeant Freeman's tank and ours under Burris were set up with us slightly behind Freeman and on the opposite side of the road, looking straight down it. Around 10:00 P.M. we heard them coming, mostly track noise. On the radio, we listened to Freeman, who would see them first, say to his gunner, 'I'll tell you when to shoot. Just a little more—okay Shoot! Shoot! Shoot!'

But there was no shot. We never found out why. Burris asked me, 'Can you see them?' I answered no. He said, 'I'll jump out and fire the .50 caliber on top of the turret. Watch the tracers. You're already pointing right anyway.'

"The .50 was only half loaded, as most of the guns were before they were really needed. Burris yelled, 'It's frozen.' He couldn't pull back the bolt. He told me to start firing and we did. Right into the blackness at point-blank. We were hitting something with our cannon. We got off six or seven rounds, traversing a little each time so we didn't always shoot in the same hole. I looked around for Burris for direction but he was gone. So were the two guys down below, the drivers. I yelled to the loader to bail out.

"As I hit the road, a tank appeared from the brush to the side. I thought it was a German who somehow got through the woods but then a flare went up and I knew he was one of us. I tried to run fast and grab on from behind. But I couldn't. Then a single round, probably from the lead German tank, let loose at the one I'd tried to jump on. I'll never know how close it was to me, but it seemed to me that I could feel something go by me and I can't describe the kind of noise it made. If that had hit me I would be, as Paul Harvey says, twenty years old, forever."

Bleak as prospects may have appeared to the cold, hungry, embattled GIs, the situation for the enemy was rapidly deteriorating. In the all-out sprint toward the Meuse, the crack 2d Panzer Division, bypassing Bastogne, had by 22 December advanced to within five miles of Dinant, where binoculars could pick out the objects of the Führer's desires, the Meuse bridges. A pair of British armored brigades guarded these strategic spans. In a skillful piece of work, the 3d Royal Tank Regiment destroyed lead enemy elements, blocking passage of the armor behind. Long-range artillery then hammered the gridlocked tanks.

The 4th Armored Division, leading the rescue by Patton's Third Army, struck at the outposts of the 2d Panzer Division. Robert Johnson recalled that while approaching Luxembourg his unit halted for the night. "Each of us stood patrol duty around the site. Near midnight, I wandered too near the German line and was grabbed. They took me to a house with a cellar where an officer tried to make me give him information. He hanged [*sic*] me by my ankles from a beam. He'd kick me and yell his questions. I never gave in to his torture. At dawn, as the 4th Armored moved forward, the Germans left, just took off, leaving me hanging. My own crew found me, stood looking at me, and laughing. They finally cut me down and I returned to duty." According to Johnson, the enemy tanks, short on ammunition and fuel, offered increasingly feeble resistance. "We walked through them like plowing new ground."

On the southern shoulder of the Bulge, the German seventh Army had never accomplished its mission, to protect the left flank of von Manteuffel's Fifth Army. They stumbled upon the rock of the 4th Infantry Division, whose isolated units refused to yield key sites. As a consequence, the German Seventh Army failed to push far enough to deter Patton's Third Army charging out of the south. And by 22 December, in fact, two Third Army contributions, the 26th and 80th Divisions, had begun to pummel the German infantrymen.

To the northwest, most of the 1st Battalion of the 517th Parachute Regiment under Bill Boyle, sandwiched between a pair of regiments belonging to the 75th Infantry Division, moved against the enemy surrounding Task Force Hogan and Arnold Albero at Marcouray. The line taken by Boyle's paratroopers stretched between Hotton and Soy. The battalion counterattacked toward Hotton to relieve GIs pinned there and ensure the safety of rear-echelon units at Soy. B Company acted as the spearhead.

According to Pfc. Mel Biddle, on the morning of 23 December, "My platoon leader said, 'Biddle, out front.' " That simple order made Mel Biddle lead scout through dense woods and underbrush as well as open ground. Snow lay eight inches deep as Biddle inched forward in the frigid air, crawling, then getting to his feet when he could detect no enemy. As he traveled over a field with less cover, several Germans, concealed in the brush, fired at him. Biddle flopped to the snow, wriggled toward the enemy position. From only twenty yards away, Biddle used his M1 to kill the trio who had shot at him.

Biddle doggedly pushed forward another 200 yards. He

ambushed a hostile machine-gun position, dispatching the two-man crew with his rifle. Still farther on, the Anderson, Indiana, twenty-one-year-old crept up until he could lob hand grenades into another automatic-weapon nest. Biddle signaled his mates that it was somewhat safer to advance. As they backed him up, the enemy focused on him with rifles and a machine gun. Again Biddle, rapidly reloading, dropped one infantryman, scooted to another position as bullets ripped into the spot he'd just left, killed a second adversary thirty yards away. A desperate grenadier swung his machine pistol in a 360-degree arc, spraying the brush with bullets. Biddle, face down, waited until the fusillade swung by, then slew his eleventh enemy. He tossed his final grenade at the machine gunners and followed up with a successful one-man charge, leaving the gunner and assistant dead; only an ammo bearer escaped.

"There was plenty of light during the day. I had great vision. I saw the faces of all of the German soldiers. I saw each of them, before they saw me and from a very short range. That was especially true in several instances when I was only about six feet away in the underbrush." The scout heard the sounds of armor and volunteered, with three others, to investigate. Bursts from an enemy patrol convinced the group it would be folly to continue. But Biddle chose to infiltrate the enemy positions under the cover of darkness.

For several hours he crept about, determining the enemy weapon emplacements, the deployment of the troops, and location of a pair of tanks. During the course of his nocturnal prowl, Nazi sentries and patrols challenged the paratrooper but their shots missed. In one instance, a searcher stepped on his hand. Biddle stifled the urge to cry out. After the enemy moved on, he slunk away. "I was out there for a very long time but I never thought about eating. I thought how cold I was, especially my fingers. I wasn't sure I could pull the trigger of my rifle. I thought I would try sticking a finger through and pull it with my left hand."

In the early hours of the morning on 24 December, the companies of the 517th, acting on the intelligence gathered by Biddle, struck again, with Biddle repeating his role as the point. American armor, aware of the precise location of the pair of German tanks, knocked both out. When a machine gun threatened to wither the attack, Biddle maneuvered himself to within fifty yards, killed the crew and two soldiers in support. Christmas Eve descended with Hotton's garrison preserved, Biddle was credited with having killed seventeen Germans after firing only twenty-nine rounds from his M1. The performance eventually won him a Medal of Honor. "I had reached a point where I would rather die than be thought of as a coward. I was terrified most of the time but there were two or three moments when I had no fear. That's when you can really operate."

Having lost their tank, Jerry Nelson and the rest of his crew sat out an engagement on Christmas Eve, a total debacle for C Company. The opposition now hurled themselves upon the smaller and outnumbered American armor along the Manhay road. Part of the German force included the Mark V, a forty-five-ton monster with a huge gun and extremely thick armor plate. Command and control, the watchwords of military tacticians, evaporated for the Americans that night in front of Manhay. Aware of the weight being hurled at the defenses, the strategists reluctantly agreed to pull back the outposts. But in the darkness, orders failed to reach some units. Others confused German armor with American or thought only infantrymen with rockets threatened them, rather than highly effective tankers. A bulldozer had neatly dug deep holes for the Shermans manned by Nelson's comrades. Theoretically, the emplacements in the snow lowered the silhouette. But according to one of the tank commanders, Sgt. Donald Hondorp, the Shermans "were standing out like black targets on a sheet of white because the rich black dirt excavated was in stark contrast." Furthermore, the pits curtailed swift maneuvering for the tanks. The enemy armor surprised C Company; some crews evacuated their tanks without getting off a round. Others left, then returned to gamely resist. A German tank commander borrowed from the American lexicon: "It was a turkey shoot." In the end, the nine Shermans from C Company lay wrecked and burning while the Germans overran Manhay. It would prove worse than a Pyrrhic victory, however. Cooler heads dissuaded General Ridgway from an almost suicidal counterattack. The winners, occupying Manhay, discovered themselves pinned by incessant artillery. Only those huddled beneath thick armor would survive.

Kampfgruppe Peiper remained trapped in the town of Stavelot, where a combination of engineers, stragglers, and Jabos barred it from crossing crucial bridges. Low on fuel, the Nazi unit no longer doubted its reversal of fortunes, becoming the prey. Unable to ford or bridge the Salm River and Lienne Creek with his panzers, Peiper, in a farmhouse at La Gleize, watched in despair as the American artillery shattered his redoubts, blasted his armor, and killed or wounded his troops. Several U.S. counterattacks, notably at Cheneaux, wreaked heavy casualties on both sides. Sometime after midnight, in the early hours of 24 December, *Kampfgruppe Peiper*'s flak tank section leader, Sgt. Karl Wortmann, was awakened by a messenger insistently crying "Merry Christmas. Merry Christmas." Befuddled at first by the greeting, Wortmann learned it was a code word directing him to blow up his vehicles and follow the escape column.

Bill Dunfee, as part of the 505th Parachute Regiment, from the moment of arrival east of the Salm River near Trois Ponts on 21 December, was, in his words, "having a very hard time with the remainder of the 1st SS Panzer Division"—Peiper's men. The American paratroopers initially ventured east of the Salm but the sheer force of numbers drove them back to a few yards of river line. To break out Peiper, the 2d SS Panzer Division advanced toward the Salm from the south. The Americans had planned to blow a key bridge near Petite-Langlir but the enemy seized the span before it could be destroyed, making it available for the oncoming panzers. A daring raid by engineers under the leadership of Maj. J. C. H. Lee Jr. penetrated enemy lines, hooked up explosives and detonated the bridge while German vehicles crossed it. Says Dunfee, "We were told that a German motorcycle, sidecar, officer, and driver went airborne along with the bridge. We 'Doggies' loved it; we were more than a little jealous of anyone who rode into battle.

"About this time my platoon leader, Lieutenant Carter, ordered me to provide riflemen to accompany a patrol led by an armored officer. We would be riding a four-wheeled armored scout car mounting a .50-caliber machine gun, pulling a two-wheeled trailer loaded with land mines. The mission was to mine an approach to a bridge. I decided Oscar Newborn and I would volunteer, since we both had BARs—never my authorized weapon, but in combat you picked the weapon you liked best. My feeling was there was no point endangering others; between us we had the firepower of four riflemen.

"We took off about midnight with the lieutenant, driver, and gunner in the scout car, Oscar and I on the trailer. We moved rather slowly, watching for German land mines. Oscar cussed me all the way, first for volunteering him, and then endangering him further by riding on top of a load of mines. I tried logic with him, explaining we were dead if the scout car hit a mine anyway, whether the trailer blew up or not. He was neither reassured nor amused.

"We made it to the bridge; it was lying in the river. Someone had already blown it. Since that bridge did not show destroyed on the lieutenant's map, he insisted we go to the next bridge, a mile farther. We were rounding a curve when we heard the crunching cadence of marching men. We knew they couldn't be friendlies. Oscar and I hopped off the trailer and headed toward the river and the oncoming troops. From there we could cover the turnabout of the scout car. That required unhooking the trailer because the road was so narrow.

"Crossing the road, I pulled back the bolt on the BAR. Not wanting to goof off a shot, I slid my finger forward in the trigger guard, hit the magazine release and dumped a loaded magazine in the middle of the road. The sound was deafening. We stopped and listened but there was no interruption in the cadence of the marchers. When the car finally turned around, we mounted up and took off. Back at the defensive perimeter, we could relax and laugh. Oscar especially enjoyed describing me crawling around the middle of the road trying to locate the magazine I dropped. In the dark I could only feel for it and besides I had a full belt of loaded magazines. It wasn't my finest hour."

The momentum of the Fifth Panzer Army swept up Harry Martin, the former Sad Sack of the 424th Infantry Regiment who, during the initial attack, had recalled the dictum, "Squeeze the trigger." Beyond St.-Vith, Martin, along with pieces of the disintegrated 424th, the 28th Division, and the combat commands of the 7th and 9th Armored, became GI flotsam flowing through a narrow corridor of escape. The route was northwest, across the Salm River where the 82d Airborne including Bill Dunfee held the way open. "On the morning of 23 December we met CCB of the 9th Armored in the snowbound hills west of Beho. We were still not aware of what was going on. Suddenly, Captain Bartel gave the frantic order to withdraw. 'Jump on anything that's moving out! Every minute counts! Every man for himself! I climbed on a light tank.

"The tank I was on was going full speed for quite some time. Just when I felt confident that we had outrun the Germans and they were left far behind, the hatch on the tank opened and the tank commander said, 'We've just received word on the radio that there is small-arms fire ahead. Come on and get inside where you will be safer.' I was very happy to get inside the tank where it was much warmer. I sat back and relaxed. I was out of the cold and I was protected by armor all around me. I thought, 'What a difference between the infantry and the armored divisions. They carry warm clothing, blankets, and food with them.' A few minutes later, machine gun bullets bounced off the tank. I might not be alive if it were not for the tank commander."

After a time, the armor drew beyond enemy fire and halted. The tankers invited the infantrymen to share their food. Martin, who had not eaten for several days, gladly accepted. He began to make plans to stay under their protection for as long as possible. But before he could even settle down for a bite, an officer rounded up the foot soldiers and led them into a wooded area. "One of the men grabbed a chicken and cut its head off with his bayonet. While the chicken was being plucked, we started a small fire. Just as the chicken was put over the fire, word came that the Germans were closing in once again. We quickly stamped out the fire. We ran down the road, passing the chicken around with each man ripping off a piece. We were so hungry that, like wild animals, we ate the chicken raw."

The small group trekked northwest, veering from the direct path a number of times as they detected the advancing enemy. After the lieutenant roused them from their fourth barn in a single night, the exhausted Martin, burdened with two bandoliers of ammunition, a canteen, mess kit, first aid kit, bayonet, hand grenades, rifle, and steel helmet, shivering with his outer wear of ordinary army shoes and a field jacket, felt he could not go on. At the last barn, when the others walked off, he slipped back and bedded down in the loft. At midmorning, Martin awoke, cautiously stuck his head outdoors and saw no one. But when he sallied forth and rounded the corner of the barn, to his horror, a huge German tank's cannon pointed straight at him. Somehow, no one noticed the lone American and he fled through the woods. He traveled in the direction of gunfire, figuring he would outflank the German lines and circle to safety.

Walking for hours, Martin lightened his load, tossing away first his grenades and then his pair of bandoliers of .30-caliber bullets. "As I crossed a snow-covered road, I saw a C ration biscuit wrapped in cellophane. It looked as though it had been run over by a dozen tanks, but I picked it up anyway. I sat down next to a small frozen brook where water flowed over the ice. I found a small package of powdered lemonade in my pocket. I filled my canteen with ice water, mixed in the lemonade powder. I opened the crushed biscuit, taking just a nibble with small sips of my drink. I savored each little nibble and sip. I was having a banquet. All of my senses were centered on this very special meal. I was no longer cold or tired; the war was completely out of my mind. I got more pleasure out of that little biscuit than any meal I have ever had. When I finished, I said aloud, 'Well, let's go and find the war and the 106th Division.' "

Miraculously, Martin apparently passed through the broken lines of the warring armies. He reached a town with American soldiers and trucks. He asked an MP, "Which way did the 106th Division go?" The soldier flatly answered he had never heard of the outfit. Martin did not pause to eat, rest, or warm himself. He trudged on, intent on meeting up with his unit. Toward nightfall, he prepared to give up his hunt and return to the town.

As he staggered back, he suddenly heard someone call his name. To his delight, the voice belonged to a sergeant from his own 3d platoon in L company. The noncom led Martin to a reunion with six others from the company. "It felt good to be back with friends and just in time for Christmas Eve. I had a lot to be thankful for, to have made it back from that dreadful ordeal, back with members of my platoon, in a warm building and finally safe from the enemy. We were with a heavy-artillery outfit. The commander invited us to stay for Christmas Eve and for Christmas Day with a promise of a special turkey dinner."

On the Elsenborn Ridge, the 99th and 2d Infantry Divisions denied the German drive to widen the salient. Mortar man Rex Whitehead, from the 99th, had been at Honsfeld only a few hours before Peiper's column captured the town and several of his buddies. He had gone through a bad patch until meeting up with elements of the 2d Division. He awoke to a pleasant sight on 24 December. "We got up and saw there wasn't a cloud in the sky, and soon we could see vapor trails coming from behind our lines. Soon we could hear and see the formations of bombers going over and you wouldn't believe anything could make a bunch of guys so happy as that sight did. Judge was waving his arms and shouting something about who said we didn't have an air corps. Formations came over for about five hours and it was a beautiful sight, the vapor trails streaming behind each motor and then the escorts weaving back and forth above them, making the sky look like a giant jigsaw puzzle. Some were shot down, for as they approached the front, the Kraut AA would open up and there were some fighters to meet them. More than anything else, we were happy to have them up there, because we didn't draw any fire since the 88s were dual, and were firing at the planes. As soon as they were gone, we started to get it though."

Dick Byers, with the 371st Field Artillery of the Checkerboards [99th], lived in a farmhouse. "The Germans had captured thousands of pounds of our mail and all the normal supply lines were disrupted. By Christmas Eve, we were feeling really lowdown and depressed without any mail for a week. A bunch of us, Cleon Janos, Bill Johnson, Gerald Krueger, Smith Eads, Henry Dewey, Paul Blackburn, and Joe Peruzzi, were on the second floor gathered around a canteen full of gasoline with a rope wick that gave out twice as much soot as light. We were trying to get high on one bottle of terribly oily cognac. Downstairs, there were about five or six young children. Some of them were the farmer's, others were orphans the farm had taken in to shelter. A battery of 240mm heavy artillery howitzers was out in the field beyond the farmhouse.

"The children were singing Christmas carols in their clear soprano voices and the sound effects went something like, 'Silent night'—BLAMM! 'Holy night'—BLAMMM! Somebody would get up and put the cardboard back in the window after the house stopped shaking from each blast. We were all just about ready to give it up as a bad job and go to bed when someone downstairs yelled, 'Mail Call!'

"There was our Christmas mail. I received two boxes from my wife [to be]. In each box was a can of candy corn and in each can was a two-ounce medicine bottle filled with good whiskey. I shared the fruitcake and the cookies with the boys, gave most of the candy to the kids. I gave just a taste of the whiskey to each man and managed to go to bed on Christmas Eve with the customary glow on."

8

End of Siege

PATTON RADIOED MCAULIFFE AT BASTOGNE THAT HE EXpected to reach him on Christmas Day. The would-be rescuers of Bastogne, the 4th Armored vanguard, stalled only four miles away due to heavy resistance. Patton chafed at the delay. His diary entry for the previous day noted: "This has been a very bad Christmas Eve. All along our line we have received violent counterattacks, one of which forced . . . the 4th Armored back some miles with the loss of ten tanks. This was probably my fault because I had been insisting on day and night attacks. This is all right on the first or second day of the battle and when we had the enemy surprised but after that the men get too tired."

Major Hal McCown, from the 119th Infantry, a prisoner of the Germans for several days, had escaped while a group of captured Americans were being led east. Thrashing through the woods at night, near the Salm River he was challenged by GIs from I Company of the 82d Airborne. Bill Dunfee remembered, "It was a cold, moonlit night with good visibility. It was too light to suit us. Ray (Mike) Maikowski was out with the point. Mike noticed movement alongside the road and eased the safety off his M1. The man hiding there made his presence known, claiming to be an American.

"Mike told him, 'Put your hands behind your head and get your ass out here where I can see you.' It was an American, Maj. Hal McCown of the 30th Infantry Division. After he got over his fright—he was sure Maikowski was about to shoot him, and knowing Mike his fright was justified—he told us he had been a prisoner of the 500 to 800 Germans that charged through our lines earlier.

"By daylight, we had reached our new positions. It was bitterly cold and windy. We were told to dig in and establish a line we could defend until the end of the war if necessary. Charles Lupoli and I selected a spot just below the high ground to our rear. It jutted out far enough to give us a clear field of fire to our right and left and across a valley. "During the day of December 25, we dug a cave and covered it with tree limbs and the dirt we removed. We had three firing openings and felt we would be safe from anything but a direct hit from an 88. That evening the roof began to sag. We were outside cutting down a tree to reinforce it when a mortar round landed between us. Lupoli caught shrapnel in his foot and I was knocked down, but uninjured. I carried Lupoli back to the company CP and he was evacuated. While at the CP they brought the mail forward. I got a box of Christmas cookies. I tried to get Lupoli to take some of the cookies with him but he refused. We shared everything and were inseparable. I would miss him. His godmother owned a bar and sent him boxes of Ritz crackers with a pint of whiskey securely imbedded among the crackers. It took a long time for our guys to figure out how we got so happy on

Ritz crackers." Dunfee settled in his new home for the following few days. There was no special meal for him on 25 December. "We went back, a day or two later, a squad at a time, for our warm Christmas dinners. It was really appreciated. After all those K rations, our bellies felt like our throats had been cut."

Christmas in Bastogne was business as usual. Jack Agnew, atop a pile of bricks, and his team started to guide in planes bearing vital supplies. German 88s attempted to disrupt the operation. A direct hit near Agnew killed eight men in a dugout. "The cold weather was the worst," said Agnew. "We only had field jackets we borrowed from an air corps pathfinder group. We were always hungry and thirsty but existed on very little food and drink. Our Christmas dinner consisted of hot C rations, an improvement over Ks, with cow beets and onions. It was so cold that I remember finding a pig a tank had run over and that was frozen stiff. I stuck it up against a tree and it looked like a bread-cutting board. Many of the dead on both sides lay frozen stiff where they had fallen. Burial details had problems putting them on stretchers. In places where the snow piled deep they were obliged to carry the litters shoulder-high. But in spite of the shells from the Germans, we managed to guide in enough supplies to fight off the enemy. It was a great Christmas present delivered by air."

At Bastogne, the greatest price was paid by members of the 101st. Schuyler Jackson earned himself a Purple Heart. "I got hit when a shell landed nearby, ripped a strip off my field glasses. I had a concussion, and my left arm was slashed. They put a little bandage on it and half an hour later I was fine. But when I saw all of the wounded it was tough. Goddamn, I give those doctors credit. They would work for forty-eight hours straight taking care of Americans and Germans."

On Christmas Eve, the Luftwaffe, taking advantage of the blackness of night, dumped two tons of high explosives, inflicting severe casualties. It got darker before the dawn, as Manteuffel, thinking the Americans might relax their vigilance on Christmas, sprang a massive frontal assault. Beginning a few hours after midnight with a huge artillery downpour, the enemy came on with soldiers hidden by white camouflage capes and white-painted tanks, difficult to spot in moonlight or even by day.

Wallace Swanson, CO for Company A of the 502d Parachute Infantry Regiment, had suffered a minor wound at Bastogne, after rifle fire apparently ricocheted off a tank and nicked his right thigh. Sulfa powder and iodine prevented any complications and he returned to duty without loss of time. "We were at Champs [in the northwestern perimeter of the donut-shaped defense around Bastogne] and about 2:30 A.M. there was an all-out barrage, artillery, cannon, mortar, and other firepower. It was raining, snowing, hailing down on our Company A positions. This was the strongest, most extensive, continuous barrage I was ever in. Their goal was to devastate our main line of resistance and all connection from the front to the back and around our strong points."

While Company B backed up Swanson's outfit, the enemy struck directly at the Rolle Château, site of the regimental HQ. Officers rallied cooks, clerks, radiomen, and even chaplains for a defense. The regimental surgeon collected his walking wounded from the stable that served as a temporary hospital, issued them rifles, and led them to defensive posts. Fortunately for the besieged, tank destroyers, along with bazooka-wielding troopers, broke up the armored assault.

Swanson had reported to battalion HQ that the enemy was on top of him, and was still talking when all communications lines to him were obliterated. Hand-to-hand fighting in the buildings and houses of Champs lasted several hours. Said Swanson, "The men held their positions on Christmas Day, securing protection, and the enemy who infiltrated the forward positions were taken prisoners. Hot meals were provided by the battalion and regimental kitchen cooks by late afternoon and evening."

Schuyler Jackson was also at Champs. "They hadn't come at our area during the first days there. The temperature, though, was around zero. There were a couple of replacements who actually froze to death while on duty. I would always have two guys go out there to keep the men awake and prevent them from freezing. When one of our planes was shot down, I took a fleece-lined jacket from the body of one of the crew. It sounds terrible but he had no more use for it. There was a bridge in front of us. We had planted explosives but the detonator froze when they hit us Christmas Day. Their infantry rode on the tanks and we were picking them off. I got myself a bazooka and hit one in the motor. The crew came out fighting. They did not surrender. We had to shoot them.

"We had originally put mines in the road but because we expected the relief column we pulled them off to the side of the road. When the German tanks came, some of the commanders must have thought the road mined. They drove off on the side and exploded our mines. We had enough ammo at our spot and stopped them cold. The last tank was turning back and going up a rise. I fired the bazooka and it was a one-in-a-million shot, dropped right down the turret. Except it didn't explode. The loader had forgotten to pull the pin on the rocket. He got some fancy cussing from me. But the tank didn't get away. Somebody else destroyed it."

Tom Poston remembered impatiently waiting an opportunity to aid the Americans in Bastogne. "It was socked in. You couldn't fly, couldn't take off because of the weather, couldn't drop anything because of the weather. You couldn't see. Every day we'd go down to the radio room, getting ready to go, because we knew the guys were desperate. Finally, around Christmas, they said, 'Okay, it looks like it's going to open up. We flew in weather all the way, got to the drop zone and pop! it was clear. We went down and dropped the parabundles. The sounds of a plane's engines are pretty loud, and there were a bunch of us, so it was pretty noisy. But the guys came out of the woods where they had been hiding and fighting and you could hear them cheer. That's how loud they were yelling. It was gratifying as hell. It suddenly seemed it was worth doing, accomplishing something."

The Christmas Day offensive was the closest call for the defenders at Bastogne. There would be one more half-hearted push on 26 December but the enemy was now very short of men and the tools of war. During the three days beginning with Agnew and company's descent into Bastogne, a total of 962 aircraft dropped 850 tons of supplies. On the day after the holiday, 11 gliders landed with doctors and fuel. The airmen paid in blood, 102 crewmen killed with 19 C-47s shot down and 51 other planes badly damaged. On the other hand, with the improvement of visibility, American fighter-bombers struck increasingly hard at the enemy, whose vehicles often left tell-tale tracks in the snow leading to seemingly concealed positions. Toward the rear of the Germans, the aerial attacks blasted any endeavor to reinforce or refurbish the German forces.

On Christmas morning, with the enemy attack halted, McAuliffe himself toured the local cemetery where he saw German prisoners, laboriously chopping holes in the frozen dirt for temporary interment of the stiffened bodies of dead paratroopers. He commented to the guards they should make certain the POWs were properly fed. Earlier, he had distributed a message to his men.

McAuliffe's communique recounted the details of the German demand for surrender and his pithy response. His Christmas message then said: "What's merry about all this, you ask? We're fighting—it's cold—we aren't home. All true, but what has the proud Eagle Division accomplished with its worthy comrades of the 10th Armored Division, the 705th Tank Destroyer Battalion, and all the rest? Just this: We have stopped cold everything that has been thrown at us from the north, east, south, and west. We have identifications from four German panzer divisions, two German infantry divisions, and one German parachute division. These units, spearheading the last desperate German lunge, were heading straight west for key points when the Eagle Division was hurriedly ordered to stem the advance. How effectively this was done will be written history, not alone in our division's glorious history but world history. The Germans actually did surround us, the radios blared our doom. Allied troops are counterattacking in force. We continue to hold Bastogne. By holding Bastogne, we assure the success of the Allied armies. We know that our division commander, General Taylor will say: Well done! We are giving our country and our loved ones at home a worthy Christmas present and being privileged to take part in this gallant feat of arms are making for ourselves a merry Christmas."

McAuliffe had caroled a less cheery tune to the VIII Corps commander, Gen. Troy Middleton, on the eve. "The finest Christmas present the 101st could get would be a relief tomorrow."

Another nut that the enemy offensive had failed to crack was on Elsenborn Ridge, manned by the 99th and 2d Divisions. Sergeant Ben Nawrocki found Christmas Day painful. "It was a day of sadness. The mail delivery came in. We were asked to send a detail of men to open individual packages of those lost in each company. We were to take out all the perishable foods and eat them ourselves. The valuables were sent back to the families in the States. Most of Company B was dead, captured, or wounded. We had a lot of food, which came in handy, nutrition for half-frozen soldiers.

"We were receiving picked-over C rations, cans of hash and beans. Men were angry at people in the rear who gave us the leftovers. The crates were obviously opened and then repacked. The food we took from the Christmas packages boosted morale and health. The sweets gave us warmth. We took the hard candy, melted it, and added prune bars begged from the armored troops along with crackers to make a jelly. The Army promised us a good, full Christmas dinner and made good with all the trimmings. It was served cold, but darn good, turkey and all. I could not understand how they did it with the biggest battle ever going on."

On 25 December, Glen Strange reported to 3d Armored Division headquarters with information on the disposition of his unit. He was ushered into the presence of General [Maurice] Rose. "I had not shaved since the sixteenth of December and had worn the same clothes since then, having lost all my others along with my toilet articles. I began, 'Capt. Glen L. Strange, with the 27th Armored Infantry Battalion, 9th Armored Division, part of Combat Command B, to make a report, sir.'

"He asked, 'Captain, are you an officer in the United States Army?'

"I answered him, 'Hell, yes, and we've been through hell, sir.'

"His reply was, 'Well, you don't look like it. Give me your report,' and he turned to his aide and said, 'See to it this captain gets a bath, in my bathroom, uses my toilet articles, gets shaved and, Major, find him some clothes to wear, even if you have to give him some of mine.' After I gave him the report, I did take a bath in his bathroom with hot water, used his razor. By the time I was cleaned up, the major had rounded up new underwear, clean ODs, and an almost new combat jacket and pants. The jacket was the general's, as it was too big and had the stars cut off the shoulder straps—you could see where they had been. This was the best Christmas present I could have received. I reported back to the battalion and was envied by many for being cleaned up and having new clothes. "

Like the 27th Armored Infantry Battalion, Dee Paris's 14th Tank Battalion was also in transit. There were no Christmas dinners, only C rations. Not far from St.-Vith, D Company of the 14th paused in an open field. Tank driver Harold Lemmenes remembered, "We were washing our feet in warm water when Lieutenant Paris came by and looked at our feet and ordered us to go to the medics."

Paris explained, "I made it a point to order a number of men to remove their boots and socks, particularly when I saw a man limping. I was no expert on trench foot—just figured that anyone having his boots and socks on for several days [Lemmenes said he hadn't taken his off for four days] should air his feet." Lemmenes and others with sore feet lay at one end of a tent with their bare feet exposed to the cold air. Most of the bunks were filled with wounded men, groaning in pain. "That night," said Lemmenes, "happened to be Christmas. The next day we had our Christmas dinner. Jack Soukup our radio man and gunner and I convinced them to let us return to our company and we did."

As Christmas Day drew to an end, Task Force Hogan, the 400-man unit from the 3d Armored, at Marcouray, broke into small groups for an attempt to sneak through the enemy encirclement. "We put dirt in the gas tanks, dismantled weapons, and buried pieces," recalled Arnold Albero. "We were told that friendly troops were to the north. I looked up into the black, dark sky trying to find the North Star. Suddenly, I wished I had paid more attention in basic training when they tried to teach compass reading at night. At dusk we started to leave, in small groups at ten-minute intervals. As each left his position, they were wished well by those to follow.

"The march through the woods and hills was rough and I mean rough. We crawled across open fields with some snow on the ground, waded cold streams. When we stopped to rest, I could not only feel but also hear my heart pounding. Then when I looked back to see if the GI behind me was still there, I was relieved to see he was relatively closer than he should have been. He actually should have been at least thirty to fifty yards behind me. When you couldn't see anyone behind, you left a trail, a cartridge belt, musette bag, anything. I prayed that the guy in front of me knew where he was going because I did not. The success of our infiltration rested on our lead man, whom I did not know. He was a lieutenant and I don't know which one but to this day I pray for that man.

"At times we were so close to the Germans, you could hear them singing Christmas carols. To my knowledge, we were challenged only once during our march. After about fourteen hours, we reached friendly infantry." In fact, the entire group of about 400, including a flier shot down while trying to airlift supplies, passed into the positions set up by Bill Boyle of the 517th Parachute Regiment. The paratroop commander was told some of the task force did not contact any frontline soldiers, probably because "in that fluid situation it was impossible to establish solid lines."

The deep penetration of the Germans required a constant readjustment of the American defenses, yielding turf won at considerable bloodshed. Vance Kidwell, a supply sergeant with the 78th Armored Field Artillery of the 2d Armored Division, had been behind the action in North Africa and reached Normandy several weeks after the division's arrival in France on D plus 1. "On October 1944," said Kidwell, "we reached Palenburg [inside Germany] and a week later the town of Ubach." Within the breakthrough, the division pulled back. "On Christmas Day we were in Liroux, a small town built along one side of a ridge, which was the main street. The night before I had slept on the kitchen floor of a house and nearly froze. It was cold and there was lots of snow on the ground. The fellows kept their engines going to keep them from freezing up and guards stood by the exhausts to keep warm. All night long, we could hear vehicles moving into a grove of trees a quarter mile away on lower ground. We assumed they were ours, but when daylight came an officer walking on the ridge was sniped at and we knew they were Germans. Our tanks lined up on the ridge and I got a bird's-eye view of our tanks picking theirs off one at a time as they tried getting away. Some of the Germans tried running across the open field toward us with their hands in the air. Some of our fellows started taking potshots at them and one German fell to the ground like he'd been hit. But as soon as the firing stopped, he got up and ran toward us to give up."

South of the Bulge, after a two-week battle at Ensdorf that established a bridgehead across the Saar River, the 95th Division, because of the Ardennes problem, received word to abandon its foothold and retreat to the village of Hayes, liberated weeks before. Carl Ulsaker had mixed emotions. "It was a relief to escape the hell of life in Ensdorf. On the other hand, it was disappointing to have to give up ground won with so much difficulty and the sacrifice of so many good men. Survival at Ensdorf provided me early in life with the nadir of my existence, enabling me to cope calmly with all subsequent crises; for nothing I have since faced has proved to be worse than that experience."

As the trucks hauled his outfit away, Ulsaker saw a fireworks show, created by demolition of ammunition stored in the town. "White phosphorus shells hurled high into the air burst into great white blossoms, brilliant against the dark sky. Rockets shot off in all directions leaving blazing trails of orange flames. The buildings in which ammunition had been piled began to burn fiercely, cooking off thousands of small-arms rounds, making a noise like a giant corn popper. Adding to the spectacle, machine gunners of the 2d Battalion fired long bursts at extreme range into the streets of the town we had so recently vacated, the red tracers resembling fiery streams from demon hoses. Division artillery added a few volleys. The roaring flames, the sporadic flashes of exploding shells, the din, and the smoke in the Stygian blackness of that last night of the fall of 1944 gave our abandoned bridgehead an appearance that could rival portrayals of Hell by such masters as Dante and Milton."

When he reached Hayes around 2:00 A.M., his advance party informed him that the men would sleep in barns. "Recalling General Patton's policy that our allies were to share their homes, I said, flatly, 'Like hell we'll sleep in barns; get me the town mayor.' After some slight delay his honor trotted up, pulling on a coat over his nightdress and looking somewhat apprehensive. I contrived my most devilish leer, looked him straight in the eye, and said, 'I don't want my men sleeping in places designed for animals. Make arrangements for the people here to share their homes with us.'

" 'But, Mon Capitaine,' he sputtered, 'there is no room.'

" 'Make room,' I said, staring at him with hard eyes, visible in the light of a kerosene lamp held by my quartering NCO, who also interpreted, although I knew enough schoolboy French to get the drift of the mayor's conversation." When the latter protested that everyone was asleep, Ulsaker responded, "We can easily wake them up," gesturing toward his platoon leaders who stood about with grenades clipped to their belts and guns hanging menacingly from their shoulders. "Listen, goddamnit, in case you don't remember, we're the unit that liberated your village from the Boche a month ago. You sure as hell were glad to see us then. Maybe you'd like us to invite the Germans back." Within an hour the company occupied warm beds hastily vacated by the host town.

For Phil Hannon of the 81st Combat Engineers, the Christmas season began his life as a POW. "The Germans walked us into the square of a small village. They were too busy to bother with us. They were learning to drive our trucks and eat our chow. The gearshift on our trucks puzzled some of them, so we had a few laughs. One Kraut got a jeep going in reverse and couldn't shift it into forward. Another seemed to think second gear was the way a truck should run. It was funny but it hurt. We should have burned our vehicles. We were herded into a courtyard with a few apple trees. I was lucky and got one of the frozen apples. They told us:

'You will spend the night, here. This is where your latrine will be'; designating a corner. 'If anyone tries to escape, all will be shot.'

"For a time we sang. Christmas was just a few days off so Christmas carols filled our minds with thoughts of home. We sang until the Germans complained that we kept them awake and if we didn't cease, we'd be shot. We lay next to and atop one another to keep warm. It drizzled all night and we were soaked by morning. None of us slept much, even though we were all dead tired. At 6:00 A.M. we were lined up four abreast in groups of 100 and told we'd get a break at the end of eighteen kilometers. About noon, after steady walking, we stopped in a village full of a Panzer Grenadier outfit. We were supposed to get food and water. Instead, they stripped us of the overshoes we had. About six spuds were thrown from a window for more than 1,000 men. The men fought for them and the Germans laughed.

"All of us were thirsty. I gathered a couple of canteens and two helmets and let some guards know I wanted 'Wasser.' Luckily, he was Polish. He took half a dozen others and me up the street to a house where he was billeted. While we filled our containers, he brought a bucket of boiled potatoes and motioned for us to stuff our pockets for our comrades. I had on my overcoat and loaded both pockets to the rim. When we rejoined the others, I had enough to hand two to each man in my platoon, which had stayed together."

The march continued, becoming increasingly more difficult as hunger, thirst, and weariness gnawed at the hapless prisoners. They slaked their parched throats from dirty puddles, gobbled raw potatoes thrown to them by French laborers, felt briefly cheered when they passed through the German city of Prüm and observed the damage inflicted by the Air Corps. Day passed into night; the men stumbled along. They sought to raise flagging spirits with song but that died out. "Most of us needed all our breath to 'pick 'em up, and lay 'em down.' " The march finally ended at a railhead around 2:00 A.M., nearly twenty hours after it began.

Water became an obsession. From a nearby stream, the POWs filled their canteens, then dumped in Halazone tablets for purification. But instead of waiting for the chemical to kill bacteria, the GIs gulped down the mixture instantly. At 11:00 A.M. the guards issued food, two bags of hardtack per man and a can of cheese to be split among seven persons. Hannon squirreled away some of his ration for future use. During the trek east, Hannon found members of his platoon and soon they were hustled toward the railyards. "Somehow we made it known we were thirsty and an old man and his wife started giving us water. Those old souls worked themselves like horses hauling water for us until the guards stopped them. Those people were helping us as best they could because they were built that way. We were their enemies but they were helping us. They weren't doing it because they knew Germany was going to be beaten. They did it because they were people, not puppets. Germany as a nation was rotten but its people are human beings with hearts and minds open to good things."

The boxcars for Hannon and the others arrived, apparently fresh from carrying horses. The straw with the droppings remained as the men boarded. Jammed together, the prisoners' body heat thawed Hannon's feet. He removed his boots and twenty-four hours would pass before he could bear to touch his tender feet. The trip descended into the depths of a nightmare. Dysentery afflicted many. Hannon, with a position beside one of the small windows, would hear a yell for "the helmet, for Christ's sake, quick!" Within a few moments, a helmet passed hand to hand would arrive at his spot and he would empty it out the window. To urinate, the men used a discarded cheese can. There was pushing and shoving, cursing, cries of pain as someone trod on another's foot. A few soldiers became delirious. Pleas for *wasser* or *essen* passed unheeded by the guards.

On 23 December, the train halted in a railyard alongside another load of POWs, wearing the patches of the 28th Infantry Division. That night an engine chugging by suddenly stopped. The engineer and fireman jumped out and ran. Hannon heard the drone of a flight of planes. "We sat there and sweated. I watched from the window and saw my Christmas tree. The lead plane dropped a flare. it burst about 200 feet in the air, took the shape of a pine tree. The burning lights were red, purple, orange, and yellow, looking quite like Christmas tree lights. Then things started to happen.

"Whomp! The first one hit and jarred us around. The engine on the track next to us kept blowing off steam like a giant hippopotamus. We prayed. Each time a bomb hit, I dropped to the floor. Guys were yelling. 'Crawl out the window.' 'If this damn train ever gets hit and starts burning . . .' I couldn't get out of the window and wasn't about to try. I couldn't see myself half in and half out when one of those babies hit nearby. Down at the other end of the car, they had better results with their helmet man. It was Corporal Stone, I think, who climbed out. A guard lying in a ditch, scared to death, spotted him and pleaded, 'Good soldier, don't run.' He ignored the guard, burrowed under our car, and unwired the door. We scrambled out as men from other cars did the same. We started looking for water and found a frozen ditch. We managed to get our fill. The bombing had stopped; the guards were worked up, shooting occasionally. We loaded back in the cars. Later, we learned eight men had been killed and thirty-six wounded during the air raid.

"On the day before Christmas, we were allowed to get water and they fed us, one-twelfth of a loaf of black bread and a daub of jam. It was more than we could handle in our weakened condition. A few of the boys were too sick to even bite it. Two of our chaplains came by and told us the bombers had wrecked the track ahead. Until it was fixed we couldn't move. They wished us a Merry Christmas and moved on to the next car. When night came, we were still in the yards and worried about being bombed again. 'They won't bomb on Christmas Eve.' 'Hell they won't! They're out to win this war. Christmas won't be celebrated this year. So we waited. From somewhere along the line of cars came a Christmas carol. Back and forth the carols went, first from our train, then from the other— *'Little Town of Bethlehem,' 'Silent Night,' 'Deck the Halls,'* and the rest of the favorites. That lasted for an hour or so. Then the Catholic boys said their Rosary while the rest of us were silent with our own prayers. The air raid siren sounded once but we weren't bothered by the bombers again."

On Christmas Day, during the morning, the journey resumed. They reached Frankfurt, where another old man sought to alleviate the perpetual thirst with buckets of water. But after a dozen trips with a bucket, it proved too much for him. Hannon's car received two helmets of water before the good Samaritan quit. The train rolled on and the prisoners reached the end of the line on Christmas Day. They unloaded, and the GIs caught a glimpse of newspaper headlines that read 35,000 AMERICANS CAPTURED. Civilians gawked at them without expression. "We drew ourselves up and tried our best to look like U.S. soldiers and did right well, considering the condition of our clothes and bodies."

They disembarked in the village of Bad Orb, then walked the final three kilometers to Stalag IX B. "The column came to a halt and the gates opened. We walked in, prisoners, Christmas Day and the gates of freedom had closed behind us. As we walked in, faces peered out of barbed-wire windows. They smiled and yelled, 'Russkies! Russkies!' Russian troops, allies, were greeting us. We smiled and feebly waved as we marched by."

Private first class Ed Uzemack, the reporter from Chicago who had become a veteran after surviving the bloody Hurtgen Forest campaign as a replacement in the 28th Division, lost his freedom on 17 December. "We could see that their tanks were in excellent condition and that the enemy soldiers were pretty sharp. Our immediate captors behaved a bit like gentlemen. The black-uniformed panzer men were young, clean-shaven and very smart in appearance. They were efficient and cocky in their attitude. They had captured us and naturally attributed this feat to their 'Aryan superiority.'

"The small group of men captured with me was permitted to secure blankets and overcoats before setting out on the march. Very few other prisoners had a similar break. We were forced to march several kilometers to a hillside air-raid shelter. We went through our first real shakedown as POWs. The German guards stripped us of every grain of tobacco and every ounce of food we carried. Many of the guards took from the GIs watches, pens, billfolds, personal letters, and other items of souvenir value. A good many men lost pictures of their loved ones."

Along with 400 others, Uzemack was forced inside the air-raid shelter, designed to accommodate only half that number. As he entered, an English-speaking guard warned, "Take a good deep breath, Yankee. It will be the last fresh air you'll get for some time." For almost two days Uzemack lived in the "pitch-black, damp, foul cave in the side of a hill. We lay in this dungeon with no food and little water. The air grew foul with the cave smell and the men became extremely irritable and hungry." On returning to sunlight after almost forty-eight hours, Uzemack noticed a change in the quality of the traffic. "The Nazi column was still rolling down the road. Their equipment looked like something out of a junkyard. Vehicles that had to be towed, horse-drawn vehicles and other decrepit pieces rolled past us all day." He also marked the passage toward the front of a number of well-marked ambulances, carrying heavily armed troops. Uzemack's group, as with the other POWs, frantically hunted for food and water. Uzemack to his own horror scratched in the mud to retrieve the remains of an apple tossed away by one of the Germans. To their surprise, almost a feast of half a loaf of sour bread plus marmalade and a small piece of cheese greeted them at a stop on 20 December. Unfortunately, the guards failed to instruct the GIs that this was to last several days. Furthermore, the excess, such as it was, proved more than many roiling stomachs could handle. Quartered in a church and unable to leave the premises, Uzemack noted, "In the morning, the vestibule was almost ankle-deep in vomit and other excreta. A great many of the men had become ill."

The following three days they marched, finally stopping after 100 kilometers at Gerolstein. The convoy was commanded by "a monocled son of a bitch, with natty breeches, swagger stick, and boots." He forced a twenty-man party to clean up an improvised latrine with their bare hands. He also relieved the men of all of their money, a collection that stuffed several thousand dollars in various currencies into his personal pockets. Locked in boxcars at Gerolstein, the

Americans heard the ominous hum of approaching U.S. aircraft. "One plane swept lower over the train, zoomed up—and then came back. This time he meant business; we heard machine-gun fire. Men pounded on the walls of the cars, screaming to be let out. A few medics in the car behind managed to get out. They waved their red cross helmets at the planes overhead and opened a few cars. Men streamed out in droves.

"Despite their fright, pain, and weakness, most headed for a vegetable patch some distance away, fell on their knees in the furrows and began grubbing out the carrots and turnips, jamming them in their hungry mouths." When the raid ended, the Germans rounded up the prisoners, firing warning shots over their heads and hitting one GI in the back. Subsequently, he died from the wound due to a lack of medical care and the hardship of the trip. Christmas Eve brought no surcease. The men abandoned efforts at caroling; the will to carry on appeared evaporating." Late on Christmas Day, shortly before midnight at Bad Orb, the authorities relented and dumped eight loaves of bread and seven meat tins amongst the nearly sixty Americans with Uzemack. "Despite the darkness, we managed to divide the food. Like many others, I decided this was the best Christmas dinner of my life."

While the 4th Armored Division spearheaded the rescue drive toward Bastogne, other elements like the 87th Infantry Division, introduced to battle early in December, followed in the wake of the tanks and half-tracks. Private first class Alan Shapiro of the 346th Infantry recalled a nine-hour truck ride to Rheims the day before Christmas. "We had a complete night's sleep, a wonderful Christmas present. Midway through the morning, many went to Christmas services given by the chaplains. We received a chicken dinner, with fresh vegetables, for lunch. For the first time in many weeks I felt as if I had really eaten."

Shapiro spent the remaining hours before dusk standing around warming fires, wondering what was to come next. After night fell, the men of the 346th once again readied themselves for a journey. "We piled onto the trucks, which were covered, and packed them to the limit. The whole platoon was in one truck and there was plenty of bitching. I had my legs doubled up under my chin, and I couldn't move without annoying somebody. I was luckier than most since my back was against the side of the truck. The fellows in the middle rested against the knees of the person behind them.

"It was impossible to sleep. There was nothing to see so we just sat there. The ride seemed interminable. Guys hollered for the trucks to stop and allow us to relieve ourselves. But during the entire twelve-hour ride, we didn't stop once to allow us to stretch or anything else. Some men were afflicted with a bit more than kidney trouble and a lot of us suffered from bad cases of the GIs [diarrhea]. We pissed in the gas cans and shit in a pile of straw. Peeing was a delicate situation since the nozzles on the gas cans were the size of a quarter and you had to be careful not to squirt all over everyone. It didn't seem funny to us and the truck hardly smelled like a rose garden. But there wasn't anything we could do. When we finally stopped and left the trucks, we didn't know where we were or even what country we were in. There were woods all around us. We marched off into them a few hundred yards away and dug in."

On the day after Christmas, Lt. Col. Creighton Abrams of the 4th Armored Division's 37th Tank Battalion poked his head up from a Sherman atop a hill three miles from Bastogne. He radioed back, "Concentration Number Nine, Play it soft and sweet." It was the code name for a Time-on-Target avalanche upon the avenue leading into the town. After 420 rounds of artillery crashed into whoever might be defending, an advance column of six tanks, followed by half-tracks packed with infantrymen from the 53d Armored Infantry, started the final charge. They ran a gauntlet of small arms and heavier pieces while blasting anyone in their way.

Abrams told correspondent Will Lang, "I like to be way out on the goddamn point, where there's nothing but me and the Germans and we can fight without reporting to headquarters." The American officer was frank in his assessment of his weakness against enemy armor. "The Germans can get any tanks we have beginning at a range of 3,000 yards and we have to wait until a Panther is within 1,000 yards before we're sure of crippling it and until 200 yards to get a Tiger Royal."

He remained firmly committed to the mission. "If those people in there need help we gotta get in there. When we move, we move with everything firing. In half a day we completely wrecked Assenois. Near Bigonville woods, we killed thirty enemy in foxholes and took fifteen POWs. We lost four half-tracks between Assenois and Bastogne. The men who were not killed or wounded continued on foot." Within half an hour after the final push began the relief force bagged 400 prisoners, killed hundreds of others, and Creighton Abrams shook hands with Tony McAuliffe. The siege of Bastogne was over.

9

Casualties and POWs

THE RELIEF OF BASTOGNE, BREAKS IN THE WEATHER THAT ENabled the Air Corps to blast the enemy, and huge infusions of fresh troops—the 11th Armored Division, the 17th Airborne Division and a host of other organizations—doomed the German offensive in the Ardennes. Patton had boasted his hand held the handle of the meatgrinder, but the crank turned excruciatingly slowly, amid substantial costs in American bodies. In fact, rather than sealing off the tens of thousands of German soldiers within the salient, the high command chose to batter the enemy in a bloody, toe-to-toe, head-on campaign. The decision ensured a casualty-strewn ordeal.

In the 87th Division, where the initiation into combat a few weeks earlier left many rifle companies with half their normal complement, Alan Shapiro tried to cope with reality. "The war still appeared peculiar to us. None of us had the slightest knowledge as to how the overall picture of the war appeared. With all our constant confusion, I couldn't see how we were winning and the Germans were retreating. I wasn't killing anybody. I didn't see any Germans and their only manifestation was in their shells and machine guns." In his only opportunity to use his rifle, Shapiro was disconcerted to learn that he and his associates were exchanging fire with another company from the division. As he trudged through the snow, the condition of his feet worsened until by New Year's Day he could barely walk. He was evacuated to England along with thousands of others afflicted with either frostbite or trenchfoot.

Similarly, Noel Robison, a runner for L Company of the 358th Regiment in the 90th Division, staggered through the snow and ice. "All of us wore 'long john' [winter] underwear, olive drab wool uniforms, cotton fatigues over the ODs, and our wool great field coat. Our clothing was so thick it was nearly impossible to respond to 'piss call' when the required stops were made by trucks." Rooting about in the snow, they uncovered buried helmets and weapons belts marked with the red keystone, mute evidence of the overrun 28th Division. In foxholes built by conscripted labor for the Germans, they huddled together for warmth, slept fully dressed in uniforms, overcoats, shoes, and with an occasional blanket.

"Early one morning when I tried to put my boots on, I couldn't. My feet had swollen. I forced my feet into my boots and didn't lace them up." Lagging behind the company, he staggered into a battalion aid station. "I sat in a corner and took off my boots. I looked at my feet. My toes were purple. The upper parts of my feet were red and looked like hamburger, raw from the chafing during the hike to the aid station." The war was over for Robison also.

Lieutenant Colonel Bill Boyle of the 517th Parachute Regiment had persuaded his regimental commander to delay an assignment to capture high ground near the Salm River until dark. The attack went off successfully but during the night, when Boyle tried to contact another unit, an enemy machine gun smashed three bullets into him. He said that as he lay bleeding in the snow, "I prayed, God, don't let me die. This was a moment when I experienced fear. I knew my brachial artery [in his arm] was severed and that I could not stop the bleeding." Fortunately, his intelligence specialist, S. Sgt. Robert Steele, got to him, administered first aid, and then goaded him into hobbling with Steele's assistance to the aid station. Although the battalion surgeon doubted his chances, Boyle clung to life and eventually was transported to a hospital.

While Boyle slowly recovered, his fellow troopers in the 517th joined the 78th Infantry Division for a renewed effort around the town of Schmidt through the bloody Hurtgen Forest. The strategists assigned the paratroopers to carry out a diversionary attack, but instead of instructing the GIs to feint and distract the foe with minimum casualties to themselves, they were ordered to forcibly confront the enemy. Error piled on error. The 517th's 2d Battalion commander, Dick Seitz, noted, "High-echelon strategists can work from a map and aerial photos, but it is an axiom of military operations that battalions or companies should never advance without firsthand knowledge of the terrain. We never had an opportunity to make a foot recon. The plan called for a night attack, which makes the need for good recon to recognize terrain features even more imperative. The plan said we were to advance with two battalions abreast. The book calls for adequate planning, rehearsals, and to proceed on a narrow front. We were unable to properly rehearse the operation. We violated all of the principles."

In the ensuing operations, units ran into a buzz saw of

enemy opposition. Lacking real knowledge of the ground, maneuvering blindly through minefields in the dark, the affair was a disaster from the viewpoint of the 517th. Although the brother infantry outfits succeeded in breaking through, the paratrooper regiment, one more victim of the Hurtgen Forest, was so chewed up that it lost its independence and was relegated to the newly arrived 13th Airborne Division in reserve, seventy miles from Paris.

Vance Kidwell, with a 2d Armored Division artillery outfit, recalled that after a break over New Year's the unit returned to combat. "We spent the first night back in a pine grove and the weather was zero and below, lots of snow. The pine trees were a hazard, for when the German shells would hit the tops of the trees they would explode, sending shrapnel downward from which we had little protection. If we had time to dig foxholes, we would take doors from houses, cover the foxhole with them, except for a small opening to crawl in, and then we would cover the doors up with dirt. If there were no doors, we would use logs of some kind."

Bill Dunfee enjoyed a brief respite from combat before his 82d Airborne unit rejoined the battle to evict the Germans from their gains. Proceeding along a road, a treeburst that no one heard coming showered his squad with shrapnel. Dunfee's close pal DiGiralamo died instantly. The blast slashed another man's foot and leg. "I was knocked down and the butt of my BAR slammed my middle finger, putting a permanent kink in it." But except for the loss of his toothbrush and toothpaste from his breast pocket, he went unharmed. As the troopers advanced Dunfee saw Germans shoot their own people when they sought to surrender.

The route taken by the 82d Airborne covered the terrain where the 28th Infantry Division in the late autumn had absorbed terrible punishment before retreating. Said Dunfee,

"The area became known to us as 'Death Valley.' There were trucks, tanks, jeeps, trailers, tank destroyers, bumper-to-bumper and all shot to hell. Tanks had thrown their tracks; trucks, jeeps, and trailers turned over, some burned. I had been exposed to the carnage of war in four airborne operations—Sicily, Italy, Normandy, and Holland—but I never saw anything that could compare. Freshly killed troops in various stages of dismemberment are gruesome enough for the average stomach. But these men had been through a freeze and thaw. They had lain there since November and their flesh had rotted and was peeling from the skeletons. Some were on litters. I hoped they were killed outright and not abandoned to freeze to death. There was complete silence in our column, each man handling this horror in his own way. For me, it was the most shocking single experience of the war. If anyone needed an incentive to fight, this gave him ample reason."

While aircraft production by the factories of the Third Reich continued in spite of the raids by the Eighth, Ninth, and Fifteenth Air Forces, the heavy attrition of German pilots due to the bomber and fighter guns sharply reduced capable flyers to man available cockpits. And the strategic bombing program created a severe shortage in fuel for planes. The absence of protective air cover enabled the Allied planes to freely attack the retreat from the Ardennes.

Cary Salter, a Mississippi country doctor's son, was a member of a group of replacement pilots who arrived in December 1944 at Le Bourget, the Paris airport made famous by Lindbergh's landing there in 1927. While the enemy had to fill its flight ranks with young men with minimal experience at the controls, Salter had accrued many hours' flying time while an instructor for students in P-40s, P-47s and P-51s. Assigned to the 354th Fighter Group, a few miles from

Toul, and in transition to P-47s from P-51s, he noted, "I was there a month and a half before I got to fly a mission. My first missions, we were cleaning them out after the Battle of the Bulge. I flew as an escort for A-26 bombers attacking bridges and railyards or else we went on search-and-destroy missions, hitting anything we saw on the ground, such as troops or trucks. We were not bothered by enemy fighters; whatever they had they generally used to go after the high-altitude Eighth Air Force bombers."

As the Americans advanced, Belgian civilians in a forest near Meyerode led them to the body of an American officer. From the papers on the remains he was identified as Eric Fisher Wood, the artillery lieutenant with the 106th Division. Seven German corpses lay nearby. There was considerable evidence that Wood had organized a guerrilla campaign against the enemy but no eyewitnesses to his feats ever surfaced. A claim by his father, himself a general, to gain a Medal of Honor for Wood was denied because of the necessity of firsthand corroboration. Instead, a Distinguished Service Cross went to his widow. Of the 600,000 GIs embroiled in the Ardennes, Eric Wood was one of 19,000 who died, with another 40,000 wounded. Casualty figures among the half-million Germans vary from 100,000 to 120,000. Most humiliating for the Americans was the matter of 19,000 prisoners, the largest number taken captive since Bataan.

The experiences of American captives varied, but at best it was uncomfortable and at worst a deadly ordeal. David Jones, the bomber pilot who escaped the enemy after the strike at Tokyo in 1942 only to be shot down in North Africa some six months later, entered Stalag III a week before Christmas. Ensconced in the East Camp, Jones recalled, "There were about forty-five Yanks. I was the first one out of North Africa so they were all from the United Kingdom. They moved British and Americans still mixed up to the North Camp in the spring of '43. It was brand new. Everything was fresh and smelled of pine and fresh air. Jeez, it was beautiful.

"It didn't last long but that's when we started working on the big plan. I was a digger, a tunneler. [There were] three Americans who were face men, who worked underground. And we had Poles and Englishmen, and all kinds of nationalities on this digging team. We had an elaborate security system, a warning system, and we had an elaborate method of dispersing sand. We had very elaborate traps. We had a square German stove that sat on a brick foundation and we lifted the whole thing and made one piece out of it and sank the tap under that. We could move the stove every time. Another trap was in the washroom where there was a slope to the center and a water trap. Someone had cut one side of it out and made it where you could lift one side, make a slab, lift that out, and we went down from there. The tunnel went down to about thirty feet, full of sand, just like Florida."

The tunnelers lay on their elbows because the confined spaces prevented them from working while on hands and knees. They carried small cans of margarine for oil and early on Jones noticed it flamed out very quickly. He kept returning it by string to those above who would relight the device. After it went out several more times he realized there was not enough oxygen to support the candle. Subsequently, as they burrowed deeper and farther, the prisoners rigged an air line using cans with the tops and bottoms cut out and then stacked to make a crude pipe. "At the bottom of the hole we had a chamber and we'd have a guy work a pump to push air into the tunnel with a big bellows. Eventually we'd tap into a light and we had electricity and electric lights."

To shore up the subterranean passageway, the captives removed boards from beds and cut them to size. Even so, there were frequent cave-ins and the trapped person depended upon the man behind to pull him out. "I was thirty feet under when a cave-in occurred. You kind of wonder, 'What in the heck am I doing here.' Of course it was imperative that you repair the hole before you get out because the effort of hundreds of people depended on you. You just *have* to fix whatever it was. And you had to get out of the hole to be counted.

"The dispersal system was very complicated. We'd move tons of sand a day in two-pound lots. We put a trolley in, two wooden rails, a little cart about two feet long and fifteen inches wide, and that's what we hauled the sand in from the face back to where it went vertical. We put the sand around bunk gardens. You'd always have diversions. You'd start fights, or have games, football, volleyball, soccer, and scuffle things around. You'd have these little bags you would wear inside your pants leg and you'd pull a little pin and the sand would trickle out."

The guards knew that the prisoners were engaged in some kind of plot. The "ferret"—a guard equipped with a long steel pole—poked the floor and heard a hollow sound. "They found the big one," said Jones, "and about that time they moved the Americans." While the Yanks occupied another compound, their former comrades, the British, continued to seek freedom through digging. In what became known as "the Great Escape" seventy-eight individuals broke out of the camp through the tunnel. According to Jones, two Norwegians and a Dane escaped completely. "They shot fifty. Some of them they turned back to camp but the Gestapo shot fifty. They had two or three in the car and they stopped to let them relieve themselves and they'd shoot them in the back of the head. The British ran a very thorough investigation after the war."

From the Doolittle raid of Tokyo, Robert Hite, a copilot, was one of the crewmen who bailed out over an occupied section of China and quickly fell into the hands of the Japanese. He and his companions underwent weeks of daily interrogations, sprinkled with physical abuse, including water torture. Lodged in a Shanghai prison, sleeping on a platform of boards with little food, the flyers were afflicted with painful boils and one crewman, Dean Hallmark, developed dysentery.

"About 19 or 20 August, the Japanese came into our cell and they took Dean and put him on a stretcher. Bill Farrow and I carried either end and took him to a truck. At Kiangwan Military Prison on the outskirts of Shanghai, we had a farce court-martial. We were all brought in and the Japanese acting as the tribunal, about four of them, had on English wigs, which I think was a mockery. There was a guard with a rifle standing in all the doorways and windows of the area. We had brought Dean Hallmark on the stretcher. They asked each of us to give our name and rank. We gave it. Dean could not; I think he was too weak to talk. Then they announced in Japanese our so-called sentence. We didn't really know what it was. The interpreter said, 'They asked me not to tell you.' They dismissed us and put us into solitary cells. They took Dean back to the Bridge House and apparently got him over his dysentery, somewhat.

"Our interpreter was a Portuguese named Cesar Luis don Remedios. About a month later we were taken out of our cells, but this time there were only five of us, three were missing. They told us that the results of our court-martial had been determined and we had been given the death penalty. That was hanging over us. Remedios said, 'But you have been reprieved to life imprisonment with "special treatment," that if the Americans win the war, you are to be shot and if the Japanese win the war, you are to be kept as slave labor.'

"That was a pretty tremendous blow. We were more or less sort of stunned. We were put back in solitary confinement and stayed there until the following April. We didn't know exactly what had happened when we realized that three of our compatriots were not with us. We felt that maybe they were holding three of the people over our heads to keep us from attempting to escape. We didn't know until the end of the war that they had been executed."

Moved to a prison in Nanking, Hite used some money he still had at the time of his capture to prevail upon the guards to buy some bread, which helped him over an illness. However, in November 1943, dysentery attacked the man in the next cell, Bob Meder, who rapidly lost weight and grew weaker and weaker. One day a guard shoved Meder, who summoned up enough bravado to throw a punch at him. He missed and fell to the ground. "That particular afternoon we tried to find out if there was anything we could do, and he said, 'Just pray.' " From his adjoining compartment, Hite heard Meder give a guard his address and ask that if he died would the man write his parents and send them his clothes. "Later, around dinnertime, when they stuck the food in Bob Meder's cell, the guard started yelling. Two or three others came running down the hall, opened the door, and went in. They kept yacking and yacking and then brought a doctor. Bob Meder had died that afternoon, sitting right in the cell."

The other Americans were given a brief viewing of their dead comrade before a cremation of the remains. We thought, 'Any of us can die at any time. We could all die and they could do away with us and nobody would ever know the difference.' It was an eerie feeling and I asked to write a letter to the prison governor. I [said] their so-called treatment of prisoners was against all Geneva conference rules [Japan was not a signatory], that our rations were outrageous or inadequate. It was a complaint letter. I asked, 'If you can't do anything else, will you please give us the Holy Bible to read?'

"I read the Bible and passed it on to Jake [Jacob deShazer]. Jake had proclaimed to be an atheist. His father was a preacher. He said he didn't believe in all that stuff. He didn't see any fruits of the so-called Christianity. It was the first time I ever—the first time any of us—had really read the Bible from cover to cover. It was sort of like a man being in the desert and finding a cool pool. After reading the Bible all of our attitudes changed. Instead of hating this enemy that we had had such hate for, we began to feel sorry for them and to see them through the eyes of Jesus or God—or through the Word, at least. It was almost a miracle to realize what happened to us. It seemed we were not afraid, to the extent we had been, at least. We no longer had the hatred. I think I lived on hate for the first year and a half. I think we were able to kind of keep ourselves living on the hate, instead of lying down and giving up."

One day while outside exercising they saw the silhouette of a B-29. "The Japanese had not seen it or heard it. Bombs dropped on the Yangtze River area and they ran us back in. These 29s were flying from way down deep in China. On Thanksgiving Day 1944 we had a P-51 raid on the airfield near the prison. When we saw the B-29 and the P-51 that really did strengthen our hope and lifted us up quite a bit."

Richard Carmichael, seized in June 1944 after his B-29 crash-landed on Iki Island, endured physical abuse from his interrogators. "They would hit me in the face with fists, books, and bookends. They would make you kneel and put these bamboo poles across your calves. Somebody would get on either end and start working on those calf muscles. They would put pencils between your fingers and start working on them."

The Japanese organized a court-martial charging Carmichael and three others with indiscriminate bombing that killed civilians. "There were three judges. We had to prove ourselves *innocent.* We were guilty until proven innocent. They had these big maps of Yawata and all the spots of the bomb burst that didn't hit the target. We didn't have any bombs on the target. We had them all killing civilians. [We were not] as in Germany deliberately bombing the cities. It was a military target, a recognized one. It was just our overage, shorts, rights and lefts. They were real serious about this. We were using high explosives. What got us off the hook was the fire raid. When LeMay brought those B-29s down to 5,000 to 9,000 feet that mass attack with firebombs, made use of the high-explosive, military target type of thing, look pretty good by comparison. So they decided not to shoot us."

The Doolittle raid flyers interned in the Soviet Union spent an uncomfortable two years, even though they had landed in the country of an ally. Living conditions were spartan and their freedom severely restricted. Visited by American brass, internee Robert Emmens reported, "In a nutshell they said, 'We are doing what we can for you guys. There is a big war going on. You guys ought to be happy that you are here and not out in combat somewhere. We will do what we can.' " For the moment that amounted to carrying out letters to families and a pledge to send toothpaste, soap, and similar items. Later a U.S. general and the ambassador appeared, an occasion for a feast but the American authorities could not assure their release.

By January 1944, Emmens and his colleagues in desperation wrote a letter to Joseph Stalin volunteering to help with training Red airmen in B-25s and failing this asked to be moved to a warmer climate. No immediate response came but subsequently a piano appeared in their quarters to provide recreation and they were treated to the opera and theatricals. Their hosts moved the crew west, through Samarkand to Ashkhabad, capital of the Turkmenistan Republic and on the edge of Persia—modern Iran. Given work in a factory, but with no prospect of freedom, Emmens and Ed York schemed to escape into Iran. They enlisted a Soviet acquaintance who with some $300 chipped in by the five Americans bribed a truck driver to smuggle them past the border guards into the town of Mashad. Once inside Iranian territory, they dashed through the gates of a British consulate. "We were transported then to Washington," said Emmens, "and we were told that under no circumstances were we allowed to say that we were part of the Doolittle raid group that was interned in Russia, that Russia was very upset at our leaving. They did not want the Japanese to know that we were out."

Initially, Emmens believed they achieved their freedom through their own efforts. But subsequently he wondered whether their escape had been a sham, a devious arrangement by the Soviets to be rid of a troublesome matter. As an added insult, the American embassy billed the quintet about $600 for parkas, tobacco, postage stamps, and medicine but no one offered to refund the $300 the escapees spent obtaining their freedom.

Those who found refuge in neutral Sweden fared considerably better. With their families assured of their safety, crews like that of Ralph Golubock, who had been forced to land in Sweden and been interned, settled into a comfortable life as tourists restricted only by the borders of the country. Golubock even spent the Jewish High Holidays with a local Jewish family. During one excursion to Stockholm the Air Corps men noticed another group of young men surrounded by Swedes as they were. Someone who spoke English informed Golubock and his colleagues that the others were all German Luftwaffe pilots.

While none of the German stalags matched the brutality or the subhuman living conditions of O'Donnell, in the Philippines, the GIs taken prisoner endured similar shortages of food, the ravages of bad nutrition, and the diseases spawned by inadequate sanitation. John Collins, who participated in a last stand before St.-Vith during the Battle of the Bulge, recalled, "Seven men to a loaf of bread, a little oleo, one cup of soup called 'scilly'—good for shaving or washing your face—and their coffee—hot water. Also we receive[d] a few potatoes at noon, if available. About three times a week, a can of bully beef or maybe horsemeat for six men." Cigarettes served as the chief currency of the Kriegsgefangeners—kriegies—40 or 50 bought a can of Nescafé, 70 or 80 bought bread. A good watch might earn between 250 and 600 smokes."

In Collins's camp they slept in huts on tiers of boards. "The barracks were infested with lice and fleas. The big fat ones stay in all tight places of clothing. You cannot get rid of them so you try to educate them by ignoring them." The filth of the latrine across the street spilled on floors although prisoners from the Red Army were supposed to clean the repository. According to Collins, Red Cross parcels went only to men who volunteered for work parties. The Americans and British refused but the French agreed to perform labor in return for the packages. Through the exchange of cigarettes, the contents of the Red Cross parcels reached some GIs.

Phil Hannon from the 106th Division observed discipline enforced by the POWs. "Any man caught stealing from another prisoner was automatically put in the 'outcast barracks.' First he was thrown into the open latrine pit, and men from the quarters where he stole stood around the pit and urinated on him. Theft from the Germans was accepted practice, so long as it didn't endanger anyone else. Others who ended up in the outcast barracks were those who fought constantly or had such disgusting habits that their associates voted them out. The outcast barracks GIs pulled the 'honey dipping detail,' emptying out the latrine and hauling the mess away. The punishment deterred a lot of thieves."

Hannon and his fellows developed unquenchable cravings for food. "I remember dreaming of a roast beef dinner with mashed potatoes and gravy. I could actually smell the gravy but I couldn't eat it and I woke myself up crying. Each of us would make up elaborate meals we would have when we got home and we tried to outdo each other. When we first became prisoners, we felt cheated, being out of the war. For a while we were hard on ourselves, as if we had been captured because we hadn't done our job properly. The attitude changed after a few days of walking and starving. We became much more individually oriented, thinking of ourselves, instead of what we failed to do for the army. Some of the men were loners. They didn't team up or seem to need cozying up. They were self-reliant, able to make it on their own. There were those rejected by everyone else because of the ways they acted or for their personal habits. They couldn't cozy up and had a difficult time. There were those, a very few, who literally gave up in the POW camp.

They'd roll over and in a couple of days they were dead. That was their escape, but their behavior was totally beyond my comprehension. I was just amazed when a person would shrivel up and die; they were not being treated any worse than anyone else."

Ed Uzemack relished a windfall of Red Cross–supplied chocolate bars, cigarettes, meat, fish, crackers, butter, raisins, sugar, coffee, powdered milk, vitamin pills, and soap. "It was explained that the boxes came as a loan from Serbian prisoners—God bless them—who had a surplus. We got one box for each four men." Uzemack said he became giddy after puffing on his first cigarette in forty-five days. During the first month at Stalag XI B, only three of the 4,000 prisoners succumbed, thanks in large measure to the work of a medical officer, said Uzemack. The figure would climb steeply in ensuing months.

Along with starvation, disease, and the deadly force from their captors, U.S. airplanes also brought destruction. Said Uzemack, "Yank planes chasing the Heinies accidently strafed the camp. Val Casados, my last buddy here, was killed. He was standing beside our bunk talking to me when bullets sprayed all around us. How those .50-caliber slugs missed me, I'll never know. One hit the bedpost a few inches from my head. Two other men were killed and twelve more wounded."

Jim Mills of the 106th Division joined a labor gang assigned to work clearing rubble in Dresden. The prisoners lived in an abandoned abattoir, later famous as *Slaughterhouse Five.* When the massive raids by RAF and the U.S. Air Corps transformed much of Dresden into a crematorium, the Germans put Mills and other POWs to work removing bodies from a basement. "There was a body lying on the floor where a hall led to the next building, and it had been hit right at the waistline with one of the incendiary bombs. The body was almost burnt in half.

"The guard pointed at the corpse as one I should remove. He indicated I take a belt off another body and put it around the one I was to remove. It's surprising how much could be communicated by hand motions. I put a belt around the neck of this man and started to drag it toward the ramp. But it broke in half. That was too much for me. I sort of lost it for a bit. I began to scream, yell, and dance around. I tried to get out of there but they wouldn't let me."

Given a draft of liquor for his ragged nerves, Mills returned to his gruesome task. "The guards forced me to pick up the top half of the body, put it on a stretcher at the base of the ramp. They made another man pick up the bottom half. He didn't like it any better than I did and told me so. We carried the remains out and put them on the street alongside several others. We then got back at the end of the line. As we neared the head of it we would slip out of the line and go to the rear, trying to avoid going back into the basement. Finally the guards caught us and put us at the front. In the cellar again, I thought I would be smart. I picked a fellow who had on a gas mask. I thought all I would need do is drag him by the mask to the stretcher. But when I grabbed the mask and pulled, it popped off his head. His eyes looked as if they were almost out of their sockets. His mouth was wide open and the whole face and mouth was covered with blood. I lost my cool again and the guards had me drink some more liquor. I remember taking out the body to the pile but the rest of the day is no longer part of my memory. From there on this was our daily job. We cleaned up the rubble and removed any bodies found."

Casual and calculated killing menaced anyone in a prison camp. The Germans housed the Ranger officers captured in the disaster at Cisterna in Stalag XIII B, at Hammelburg. Clarence Meltesen recalled, "The shooting of Lt. John Weeks was cold-blooded murder by a German gate guard. On the sixteenth the guard in question had been noticed at his post and muttering to the men as they passed on their way. Later an explanation was offered that the guard had recently lost his wife in an air-raid attack. When Weeks went by, and after turning the corner, the guard steadied his rifle on the wire and shot him in the back of the head." The camp commandant apologized to the senior American officer and a brief funeral interred the lieutenant in a cemetery with a growing number of residents from XIII B. Bing Evans, a Ranger captured at Cisterna, said he witnessed so many incidents of abuse and murder that he developed a lifelong affliction of periodic black rages.

The sustained, massive bombing that did not spare civilians added to the jeopardy of those airmen shot down. German police and civilians clubbed, shot, or stabbed to death four members of a crew, including the pilot, Capt. Herb Newman, after enemy fighters knocked their plane out of the sky. While evadee pilot Howard Snyder, who had trained as an infantryman before volunteering for the Air Corps, joined the Belgian Maquis, other members of his crews also hid out with local people. On the morning of 22 April 1944, eight American airmen, including George Eike, Snyder's copilot, his navigator Robert Benninger, and gunner John Pindroch, ate breakfast in a hut owned by a Belgian farmer. Plans had been set for the evadees to seek safety. They were given money, some received civilian clothing. Suddenly, a party of as many as 1,500 soldiers, Gestapo and Belgian collaborators descended on the area and seized the Americans along with those who harbored them.

The captives were taken to a nearby schoolhouse for interrogation. All of them still had their dog tags, which identified them as military personnel, but, except for Eike and Benninger, were out of uniform. Around 2:30 in the afternoon the Americans were loaded into a truck and under guard driven to a nearby woods. Lined up in single file, with a pair of soldiers behind each one, they were marched into the forest. Some 500 feet from the road, each airman was moved in a separate direction, still accompanied by his two Germans carrying pistols. Upon a prearranged signal, the soldiers shot the captives in the back three or four times and left them for dead. Sometime later, the bodies were buried in a common grave. A pair of Belgians who had been acting as hosts to the evadees disappeared into concentration camps.

The behavior of those held by the Germans varied considerably. Fighter pilot Henry Spicer, the senior officer in his camp until the arrival of Hub Zemke, became a sharp thorn to his captors. Interviewing newcomers Spicer heard tales of mistreatment by civilians and soldiers. He may also have had an opportunity to witness the brutality meted out to Soviet captives. In any event, Spicer soon became the instigator of resistance to the camp routine as the captives harassed guards, mucked up their roll call counts, and challenged any behavior proscribed by the Geneva convention. When Zemke came to the camp and became the prisoner leader, he supported Spicer's campaign. On a frigid November morning with the entire population rousted from the barracks to stand shivering in the open air the guards exacted their own revenge as they stretched out the count from the normal fifteen minutes to two interminable hours.

At this point, according to Lt. Philip Robertson, "Colonel Spicer dismissed us, over the loud protestations of the German guards. He then called us over to his barracks, and we gathered around him, as he stood on the steps about three feet above us and began to talk loud enough for the guards to hear."

Captain Mozart Kaufman, in the audience, and who later reconstructed with others Spicer's speech, said the outspoken fighter pilot first recounted an incident in the stalag. "Yesterday an officer was put in the 'cooler' for two weeks. He had two counts against him. The first was failure to obey an order of a German officer. That is beside the point. The second was failure to salute a German officer of lower rank.

"The Articles of the Geneva convention say to salute all officers of equal or higher rank. The Germans in this camp have put out an order that we must salute all German officers, whether of lower or higher rank. My order to you is salute all German officers of equal or higher rank." Spicer then shifted to other matters. "I have noticed that many of you are becoming too buddy-buddy with the Germans. [Irwin Stovroff saw officers, including ones of higher rank, cozy up to their captors in return for small favors, such as an egg.] Remember we are still at war with the Germans. They are still our enemies and are doing everything they can to win this war. Don't let them fool you around this camp, because they are dirty, lying sneaks and can't be trusted."

The prisoners cheered loudly and a German major, outraged at the tirade, ordered Spicer into the "cooler," a small cell about six by eight feet. The camp authorities held a court-martial, charging him with inciting a riot. The initial sentence was six months in the cooler and then death by firing squad. When the men happened to be led past Spicer's cell they yelled encouragement and Spicer would reply with words like, "Keep fighting! Don't give in to the bastards." After he had endured a number of months in solitary, his jailers relented, canceling the orders for execution and returning him to the general population.

Conditions in the prison camps had begun to deteriorate further as the Soviet armies to the east and the Americans and British to the west squeezed the area controlled by the Germans and food supplies shrank. Bombardier Irwin Stovroff, shot down in August while aboard *Passion Pit,* had taken the precaution to toss away his dogtags, which identified him as Jewish. But on 19 January 1945, with the entire compound population drawn up for the usual roll call and count, the commandant ordered all Jewish prisoners to take one step forward. Before anyone could respond, Spicer, backed by Zemke, shouted for all of the Americans to step out. None of those present hesitated and all obeyed. The solidarity by his comrades in incarceration heartened Stovroff but to his dismay, he and the others of his faith were soon segregated. Luftwaffe intelligence apparently already knew the background of most of their captives.

P-47 pilot Paul Ellington recalled, "The commandant, von Mueller, went to Hub Zemke and asked him for a roster of the Jews. Zemke told him, 'We're all Jews.' I guess von Mueller thought he'd make his job easier. But they knew who the Jews were and put them in some buildings separated from us by a fence. At night, we cut up the fence so people could move back and forth and they never repaired it. Some of the Jews had been treated badly. There was a fellow named Goldstein, from the 56th Fighter Group, and he had been cut badly on his shin when shot down. He was picked up by the Gestapo and they kept kicking him with their steel, pointed boots in that shin. When he got to the camp, his shin was a terrible mess, all scarred. Somehow, they didn't have his name when they separated out the Jews. He went to Zemke and said, 'I feel I ought to go with my people.' Zemke said, 'You've had enough trouble already. Keep your mouth shut.' "

For the next four months, Stovroff and those with him feared the worst. Spicer, who once again had annoyed the authorities, drew no extra punishment for his attempt to shield the Jewish prisoners. Apparently, the camp officials accepted him as a hard case. Although Stovroff had been fearful of his future once the officials separated the Jewish prisoners, he experienced no ill treatment. Stovroff recalls a brief visit to camp by Max Schmeling, the former world heavyweight boxing champion, who said, "I wish you all luck and hope to see you in the States." He handed out photographs. "We put them in the urinals," says Stovroff.

Perhaps the most dangerous status of the prisoners was to be in transit. Jim McCubbin said, "A German army sergeant told a group of us, consisting of about one hundred, that we were to be transported by train to a prisoner of war camp in Nürnberg. He [said] he had taken this trip with other prisoners twenty-six times and had been strafed by our fighters twenty-five times. The train was an ordinary passenger one with three boxcars attached to the end with a flak car between. Half of the car was roped off for the guards, and some thirty prisoners shared the other half. There was only room for a few to sit. The remainder had to stand. There were two openings high up on the side walls through which one could gain a limited view. We had only been traveling several hours when the 'lookouts' shouted that two Mustangs were strafing the locomotive. The two lookouts dived for the floor, allowing several others and myself to then gain access to the view. I was just in time to see the fighters starting a run down the length of the train. As I turned to join the heap on the floor, the only opening was on the top. I shall never forget the sound of those .50-caliber bullets crashing through the wood and bodies. It reminded me of the game played in bars where you shake five dice in a wooden cup for drinks. There were two passes, but I didn't hear the second. That time I was thankful for the German flak car. If it hadn't been for them, I know the planes would have made several more passes." McCubbin adds, "I should know. I had done this frequently.

"In all, there were about sixteen prisoners killed, about the same number of civilians, and many wounded. Later, after the bodies were laid out and the wounded identified, a German medical officer and several orderlies began to attend to those in need. I was impressed to witness how the wounded were attended without regard for nationality." Marched to another rail line to resume the journey, McCubbin endured a dive-bomb attack from P-47s. Watching the bombs leave the wings, he says, "I remembered that you were supposed to lie down but to keep your stomach off the ground. The bombs landed so far away I hardly noticed them. But that gave me a feeling of life in the infantry. I was much more scared than I had ever been in the air."

As the Soviet armies advanced toward the German border, the Nazis started to drive prisoners housed in the east toward the Americans and British, perhaps to use as bargaining chips. It became a death march as weakened kriegies collapsed from unhealed wounds, disease, or hunger and either froze to death or else guards murdered them. In some instances, the prisoners carried a sick man to the door of a house and after knocking left him there, hoping for mercy from the inhabitants.

In his role as medical officer, Lu Cox tended the sick and injured, but his supplies were so limited he could mostly offer only Band-Aids for blisters. The torturous hike in the worst snowstorm Cox had ever seen covered 100 miles, and all along the way they saw a vast caravan of German refugees, old men and women, small children and babies, in farm wagons pulled by oxen or on foot, also fleeing the oncoming Soviets. At the end of a nearly six-day journey, the surviving prisoners crowded into boxcars that carried them to their new home, a huge camp that eventually held more than 100,000 Allied prisoners. In his compound Cox says, "A thousand men were flat on their backs suffering from advanced stages of diarrhea, flu, pneumonia, dysentery, malnutrition, exposure, frostbite, frozen feet, and irritated and reopened wounds. There were no doctors, next to no medical supplies, not even a place fit to lie down. After appealing time after time for medical help from the Germans, the worst patients were taken out of the camp and given showers and deloused and moved into another compound. The most serious were removed to the hospital." Cox and the others in better condition now coped with the omnipresent frigid temperatures, sanitation problems, and a diet he describes as "unfit for pigs to eat, for it contained bits of wire, wood, worms, bugs, and sometimes a dead mouse."

While some felt escape was hopeless, others persisted in their attempts. Bill Topping said, "I tried five times to escape, digging tunnels. Hell, the Germans knew we were digging them. They'd let us alone and by the time we were ready to pop out, they'd swoop in and catch us. It gave us something to do and kept us busy. I played so much bridge in the camp that I became sick of it. I played solitaire, listened to stories that got bigger and longer as you stayed there."

Marshall Draper, the bombardier shot down on the fourth of July 1942, endured one of the longest stays of an American behind the wire. He reported, "Most of the activities of the camp revolved around escaping. The accounts I have read or seen about tunneling or other escape efforts at Stalag Luft III seem to indicate that these were primarily activities of men from the RAF. As a matter of fact, the Americans were heavily involved and supplied a good deal of labor and technical expertise for such enterprises. I was number 101 on the priority list to go through a tunnel if and when it was completed. I contracted diphtheria in the summer of 1943 and was quarantined in the sick bay for a couple of weeks, during which time one of the tunnels was discovered. A few days later, the Americans were separated from the RAF and moved to a different compound, away from the two other partially built tunnels.

He confirms the account of David Jones. "Of these two, one was discovered by the Germans, but the other, closed down for the winter, was successfully completed the following spring and resulted in the exit from the North Compound of seventy-six RAF men. Three of these, two Norwegians and a Dutchman, made it home. Fifty of the recaptured men were shot by the Gestapo, fifteen returned to the camp, and eight were sent to the Oranienburg concentration camp. In point of fact, only a few men made good their escape. The remainder could only wait for the arrival of the advancing troops."

10

The Battle for Manila

THE FLYING COLUMNS THAT PENETRATED THE MANILA OUT-skirts struck from the northeast. At first the overall plan envisioned a move by the 11th Airborne parachutists and glidermen that would block any attempt to relieve the Manila garrison from the south. Subsequently, Gen. Robert Eichelberger, in charge of the U.S. Eighth Army, received permission from MacArthur to change the mission and attack Manila from the south, penetrating what was known as the Genko line. With two glider-infantry teams ashore from a seaborne operation that placed them a scant forty-five miles from Manila, the script posited an airborne drop on Tagaytay Ridge, heights that overlooked the strongest fortifications of the defenders. Building upon the former U.S. installations of Nichols Field and Fort McKinley over a three-year period, the Japanese had constructed reinforced concrete pillboxes dominating the avenues into the city. In the passage of time nature contributed vegetation to augment skillful camouflage.

The glider-infantrymen progressed swiftly toward Manila until they bumped up against an enemy dug in along the slopes of the mountains between them and the city. Medic Al Ullman scribbled in his diary for 2 February, "Tired of marching, slept on the ground last night. Expect trouble soon. At noon it happened. Jap artillery opened up, everyone dived for ditches but some were not so lucky. At least 10 killed and no wounded. Assisted major in performing an amputation in a ditch with a trench knife, artillery landing around us. A miserable day. That night was on guard, boy, was I scared."

After some debate about the risks of an airborne drop on Tagaytay, Gen. Joseph Swing's paratroopers crowded aboard C-47s on Leyte on the morning of 3 February, the same day the first Americans burst into Manila from the northeast. With only forty-eight transports available, the troop carriers flew a dangerous three-shift operation, one in which the last two serials could anticipate deadly antiaircraft fire from an alerted enemy.

William "Buzz" Miley, as leader of the 2d platoon in Company G, said, "We were in the first echelon. I will always remember the beautiful sight of Lake Taal as we approached from the south, made a wide circle around the lake, and dropped on an east-to-west pass. Even though later reports stated we jumped early, I don't believe my stick did since we landed just north of the Manila Extension Hotel, about 200–330 yards from the highway. We landed without incident, assembled, and started moving south to the highway. We smelled a terrific stench and discovered a dead Filipino next to a small fire. His feet had been burned off. We naturally assumed that the Japanese had done it but none were sighted until that afternoon."

Although Miley describes an uneventful drop, as happened so often, the deliveries significantly missed the marks. As the first seventeen aircraft dropped men right over the target, the lead ship of the second section dumped its equipment bundles. Figuring this was their cue, jumpmasters standing in the doors of the trailing planes signaled go. The parachutes of 540 troopers blossomed and the jumpers touched down four to five miles away from the drop zone on Tagaytay Ridge. After the planes returned to Leyte and loaded up again they repeated the mistake, as the jumpmasters, peering down, cued on the discarded chutes of the earlier jumpers. Purely by luck, and unknown to the descending paratroopers, the Japanese had not posted any troops on Tagaytay Ridge. The Americans who landed there escaped serious consequences from the error. A day later, the final batch of troopers dropped in the proper place.

The men of the 11th forging toward Tagaytay Ridge on the ground joined their comrades who came by air. Troopers and glidermen attacked the foremost enemy emplacements. Hard fighting followed as the outfit forced a crossing over the Parañaque River. Al Ullman's diary reports, "Today we had 19 wounded men to be evacuated. By now a man's guts are no new sight to me. Today the first of my buddies died from his wounds. I kept saying my prayers."

As the airborne GIs slogged toward Manila, the 1st Cavalry began the job of evicting the defenders. "We beat the 37th [Division] into Manila," recalls Sal DeGaetano, "but only after crawling across bombed-out bridges and past dead civilians. We came into a courtyard and spotted some Japs across Malate Circle at a gas station and house. We crossed to the opposite side of the street to the station where the Japs had disappeared. I heard voices from a basement window, level with the ground. I recognized the language and tossed a grenade, at the same time as one came out. I had dropped to the ground and when I heard my grenade go off, I raised up and got bits of shrapnel in my wrist, head, and shoulder. Luckily, I had raised my hand or I might have been hit in the left eye." Medics evacuated DeGaetano to a hospital in Quezon City.

From southwest of Manila, the 38th Division, with the 34th Regiment of the 24th Division attached, expected to cut across the top of the Bataan peninsula and meet the troops driving down from Lingayen Gulf on the highway between Clark Field and the city. Paul Austin, promoted from company commander to executive officer of the 34th's 2d Battalion, endured a miserable march of nineteen miles in the heat before his outfit reached the now-deserted town of Olongapo. From there the GIs traveled east along a road known as Zig Zag Trail. It was a mountainous area and all the terrain sloped down toward the south to the edges of the road, which zigged and zagged around each ridge.

"We were in reserve when the 38th made contact with the Japanese," said Austin. "They had had two and a half years to prepare their defenses along Zig Zag Pass and done their work very well. Back on the highway, three or four miles behind the 38th, we saw those two-and-a-half-ton trucks haul men out of there, bodies piled in the back like cordwood. They had the road under observation and as our troops moved into a certain area, all they had to do was go to their reference table, put the gun to a certain setting, fire half a dozen rounds, and literally blow men to pieces. It was that accurate.

"We moved up closer on February 3d. We hiked in under a 90mm mortar barrage. It came walking down the road and as the shells got closer and closer, I grabbed the base of a tree trunk and flung my body over the edge of a deep dropoff. I hung my body over that gully, while clinging to that tree. I was scared. There is nothing more terrifying than those mortar shells. You cannot hear them coming. You have no warning. Before you hear anything at all, it has already exploded, thrown, or torn your body. I managed to get back up and we moved on.

"The 38th was pulled back for reorganization and rest. They had suffered tremendous casualties. We continued up the road. We had a couple of tanks with us, artillery firing coming over constantly. We drove 'em back probably a quarter of a mile. The next day we made maybe half a mile. On February 6, we ran into several mortar barrages that literally destroyed the 2d Battalion. F Company walked into a forty-round barrage and they came out with just twelve men. A sergeant came to me crying, tears running down his face. He was devastated. All his friends were gone. It was a family thing and it tears at a man's guts when the family he's been living with, trying to survive with, the men he loved and respected and that loved him, and they're all gone."

Joe Hofrichter, the onetime engineer reassigned to F Company, had developed a blister from ill-fitting shoes and the extended marches to Zig Zag. "We had two Sherman tanks that led our convoy of a few vehicles, and a truck with ammunition and other supplies followed. I asked the driver if it would be okay to ride on the back of the truck until we got up through the pass. He said 'Hop on,' and I did. Slowly the tanks and truck crawled forward. About three-fourths of the way to the summit, we came to a wide curve and relatively straight piece of exposed road. Suddenly, to the right and above us, all hell seemed to come alive. I saw the first tank get hit and begin to burn. Almost immediately, the tank in front of my truck was struck a glancing blow that spun it to the right. An antitank gun trained on the rear of that tank missed its target and hit the left front of our truck, blowing it and everyone in it over the side into a ravine in the dense jungle.

"As I flew into the air, I saw a shoe flying by. What's my shoe doing there, I wondered! In a split second it was over. I have no recollection of where or how I landed. After seeing the shoe, my mind went blank. When I opened my eyes, it was dark and I was lying on a cot. I had no idea where I was, how I got there, what time it was, nor for that matter, what day it was. I next became conscious that I was in great pain. My legs were numb and my back hurt so badly, I could hardly breathe. To my left I saw what looked like a huge person, lying completely still. To my right was a man on a cot, leaning on his elbow and looking at me. In a thick Southern accent, he whispered, 'How ya all doin? I heard ya moanin.'

" 'I hurt,' I replied. 'Where in the heck am I?'

" 'Youse in a hospital in Olongapo.'

"About that time someone walked between our beds and turned on a flashlight. I thought I had died and gone to heaven. A foot away was the face of a beautiful woman. She said, 'Hi, I see you are awake. I'm Lieutenant Powell.' She told me I was brought in late that afternoon. They had dug some shrapnel from my back, which was severely damaged. She gave me a shot of morphine and I drifted off to sleep. When I awakened I saw I was in a room with thirty wounded men. The fellow next to me with the Southern accent was a black man from South Carolina. He was a cook and was burned on the legs when a field stove blew up. After watching them administer my first injections of morphine with three needles, he would often say, 'Man, how in hell can ya take those long-ass needles.' He couldn't understand that I looked forward to them to manage the pain. The big fellow to my right had a severe wound in his stomach. He was in bad shape and had gone into shock. Brought in with me, he died three days later."

Wireman Han Rants with the 2d Battalion Headquarters Company had placed telephone lines for communications. Around 4:00 P.M. he heard the sound of heavy blasts in the E Company sector. Notified that communications were out, Rants led a wire section to repair the telephone system. "Each of the shells that had come in had been a direct hit, as if someone had been looking at the men and dropped the shells right on them. The shock was seeing a body lodged up a small tree. There were bodies blown in all directions. They had thirty-four killed and many wounded. We established a new line, got the wounded and the bodies of the dead back to Headquarters Company for the move back to regiment.

"We were just settled, the time probably about 5:00 P.M., still daylight. We heard five more thunderous explosions like those that had hit E Company. These were in the direction of F and G Companies. We just assumed they had been hit horribly with the same big mortars. It was such a sickening sound. Again we took off to be sure the line was in place. We took some able-bodied soldiers, plus medics because we knew there would be casualties again. The sight was almost the same as seeing E Company. There were many guys blown apart, badly wounded with lots of need for medics, and many, many dead. We repeated the same operation we had with E Company but just could not get all the dead because it was getting late at night."

On the following morning, the huge mortars zeroed in on the Headquarters Company position. "I was perched on a field telephone, sitting just off the ground, eating some breakfast after the days of heavy, heavy work and fighting. Even in the fear, hunger came through. As I sat there, these shells exploded and I was blown some six feet into a hole."

The carnage was fearsome, wiping out close associates, exposing Rants to sights of dismembered dead comrades. One man could only be identified by a ring and watch still around the remnant of an arm.

Austin spent an anguished night in a foxhole with Major Snavely, his CO, and in the morning greeted a handful of men on the road. "There was an artillery observation team sitting there, two or three medical jeeps with aidmen eating their breakfast, C rations. I squatted down talking with the sergeant of the observation team when I got a funny feeling. Something was going on in my gut, maybe diarrhea. It got very intense, a feeling I had to move and which I couldn't resist. I walked back up to my foxhole, put on my steel helmet, wondering why I was doing it. At that instant, three 90mm mortar shells hit in the area. One struck dead center of the forward observation team. Another landed in the road and destroyed the jeeps with the medics. The third exploded in the foxhole with the battalion sergeant major and killed him. That was it. They fired just these three rounds. I went back down the road. All of the men I had been talking to were blown to pieces. Body parts lay all around the rations; the medics had shrapnel wounds that tore their bodies up. One man was blown in two and I saw a boot with a leg still in it.

"About that time, Major Snavely and the battalion surgeon, Dr. Cameron, showed up and told me to take every man I could find down into a gully. Just as we got everybody under cover, the regimental CO, Col. [William] Jenna, rode up in a jeep. He stopped and immediately wanted to know what we were doing, standing there when we were supposed to be moving up the road in an attack. He said to me, 'Captain, get those men out of that ditch and up on the road and start moving.' I said, 'Yes, sir.' I was in a battlefield situation in the face of the enemy and my colonel had given me an order and the only thing I could do was obey.

"Dr. Cameron asked if he could speak with Colonel Jenna and when given permission told him the situation of the 2d Battalion. He said he knew where all the units were, and their approximate strength, and in effect told the colonel, 'You don't have a 2d Battalion anymore.' Colonel Jenna said, 'I didn't know this. I'll have trucks up here in an hour and you're going back to a rest area.' We went back to our holes and sure enough trucks came and carried us back twenty miles to a bivouac area on a stream with shade trees. I spent several miserable days there as I thought about our friends and what had happened to them."

"On the first night just out of Zig Zag Pass," says Rants, "I made a decision that has made my entire life a series of blessings in God's service. I had believed I was a Christian because I believed in God and lived the kind of life I thought he would want me to live. An occasional trip to church perhaps three or four times a year was a way of confirming my support. I was very grateful to God for the physical gifts I had, but I really thought that I was the one who performed the deeds and God simply said, 'Well done.' This night I realized that I was not in control at all and that I had been accepting credit and compliments for achievements which he was responsible for. The fact that I had been blown through the air and received only a small wound was one more in a series of miracles, a blessing, if you will, which I finally realized God was providing. He gave me direction in the kinds of things I did, had me in the right place at the right time. As I prayed and talked with God, I asked forgiveness for feeling that I had done so much and I surrendered all credit to his glory. I told him that whatever amount of days or nights I had left in my life would all be dedicated to his service."

The official figures reported 325 battle casualties for the 34th Infantry and 25 psychoneurosis cases in less than a week, nearly half as many as were lost during 78 days of combat on Leyte. Austin insisted the total was closer to 1,200 at Zig Zag, but he may have included the losses to the 38th Division in his count. The results at Zig Zag brought the dismissal of the 38th Division commander as well as assorted regimental and staff officers for a "lack of aggressiveness." Austin, from his perspective, responds, "From General MacArthur on down, every one of our leaders knew that place was fortified, but they sent us in there, men with rifles and grenades, and they chewed us to pieces. We had no air support, did not bomb the area before we went in, didn't napalm it, nothing to soften it up for the infantry. Later they fired the entire load of 105 ammo from a Liberty ship into the Japanese on Zig Zag Pass. They marked it off in sections and gave a section to each gun, literally blowing the area to bits. Finally, when the boys with rifles got up there, they could pretty much walk through with no problem." In addition, planes from the the airfield on Luzon repeatedly bombed the area.

While the GIs waged a deadly contest for the route from the west coast, the 37th Division, on the right flank, beaten into Manila by the 1st Cavalry with its more mechanized troops, nibbled at the edges of the city on 4 February and after a respite at a brewery, where they slaked their thirst, the GIs moved out. They walked cautiously down Rizal Avenue toward Bonifacio Monument, with nary an incident other than outbursts from cheering throngs. By nightfall, the beery battalion settled in a few miles from Bilibid Prison with its imprisoned Americans from 1942. On the following day, an advance element of the 148th approached Bilibid, bearing in mind an intelligence report that said the Japanese planned to blow up an ammunition dump in the prison when the GIs came on the scene.

As members of F Company approached Bilibid, an enemy machine gun sprayed the boulevard and snipers let fly. The soldiers, lounging on the curbs along with the Manilans showering them with greetings and offerings, scattered. A ten-man patrol led by Sgt. Rayford Anderson cautiously attained a vantage point from which they saw a pair of Japanese sentries lolling about the main entrance of Bilibid. Anderson gave the word and a fusillade of bullets cut down both guards. The commotion aroused hostile but ineffectual bursts from a nearby machine gunner.

Rather than confront that automatic weapon, Anderson chose to reconnoiter the rear of the building. A member of the patrol shot off the lock from a side entrance and broke into a storage area. Prowling the building, they came upon boarded-up windows. When Anderson pried the slats off he peered out into the prison courtyard and saw about fifty people huddled together. The Americans realized these were Caucasians and probably prisoners. They called out to them, urged them to open a locked iron gate. To the inmates, the unfamiliar silhouettes of the American helmets and their rifles, gear that postdated their knowledge, generated the suspicion that the armed men were Japanese assigned to murder them. The crowd refused to budge. Not even a few verses of "God Bless America" sufficed to convince them. Sergeant Smith tossed in some Philip Morris cigarettes and the smokes persuaded the prisoners. In short order, the entire battalion occupied Bilibid and the surrounding streets, liberating 1,200 people, including several hundred military men, most of whom were in the hospital on the verge of death from their injuries, disease, and malnutrition.

The 754th Tank Battalion with gunner Tom Howard in

Company A had checked in with the 37th Infantry Division and expected to face ferocious opposition as they entered the city streets. Instead it was more like a spontaneous Mardi Gras parade than a war. "The Filipinos came from their homes, their shops, appearing from everywhere to greet us, waving and yelling. Some Filipinos invited us into their homes and set up the drinks. One elderly Filipino man brought out an old bottle of Three Feathers whiskey that he had hidden during the Japanese occupation. He said he had saved it for just this occasion. We gladly helped him drink it. Someone played the piano and others cleared the floor for dancing. To hell with the war. Forgot about eating lunch. 'Snake' [the company commander] came looking for us and even he is dancing."

The 754th tanks rambled deeper into the city, trying to draw a reaction from Japanese soldiers and their locations, but fierce blazes consuming Manila kept both sides from contact. Howard's tank, Boozer 3-4, stopped at Bilibid Prison, now liberated, and then Santo Tomas before it entered the downtown section. With the rear of the tank backed into the entrance of the Commonwealth Life Insurance Building the crew overlooked the strategic Jones Bridge over the Pasig River and received orders to hold the span whatever the cost. Howard remarked, "We had to button up inside the tank because of sniper fire."

Across the Pasig, along its banks and behind fortified emplacements, perhaps 15,000 soldiers and sailors prepared to battle the Americans. To confound their attackers, the defenders detonated preset charges that ignited everything flammable. The fires on the Japanese side leaped the Pasig, raking Manila with a huge, uncontrolled blaze. GIs from the 37th coped with intense heat, ever-prevalent snipers, and pillboxes that dominated approaches to the river.

Tom Howard's 2d platoon led foot soldiers of the 145th Infantry Regiment toward their objective. Howard noted, "The tank commander reported an antitank gun and directed his gunner's fire upon it. The weapon was completely destroyed. Platoon credit for the engagement was 12 dead and was instrumental in killing 113 of the enemy." Subsequently, while protecting the Quezon Bridge, Howard halted a charge by the enemy with rounds of 75mm canister. "The state of siege had settled down into a condition where bodies of civilians and Japanese were still strewn over the streets, in gutters, on lawns, and in the middle of the pavement. Attempts to remove them were met with sniper fire, so instead of removal, when dusk came, the bodies were covered with quicklime to hasten their deterioration and to stifle the smell. Upon entering any of the buildings on sniper patrols, the halls, corridors, and rooms had scattered Japanese bodies that it was impossible to get rid of. To keep from being tricked by a sniper pretending to be dead, we pulled all the bodies to the walls and sat them up leaning against the wall. We proceeded to shoot each one in the forehead regardless of whether they were already dead. In this way, we could immediately tell upon entering a room or a hall if any bluff was being pulled. Anything that lay in the middle of the floor was shot again, then placed against the wall. It was a grotesque, gruesome picture to see these row-by-row bodies along the walls. These were the day-by-day necessities to survive one day more."

From the buildings overlooking the Pasig River environs, the tankers provided an observation post for U.S. artillery, carefully avoiding the eyes of enemy troops who would then shell the structure. "We had to watch while the Japanese soldiers dragged out nuns in their habits and tied them to the flagpole and proceeded to whip them. We had to endure the sight of a group of Japanese soldiers drag Filipino women out into the open and rape them. It was hard to hold fire and observe the events. There was no way to describe the emotion of hate of the Japanese and the anguish of not being able to help the women, but orders were orders."

From the southwest, platoon leader Eli Bernheim of the 11th Airborne contrasted the catch-as-catch-can confrontations in Leyte, where front lines hardly existed, to the fight for Nichols Field. "We had the classic coordinated attack on Nichols Field, airborne artillery, 75mm pack howitzers, against Japanese 5-inch naval guns in concrete pillboxes and many 20mms. It was very, very difficult. My battalion took friendly fire from marine dive-bombers. A 500-pound bomb hit a platoon CP." The struggle for the airbase lasted four bloody days.

The Shimbu Group, an army under Gen. Shizuo Yokoyama, within whose purview Manila came, entertained the notion of a counterattack against what its intelligence faultily described as a limited U.S. presence in the city. At the very least, Yokoyama believed he could open an escape route for Admiral Iwabuchi's men. General Tomoyuki Yamashita, however, angry that Iwabuchi had been permitted to attempt a defense, needlessly sacrificing people, scotched any ambitions of an offensive. He ordered that his subordinate only attempt to extricate the naval soldiers in the city. Yokoyama achieved dismal results. The 1st Cavalry, aided by devastating artillery, slaughtered the Japanese seeking to open a route out of Manila.

At the same time, the paratroopers of the 503d Regimental Combat Team prepared for another daring adventure, the capture of Corregidor. The combined airborne-amphibious operation assigned a battalion from the 24th Division's 34th Regiment to assault the tiny island's beaches. Intelligence figured the Japanese garrison numbered only 850 and with 2,000 GIs dropping from the sky and another 1,000 coming from the sea, the prospects of overwhelming the enemy, particularly through the surprise element of chutists, seemed excellent.

What read well on paper again missed reality and ignored critical factors. Instead of 850 defenders, Corregidor bristled with about 5,000. The highest portion of the island, Topside, 500 feet above sea level, afforded the residents the most devastating opportunities to beat off waterborne invaders and anyone landing on the lower ground. For that reason the Sixth Army planners chose the small areas of the old parade field and golf course on Topside as the drop zones. The restricted size of these targets, the tricky winds and steep cliffs alongside, and the tangle of shell holes and wreckage from the 1942 Japanese attack along with the coarse vegetation, hazarded troopers falling to earth. A shortage of troop carrier planes and the tiny area for the chutists dictated a series of flights, which meant those who arrived first would have to hold off defenders intent on repelling further airborne deliveries.

In the Americans' favor lay the conviction of the defenders that no one would be so foolhardy as to attempt an assault by air. Furthermore, the Japanese underwent a furious bombardment by Air Corps planes and from the Navy. Meanwhile, on Mindoro, paratroopers at dawn on 16 February loaded onto their C-47s. Rod Rodriguez, as a member of G Company of the 503d, recalled the drop. "The 3d Battalion was scheduled to jump at 8:40 A.M. That was H minus 2, two hours before the main assault by sea, and we were to secure the golf course and parade ground for the subsequent jump of the 2d Battalion. Our mission then was to provide fire support for the infantry assaulting Black

Beach, destroy the Japanese positions dug into the cliffs of Topside, and methodically move down the island eliminating the Japanese garrison.

"On the flight over I was a bit tense. I was concerned that the men seated on the other side of the plane and facing me might note my apprehension. I nonchalantly rose and walked to the plane's door, which was removed, to look around. What I saw raised my spirit. There was an impressive array of U.S. power all around us. Above the C-47s were protective flights of P-38s and flying below us were flights of P-47s. In the sea below, the LCIs carrying the 34th Infantry to the beach were already underway. They were being escorted by cruisers and destroyers. It was an inspiring sight.

"We jumped at about 400 feet. I believe this was one of the lowest-level combat jumps made by U.S. parachute troops in World War II. The purpose was to minimize descent time, during which we would be a floating target. Because it takes about 175 feet for the parachute to open, it meant the average trooper had about 225 feet of float time, not very long. The flip side is that any delay in opening may be fatal, and because one has very little time to stabilize the parachute once it opens, jump injuries can also mount. I was just a little over the treetops that lined the golf course when my parachute blossomed. I came crashing down on the edge of the course. The other guys from the platoon landed around me. I quickly slipped out of the harness, ran to the assembly area, and we established a perimeter around the golf course.

"The enemy was caught by surprise and our battalion encountered only sporadic opposition on the jump. It would be different for the 2d Battalion when it jumped two hours later. From our perimeter I could see a number of troopers hit in midair by rifle fire and ack-ack weapons. Others were hit as they landed and for the most part were men who missed the drop zone and came down in the cliffs outside the perimeter.

"A fortunate break occurred when the Japanese commander, [Naval] Capt. Akira Itagaki, was killed by our troops minutes after the landing. With an armed escort he had left his command post on Topside to inspect positions in the cliffs below and observe the amphibious operations. Suddenly, paratroopers who had missed the drop zone landed in his midst. Several of them were killed but Itagaki and virtually all of his armed escort were destroyed in the ensuing firefight." Rodriguez and the others on Topside settled in for the night, setting up machine guns to help cover the amphibians, fortifying their airhead, setting up fire lanes and patrols, tending to the wounded and injured—while combat losses had been low, about 25 percent of the first jumpers had been hurt crashing into ruins of buildings, trees and the ground itself.

"About 4:00 A.M. the man on guard in our three-man foxhole nudged us awake and pointed to the road. There were, perhaps thirty yards from our position, troops moving toward Bottomside. We were pretty sure that they were Japanese, because our troops did not generally move at night. They were not moving directly at us, so to avoid giving away our position, we held our fire. At that moment a flare was fired and illuminated the night sky. It was indeed a Japanese platoon marching toward the beach. Carrying satchels of TNT they raced toward the beach and were met by withering gunfire. Several saw the folly of attempting to penetrate the beach and turned in our direction. We held our fire until they were almost on us and then riddled them.

Four died in front of our position and about thirty were killed in this rather senseless suicidal attack."

To the delight of commanders, the first four waves of landing craft beached their men without opposition. The barrage by naval vessels, the bombs dropped from the air, and the parachutists stunned the defenders, who stayed under cover until the fifth wave made for the shore. By then, the GIs of the 34th Infantry held their initial objectives.

"For several days," says Rodriguez, "we were mainly busy eliminating enemy positions along the cliffs of Topside. They consisted of bunkers, underground tunnels, and caves. Usually a small team would move forward to the target after softening up by artillery or other heavy weapons. The machine guns, BARs, or mortars would lay down fire, while the squad approached the mouth of the fortification. Once you were close enough, the flamethrower or phosphorus grenade did the rest of the job. In other cases, we had air observers attached to our unit who would radio in map coordinates. Once the target had been identified, pilots would dive and drop a napalm bomb with pinpoint precision into the mouth of the bunker or tunnel. The sight of those soldiers running out of their bunkers, engulfed in flames, is a vivid memory."

The climax of the battle for Corregidor occurred about ten days after the troopers descended upon the Rock. An arsenal, cached under Monkey Point, detonated in an enormous blast, caused either by an act of suicide or a U.S.-fired tank shell. "Most of the 1st Battalion," says Rodriguez, "was on top of the hill and the explosion caused many deaths and injuries. We must have been 1,500 yards behind the 1st and yet we had huge rocks and boulders raining down on us. Fortunately, we had enough time to reach cover." The explosion tore apart the bodies of men from both sides, buried some under rock slides and threw a medium tank fifty yards in the air. At least 200 Japanese died instantly, while the Rock force lost about 50 killed, 150 wounded.

When MacArthur set foot on Corregidor, nine days short of three years since he boarded Bulkeley's PT boat, more than 4,500 Japanese were counted as dead, with perhaps another 500 either sealed in demolished caves or drowned while attempting to swim for their lives. Only twenty prisoners were taken. The American casualty count added up to more than 1,000.

During the battle for Corregidor, another foray tried to save the remaining captives on Luzon, the 2,147 people, including Navy nurse Mary Rose Harrington, held at Los Baños near Laguna de Bay. For this expedition, the Sixth Army marshaled elements from the 188th Glider Infantry, paratroopers of the 511th Parachute Regiment, guerrillas, the vehicles of the 672d Amphibious Tractor Battalion and supporting tank and tank destroyer outfits.

Amtrac gunner Art Coleman recalled, "After a couple of weeks at the racetrack, we got word to make contact with the 11th Airborne. We were told we were going to liberate those held at Los Baños and could expect one-third casualties. Two-thirds of the prisoners might be lost. Going through the city, we saw bodies everywhere, mostly natives but also combatants from both sides. The sports stadium was overflowing with dead.

"At 2:00 A.M. 23 February, loaded with two companies of troopers plus artillerymen, jeeps and guns, we set off across Laguna de Bay toward Los Baños on the southeast shore. We were told paratroopers would jump at dawn. At first light we had eyes glued straight up as we neared the lakeshore. Suddenly, at treetop height, nine C-47s rounded a hill and 120 paratroopers poured out and in split seconds were on the ground. We could not believe it, dropping from planes so low. Some troopers later said they couldn't either. We crawled ashore and unloaded our troopers who went into the jungle and set up a defense of the area. We proceeded to the camp."

Eleventh Airborne commander, Maj. Gen. Joseph Swing, described the action. "The camp has a morning roll call at 7:00 A.M. Timed everything to hit at that hour. There wasn't a hitch—the recon platoon murdered every sentry as the roll call gong was ringing, barged into camp, and kept the main barracks under fire until the parachute company came in and exterminated them. [Some on the scene say the garrison was on the ballfield in loincloths partaking of morning calisthenics.] The amtracs hit the beach at 7:00, grabbed a small beachhead and kept right on inland two miles to the camp while a 75mm battery kept the Baños garrison quiet. Another battalion attacked south from Calamba and drew all reserves in that direction. We loaded the people in the amtracs and shuttled back to my lines. At 5:00 P.M., 2,134 evacuees removed—had withdrawn from the beachhead to the bridgehead at Calamba. Three evacuees slightly wounded; my own casualties, two KIA, three WIA and not a d—— Jap got away".

Navy nurse Mary Rose Harrington, one of those incarcerated at Los Baños, said, "We had word in advance that they would try to liberate the camp. We weren't given any details but we had people who regularly went through the wire and contacted the guerrillas. Of course they always made roll call in the morning. Peter Miles had been in and out a number of times and he was gone a couple of days. I was outside hanging up bandages when I felt these vibrations on the ground from the amtracs coming toward us. Then when I looked up I saw the planes and something came out of one. I thought it was a bundle of supplies—the man had his body doubled up—and thought it's going to land outside the camp. But once the paratroopers started to land, the guerrillas and the men on the ground attacked the pillboxes. It was all over very quickly."

On the whole, those at Los Baños were not as physically debilitated as the internees at Santo Tomas. "There was less competition for food out where we were," explains Harrington. "We probably ate a little better. Still, toward the end, they sent about 100 old men to us. Some of them undoubtedly needed help or had to be carried to the vehicles."

With between thirty or forty people on the amtrac, Coleman's crew headed for Laguna de Bay. "A Filipino boy pointed to a sheet-metal-covered building, mouthing, Japs in there. Every available machine gun opened up, turning the place into a junk heap. No one approached to see the results. We entered the water, instructed to stay away from the shore on the return. The 1st platoon, wanting more action, went close in with all those people on board and promptly the enemy opened up. They turned away and the bullets struck the tailgates, which could withstand the fire better. No one was injured. On reaching the safe shore, the freed people boarded trucks and ambulances. We immediately returned to Los Baños and brought out the paratroopers. As we entered the water, mortar and artillery fire descended on us but not one round found its target. The commander of the task force, Maj. Henry Burgess, later told me he could hear the Jap officers giving commands as we withdrew. The operation took less than one day."

Within Manila, however, the trapped defenders refused

to quit. A considerable number holed up inside Intramuros, an old walled Spanish city that backed up on the bay. Great stone blocks piled as high as twenty-five feet and as much as forty feet thick at the bottom surrounded the mostly stone structures. Units from the 1st Cavalry and 37th Divisions with supporting outfits assaulted Intramuros and large government buildings in the environs.

The 754th Tank Battalion brought its armor and 75mm guns to bear upon the targets, blasting away at the downtown edifices. On 15 February, Tom Howard's 2d platoon had rumbled out of the Bilibid Prison yard, site of the Company A command post. As Howard's tank crossed a pontoon bridge over the Pasig River, a lone enemy plane flew over Bilibid and dropped a bomb. "It landed about five feet from the command tank, killing company commander Coy 'Snake' Rogers and three of his crew; driver Earl Bartling, gunner Fred Kassman, and bow gunner Russell Cattamelata. Nine men were wounded. Since the CP had been carefully selected to hide the tanks, a spy, an enemy observer, a collaborator must have reported our whereabouts and pinpointed our exact location.

"Garbled communication had been received all morning concerning the events at the CP. It was unbelievable. We couldn't comprehend what happened. Here we were at the front, on the firing line, and those in relative safety were gone. It was definite that 'Snake' was among the dead, as his arm had been found and the tattoo Panama easily discernable. We felt like our head had been cut off or that we had lost a parent. We were like orphans waiting for word on what would happen next or who would assume control."

In the middle two weeks of February, Howard's A Company listed twenty battle casualties, including six dead.

Other medical problems, malaria, amebic dysentery, hepatitis, and routine cuts and bruises while operating the tanks, depleted ranks further. "We had started with seventeen tanks at the time of the landing but now we had eleven that would run, but only enough men to man eight, using the cooks, mechanics, and administrators. We would recruit infantrymen to fill positions of machine gunner or loader for the 75mm cannon. Although we could never get a volunteer to come back a second time, we were able to get men on direct orders from the infantry officers."

In a moment of tranquility, Howard and his mates pondered the question, "Why them, not us?" They mourned their losses, reminisced about the past—"Proud, arrogant, stately, yet one of us, 'Snake' Rogers; Fred Kassman, our prized basketball player when we were on Bougainville; Theriot, with his blond hair, handsome features and a body he was always developing by exercise and weights. We who were left were a motley-looking crew, unwashed, unshaven, clothes in tatters. I existed as the rest did by stripping dead Japs of their jackets and pants and stockings. We were tired, absolutely weary. I remember I sat and cried for no apparent reason, uncontrollably, unashamed, and not cold, but spent, exhausted. I had forgotten when I had last eaten a hot meal, instead of picking on a cold can of C ration, had a full night's sleep, had taken a crap—must have been constipated since the attack of dysentery."

On 21 February, their tanks serviced, restocked with ammunition, food, water, and first-aid kits, Company A in support of the infantry zeroed in on the Manila Hotel. MacArthur was close enough to the site to watch as the Japanese inside supposedly set fire to his prewar penthouse suite. "We were told to zero in on the hotel and then hold fire until the word was given. Each of the five tanks se-

A rescue launch plucked from the water a sailor who jumped overboard from the shattered battleship *West Virginia*. (National Archives)

During the infamous Death March after the fall of Bataan, captives improvised litters for those unable to complete the hike to a prison camp. (National Archives)

The U.S. carrier *Yorktown* listed badly after being hit during the Battle of Midway. (National Archives)

Battle-weary and malaria plagued, leathernecks from the 1st Marine Division relaxed behind the lines on Guadalcanal while fresh forces relieved them. (National Archives)

P-40s flew off the deck of a carrier to support the ground forces in North Africa. (National Archives)

Working with a Sherman tank, infantrymen expanded the beachhead on Bougainville in the South Pacific. (National Archives)

Shattered palms and flame-thrower smoke marked a marine assault upon a sand-banked blockhouse on Tarawa. (National Archives)

Torpedo bombers from U.S. carriers ranged the skies over a Japanese armada in the South Pacific. (National Archives)

Near Italy's Rapido River, an antitank squad defended against an enemy counterattack. (National Archives)

Crewmen aboard the U.S. Coast Guard cutter *Spencer* watch a depth charge explode during a successful attack upon a German submarine, the U-175, which menaced a North Atlantic convoy. (National Archives)

During the bomb run of B-17s from the 94th Bomb Group over Berlin in May 1944, *Miss Donna Mae* drifted beneath another Fort as it released its 500-pounders. The camera in the aircraft dropping the ordnance captured the images.

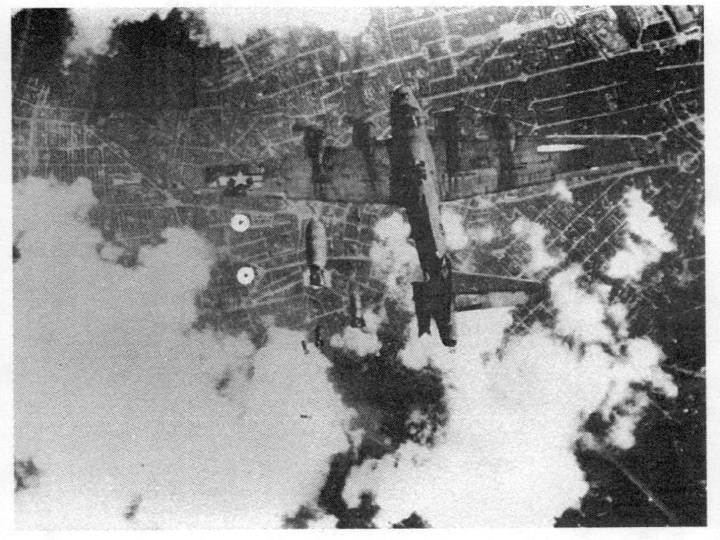

The doomed *Miss Donna Mae*, still level, has lost the elevator and the plane soon plunged to earth. There were no survivors. (Wilbur Richardson)

Half-drowned soldiers in the English Channel on D day were hauled on an inflatable raft to Omaha Beach. (National Archives)

In September 1944, U.S. infantrymen first broke through the formidable German defensive wall known as the Siegfried Line. (National Archives)

The aircraft carrier *Princeton* suffered a mortal blow from a suicide raider during the Battle of Leyte Gulf. (National Archives)

Boyd's Boids, a B-17, managed to stagger back to England before it crash landed and broke apart. (Dick Bowman)

Troops fought house to house to capture Cologne. (National Archives)

On Iwo Jima, marines crawled over the black volcanic ash deposited by Mt. Suribachi, whose summit overlooked them and provided a deadly observation post for the enemy. (National Archives)

The capture of the Remagen Bridge over the Rhine hastened the Allied advance into Germany. (National Archives)

Soldiers in an amphibious truck broached the last formidable natural defenses of Germany in March 1945 as they crossed the Rhine River. (National Archives)

Marine Corsair fighter planes operated from landing strips in the Philippines to provide ground support for army troops. (National Archives)

Flames threatened to explode a Navy Hellcat fighter aboard the carrier *Enterprise* after an errant antiaircraft shell aimed at a kamikaze sprayed the deck with hot shrapnel. (National Archives)

Struck by a kamikaze off Okinawa, the aircraft carrier *Bunker Hill* spewed fire and smoke as more than 350 men died and another 250 were injured. (National Archives)

lected a partition between two windows and sat tight. Lieutenant William Dougherty, on the ground outside his tank, was to give the command to fire. We had never rehearsed a command not to fire. When 'Junior' gave us the sign, we opened fire and the building came tumbling down. We continued to rotate our turrets so that the 75 mm cannon would pour shells into the interior with the shells exploding inside and the shrapnel tear the Japanese to pieces. Unknown to us, the order given was supposed to mean not to fire since MacArthur wanted to save the hotel as best as possible."

Impatient with any delay in the liberation of the city, MacArthur virtually trod on the heels of the combat soldier. Platoon sergeant Cletus J. Schwab of the 37th Division participated in the block-by-block fighting. "We were pushing the Japanese toward Manila Bay this day and about to be attacked on our right flank when one of my sergeants hollered to me that General MacArthur and his escort were coming up the street we were fighting in. I hurried back to stop them. I reported to the general my name, rank, and reason for stopping him. He wanted to know how long the Japanese could hold out. About that time all hell broke loose. It was about half an hour before the general and his staff could retreat to safety." About a week later, Schwab received a battlefield promotion to second lieutenant and a transfer to another company.

To better support the foot soldiers and reduce turnaround time, the maintenance and ordnance details moved closer to the tanks at the front. Armor with flamethrowers trundled forward spouting napalm that adhered to the stone and concrete sides of buildings, even flowing around corners. But the 75s could not seriously dent the walls of Intramuros. The heaviest-caliber artillery, 155mm and

240mm guns, methodically blasted breaches in the walls of Intramuros and stalwart government buildings. Still, infantrymen, aided by tanks, underwent the ordeal of a room-by-room struggle against an enemy resigned to death with his boots on. Iwabuchi's men held thousands of Filipinos as hostages inside. Many died from the shelling or were murdered by the defenders. The attack halted temporarily when the GIs who ran through the shattered walls discovered 3,000 civilians who took sanctuary in the churches within Intramuros. The refugees, mainly women and children—most males had been executed—were escorted out before the Americans resumed firing. About 1,000 Japanese died in the warrens of Intramuros.

The last stages of the Battle of Manila centered around a complex of government buildings constructed along the lines of those of the U.S. in Washington, D.C. Massive piles of thick concrete, they slowly collapsed from an onslaught of heavy artillery bombardment. Late on 3 March, a month after the siege began, the corps commander, General Griswold, advised Sixth Army chief General Kreuger that organized resistance in the Manila area had ceased. In and around the city, the Americans had killed about 16,000 enemy while casualties for the GIs totaled 1,000 KIA and 5,500 wounded. One estimate claimed 100,000 Filipino civilians lost their lives. Manila itself was wrecked, without power, water, or sewage systems. Few buildings escaped damage if not total destruction. With much of the housing demolished, those residents who survived occupied condemned hulks of structures or simply camped outdoors. Men and children begged the troops for food, as women peddled their bodies for something to eat. Giant holes and heaps of debris rendered many streets nearly impassable. Little more than chunks of concrete remained of landmarks like the 400-year-old Intramuros.

MacArthur had achieved his strategic aim, isolation of the three Japanese armies on Luzon. However, although they could no longer support one another or exchange men and equipment, they fought on, determined to exact as high a blood penalty as possible.

11

Firestorms

ONCE THE MARIANAS WERE CONQUERED AND THE AIRFIELDS made suitable, Air Force chief Hap Arnold transferred the B-29s from their fields in India to bases at Saipan, Tinian, and Guam. David Burchinal, who had been a test pilot checking out all types of multiple-engine planes after they rolled out of a depot, and on the staff of the 73d Bomb Group on Tinian, volunteered to accompany a mission from Saipan to the target area. "It was against a place called Nakajima Aircraft, an engine factory in Nagoya. That was a long haul [roughly 1,500 miles each way]. We didn't know too much about the B-29s. We were in a new business; everybody was. Thank heavens they built those runways about a hundred feet above the water, because with the loads on those airplanes at the temperatures we were operating, you had to have a little bit of headwind. You got the plane off the ground and dove it over the runway toward the water and you could pick up enough flying speed then to clear yourself up and get on the way. We found we were literally burning fuel to haul fuel.

We were loading the airplanes so heavily with fuel it would cost us fuel consumption. A lighter airplane was more efficient, had more range, and much better takeoff performance. It took us time to learn.

"On that first mission, we were bombing as high as they could get the airplane, practically in a stall, up to 31,000 feet, scared to death of the fighters. At that altitude we suddenly ran into these terrific jet winds that no one had run into before. They were well over 100 knots, sometimes you'd get up to 200. That first bomb run against the airplane-engine factory, we never saw it. We were going so fast downwind that there was no way the bombardier could get on the bombsight, look through it, using radar or anything else, and synchronize anything. It was beyond the capability of the system. The bombs would fly into the fields. It was the most ineffective mission I believe I have ever been on."

Too many times, crews and their craft were unable to deal with the hazards of long-distance flights, hampered by vagaries of weather and the continuing problems of maintenance. While operations out of the Marianas had shortened distances and eliminated the difficulty of bringing in materials over the Hump, the Japanese base on the island of Iwo Jima, midway between Saipan and Tokyo, not only provided the enemy with an early-warning site but also its fighters threatened the American bases and the bombers.

Burchinal recalled, "The bases in the Marianas would get attacks from the Japanese from Iwo Jima. They would fly the Bettys down, mostly at night. They did rip up the 73d Bomb Group pretty badly one day, early in the morning. They laid a streak of bombs right down the runway where the airplanes were parked wing tip to wing tip. [Apparently the lesson of Clark Field in 1941 had escaped the notice of the base commander.] They had a pretty good fire going on the ground.

They would come over our way [Tinian] and we'd go for the slit trenches. The antiaircraft would open up. They never hit anything." To avoid interception, formations out of the Marianas navigated a fuel-burning, navigationally challenged dogleg course to their targets.

Arnold installed Curtis LeMay to improve results. At first he was no more successful than his predecessors. As in Europe, LeMay focused attention on tight box formations and extended practice to enhance accuracy. "We weren't bombing very well in that formation," said Burchinal, "but we weren't getting shot down or rammed either. Then he brought us right down in altitude. He said, 'You're not going to get anything at 32,000, 30,000 feet, so come on down to 24,000, 23,000, 22,000. We started to hit targets. We weren't taking any losses to speak of. We were increasing the bomb load and the winds dropped off. We had a pretty decent attack going."

But the big change came with the conquest of Iwo Jima, some 650 miles from Tokyo. Navy strategists had long coveted Iwo as a potential base for an attack into the Ryukyu Islands—Okinawa—and the imperial homeland. LeMay and his associates envisioned Iwo as a welcome emergency field for distressed bombers and in American hands allowed Superforts to fly a direct route to Japan. Capture also would end Iwo's role as an early-warning outpost.

At most only four and a half miles long and two and a half miles wide, volcano-spawned Iwo sprouted from the Pacific like a noxious wart from whose pores wafted the sulphuric aroma of rotten eggs. Its one distinguishing natural landmark was a modest 550-foot hill, Mount Suribachi, a burned-out hulk. The Japanese had scraped away Iwo's covering of volcanic ash to complete two airfields, with another under construction. The mix of the ash with cement produced a concrete divinely suited to the construction of bunkers and pillboxes. In their inimitable way, the defenders burrowed beneath the surface for extensive underground fortifications with multiple entrances and exits all connected by a weave of tunnels. The caves, shielded by thirty-five feet of overhead cover, could withstand the biggest bombs or shells. Engineers erected air shafts for ventilation and the sharp corners to the underground maze protected against flamethrowers. The garrison commander, whose own redoubt lay seventy-five feet beneath the ground, led 21,000 men, well equipped with artillery, mortar, antiaircraft guns, and other deadly hardware. Neither he nor his men had any doubts of their destiny. They expected to fight to the death. For several months American aircraft regularly and ships occasionally visited Iwo, blasting at the fortress. All reported significant retaliatory reactions.

While naval historian Samuel Eliot Morison wrote of the Iwo invasion, "The operation looked like a pushover," the Marines most closely involved with the affair regarded it with trepidation. The V Amphibious Corps under Maj. Gen. Harry Schmidt requested a ten-day softening-up barrage by ships before the first Marine stepped into a landing craft. But other activities, the engagement in the Philippines and a carrier-based strike at Japan, siphoned off ships. The Marines would have to make do with just three days of preparatory shelling.

The bombardment, from the sea and the air, inflicted slight damage during the first two days, but on the third, 18 February, it appreciably battered the positions guarding the landing beaches. On the following day, the battleships and cruisers approached to within a thousand yards of the shore to pour point-blank cannonades at blockhouses and pillboxes until 8:05 A.M. They paused long enough for some

120 carrier-based dive-bombers and fighters to shoot up defensive sites. A squadron of B-29s from the Marianas dumped tons of explosives, stirring up old lava and sand. Finally, gunboats cut loose with rockets and even mortars.

Observers could not believe anyone near the beaches could have survived. A wave of amtracs churned to the shore while spouting 75mm pack-howitzer shells and machine-gun bullets. The black beach seemed inert, lifeless. For a few moments, the Marines hoped for the unthinkable, but the first big splashes among the landing craft signaled the presence of a malevolent enemy. A direct hit sank an amtrac, drowning some unable to divest themselves of packs and weaponry. Bullets rattled against the armor plate. Still, with relatively few casualties, seven battalions landed abreast on 3,500 yards of Iwo Jima adjacent to the right side of Suribachi.

Richard Wheeler, a corporal in the 28th Marines, undergoing his baptism of fire, stepped onto the wet sand on the extreme left flank, closest to Suribachi and where the tip narrows to only 700 yards in width. Suribachi provided the Japanese with observation of almost the entire island, and was an immediate objective for Wheeler's battalion. As they moved toward it, Wheeler remembered, "We [realized] we could hardly make a move that escaped Japanese notice. We troops in the Suribachi area would be particularly conscious of this. We would seldom be more than half a mile from the volcano and much of the time we would be plainly exposed to the view of observers, gun crews, and riflemen in the caves on its slopes and at its summit. Even when we were in holes we wouldn't feel undetectable, however low we pressed ourselves. This sensation of being watched over gunsights by hundreds of hostile eyes would be very nearly as unnerving as being actually under fire.

"The loose sand was hard to negotiate. We wanted to run,

in obedience to our training and our instincts, but loaded with gear as we were, we could only plod. Our route was crowded with Marines. Some were lying prone or were digging in, while others were climbing the terrace and moving inland. Troop congestion was mounting dangerously. We were all aware of the importance of dispersion in combat. . . . We passed a number of tallow-faced casualties who were being treated by corpsmen and saw a blinded man being led to the water's edge for evacuation."

Glancing back to the sea, Wheeler glimpsed terrifying scenes. A landing craft approached the beach with a large American flag flapping by a gunwale. "A bold gesture," said Wheeler, "since they must have known the flag would invite a concentration of enemy fire. The Marines were carrying their display of defiance to the limit, for they were shouting lustily as their vessel cut through the surf and thrust its prow against the shore. Then as the ramp dropped to the sand and the men bolted out they took a direct artillery hit and their spirited shouts were instantly replaced by cries of anguish and confusion. Another appalling sight presented itself. About a hundred yards to our left-front, a Marine was blown high into the air. Like a great rag doll, he went up end over end and seemed to rise at least fifty feet before plummeting back to the earth."

His unit halted before a mound of sand, innocent-looking except for a dark rectangular opening that indicated a concrete gun emplacement. The sand provided both camouflage and protection for the inhabitants. "We all knew how a rifle platoon was supposed to handle a problem like this. While one man semicircled his way to the pillbox with a demolitions charge, the rest were to deliver concentrated fire at the aperture and make it impossible for the gun crew to operate. When the demolitions man was close enough to make a dash for the aperture and push his charge inside, the others were to cease firing—but only long enough for the man to make his play. The moment he turned away, the firing was to resume so the charge couldn't be expelled.

"As we lay in our places of skimpy concealment and considered the obstacle before us, the prescribed method of dealing with pillboxes seemed suddenly unfeasible. Few of us felt like poking our heads up high enough to fire our rifles and the idea of a man's rising and venturing across that barren sand seemed absurd. But if Wells [the platoon lieutenant] gave the order the measure would be tried." To their relief, a pair of Sherman tanks clattered to the rescue. Coming around their flank, the armor aimed its 75mm cannons at point-blank range, turning the pillbox into a tomb. But the tanks themselves were vulnerable to well-sited antitank guns and lacked opportunities to take cover.

During the first hour the enemy had remained almost quiescent. To make the Americans pay dearly for every yard, the commander of the detachment had established a defense in depth, rather than the earlier mode that tried to halt invaders at the water's edge. On the beach, men and machines piled up in a small area as a mounting crescendo of mortars, artillery, and automatic weapons cascaded over the area. A 5th Marine Division history reported, "Wounded men were arriving on the beach by the dozen where they were not much better off than they had been at the front. . . . The first two boats bringing in badly needed litters were blown out of the water. Casualties were being hit again as they lay helpless under blankets awaiting evacuation."

Most of the corpsmen who expected to move inland to treat the wounded never left the beach area as casualties streamed back. Crawling about to sew chest wounds, bandage lacerated limbs, and inject morphine to ease pain, the medics themselves absorbed cruel punishment. In one battalion, their first-day casualties ran higher than for most assault groups. Indeed, for many of the reserve outfits that followed the first waves several hours later, the onslaught was much fiercer. Captain LaVerne Wagner, who brought in K company of the 23d Regiment, said, "One of the first sights I saw was a Marine blown in half. The beach was crowded with Marines as far as I could see. Enemy artillery fire was very hot and it seemed to me that almost half the men on the beach had been wounded and were waiting to be evacuated.

"We had indoctrinated all our men with the necessity of getting off the beach fast, and had even picked out prearranged assembly areas. But before we had a chance to move forward our men began to drop. The machine gun that had fired on us in the water was still in action and as we jumped from shellhole to shellhole it followed us, firing from our flank. Ahead of us were literally dozens of pillboxes and many blockhouses. You couldn't move twenty-five yards in any direction without running into some kind of position. Most of them had been knocked out and had dead Japanese in them. One blockhouse greeted us with a burst of machine-gun fire. We got one of the tanks to come up and work it over, but the walls were three and four feet thick and the tank didn't do much damage. Finally, the company on our left threw some grenades into the rear entrance. Suddenly, what seemed like about eighteen grenades came flying back at us. We kept throwing our own grenades into the entrance and finally killed the Japs—three of them. We found seventy-five grenades lined up in a row, ready to be thrown. We realized that the Japs were going at this systematically."

While fellow Marines slowly ascended the lower elevations of Suribachi, the 23d Marine Regiment concentrated upon the biggest airfield, Motoyama Number 1. By midafternoon, the leathernecks approached the twenty-foot-high slope that bordered it. Hard fighting killed many defenders and when the remainder suddenly disappeared, the Marines, accompanied by tanks, climbed the sandy embankment only to come under intense fire. The Japanese had crawled through huge drain pipes and resumed the battle from positions across the landing strip.

LaVerne Wagner and his company joined the effort to wrest control of the place. "Our first big surprise was to find that no one had started across the airfield. One reason we discovered, was that a Jap antiaircraft gunner had depressed his gun level with the field and was shooting at anyone who stuck his head up. We sent a squad of men to work around behind him and one of our men shot him in the head. The bullet went in his forehead and came out his temple and despite the fact that his brains were actually oozing out through the hole, he lived. In fact, he would walk and talk. We took him prisoner—the first Jap captured on the beach. It had taken us two hours to get from the beach to the field and join the battalion ahead of us. And this was a beach that had been fought over all morning and was supposedly cleared. Already, we had lost thirty of our men. Theoretically, we hadn't even been committed to the battle. We were still in reserve."

By the end of the first day, 40,000 Marines from the 4th and 5th Divisions were digging in, with the former still on the edge of Motoyama No. 1 and the latter having cut across the lower tip of the island to isolate Suribachi. They weathered night-long volleys from artillery and mortars and choked off a battalion-size counterattack. Sporadic rifle fire rattled the darkness as star shells from the fleet, illuminating infiltrators, lit up the night.

On the second day, the Marines resumed the effort to capture the old volcano. Flights of Marine and Navy planes roared in at low altitude to smash targets with rockets, bombs, and machine guns. Napalm erupted in balls of flame and from the sea the big ships hurled shells and rockets. Tanks and half-tracks lurched forward to blast away at the lower reaches of enemy defenses. The infantry painstakingly inched toward Suribachi and poised for an attempted ascent.

Richard Wheeler participated in the assault that began after the customary barrages from ships and planes. "For a few moments the hulking fortress remained still. Then it began to react. First came the crack of rifles and the chatter of machine guns. This quickly grew to a heavy rattle, and bullets began to snap and whine about us. Then the mortars started coming in, some being visible as they made their high arc, and shortly the area was being blanketed by roaring funnels of steel and sand. The noise and fury increased until our hearing was numbed and our thinking impaired. It was as though the volcano's ancient bowels had suddenly come to life and we were advancing into a full-scale eruption.

"We were now part of a real hell-bent-for-leather attack, the kind the Marines are famous for. But there was nothing inspiring about it. None of our ex-Raiders shouted 'Gung ho!'; none of our ex-paratroopers shouted 'Geronimo!' and none of our Southerners let go the rebel yell. We felt only reluctance and enervating anxiety. There seemed nothing ahead but death. If we managed somehow to make it across the open area, we'd only become close-range targets for those concealed guns. I was seized by a sensation of utter hopelessness.

"It is in situations like this that Marine Corps training proves its value. There probably wasn't a man among us who didn't wish to God he was moving in the opposite direction. But we had been ordered to attack, so we would attack. And our obedience involved more than just a resignation to discipline. Our training had imbued us with a fierce pride in our outfit, and this pride helped now to keep us from faltering. Few of us would have admitted that we were bound by the old-fashioned principle of 'death before dishonor' but it was probably this, above all else, that kept us pressing forward."

His closest comrades started to fall all around him and the cry of "corpsman" rose above the din of explosions. Wheeler and four others jumped into a crater left by an aerial bomb. Suddenly, a shell exploded on the rim of the big hole. "My rifle was torn from my hands and I reeled under a hard, ear-ringing blow to the left side of my face. I thought for an instant that I had taken only a concussion but when my hand leaped reflexively to the affected area, the tip of my thumb went through a hole at my jaw line. A fragment had broken my jaw, smashed through the roots of two molars and lodged in the muscles beneath my tongue.

"My wound started to bleed profusely, both externally and inside my mouth. While [Howard] Snyder [his squad leader] stuck up his head and shouted an urgent call for a corpsman, I took off my helmet, pack, and cartridge belt and sat down against the crater's slope. Spitting out a stream of blood and the crown of a tooth, I wondered worriedly how my injury's two-way flow could be stanched. I was afraid my jugular vein had been hit." Corpsman Clifford Langley applied compresses inside and outside Wheeler's mouth to halt the stream of blood.

Except for one other slightly wounded man and Langley, the others who had taken refuge with Wheeler departed to continue their climb. A few minutes later, another savage explosion rocked the crater. Shrapnel ripped away Wheeler's trouser leg, his canvas leggings, and a chunk of flesh from his left calf. Langley immediately sprinkled sulfa powder on the new wound and bandaged it. The corpsman himself was wounded slightly and the other Marine killed.

The still functioning members of Wheeler's platoon doggedly advanced toward the crater of Suribachi. Donald Ruhl, known as the unit's malcontent, threw himself on a grenade and won a posthumous Medal of Honor. Native American Louie Adrian, a close friend of Wheeler's, fell, mortally wounded, while triggering his BAR. A mortar shell burst among a quintet of Marines, seriously wounding platoon leader Lt. John K. Wells. Tossing grenades almost like confetti, closing in on bunkers with flamethrowers, aided by tanks, the Marines forged forward.

The last few of the 2,000-strong force that defended Suribachi hunkered down at the edge of the crater. On D plus 4, Lieutenant Colonel Chandler Johnson, the battalion commander, dispatched a forty-man patrol composed of survivors of Wheeler's platoon augmented by men from other outfits to capture the final outpost. Johnson handed the patrol leader, Lt. Harold Schrier, a folded American flag. "Johnson's orders were simple," said Wheeler. "The patrol was to climb to the summit, secure the crater, and raise the flag." On reaching the crater rim, the leathernecks encountered a few holdouts, but grenades and rifles disposed of them. The Marines scrounged a piece of pipe that became a flagpole from which the Stars and Stripes soon whipped about in the wind atop the volcano. Some three hours later, battalion commander Johnson decided to replace the small flag with a much larger one. Associated Press photographer Joe Rosenthal accompanied the group that bore the new banner to the top and snapped the famous picture.

There were other eyewitnesses. Offshore, Walter Vogel, promoted to the rank of chief petty officer and transferred from the *Downes*, was on the bridge of the destroyer *Hyman* where he trained his long glass on the island whenever permitted by his duties. "The commander came to me and said, 'Put your glass on Mount Surabachi.' Everyone that had binoculars was watching. All of a sudden about seven or eight Marines put the American flag that was on a pole up in the rocks. Everyone yelled. It was a great thrill to see this and then we knew it would be a short time before we left."

About 900 Marines from the 28th Regiment became casualties during the attack on the old volcano and in the 3d platoon to which Wheeler belonged, 91 percent of the leathernecks were killed or wounded. But the fight for Iwo was far from over. The northern end of the island still featured shore-to-shore caves, tunnels, bunkers, pillboxes, and obdurate defenders. Fresh forces from the 9th Marine Regiment, supported by tanks, slammed up against a ridge that overlooked Motoyama Number 2, half of which still remained in enemy possession..

Three tanks, *Angel*, *Agony*, and *Ateball*, cranked ahead, only to be rocked by a fusillade of antitank shells. *Angel* and *Agony* started to burn, while *Ateball* lost the ability to move forward. Corporal William R. Adamson squeezed out of the hatch of *Agony* and dropped to the ground. As other tankers followed, looking for protection in shell holes, a bullet hit Adamson in the leg. He rendered first aid to himself with a tourniquet and then noticed the muzzle flash of the gun that had knocked out his vehicle. Adamson crawled to *Ateball,* whose crew could still operate its weapons. With his arm, he indicated the position of the enemy piece. *Ateball* responded and blew it away. Adamson then detected four machine-gun nests in the rocks ahead. Again he signaled to the disabled tank and its 75mm smashed all four guns. A Japanese soldier tried to sneak up on the tank with a satchel charge but the intrepid Adamson spotted him and directed machine-gun fire that cut him down. Some thirty infantrymen ran forward to destroy the nettlesome tank and Adamson, but *Ateball* repulsed them with artillery and machine-gun fire. Other tanks came forward, and under their cover the *Ateball* crew and Adamson retreated to safety.

The killing continued day after day. Gains could be measured only in yards and along with map designations such as "Hill 383" and "Turkey Nob" the sectors earned grim names, "the Meat Grinder," "Bloody Gorge" and "Death Valley." Wheeler's platoon sergeant Ernest Thomas, who helped raise the first flag atop Suribachi, took a fatal bullet through the head. Sergeant Henry O. Hansen, who appeared in the Rosenthal photograph of the second flag, was killed. A shell burst cut down the intrepid battalion commander Chandler Johnson. Ambushes and stalwart defenses occasionally forced the Marines to retreat, sometimes unable to take all of their wounded. These unfortunates lay there, feigning death. Any sign of life meant skewering by an enemy bayonet.

Carrier-based aircraft attempted to aid the ground forces. Pittsburgh native Harry Jones, who flew a torpedo-bomber from the *Hornet*, said, "It was a little like watching a football game from the air. The Marines put down these orange panels so we would know where to drop bombs ahead of our people. We tried to hit the caves but we couldn't see the openings from the air."

For the most part the Japanese, offered numerous opportunities to surrender, replied with bullets, grenades, and mortars. Near the third airfield, still under construction, the Marines advanced beyond a rocky ridge. From their rear, a machine gun secreted amid the ruins of blockhouses and boulders suddenly opened fire. Pinned down, those leathernecks awaited tanks and demolition teams. They repeated the tedious but deadly job of destroying anyone in the myriad openings. Methodically, the tanks fired into each hole, followed by grenades and packages of explosives. Through tunnels the inhabitants moved quickly to new positions from which to shoot. The ultimate weapon of attack, the flamethrower, threw long jets of searing napalm, which, unlike bullets and shells, bounced off the curved walls and traveled around the 90-degree angles. A correspondent reported, "The Marines heard the Japs howling. A few rushed out of the caves on fire. The Marines shot them or knocked them down and beat out the flames and took them prisoners. When the Marines began to hear muffled explosions inside the caves, they guessed that some of the Japs were blowing themselves up with hand grenades. The scene became wild and terrible. More Japs rushed screaming from the caves. They tumbled over the rocks, their clothes and bodies burning fiercely. Soon the flamethrowers paused. A Marine lifted himself cautiously into view. There were no shots from the caves. A Jap with his clothes in rags hunched himself out of one hole with arms upraised. The Marines stood up behind the rocks and waved to him to come out. The Jap indicated there were more who would like to surrender. The Marines motioned him to tell them to come out.

"Almost forty scared and beaten men emerged from different holes. Some of them had round pudding faces. They grinned nervously and said they were Koreans. They had been forced by the Japs to stay in the caves. They said that everyone else in the caves had either been burned to death or had committed suicide. The Marines sent them to the rear. Then they groped cautiously among the rocks from hole to hole, examining each entranceway. Dead bodies, some hit by bullets and grenade fragments, some burned into frightful black lumps, lay in the holes. The smell was overwhelming and the men turned away in disgust." Few Japanese soldiers surrendered. At one point eleven soldiers simply stood up and faced the Americans, who shot them down.

On D plus 25, the American command declared Iwo Jima officially secured. More than 20,000 of the enemy fought to their death. The Marines counted 6,821 dead and nearly 20,000 wounded. This was the only campaign of the island war in which the U.S. absorbed more casualties than the enemy. Twenty-seven Marines and navy corpsmen earned Medals of Honor in providing the Air Force with the emergency landing site for which it lusted.

Anxious to prove the worth of B-29s flying out of these islands, the strategic bomb experts sought to justify their presence. Prior to the shift of Superforts to the Marianas, one mass raid on Hankow, China, wiped out much of the dock area although debriefers concluded that less than 40 percent of the bombs struck in the target area. But because incendiaries that employed napalm dominated the ordnance, fires wrought enormous damage. The bomber command decided to try the method against Japan itself.

"Toward the end of February," said Burchinal, "we were ordered to load up pretty heavily with incendiaries. It was high altitude, 26,000 feet against Tokyo. I was to fly deputy lead for the wing. Our wing led all the wings in this first

200-plane attack on Japan. The idea was to take off from all the different bases and head north of Iwo Jima. We were to assemble over the water, putting phosphorus flares out for marking the assembly point. The airplanes would come in, look at the different colors, and assemble into their formation and then a line of formation.

"I was a lieutenant colonel and had been designated the leader for the whole command. We had one brigadier general, a couple of other wing commanders, a group of colonel types along with their own outfits. They didn't like all this forming up over the water because it was going to take a while, thirty to forty minutes to bring that gang together. They said, 'We're going to head for Japan.' I got on the radio and said, 'You'll see me in LeMay's office and I'll be preferring charges. Your job is to stay and form this formation.' " And they did.

"We burned up a pretty good chunk of Tokyo that day from high altitude. We didn't have much of a bomb load on the mission but it proved a point. LeMay wanted to find out if that damn place would burn, and if it was really a prospect for incendiary attacks. That pretty well proved it. A couple of nights later, a real gutsy commander volunteered to see what the Japanese defenses would look like at night, low level. He took a B-29 by himself over Tokyo at 5,000 feet at night and didn't get a scratch. He came back and said, I think we can do it. LeMay said okay and that's when he started the low-level night incendiary attacks, first on the four major cities, Tokyo, Kobe, Nagoya, Osaka.

"The third mission was Kobe and I went on it, [on a jump seat next to pilot Bill Pitts] flying deputy lead again for the group. We came up over the bay into Kobe. At 5,000 feet we had a cloud layer so we dropped under it, which put us down around 4,200 feet. I have never seen such fireworks in my life. They were throwing everything at us in the way of antiaircraft and searchlights. My God, the night was really lit up. Right ahead of us was the lead crew—good friends of ours. We got just about a minute or so from bomb release and up he went, a direct hit from AA. That was the end of him. Then the tail gunner called that another one right behind us had been hit by AA and down he'd gone. That was two out of the first three."

Burchinal watched as his pilot, "cool as a cucumber, flew right over that town, put those bombs, all those incendiaries, right where it counted and all the other guys right after him. I was a little edgy and after we got the bombs away, he just kept driving straight. You could still see the stuff coming up and I said, 'It would be a good idea to get out of here, wouldn't it?' He said, 'The best way is to keep right on going, it's the fastest we can get out of it. All of a sudden we were back in the night, climbed up, and headed home.

"After that we began to clean up Tokyo. The first night we'd gotten a whole chunk of it but there was lots left, because it was a hell of a big city. Lots of defense industries. We got a little more scientific. At the time we were still bombing at medium altitudes, daytime, at 25,000–26,000 feet. LeMay called a critique after one of those missions because our results had not been very good. I was fairly critical of some of the tactics we were using and the ways we were bombing. I didn't like the formation he was making us use. He listened and just grunted. I said what was in the minds of a lot of the crews and the ops staffs."

The problem lay in the amount of time it took to generate fires to aim upon and bring the bomber stream into position to exploit the existing conflagration. "We would spend maybe an hour and a half over the target. By the time they got a fire going, those damn flames would be up to 15,000–18,000 feet. The area was small, the updrafts tremendous.

You'd bounce as high as you could see flames—it would take an airplane up like a leaf. There was one particularly bad night, attacking the Yokohama area and Kawasaki area. The naval AA was particularly good. We had planned a breakaway down Tokyo Bay, which was still in range of the naval guns. The timing had gotten screwed up and the tail end was straggling. I watched twenty-three B-29s shot down at the end of the formation. I tried to divert them to take another route but it was too late.

"We knew we were going to have to concentrate the string more. We had had one midair collision, and at least one airplane came home with a piece of another's tail in the intake. The other airplane didn't come home. We worked to bring in parallel strings. We compressed the time of attack. They could handle singles pretty well with some of the sharp AA but they couldn't deal with the mass stuff because they all had their heads down.

"When we got on Iwo Jima, we got our first long-range fighters, P-47s. We then had escort over Japan. They would also run independent fighter sweeps. The kids couldn't navigate themselves in those fighters all the way from Iwo up to the empire and back. We arranged for them to join the bomber formations. We'd escort them up and they would break off and go in. They would make a sweep ahead of us, escort us or whatever their mission. We also developed our air-sea rescue because our crews were a long way from home if they had to ditch off Japan or even on the way back. We had submarines the Navy couldn't use because there were no targets left for them and surface craft also. My friend Bill Pitts came off the target badly shot up one day and just managed to get off the coast. We had definite rendezvous points for these subs and he called his position in with such code words as 'Nellie's Belly.' He headed for one, bailed out his crew, then bailed himself. He said he was in the water maybe a minute and twenty seconds before a submarine had come and picked up his whole crew. Of course he was out of the war for about two and a half weeks—it took that long to get back to Tinian from the empire on that submarine."

Onboard a B-29 named *City of Los Angeles*, radio operator Sgt. Henry Erwin had completed seventeen missions when his 52d Bomb Squadron began to congregate for an attack on Koriyama, Japan. *City of Los Angeles* usually led the unit, serving as a pathfinder on night raids, when it would light up the target for the bomber stream, and as the lead during daylight raids. As radioman, it was Erwin's task during the assembly maneuvers about fifty miles from the enemy coastline to drop two or three phosphorus bombs down a three-and-a-half-foot chute that provided guidance for the bomb-approach formation.

According to Erwin, "There was about an eight- or ten-second delay from the time you pulled the pin [on the phosphorus bomb] until you threw it down the tube. On this particular mission, I recall throwing some prior, but on the last one, we either hit an air pocket or there was a malfunction in the bomb. I knew it was coming back and I tried to put my foot on it and kick it out, but it came on into the plane and exploded at my feet." After ignition, the phosphorus reaches a temperature of from 1,500 to 2,000 degrees.

"Instantly, it put my eyes out, burned my ear off, burned my hair off, and my uniform was on fire. I thought to myself, 'I can't see.' I was always taught, 'Don't panic.' If you panic you are not going to be able to do anything. The first inclination, even after all this teaching, is self-preservation; how do I get out of here? I am in this radio operator's shack, back in the corner, obstructed behind the navigator. This thing is at my feet and I'm on fire and I'm burning." The smoke quickly filled the airplane and the command pilot, Capt. George Simeral, dove down toward the sea.

"I said, 'Lord, I need your help *NOW!*' And instantly, I knew that there was somebody else in that plane. I reached down. I grabbed it with my right hand. I began to crawl. I remember opening the navigator's table [to get past it], crawled by the flight engineer on the right, went up between the pilot and the copilot. I told Captain Simeral to open the window and I flipped it out. One reason—we were at 300 feet over the water—the phosphorus gives out a lot of smoke and the pilot couldn't see his instruments. He couldn't understand what was happening. They were at sort of a loss. It happened so quick. But just as soon as he opened the window and I pitched it out, then the breeze sucked all of the smoke out.

"They saw me, and Captain Simeral said, 'My Lord, what's wrong?' They instantly began first aid. The first thing they had to do was take a fire extinguisher and put out the fire. I was completely aflame. Then they began wanting to give me morphine. In addition to the radio operator I was the first-aid man on the plane. They gave me one Syrette. I never was unconscious. I was still alert; I couldn't see them, I could respond to their talking. 'Red, are you all right?' 'I'm fine.'

"Colonel Strouse [Lt. Col. Eugene O.] who was our squadron commander, did something normally no commander would ever do. He told the bombardier. 'Open those bomb-bay doors and drop those bombs right here now. We are going to head for Iwo Jima.' We turned and headed for Iwo Jima. They wanted to give me some more morphine. I said, 'Don't give me any more of that stuff; you are going to kill me with morphine.' " One of the side gunners administered plasma to the stricken sergeant.

When *City of Los Angeles* touched down, Erwin began a thirty-one-month period in hospitals as doctors treated his injuries. For nearly a month, the grains of phosphorus embedded in his eyes and skin smoldered whenever exposed to oxygen. He regained sight in one eye while undergoing extensive skin grafts and reconstruction of his right hand. For his valor he was awarded a Medal of Honor. By the time the war ended, more than 2,000 B-29s had used Iwo as an emergency field, perhaps a partial payment on the investment of so many lives and bodies to capture the island.

The campaign of fire ravaged much of Japan. The 300 B-29s that hit Tokyo on 9 March ignited a holocaust that killed 83,000 people and destroyed 267,000 buildings within a sixteen-square-mile sector. The conflagration generated temperatures that boiled canal waters while towering clouds of soot and smoke blotted out the sky. The devastation surpassed the firestorms of Hamburg and Dresden. The B-29s added minelaying to their operations, sowing them extensively in Japan's Inland Sea where they sank a considerable number of ships. Leaflets dropped from the sky rained down on the residents of cities, warning them they were next on the list for the fire raids. Many people headed for the countryside, weakening the war production effort. However, although the war had now been brought to the home islands, the Allies detected no signs of weakening resolve in the military.

12

Over the Rhine

THE MAPS INDICATING THE FRONTS OF THE ALLIES AND THE Germans in the west showed little change between those that charted the situation in mid-December and the first week of February. But the collapse of the attack through the Ardennes and the severe losses inflicted upon men and armor, some of which had been diverted from the eastern front, brought the Third Reich to the brink of extinction. While the Soviet armies rampaged through the depleted ranks of the Wehrmacht, the Americans and British, fortified by fresh infusions of men and materials, opened up the final drive against a much weaker enemy than had faced them three months earlier.

The last natural barrier before the Rhine was the Roer River. The 2d Ranger Battalion prepared to join an assault culminating in a crossing of the Roer. Medic Frank South said, "The day before while making sure that our aid station equipment and such were set to go, we heard the familiar cry of 'Medic!' Grabbing my aid kit, I ran out of the ruined building we were in and started across the field from whence the cry had come. Just as I heard the also familiar 'crump' of a mortar round, I felt a tug at my knee and I was on the ground. I had been hit again and while I could move my leg it wouldn't support me dependably. Within a few minutes Bill Clark was at my side, compressed bandage ready and applied, and supported me back to the aid station. After glancing at the wound, dusting it with sulfathiazole and immobilizing the leg, our new medical officer, Capt. Max Fox, had me loaded into an ambulance. The hospital was in Liége where a bit more surgery was done, and I was confined to bed while the battalion was crossing the Roer and taking casualties.

"Two other recovering patients, a B-17 waist gunner and a 2d Division infantryman and I, got passes to go into town. We had a fine time wandering about, two of us with an arm in a sling and one hobbling about on crutches, inspecting girls and comparing the merits of bars. All went well until while making our way down a fairly steep street, there was a loud explosion almost at our elbows. Our reaction times well polished, both the 2d Division man and I hit the ground. Looking up, we saw the gunner staring at us in puzzlement and a ring of concerned Belgians surrounding us. It had been a semitruck and trailer that had backfired. Sheepishly we continued on. I hoped the Belgians thought that my crutches merely had slipped."

The period following the Ardennes campaign revealed war at its nastiest to Dee Paris with the 14th Tank Battalion. The 9th Armored Division, of which his unit was an element, had regrouped following the Bulge and become an integral part of the First Army's drive toward the Rhine. But faulty intelligence continued to dog his tracks. "Originally, since horses do not have radios, the cavalry used motorcyclists to carry messages. When they did away with this method, our cyclist was devastated. I made him a gunner in my platoon sergeant's tank. We received some incorrect information and were caught in direct antitank fire. I was in the lead tank on a road approaching a village when an antitank round passed just above my head. The weapon fired two or three more times, each time the round just about a yard over me. I figured he had the gun dug in and couldn't lower his gun tube enough to hit me. The shell passing overhead made a fluttering sound—like when you expel air through your mouth, fluttering your lips.

"The shells missed me. But the platoon sergeant, looking out his turret, was decapitated by a round. When the motorcyclist-made-gunner turned to him for orders, he saw the headless body and just about lost his mind. We got the tank back to safety, but now the gunner was a mental case. He couldn't face that experience again so he was assigned as a driver, which placed him in the lower left part of the chassis. Subsequently, his tank came under fire and was struck by a round. I neutralized the German gun and went forward to survey the damage. The shell from a German 75mm antitank piece had hit the pavement in front of the tank and pierced the thin bottom of the tank. It split the body of the driver. I was devastated. I leaned against the tank and cried.

"The battalion commander and an officer from higher headquarters arrived. This officer peered into the hatch and I lost my temper, shouting, 'If you want to see blood, why don't you come up here and fight!' My commander restrained me until I calmed down. But no matter what you've been through before, you can still feel a loss to the point where you ignore discipline and verbally attack a senior officer. I understand that as a result of my behavior, he disapproved a valor award recommendation.

"Then there was an officer who had been wounded and evacuated during the Bulge. He returned just as we left on the mission that ended in the death of my platoon sergeant. He, too, was killed. At the time he was carried as missing in action. His wife, who'd lost a baby just before we went overseas, wrote, saying, 'God couldn't be so mean as to take my child and my husband at the same time. He can't be dead.' Against all regulations, I wrote back telling her not to prolong her grief with hope. Her husband, my friend, was dead. It was another terrible moment."

Major Glen Strange of the 27th Armored Infantry Battalion of the 9th Armored Division became part of Combat Command B, an eighteen-mile-long column, as it wound its way through Belgium, into Germany, and across the Roer River on the last day of February. According to Strange, progress slowed perceptibly. "Some of the companies had lost too much leadership. I had been told many times not to volunteer in the army but something made me feel these wonderful men whom I had helped train and been through so much needed me. I told Major Deevers, 'Give me a task force and we will move.' "

Deevers arranged for Strange to lead two companies of the 27th AIB, one from the 14th Tank Battalion, artillery support, and a platoon from the 89th Recon Battalion. The task force achieved its first objective, Lommersum on the Erft Canal, a few hours after its creation. "On the morning of March 4, a sergeant who piloted an L-5 [observation plane] landed in a turnip patch just behind my lines. I had flown with him before and he took me up. It was a hazy day but we could see the Rhine River and the Ludendorff Bridge at Remagen. I reported this to Gen. William Hoge, Combat Command B commander, and his comment was, 'It won't be there when we reach it.' "

From Lommersum, Strange's task force assaulted Bodenheim. "I took A Company from the 27th Armored Infantry Battalion and a platoon of the 14th tanks and captured it with some losses in about one hour. The history books say General Hoge led this attack. He did show up and was right with me to the end of it. But I gave all the orders and directed the attack. He never countermanded anything I said and it was nice to have him there, although he had no business being on the scene and his aide was killed during the fight."

On the following day, Strange was part of a party assaulting the village of Esch. "About 2:00 P.M. I was on foot and with the leading element. I was shot by a .30-caliber machine gun located in a church on the outskirts of Esch. My military career was over. I was evacuated and reached a field hospital in Liége on the morning of March 6." The bullet severely damaged Strange's spine and he began an eleven-month ordeal of hospitalization with a prognosis that he'd never walk again.

Glen Strange, his task force, and Combat Company B of the 9th Armored were engaged in a race to cross the Rhine, the last sùbstantial natural barrier in the west. In the vanguard of Combat Company B was Dee Paris with the 14th Tank Battalion. On 6 March, "Colonel [Len] Engeman [Paris's CO] called me, 'Squirrel'—that was my radio code name, he was 'Gopher'—'Go up there and look at that bridge.' I tried to tell him we didn't have enough gas but he ignored me. I did not want to go in the worst way. I hated night operations, you can't see and the tanks roll off into ditches and crash into trees. At five minutes to nine, just as I told the guys to crank up the engines, I received a call to cancel the mission. The Ludendorff Bridge at Remagen, on the west side of the Rhine, was still standing but there was a big hole in front of it. Meanwhile, there were German guns on a hill that was actually behind us. We'd be sitting ducks for them if we tried to reach the bridge. I was told to take some tanks and take out those guns. I couldn't get close enough with the tanks so we dismounted and swept the hill like infantry. That silenced the guns. We moved into Remagen."

For years the alumni of various organizations have argued over who deserves credit for the events surrounding the Ludendorff Bridge. Engeman, the 14th Tank Battalion CO, offered the most authoritative account. "We made reasonable progress across the Cologne Plain toward the Rhine River, crossing the Erft Canal and the Neffel River and overcoming the German resistance. We lost ten medium tanks, and two light tanks. In the late evening of 6 March, in Stadt Meckenheim about fifteen miles from the Rhine River, I met with General Hoge. I received orders to advance at daylight 7 March to seize the cities of Remagen and Kripp and to be prepared to cross the Ahr River to join up with General Patton's Third Army advancing from the south." For the job, Engeman led a task force of tanks, armored infantry, a mortar platoon, and an engineer unit.

"When we received our orders, mention was made that the Ludendorff Bridge over the Rhine River at Remagen was still standing. We thought nothing of it as it was normal for the Germans to wait until we were almost on a bridge before they blew it up in our face. We moved out of Stadt Meckenheim at 0820 on the morning of the seventh. The city had been badly bombed by us so it took a little time to clear paths through the town. We had one tank in each company equipped with a tankdozer that would clear almost anything in a roadway. Then we had tank recovery vehicles that could tow and maneuver heavy units around. We finally left the city and Task Force Engeman proceeded on our route to Remagen. We had light opposition. Mostly roadblocks and small-arms fire. No German air nor much artillery. I was riding in my jeep as usual back of the lead tank platoon commanded by Lt. John Grimball. At about 1300 Grimball reported that the bridge was still standing. I was surprised but realized that they would probably blow it before we could get to it. I moved up with Grimball and saw the bridge. I requested artillery fire to burst over the bridge and called together Major Deevers and the other commanders involved. I decided to move the infantry dismounted down the highway into the city. We were on a high point overlooking the city and the river so we had great observation.

"I started the dismounted infantry down the hill on the left side of the roadway. A little later, about 1415, I ordered Grimball and the rest of the units to proceed down the road and told Grimball to get to the bridge as soon as possible and cover the bridge roadway with fire to prevent the Germans [from] getting on the bridge [to] destroy it. There were two trains across the river and I told him to take out the engines while he was going down the hill. About the time I was ready to head down the hill, General Hoge roared up in his jeep. I informed him of what I was doing. His only comment was to the effect that it would be nice to have a bridge. I left him and headed for the bridge. On the way, I told Grimball on my radio to get to the bridge as soon as possible. His reply was, 'Suh, I am already there.' When I arrived at the bridge I found that Grimball had lined up his vehicles on the road and was firing on the bridge roadway. I had my driver park our jeep by a house near the entry to the bridge. About this time a tremendous explosion went off on the side of the bridge near where I was standing by my jeep while using the radio. The debris from the explosion rose several hundred feet into the air. I fully expected the bridge to dump into the river and was totally surprised when the debris settled and the bridge was still standing. I immediately called Major Deevers and ordered him to get his infantry across the bridge and build up a defensive position on the other side. There was a small village and a high hill on the east approach to the bridge. We discussed getting heavier weapons up on the high ground.

"Deevers took off and I called for Lt. [Hugh B.] Mott, who commanded the engineer platoon attached to me. When Mott reported in I directed him to get on the bridge with his platoon and thoroughly check to see that all demolitions were destroyed on the bridge. Then to report back to me when we could move tanks across. The infantry continued to move over the bridge as they had taken care of the German defenders in the bridge towers and most of the German defense was broken. We still got a lot of small arms and medium artillery fire. Lieutenant Mott reported that they had destroyed any remaining demolitions on the bridge and the roadway needed repair before we could get tanks across. If he could find timbers he would have it ready by midnight."

Deevers had told Lt. Karl Timmerman, newly appointed CO of Company A, to get men across the bridge. They had been about to start when the explosion mentioned by Engeman occurred. According to author Ken Hechler in *The Bridge at Remagen,* when the debris and dust settled, Timmerman waved his arm overhead signaling the troops, "Follow me." Three squads led by Sgt. Joe DeLisio, Sgt. Joe Petrensik, and Sgt. Alex Drabik sprinted over the planking in the face of fire from the other side. An American tank threw a few rounds at a tower on the opposite bank, suppressing the enemy action.

DeLisio reached the towers, charged up a circular staircase in one, and leveled his weapon on three German machine gunners. They quickly obeyed his cry of "*Hände hoch!*" When DeLisio tossed their weapon out the aperture, the GIs still on the bridge dashed across. The Americans overwhelmed German engineers intent on blowing up the bridge and set up a perimeter defense on the east side of the Rhine. They organized roadblocks and set out mines.

On the west bank, Engeman said, "About 1600 I realized that I had no direct orders to take the bridge and felt I needed verification that our actions were approved by higher command so I had a coded message sent back to CCB to the effect that we had sent the infantry across the bridge, which was still intact. I asked for their plans. At about 1855 [almost three hours later] I received a reply from CCB. They stated in effect that they were backing me with everything they have. I was to build up my defenses on the east side and they would protect my rear and a battalion was on the way to help me."

Engeman set up his command post in a large, empty wine cellar below street level and installed radios from vehicles to provide communications. A company of tank destroyers, a recon troop, and a battalion from an infantry regiment reached the scene. Meanwhile the engineers led by Mott labored in the black of night to repair the bridge roadway. About 1:00 A.M., said Engeman, "General Hoge stormed into the wine cellar. He was upset he had lost his radio communications on the way down the hill when his half-track tipped over. He asked me to let him use our communications, which was fine with me. We spent the rest of the night poring over maps and planning our moves to expand the bridgehead. About 0200, a platoon of Company A [a tank unit] was ordered across the bridge following a report from

Mott that the bridge would hold the tanks. He had strung white engineer tape on both sides of the roadways so that the drivers could see the edges. It was pitch black. The platoon made it across and took positions on the far side of the bridge. I then ordered a company of tank destroyers to proceed across. Unfortunately, the tank destroyer had steel tread as opposed to our rubber tread, and the first one slipped off the roadway on the bridge and down onto the main support girders. We got the maintenance platoon to get a tank retriever with a hoist and they managed to get the TD out in a couple of hours.

"I later learned that when news of the bridge capture had been reported to General Eisenhower he was ecstatic and approved General Bradley's plan to put four divisions across the bridge. These units were moving piecemeal beginning the morning of 8 March. At 0635 [that day], General Hoge and I crossed the bridge and we set up headquarters downriver. I moved into a big house right on the east bank of the river. Shortly afterward General Louis A. Craig, 9th Infantry Division commander, assumed command of the bridgehead units. They began to assign my tanks to support the infantry units pushing out of the bridgehead so that I eventually had little command left. General Craig came into my headquarters and asked if he could move his command staff into a wine cellar directly in back of the house I occupied. It was the first time a general asked for something instead of ordering it."

A key figure in the exploitation of the Ludendorff Bridge was then-Lt. Hugh B. Mott of the 9th Armored's engineers. A 1939 ROTC honor graduate of high school in Nashville, Mott had married a childhood sweetheart. This prevented him from accepting a later nomination to West Point. Mott remembered, "People in town had informed us the bridge was to be blown up at four o'clock. We knew if anything was to be done, it had to be done quick. Colonel Engeman called me down to the foot of the bridge and we had the full bridge in sight and decided we'd go ahead and try to take the thing. It looked awful long and awful dangerous to me. I said, 'Lemme go and get a couple of my men and my tools.' I got two of my good sergeants, Sergeant Reynolds and Sergeant Dolan, brought them back down there. There had been no Americans across the Rhine yet. I told Colonel Engeman to give me all the fire cover he could. They had two main charges at the center of the bridge and a number of twenty-pound packages of TNT in a number of places underneath where there was a scaffolding that covered everything up. Having no knowledge of the system layout we just cut all of the wires we could and hoped to get the one that controlled the whole electrical setup for all of the charges. As we started on the bridge, the infantry scouts came along with us. We attempted to cut every wire while the infantry boys were going across the bridge. We were getting pretty good fire from the other side. We really didn't know what to expect. Sergeant Dolan worked out a little bit ahead of me and Sergeant Reynolds, and he found what he thought was the main conduit for the electrical charges and blew it in two with his rifle. We never did know whether that was the right one, but the rest of the charges didn't go off.

"Our next problem was to get armor across but with that big hole in the middle of the bridge we couldn't. We worked on up into the night, pitch black night with no flashlights, with sniper fire, enemy fire hot and heavy. About midnight, we finally told them it was ready. Their armor lined up bumper-to-bumper. When the tank destroyer slid into a hole we got some cross ties, put them behind it, and they were able to pull the thing out."

As armor and men flowed across the Ludendorff Bridge—Dee Paris guided his platoon of tanks over on the morning of 8 March—the Germans attempted to destroy the span. Engeman remembered, "For the next several days the Germans blasted the bridge with artillery and tried but failed to hit it with bombs from their planes. We had moved so many anti-aircraft [weapons] into the area that the Germans' aircraft had no chance. I really felt pity for the pilots who were repeatedly knocked down or dropped their bombs long before they neared the bridge."

To facilitate passage over the Rhine, GIs constructed a pair of pontoon bridges, one above and one below the Ludendorff. "The German artillery," said Engeman, "hit them repeatedly but the engineers managed to get them across. On 17 March, at 1505, my adjutant burst into headquarters and informed me that the bridge had collapsed into the river. I rushed to the site and found it had fallen and medics and others were rescuing the engineers who had toppled into the river with the bridge. In all twenty-eight men were killed and sixty-one injured. They were primarily men from an engineer construction battalion, repairing the bridge at the time. It had been closed to traffic while repairs were going on and we were using the two pontoon bridges." Although official records credited the 9th Armored Division commander Maj. Gen. John Leonard and Combat Command B's leader Brig. Gen. William Hoge, both West Pointers, with the decision to send the troops across the bridge, neither officer ever issued such an order. Erroneous accounts even place Hoge at the scene when the first GIs dashed onto the structure, but it was well after dark before he arrived. Instead, it was Engeman, an ROTC product of the University of Minnesota, on his own, at considerable risk since he had been given a mission of linking up with the Third Army south of him, who directed the crossing. Major General George Ruhlen, who bossed the division artillery, said, "Colonel Engeman and Engeman alone made the decision to attempt to capture the bridge. He and he alone gave the order to the 27th Armored Infantry Battalion to do it."

More than two weeks after the 27th Armored Infantry Battalion jounced across the Ludendorff Bridge at Remagen, Patton boasted that his Third Army had achieved the first successful assault crossing of the Rhine. He celebrated with several histrionic gestures, peeing into the river from a pontoon span thrown up by his engineers, grabbing handfuls of dirt on the eastern bank in emulation of William the Conqueror and topping off his performance with a telephone call to Omar Bradley: "For God's sake, tell the world we're across. I want the world to know Third Army made it before Monty starts across!"

Assault boats began to ferry thousands of GIs from the Ninth Army across the Rhine a day later. A barrage of 2,000 artillery pieces along with massive air raids preceded the crossing and the defenders offered relatively weak resistance to the 79th and 30th Divisions. Bill Kunz, as a member of the 3d Infantry Division's artillery, recalled, "Early on the assault morning, we fired a barrage of 10,000 rounds onto the Rhine east bank in less than 45 minutes. In one of my more stupid moves, I managed to get our jeep hung up crossways on the pontoon bridge. Luckily it was only temporarily stuck. Once across, our advance started to gain some momentum, and the amount of prisoners increased."

On 24 March, Operation Varsity carried 21,680 parachute and glider troops, mostly from the 17th Airborne Division, over the river for a daylight drop north of the main pontoon and assault-boat operations. Paratroopers rode in C-46s, whose doors on either side of the ship permitted a faster exit than the single-entrance C-47s. But the less-protected fuel systems of the C-46 resulted in deadly fires.

Pete Buckley flew a glider towed by a C-47. "It would be the first landing in enemy territory not secured in advance by our own paratroopers. My copilot, flight officer Bill Ryan, and I introduced ourselves to the men from the 194th Glider Infantry whom we would be carrying. Bill and I up to this point felt secure in the knowledge that they were experienced combat soldiers, having been blooded while fighting in the Ardennes. One of the young troopers came up to me and mentioned the fact that most of them in my glider were replacements who had been transferred from another airborne unit and had not been in combat. They sure hoped that Bill and I knew what we were doing. With a sinking feeling in the pit of my stomach, I put on a very straight face and told him that Bill and I had landed in Normandy and Holland and assured him this was going to be a piece of cake. Little did I know that it was going to be the toughest mission to date for the tow plane crews and the glider pilots. It would also be the first time that the glider pilots, after landing, would be organized into fighting units under the direct command of their own and senior airborne officers.

"The takeoff for the whole group went smoothly and quickly. In a very short time we had formed up and started to blend in with hundreds of other C-47s and their gliders that had taken off from fields all over France. The end result was a massive formation of aircraft that stretched as far as you could see from horizon to horizon, all headed for Germany. The only drawback was the extreme turbulence in the air caused by the prop wash of hundreds of planes ahead of us. You couldn't relax on the controls for one minute.

"About an hour into the flight, a glider on a tow ahead of me shed a wing and then broke up completely in midair spilling its cargo of men and a jeep out where they seemed to float down in slow motion, mixed in with pieces of the glider. When all these glider pieces and the jeep hit the ground a big cloud of dust settled over the wreckage as we flew directly over it. This gave me the cold sweats for a few minutes and Bill took over the controls so that I would have a minute or two to compose myself. I didn't know whether the glidermen sitting behind us had seen this terrible accident but I hoped not.

"As the Rhine River came into view, Bill and I noticed to our mutual horror that all of the LZs and DZs on the other side were almost totally obscured by smoke and haze. Murphy's Law, which always seemed to haunt these airborne missions, was coming into play. The cause was the smoke screens the British were pumping out all along the banks to mask the crossing earlier that morning of their Commandos, who were assaulting the town of Wesel on the western edges of the landing zones. The RAF had also bombed Wesel and the smoke and dust from this combining with the smoke screens on the river had blown over the drop and landing zones.

"The moment that we crossed the Rhine, heavy flak and small-arms fire started coming up at us, the worst I had seen to date. The closer we got to the landing zones, the heavier it got. Tow planes and gliders were getting hit and going down in flames. A C-47 in front of us, with one engine out and with flames streaming back over its wing, held to a steady course, determined to get its two gliders to the LZs. In many cases they succeeded but by then their chances of bailing out were nil. All through this hell in the air, formation discipline was fantastic. The tow planes tucked in closer and bored straight on toward the landing zones with no attempt at evasive action.

"In a very short time the green cutoff light came on in the astrodome of our tow plane. I reached up and smacked the tow-rope release and started a 360-degree turn down into the smoke and flak. The closer we got to the ground, the more details became visible, details you really didn't want to see. We were looking right down the throats of the Germans who were manning their slit trenches and flak guns and were firing at us with everything they had. Gliders were coming down from all directions, at all speeds, into fields criss-crossed with tracers, artillery bursts, and mortar explosions. Some were touching down smoothly, while those that came in too fast usually ended up in a twisted ball of wreckage from which no one emerged. Almost everyone became engaged in some form of hand-to-hand combat the instant they left the glider. Some poor souls never left their glider.

"Four gliders that landed in front of a well-entrenched 88 field gun were blown to bits with no survivors. Three others in this same field caught fire when the gas tanks in the jeeps they were carrying were hit by incendiary bullets and exploded. The pilots and glidermen were still sitting in their seats, burned to unrecognizable black crisps. If any place could be described as Hell on earth, this little corner of the world at this particular time had to be the place.

"By now I was so low that I had to decide fast what field we were going to land or crash on. The biggest field that we had just flown over was completely filled with wrecked, burning, and intact gliders with no opening in between except close to the 88, which was still firing. I spotted a small field dead ahead, surrounded by tall trees and with only one glider in the corner. By now we were getting hit by some small-arms fire, and were so low that it had to be this field. I pulled the nose of the glider up to kill off the air speed. Bill held on full spoilers [devices that manipulate air flow over a wing] and in a nose-high sideslip just above stall speed, just before touchdown, I kicked it straight and we settled into a smooth, three-point landing. I rammed the nose down into the soft dirt and we stopped so quickly that I thought for a moment we were going to flip over. Bill and I yelled, 'Everybody out!' and when we turned around we were alone in the glider. I think the glidermen must have been jumping out while we were still rolling. I can understand this because I could hardly wait to get out myself but I couldn't because I was still at the controls. The important thing was we were down on terra firma, all in one piece, huddled in a wet ditch on the edge of the field.

"I wasn't sure where we were but for sure the enemy were in fields all around us and heavy fire was going on at all points of the compass. The sergeant in charge of the glidermen pulled out a map and I pulled out an aerial photo of the area to ascertain where we were with no luck. We all climbed out of the ditch and started off single file down a narrow dirt farm road in the direction of the heaviest firing. As we proceeded, we could hear the cry 'Medic, Medic' coming from both sides of us. There was very little we could do to help because we were under continuous sniper fire from all sides. We could see medics under continuous enemy fire bending over treating the wounded and trying to assist troopers still trapped in smashed gliders.

"As we passed a small farmhouse, surrounded by a stone wall, a sniper let loose from the upper window. We ducked behind the wall. While plotting out our strategy to cope with this problem, we heard a strange noise coming up the path. Like a Hollywood sketch, with a thunder of hoofs, six airborne troopers rode up on liberated farm horses, circled the farmhouse shooting into the windows. Finally, one trooper stopped and lobbed a rifle grenade through the second-story window and the sniper fire stopped. These crazy characters then galloped off down the road, into the sunset, as they say in cowboy movies. It seems funny but at the time it was a deadly serious game. Airborne men always seemed to find horses no matter how hot things got."

Buckley said he separated from the group to try to find other pilots. He paused briefly to reassure a wounded lieutenant that a medic would soon attend to him, then headed into the big field where so many gliders had been wiped out. "In the middle of the field I came across a glider pilot lying on his face about twenty feet in front of his glider. He was dead, with a bullet hole in the back of his head. I gently rolled him over and saw that when the bullet came out it took most of his forehead with it, making it impossible to recognize him. I checked his dog tags and much to my horror discovered that he was a friend and we had flown together during training.

"While sitting there on the ground beside the dead pilot, feeling quite depressed and downright scared, I heard a low rumbling noise in the distance. It came closer and closer until the ground began to tremble under me. Then with a horrendous roar, 240 Eighth Air Force B-24s came over right on the deck dropping supplies by parachute. It was the same outfit that resupplied us during the Holland mission. It was beautiful, awesome, and thrilling. I jumped up and waved and cheered them on. The tragic part began when the Germans in and around the perimeter opened up and shot down fifteen of them. At that low altitude it was almost impossible to bail out and most of the crews had to ride the planes down.

"Later in the day, I finally linked up with a group of glider pilots and we were assigned a section of the perimeter to hold until daylight. We settled down in some abandoned German dugouts in an apple orchard behind a farmhouse. Most of us crawled in and promptly fell asleep. Around midnight, all hell broke loose at a crossroads. Just over the hill from our position, glider pilots of other groups had been assigned this section around a key road junction to block any attempt to infiltrate into our lines. That is exactly what happened. Two platoons of German infantry with two tanks and a 20mm flak wagon were advancing straight up the road on a collision course with the glider pilots who were backed up by a .50-caliber machine gun manned by glidermen of the 194th. The battle raged off and on for most of the night before tapering off. During the fight, one glider pilot managed to knock out a tank with a borrowed bazooka.

"When the sun came up, the glider pilots at the crossroads took stock of their night's work. They found at least twelve German dead in front of their positions and more than forty wounded. Two tanks had been put out of commission; one 20mm antitank gun was destroyed and approximately eighty-four enemy infantry in and around their positions were ready to surrender. Not a bad score for a bunch of so-called undisciplined glider pilots. Their own casualties were three dead glidermen who had manned the machine gun and two wounded glider pilots. By late afternoon of the second day, things had stabilized to the point where glider pilots were authorized to withdraw back over the Rhine. They brought back with them 2,000 prisoners, some of whom they had captured themselves. A funny thing about these prisoners. A short time before, when they had their weapons, they fought like hell trying to kill you. Now with no weapons they were as docile as cows and seemed to sense that they had lost the war. It was much different in Normandy and Holland. Most of the POWs captured at that time remained surly and arrogant, convinced that they were still going to win the war."

Within three hours of the first drop, American paratroopers linked up with British forces. Three entire German divisions plus other units were destroyed between the Allied airborne contingents and the armor and infantry crossing the Rhine in great numbers. U.S. forces, however, incurred losses of ten percent and the British suffered triple that number. But it was now only a question of how far the soldiers in the west could travel before meeting the Red Army.

On 25 March, the 4th Armored Division, with Capt. Abe Baum of the 10th Armored Infantry Battalion, had advanced to the Main River, capturing bridgeheads at Hanau and Aschaffenburg. Now Patton proposed to send men of the 4th Armored on a daring rescue mission, the liberation of Stalag XIII A at Hammelburg, forty miles away, and where Lieutenants Lyle Bouck and Alan Jones Jr. were confined with other officers. Patton explained on 30 March, "I felt I could not sleep during the night if I got within sixty miles and made no attempt to get that place." He claimed the inhabitants were in dire peril since the Nazis were murdering POWs.

Patton handed the mission to Gen. Manton Eddy, commander of the XII Corps, and Gen. William Hoge, promoted to head the 4th Armored. Both of them objected strenuously to the concept of a foray by a force containing 3,000 men, 150 tanks plus artillery and other support. Omar Bradley was not in favor of the raid either. In the end, Patton yielded on the numbers, but his persistence brought a deadly compromise, that instead of the equivalent of a full combat command, the strike force be little more than one-tenth that size, about two companies' worth of troops.

Although Patton professed his motivation was the welfare

of all of the officers confined at Hammelburg, there are strong signals he was concerned about one individual in particular, his son-in-law, John Waters. There was intelligence that indicated Waters had been moved from a prison camp in Poland and most likely was at Hammelburg. The idea of a sudden dramatic strike to liberate American prisoners obviously appealed to Patton. MacArthur had scored huge headlines with the operation that freed 5,000 U.S. prisoners in the Philippines. While lobbying for support with Hoge, Patton boasted, "This is going to make MacArthur's raid on Cabanatuan peanuts." Al Stiller, a Patton aide, repeated the general's comparison with the MacArthur feat, changing the "peanuts" to "look like a Boy Scout hike."

Nomination of those who would go on what he perceived as a near suicide mission devolved to Col. Creighton Abrams, newly elevated to lead the 4th Armored Combat Company B. Actually, his first choice would have been Abrams' former regular partner on missions, Harold Cohen, and members of the 10th Armored Infantry Battalion. But Cohen was still recovering from a painful case of hemorrhoids.

With Cohen not available because of his painful rear end—he was excused only after personal inspection by Patton—Baum became the choice. After Baum heard the bare essentials of the mission at a meeting, Patton drew him aside, and in a conspiratorial whisper, said, "Listen, Abe—it is Abe, isn't it? You pull this off and I'll see to it that you get the Medal of Honor."

When he learned what was expected of him, Baum says he never considered refusing the orders—perhaps a consequence of being an aggressive twenty-four-year-old. He remarked to Abrams and Cohen, "You won't get rid of me this easy. I'll be back." In retrospect he said, "When a mission is created, nobody says this or that might happen to you. There usually isn't the intelligence available to say what could occur."

Al Stiller actually supplied the details of the operation. He spoke of 300 officers being held at Hammelburg, an error that would give the affair even less chance. He reassured Baum there would be air cover where possible, and that because Patton's Third Army was headed for another sector, the Seventh Army would be prepared to render assistance once Task Force Baum broke away from Hammelburg to return to the U.S. lines. Stiller casually mentioned Patton's son-in-law as one of the inmates to Baum.

The column jumped off on 26 March. It included 10 Shermans, 6 light tanks, 27 half-tracks, 3 105mm assault guns, a medic weasel for evacuation of wounded; these and jeeps, all loaded with extra fuel and ammunition. These vehicles bore 293 soldiers, most of whom had slept but one out of the previous four days of movement and battle. The mission began on a foreboding note as Task Force Baum had to run a gauntlet through the town of Schweinheim, after a TOT artillery cannonade opened the proceedings around 8:30 P.M.

With their path brightly outlined by burning buildings, and snaking between the parked tanks down the narrow street, Baum's column bolted through Schweinheim, nicknamed "Bazooka City" for the prevalence of antitank rockets. Once beyond the fires and in the blackness of night, the column used follow-the-leader navigation, relying on the glow of exhausts and specks of illumination from blackout lights. The swifter light tanks assumed the head of the mile-long column that now hurried through the darkness at fifteen miles per hour. Overhead, a liaison plane dallied long enough to relay radio messages from Baum.

At the Berlin headquarters of the Wehrmacht, news of the

fight at Schweinheim trickled in, but the defenders could not accurately report the size of the American contingent. The Germans concluded Patton had engineered another daring thrust with a considerable force, rather than the small self-contained group under Baum. The foe quickly mobilized to stop this threat.

The task force smashed through a roadblock and demolished a German truck convoy in which the main casualties turned out to be German flak girls assigned to antiaircraft duties. At Gemünden the GIs blasted several trains, but when the foe dropped the only bridge over the Saale River into the water, the armored column had to locate another less direct route. At the same time, several tanks had been disabled and about twenty men killed or wounded. Overhead, however, spotter planes appeared to track the path of the task force.

After several more skirmishes, the tanks and half-tracks reached the Hammelburg camp. German soldiers tried to defend the place from foxholes, but they were outgunned. The commandant agreed to yield. With all of the confusion and shooting, however, it was necessary to send out a truce team from the camp. John Waters volunteered and, with several other Americans plus a German officer, set out, carrying a white flag manufactured from a bed sheet. When the party passed through the gate, a German soldier suddenly appeared, leveled his rifle, and squeezed off a shot. The bullet hit Waters below the right hip, smashed off bone, and then chipped his coccyx as it exited from his left buttock. The German officer with Waters and the others engaged in a furious discussion with the soldier, who seemed inclined to shoot everyone. But at last he grasped that his commandant had agreed to the surrender. The badly wounded Waters was carried in a blanket to the POW hospital operated by Serbian prisoners. The task force battered down the barbed wire, then parked in a field just beyond the camp.

Lieutenant Alan Jones Jr. from the 106th Division says, "The attack on the camp was totally unexpected by me. I was sitting there when suddenly I heard the firing. We moved quickly to another barracks, which was made of stone and would protect us better. But we were all at the windows watching, cheering our guys on. I saw Lieutenant Colonel Waters go out with the others and I saw him being shot. Then, as darkness came, the tanks moved into the camp."

Baum was dismayed to learn that instead of the 300 officers Stiller claimed were held at Hammelburg, the number was about 1,500. He could not possibly accommodate that many in his half-tracks or on his tanks. As a kriegie, Lyle Bouck thought in terms of the Allied advance rather than a raid as the engine of his liberation. "Early in the morning, I heard small-arms fire. We thought it meant that the front lines were approaching. Somewhere before dark, we saw tanks and the next thing I heard stories that a task force had come to get us. There was much confusion. A lot of people were standing around, Yugoslavs and Americans, amid the tanks and half-tracks. We found the task force couldn't take all of us." Actually, Baum had asked the senior American prisoner, Col. Paul Goode, to pick the limited number of lucky ones who could ride with the task force, fewer than 300 because of Baum's losses. When Goode failed to make a selection, rumors circulated. "There was a story that only field-grade officers would go," remembered Bouck. "Some of the guys said to one another, 'I'm promoting you to major,' and the other would reciprocate."

Baum never sought to limit the rescue to field-grade officers. But he was forced to make the discouraging announcement to the crowd of kriegies. He explained that there were far more men than had been expected. He could take some but the rest would have to decide whether to take their chances walking westward toward the advancing Seventh Army or remain in the camp until the front lines swept past them. Those who accompanied his column would risk attacks directed at the task force. The frustrated Baum, aware of his losses in what was clearly a long shot with no real payoff, says he fought back his tears as he spoke to the prisoners.

While Baum dealt with the main body of prisoners, Al Stiller sought out the one man for whom the entire operation was designed. He found Waters recovering from emergency surgery by Serbian physicians. He obviously was in no condition to be moved and he still faced the danger of infection or paralysis. Stiller visited with Patton's son-in-law, then made his way to the task force. Baum hurriedly ordered engines cranked up for the start back, knowing the Germans would come after his task force and its cargo. Hundreds of prisoners, evaluating the odds or considering themselves too weak to attempt to travel the forty to sixty miles to the American lines, shuffled back into the camp. Many others walked off on their own, hoping to remain free. And a generous number clambered aboard the tanks and half-tracks.

Alan Jones and a buddy, Lt. Bud Bolling, whose father also commanded a division (84th Infantry), boarded a tank, but the crowd was too much for the Sherman's commander. He couldn't traverse his gun and he ordered a bunch off, including Jones and Bolling. "Bolling and I started to walk. My feet were still bothering me and I couldn't go very fast. In the morning they found me and brought me back to camp. But Bolling got away."

Lyle Bouck and a friend, Matthew Reid, stuck together,

hauling themselves aboard the second tank in the column. The convoy started off, trying to take a different path to avoid discovery and roadblocks. "One of the guys gave each of us a grease gun. We were making pretty good progress when the tank in front of us exploded and started to burn. I see that I'm in the middle of a sea of tracer bullets. I'm hit in the left knee. It felt very hot and I couldn't tell where I could move. Reid and I ducked into some small saplings. From there we could see where the stuff was coming from, crew-served weapons. I hollered, 'Let's charge 'em' and we did, firing the grease guns. We could see them dropping.

"I yelled to the tankers to call the commander and tell him we knocked out the roadblock and he could move around it. We climbed on the last tank and then pulled up in an area where they put out a perimeter defense. We had some wounded and they were all put in a kind of outbuilding made of stone. They put a white flag on the rocks."

The task force commander, aware his men had had no sleep for forty-eight hours, decided to wait until dawn to make a last desperate dash to evade his pursuers. He ordered gasoline siphoned from some half-tracks to fill the vehicles that would make the final run. Reid and Bouck got into a half-track. But during the night, the Germans had moved a substantial force into position. Bouck remembered, "All of a sudden we were hit. We took off for the woods. But they had goddamn dogs all around us and they began rounding us up. Some of the tankers took off their coveralls and the Germans got angry because they couldn't tell who was from the task force and who had been a prisoner. They went around looking at faces, trying to see who was well fed."

A salvo crashed into the building with the wounded. The walls collapsed on the hapless victims; none survived. As if in a shooting gallery, the Germans methodically destroyed every vehicle in a firestorm of shells. Baum with Stiller and another man fled to the forest. But the dogs picked up their trail. The enemy closed in. Baum was prepared to shoot his way out, if possible. "I tried to pull up my mackinaw to reach my .45 and I saw this German. While I watched him, he pulled out his P38 [pistol] and shot me inside the thigh of my right leg. 'You son of a bitch, you nearly shot off my balls,' I said. He laughed. He understood English; he was from Bridgeport and serving in the Volksturm, the home guard." Baum managed to discard his dog tags, which identified him as Jewish. He was now a prisoner, a seriously wounded one at that.

Other captives persuaded the Germans that Baum was just another inmate caught in the crossfire. They half-carried him back into camp and placed him in the care of the Serbian medics. When the 14th Armored Division overran Hammelburg little more than a week later it liberated both Baum and Waters. While they recuperated in a hospital at Gotha, Patton visited them both, presenting each with a Distinguished Service Cross. Waters earned his in North Africa and Baum's was the payoff for the task force operation. An intelligence officer had already warned Baum that the mission must remain top secret. He also realized that Patton could not afford to recommend a Medal of Honor, for that would require a public airing of the circumstances.

The great Hammelburg raid failed to free John Waters, and only a few prisoners and would-be rescuers slipped through the German lines to safety. Every piece of equipment was lost; nine men were officially identified as dead and an additional sixteen were never accounted for. Most of Task Force Baum endured several weeks in the stalags.

Some military historians point out that whatever the motivation behind it, the mission wreaked havoc upon a substantial number of German troops and caused a diversion of forces that the Americans exploited. Patton never conceded the purpose of the expedition was the liberation of his son-in-law. Abe Baum, who became friendly with Waters, asked him at the time if he had ever discussed the matter with Patton. "He said he had asked his father-in-law, who answered, 'If I did know I wouldn't tell you, because that would jeopardize our intelligence.' " Baum had no doubts that Patton was aware of Waters's location.

13

Operation Iceberg

THE FIRST DAY OF APRIL SAW ALLIED ARMIES IN EUROPE ON the western front sweeping across the Rhineland toward Berlin and a rendezvous at the Elbe River with the Soviet forces careening through Czechoslovakia and Austria before bludgeoning their way into Germany. The advancing troops bagged thousands of prisoners and overran the Third Reich's war factories as the bombers of the RAF and U.S. began to run out of targets.

In the Pacific, GIs continued to liberate chunks of the Philippines while a mighty armada bore down on the Ryukyus intent upon a base only 350 miles from the Japanese home islands. The advance across the Pacific toward Japan had almost wiped out every acquisition of the Empire, though the ultimate aim, as in Europe, was not simply to roll back the enemy but to defeat them on their home turf. Ground troops were required to achieve victory in Europe in spite of the terrible pasting delivered to the Third Reich from the air, and it was believed that only when GI boots tromped on the streets of Tokyo would the warlords accept unconditional surrender.

Beyond the Philippines lay two candidates for the last stage before an invasion of Kyushu, the southernmost Nipponese island, the large Chinese island of Formosa (Taiwan in today's lexicon), and the biggest of the Ryukyu Islands, Okinawa. U.S. Army strategists estimated conquest of Formosa would require nine combat divisions plus the requisite service troops. With the war in Europe still blazing, there simply would not be enough men available.

Okinawa, closer to Japan than Formosa, and in an early intelligence report defended by fewer than 50,000, seemed more manageable. For the purposes of establishing supply and airbases to support an invasion of Kyushu it was eminently qualified. Okinawa beckoned with first-rate, protected anchorages for a fleet striking at Japan. The vast stockpiles of supplies required for the million men deemed necessary to shatter the last strongholds of resistance could be safely warehoused on Okinawa. It would provide an unsinkable aircraft carrier, close enough to the targets for fighter planes to shepherd the bombers. Formosa could be bypassed. Attempts to interdict the Allied operations from that island could be blocked by naval and air forces.

Known sometimes as "Loochoo" or "Lew Chew" in Chinese and Japanese dialects, the roughly 140 Ryukyu Islands consist of the remains from mountains and some now-dormant volcanoes that thrust up from the East China Sea. The biggest of the bunch, Okinawa, "the Great Loochoo," includes a quarter of the land mass and lies in the middle of the chain. Its closest companions were a clump of small islands known as the Kerama Retto and one of sufficient size to maintain a large airfield, Ie Shima. Fully vested citizens of Imperial Japan, Okinawans were regarded by those who came to govern, manage, and defend the place as rustics and perhaps inferiors. However, the soldiers stationed on Okinawa never generated the hostility manifested by the peoples of the occupied territories like the Philippines, Solomon Islands, or other lands conquered after Pearl Harbor. The native inhabitants may have resented the attitudes of those from the original Japanese country, but they considered the Allies their enemies and they were willing to fight for their homeland and Japan. To the 80,000 troops from various parts of Japan hunkering down to defend Okinawa were added 20,000 Okinawan conscripts. Their officers from the Japanese army had no complaints about their performance under fire.

The American figures on Japanese strength on Okinawa and the surrounding islands considerably underestimated the number of troops. Interrogators collected scraps of information from documents and an occasional prisoner taken elsewhere, but their knowledge of the Ryukyus was scant. A submarine dispatched from Pearl Harbor to photograph the beaches disappeared. The only real source of intelligence lay in aerial reconnaissance, and early in the game the enemy had gone underground. To the prying eyes of the pilots and to the lenses of the cameras, Okinawa began to look as if it were devoid of humans. Photographs indicated defenses around Naha, twenty miles behind the western Hagushi coast beaches, and along a ridge known as the Shuri line that centered on an ancient walled city dominated by a castle.

On Okinawa, subterranean defenses, as at Tarawa and Iwo Jima, burrowed into nearly impregnable coral for their emplacements, rendering themselves all but invulnerable to the usual insults of artillery and heavy naval guns. The defenders developed coordinated tactics with snipers to pick off assault teams with flamethrowers and explosives. Anti-incendiary devices like wet mats or blankets smothered fires. Ventilation systems became well disguised and less susceptible to attacks. For close to two years, the Okinawa commanders drove their men to dig, ever deeper.

This industry and ingenuity created a honeycomb of underground bunkers, some as much as five stories below ground, and many of these connected through a web of tunnels, as much as sixty miles of subterranean corridors. A single cave could house as many as 1,000 men, and trucks, and even tanks, could be parked inside. Intersecting automatic weapons fire forged deadly mutual protection for entrances. Openings from inside the caves allowed positions to shift during artillery and air bombardments. Egress was artfully concealed. Spider holes—small, well-hidden pits—sited near entrances provided sentries clear and surprise fire lanes upon interlopers.

The U.S. forces focused on three other principal objectives in the Ryukyus, the Kerama Retto, Keise Shima, and Ie Shima. The first of these consisted of eight mounds of steep, rocky slopes that poked 400 to 600 feet out of the water. The largest added up to only a few square miles and provided sustenance for a handful of inhabitants. There were no roads on the Kerama Retto, merely trails for pack animals or humans. The Kerama Retto offered one irresistible asset. Lying only ten to fifteen miles from Okinawa, within the waters of the otherwise unprepossessing clumps of real estate, was nestled a spacious, well-protected deep anchorage.

It apparently never occurred to the Japanese that the enemy would find the natural harbor within the Kerama Retto so attractive, for little effort had been made to install strong points capable of fending off attacks. Instead, they based only about 100 troops there, supplementing them with some 600 Korean laborers. But one additional and potentially dangerous element consisted of several squadrons of plywood motorboats armed with depth charges.

The sea raider squadron crews were trained to dump their 264-pound explosives as close to the vital areas of a ship as possible. Once the devices rolled off the racks at the back of a speedboat, the pilot had five seconds before they went off. The thin-hulled, slow-moving, and poorly built craft probably would not survive the blast, but it was not considered suicidal in the same terms as a kamikaze. Altogether there were 350 of these Q-boats squirreled around the Kerama Retto.

The island of Ie Shima, about ten square smiles in size, stood less than four miles from the tip of an Okinawa peninsula about twenty miles north of where the initial attack on the Great Loochoo would occur. Flatter than most of its sister islands, Ie Shima boasted a large plateau over much of its interior. Aware of its topographical advantages in an area where few existed, the Japanese had started to construct no fewer than three airfields on Ie Shima. Only at the southern end was the level terrain radically broken. Iegusugu Mountain, a 600-foot, sheer outcrop of rock, dubbed "the Pinnacle" by GIs, jutted above the rest of the oval-shaped plateau and its airstrips like the control tower of an aircraft carrier stationed in the East China Sea. South of the Pinnacle, in the town of Ie, many of the 5,000 civilians who remained when the war reached the Ryukyus, occupied 300 houses. Ie Shima, as one more objective in the overall scheme for the conquest of the Ryukyus, also drew the attention of aerial reconnaissance.

The American strategists, using four army and two marine divisions plus naval and air forces, planned to commit 172,000 combatants supported by another 115,000 troops to invade Okinawa. That required a seagoing component of more than 1,200 vessels, including transports and warships. These would of necessity be supported by ships for screening and attack purposes. The total amphibious forces added up to more than 1,200 vessels. The number does not include ships from the Royal Navy, VAdm. Marc Mitscher's Fast Carrier [Aircraft] Force, and some other units from other groups. At least 1,500 Allied craft would participate in Operation Iceberg.

To keep the enemy back on its heels, in mid-March, the Allied navies punched away at Japanese ships and installations on Kyushu. The foe counterattacked mainly with kamikazes and conventional bombing raids. Over a number of days, the attacks scored hits on a number of aircraft carriers—*Enterprise*, *Intrepid*, *Yorktown*, *Wasp*, and most devastatingly on *Franklin*. A series of explosions and fires rocked the huge ship and the final count showed 724 of the crew killed or missing and another 265 wounded. Another 1,700 owed their lives to rescue efforts by nearby cruisers and destroyers that plucked them from the water after all but key personnel received the abandon-ship order. After the fires aboard "Big Ben" were extinguished, it managed to stay afloat under its own power on a 12,000-mile trip to New York for repairs.

A critical decision in the design of U.S. carriers had specified wooden flight decks rather than steel ones. The use of the lighter-weight material enabled U.S. carriers to carry a greater number of planes compared to the complement aboard British ships, which had steel decks. But Japanese bombs penetrated the thin, flammable wood and crashed through to explode amid hangar decks, munitions magazines, and power plants. (The *Wasp* had a missile smash through before going off between the second and third decks, but the crew quickly extinguished the blaze.)

The trade-off, additional firepower and speed in place of safety—the weightier decks introduced a top-heavy quality and slowed the British carriers—was partly compensated for by intensive instruction in fire fighting. Experts who had served with the New York City and Boston fire departments convinced the Bureau of Ships to issue new fog nozzles that produced a fine spray and snuffed out flames more quickly than a heavy stream of water. Big ships installed fire mains that worked independently of a vessel's power plant, which often shut down after a big hit.

The invasion of Okinawa was scheduled for Easter Sunday, 1 April, and coded "Love Day" since "D day" had come exclusively to signify the Normandy landings. As Love Day approached, the extensive casualties for the Navy continued because of the need to sweep the waters off the Ryukyus clear of mines. During the sanitation of 2,500 square miles of ocean the fire-support destroyer *Halligan* struck a mine that detonated her two forward magazines. Smoke and debris rose two hundred feet in the air and the ship was abandoned with a loss of 153 dead and 39 wounded.

On Palm Sunday, one week before Love Day, U.S. warships began a bombardment of Kerama Retto. Under the cover of this fire, teams of frogmen swam in toward the beaches to map the reefs and mark spots where coral threatened landing craft. When they completed their tasks, on 26 March amtracs raced ashore. Four battalion landing teams from the 77th Division clambered out of their amtracs in the early morning on the beaches of four islands in the Kerama Retto group. Thanks to the preparations and practices carried out in the Philippines, the troops landed at the right places and almost all on schedule. The covering fire had been so effective that not a single man or amtrac was lost.

Official accounts declare that the ragtag defenders, a small complement of soldiers bolstered by the Q-boat pilots and Korean laborers, offered only sporadic resistance with minimal effect. However, in several instances where the U.S. forces headed into the hills, the Japanese and some of their Korean conscripts fought hard. On the island of Zamami hand-to-hand combat brought out Japanese wielding rifles, pistols, and sabers. "The GIs did not think it was so easy," remarked liaison pilot John Kriegsman. "The only way to snuff out the Japs was to walk over the rock mountains. The boat crews did not give up easily. Navy destroyers poured 5-inch shells into the caves to neutralize them." When the Kerama Retto operation ended, the Americans listed 530 of the enemy killed, 121 prisoners, and almost 1,200 civilians rounded up. The 77th Division mourned 78 dead and 177 wounded. Close to 250 suicide boats were seized and eventually rendered harmless, although one officer who attempted to joyride in one lost his life to a booby trap. As many as 300 Japanese soldiers and Korean laborers hid out in the backcountry hills of the rugged islands and they would not actually surrender until after V-E Day.

The 1st and 6th Marine Divisions, which composed the III Amphibious Corps commanded by Maj. Gen. Roy S. Geiger, were to be responsible for the the northern stretches of the Hagushi beaches on Okinawa itself. "I was aboard a troop transport and it was the evening before we stormed onto Okinawa," wrote Ernie Pyle. "We were carrying marines. Some of them were going into combat for the first time; others were veterans from as far back as Guadalcanal. They were a rough, unshaven, competent bunch of Americans. I was landing with them and I felt I was in good hands.

. . . We were nervous. Anybody with any sense is nervous on the night before D day. . . . We would take Okinawa—nobody had any doubt about that. But we knew we would have to pay for it. Some on the ship would not be alive in twenty-four hours."

Pyle awoke before a predawn breakfast of ham and eggs. "Our assault transport carried many landing craft on deck. A derrick swung them over the side, we piled into them as they hung even with the rail, and then the winch lowered them into the water. I went on the first boat to leave our ship. It was just breaking dawn when we left and still more than two hours before H-Hour. Our long ocean trip was over. Our time had run out. This was it. . . .

"An hour and a half before H-Hour at Okinawa, our vast fleet began its final, mighty bombardment of the shore with its big guns. They had been at it for a week, but this was a concentration whose fury had never been approached before. . . . Great sheets of flame flashed out from a battery of guns, gray-brownish smoke puffed up in a huge cloud, then the crash of sound and concussion carried across the water and hit you. Multiply that by hundreds and you had bedlam. Now and then the smoke from a battlewagon would come out in a smoke ring, an enormous one, twenty or thirty feet across, and float upward with perfect symmetry.

"Then came our carrier planes, diving on the beaches and torpedo planes, carrying heavy bombs and incendiaries that spread deep-red flame. Smoke and dust rose up from the shore, thousands of feet high, until finally the land was completely veiled. Bombs and strafing machine guns and roaring engines mingled with the crash of naval bombardment. . . .

"H-Hour was set for 8:30. By 8:00 A.M. directions were being radioed and a voice boomed out to sea to form up waves one and two, to hurry up, to get things moving. Our first wave consisted solely of heavy guns on amphibious tanks which were to get ashore and blast out the pillboxes on the beaches. One minute behind them came the second wave—the first of our foot troops. After that waves came at about ten-minute intervals. Wave six was on its way before wave one ever hit the beach. Wave fifteen was moving up before wave six got to the beach."

"Word came by radio that waves one and two were ashore without much opposition and there were no mines on the beaches. So far, so good. We looked at the shore through binoculars. We could see tanks moving across the fields and the men of the second wave walking inland, standing upright. There were a few splashes in the water at the beach but we couldn't make out any real fire coming from the shore.

"It was all very indefinite and yet it was indicative. The weight began to lift. I wasn't really conscious of it, but I found myself talking more easily with the sailors and somehow the feeling gradually took hold of me that we were to be spared." With the seventh wave, Pyle chugged toward the now less ominous shore, transferring to an amtrac to cross the reef. "I had dreaded the sight of the beach littered with many mangled bodies, and my first look up and down the beach was a reluctant one. Then like a man in the movies who looks away and then suddenly looks back unbelieving, I realized there were no bodies anywhere—and no wounded. What a wonderful feeling.

"Our entire regiment came ashore with only two casualties: one was a marine who hurt his foot getting out of an amphibious truck; the other was, of all things, a case of heat prostration! And to add to the picnic atmosphere, they had fixed me up with a big sack of turkey wings, bread, oranges, and apples. So instead of grabbing a hasty bit of K rations for our first meal ashore, we sat and lunched on turkey wings and oranges."

Marine platoon leader Bob Craig, as part of the 1st Division reserve, headed for the shore with his men in midafternoon. "Our LCVP [Landing Craft, Vehicles and Personnel] stuck on a coral reef about 200 yards out. Waded ashore, and moved inland about 200 yards and started to dig in. Lost one squad leader, Corporal Boris. Dropped a rifle on his foot and hurt it. He should be back.

"About dusk (6:30 P.M.) we moved up the hill toward Yontan Airfield. Were halfway up when a Jap plane came over. All the ships opened up with their AA. While we dodged falling shrapnel, the Jap landed on the airfield and got out of his plane. When he tried to run, some boys in an amtrac got him. We moved across a corner of the airfield, past a motorless Jap plane. Made first contact with the enemy. A sniper. I dived into a shell hole as two shots zipped through the grass near me. Too dark to do anything, so moved another 100 yards and dug in for the night, just east of the village of Sobe. Awake most of the night—partly in fear and partly because the fleas in the grass really bothered me. The only activity of the night, aside from the regular naval bombardment, was the appearance of another Jap plane on the Pacific side of the island. We saw a little 20mm AA but with no results."

Company A of the 7th Marine Regiment, with Don Farquhar in command of the machine gun platoon, drew the assignment of reserve. "We were in the third wave," said Farquhar. "I wasn't scared; the feeling is just like playing football in college, nervous as can be until you get in the game then the jitters are gone. It was a great relief to find the beaches not defended and a real surprise. We had been trained in kill or be killed, and I had taken some special training in bayonet fighting, so I was rather looking forward to being able to use my special training."

Jim Moll remembered, "They told us Okinawa would not be easy because we were getting closer to Japan proper. There were some larger cities we would have to take, more occasions when we would be up against larger concentrations of enemy troops than what we had met in the past, and also more concentrations of civilians. It was a blessing to land on the beach without a single casualty. I don't think anybody, including the highest brass, expected this but whoever planned the operation deserves the highest medal."

Sergeant Harry Manion, with the recon company of the 6th Marine Division, who developed his expertise at scouting and patrolling while mopping up on Guadalcanal and then applied his skills on Guam, recalled: "Recon Company went ashore and moved directly inland. Came across some caves, with civilians and perhaps some military. Called out in Japanese for the people to come out. Reply was one shot. In goes WP [white phosphorus grenade]. Out come some civilians. No soldiers. We left them for the civil affairs people. Still plenty of daylight. Moved off the left flank of the division. Dug holes, put out security, and flaked out. Later, after dark, we heard firing coming from Yontan Airfield area. We learned that a Japanese pilot landed his fighter on the field. Always some who don't get the word."

Earl Rice, who had almost been transferred out of the 1st Marine Division for misbehavior, feared another debacle like Peleliu. "There were so many boats out there," said Rice, "it was like land rather than water. Before we got on the Higgins boat they gave us only a piece of fruit and some water. Those Higgins boats went up and down, up and down, so the idea was to keep us from getting sick. I puked over the side and then I felt fine after that. The guy says,

'Fix bayonets.' You don't know who the hell is on that beach, what you're heading into. I remembered what I saw at Peleliu. You fix that bayonet and see everybody doing the same. Then you hit the ground, the boat touches the shore, you can hear it. You know you're going to be getting off. Then you see everybody, myself included, blessing their selves, everyone's full of religion."

"The religious had attended services at 3:00 A.M.," said Bob Jackson with the 96th Infantry Division. "It was a gorgeous Easter/April Fool's Day. We embarked into the landing craft and spent the usual two hours boating around in circles, under an azure sky—I can't help the cliché. There was no shore activity except that of our shore parties so we rode in basking in the cool but sunny weather that reminded me of San Francisco on such a day. The landing, with those expert seamen, was dryfooted, unlike most of our previous experiences with Army boat commanders. We came ashore, got into columns of companies, and moved inland as if it were a school exercise."

In the southwest, the 2d Marine Division loaded men from troop transports into landing craft and seven waves consisting of 168 LCVPs set course for the Minatoga beaches on the southeastern side of the island. At 08:30, as the first GIs and leathernecks stepped onto the Hagushi beaches, the vessels bearing the 2d Marines reversed course and returned to the mother ships. The feint drew one salvo of four rounds. But the official communiqué from Japanese headquarters triumphantly announced that "an enemy landing attempt on the eastern coast of Okinawa on Sunday morning was completely foiled, with heavy losses to the enemy."

By the time darkness fell on Love Day and all of the invaders had burrowed into the ground for the night, the beachhead stretched along more than twelve miles of the Okinawa coastline. In some places the troops had pushed inland for three miles. The 17th Regimental Combat Team of the 7th Division had occupied a now deserted Kadena airfield shortly before noon. Patrols from the 17th gazed upon the east coast waterfront of Okinawa in midafternoon. With the two Marine divisions making swift progress into the lightly defended north, the island had been virtually chopped in half in less than twelve hours.

Marines from the 6th Division took over Yontan, the bigger and better developed of the airstrips, without any opposition. The booty included shattered Japanese planes and supplies, destroyed by the preinvasion bombardments. The swiftness of the advance surprised not only the Americans but obviously the enemy, which explains the fate of the unfortunate pilot who sought to land at Yontan after it had fallen. Statisticians figured at least 60,000 men reached shore on Love Day. The bulk of these were foot soldiers backed up by divisional artillery and tanks plus a generous number of service troops. The only serious opposition came from the air. A suicide plane crashed into the battleship *West Virginia*, another splashed down close enough to damage some transports, and two kamikazes off Minatoga struck an LST, killing 24, injuring 21, and a transport with a loss of 16 dead and 39 wounded. While these losses, from a strategic viewpoint, were negligible, they signaled the coming challenge to the Navy.

Americans also had seen individual Japanese pilots try to crash into them, or strike ships, certainly more frequently than such tactics were employed by U.S. servicemen, but until late 1944, it was not recognized that this was now a deliberate strategic weapon. The series of defeats suffered on land, at sea, and in the air after the loss of Guadalcanal convinced some Japanese military theorists that the last hope lay in assaults that would destroy the principal weapon bringing the war to Japan, the aircraft carrier. American land-based bombers could never have hoped to reach the homeland had not the floating airfields that destroyed the Japanese Navy provided tactical support. The fleet air arms enabled soldiers and Marines to conquer islands that now served as bases for the big planes. And with the Imperial Navy vanquished, carrier task forces would bring their short-range bombers to the Japanese doorstep.

The immediate inspiration for the suicide airplane came from RAdm. Masbomi Arima, who commanded aircraft squadrons that were being defeated in the Philippine skies. On 15 October, five days before the invasion of Leyte, Admiral Arima aimed his own plane at the carrier *Franklin.* A U.S. combat air patrol, hovering in the vicinity, spotted Arima and shot him down, just short of his target. (Some historians erroneously continue to claim Arima actually crashed into the carrier.)

The grand if unsuccessful gesture by Arima confirmed a program already in progress under Admiral Takajiro Ohnishi. He had been encouraging navy pilots to take such an initiative as a last resort. Now it would become the basic goal of a corps of fliers. Their acceptance and participation in the program that obligated their deaths during the final nine months of the war indicates the deeply ingrained belief in Imperial Japan with its emperor.

Onishi dubbed his group *Kamikaze Tokubetsu Kogetitai,* which roughly translates as the Divine Wind Special Attack Corps. The word kamikaze bore special meaning. Japanese history told of a sixteenth-century Mongol emperor who organized a huge amphibious force to conquer the country but a "divine wind" in the form of a typhoon blew away the Chinese-based fleet.

Anything that could fly, from trainers to bombers and fighter planes, eventually even pre–World War II ones with fabric-covered wings, and gliders, were adapted for use by the special attack forces. In addition, engineers designed a 4,700-pound, rocket-propelled flying bomb, the *ohka* or cherry blossom (known to Americans as the *baka,* meaning screwball). The *baka,* launched from a Betty-model bomber, carried a pilot to guide the missile on a one-way trip.

The tactic of suicidal missions expanded to include the kind of suicide motor boats found in Kerama Retto. An even more primitive approach, the *Fukuryu*—Crouching Dragon—called for men with scuba equipment to blast ship bottoms by using mines attached to poles. To Americans all these fell under the label of kamikaze, but strictly speaking the Japanese applied the term only to the naval air operations.

Neither conventional aerial raids nor kamikazes seriously interfered with the Love Day operations. But the fleet absorbed some hard punches that night. A pair of transport vessels were struck by kamikazes. One blow fell at twilight, 7:10 P.M., and the other at the seemingly safer hour near midnight. Both ships remained afloat and able to unload their cargo before steaming off for repairs. But another 21 sailors died and 68 were injured.

On 2 April, the ships in the Kerama Retto anchorage and off the Hagushi beaches reeled from lashes inflicted by the divine winds. Mindful of exposure to the enemy, a group of transports carrying soldiers from the 77th Division after reembarking them from the Kerama Retto operations, headed toward a position that would remove them from harm's way. A flock of kamikazes, at least ten planes, bore down on the fifteen-ship convoy. The destroyer *Dickerson* took a direct hit on the bridge. The fifty-three dead included the skipper, and the unsalvageable ship was towed to sea and scuttled. Two other warships escaped with lesser damage from attacks on them.

That night, the bulk of the 77th Division's 305th Infantry Regiment was aboard the *Henrico*, the flagship of Transdiv 50. Dick Forse, the crewman for an M8—self-propelled, armored 75mm gun—remembered, "There was no general quarters signal, although there was some firing from other ships. I had noticed that the radar dish on the mast was not going around. I had been sitting on a hatch cover on the main deck, forward. I got up and went on a line for ice cream. We heard the sound of planes coming in. We couldn't see them because the ship's forecastle blocked our view to the front. But I got a glimpse of the tail of a plane as it went by. I dismissed it as the tail of a Hellcat from the U.S. Navy.

"An instant after glimpsing the tail, I heard a 'kerchunk.' I don't remember it as being very loud. The Jap plane, a Frances [two-engine navy bomber], hit the *Henrico*'s superstructure [bridge area], near the spot where I had previously been sitting. One engine broke off and rolled, flaming, down a corridor into the wardroom where many officers were writing or just batting the breeze. One of the bombs on the plane also exploded.

"I ran to the side and saw a big hole in the superstructure with showers of sparks and clouds of heavy gray smoke pouring out. The *Henrico*'s steam whistle went off and continued one long shriek for about fifteen minutes before it finally ran out of steam. Another guy and I ran inside the forecastle to get out of the way, but we found ourselves in the way of four navy men who were getting into asbestos suits. There were several fires in the superstructure and the ship was dead in the water. There was no power whatsoever and fire hoses couldn't be used. They lowered small water pumps into the sea, but most of them stopped working when they hit the water.

"The steam whistle that continued to scream scared us. I must have checked my life preserver fifteen times an hour, hoping it would work if we had to abandon ship. I went below deck to stay out of the way. Battery power lines were being set up everywhere because there was no electricity. There also was no drinking water and no water in the heads. I realized that the ship was listing to starboard which really concerned me. Soon after, all able bodies were called topside and told to stand along the rail on the port side because of the ship's list. A destroyer passed by us up close, trying to hose down fires on our ship. But the sea was too choppy. First the hose would point toward the sky and then down into the ocean. Later they tried to shoot a line to us so we could be towed. They tried four or five times but the line missed. Everytime they fired the line I jumped a foot.

"The rest of the convoy continued on after the attack. Soon we were alone, out in the ocean. I looked out on the horizon and could see two ships burning. Then the moon came up. It was the biggest moon I have ever seen, a full moon that could silhouette the *Henrico* for the Jap subs. My morale was not very high at this point. But no subs attacked us and we were later towed by another APA [attack transport] into the Kerama Retto anchorage. It was loaded with ships crippled by kamikazes. Four or five of us slept in the paint locker that night. None of us had any desire to sleep in our quarters, which were two decks below. For breakfast we got an apple and an orange and two cans of beer. That's the only time I know of when the Navy issued alcoholic drinks to enlisted men in a combat zone.

"The *Henrico* tied up next to another APA, the *Sarasota*.

We were to transfer to it. We heard that someone was inside the pitch-black *Henrico* and would not come out. One of the last men taken off it was this soldier. He looked like a teenager, and with great difficulty, some sailors had made their way through equipment below deck, brought him up two sets of stairs to the main deck. He was very distressed, shaking, tears streaming down his face, snuffling, shuffling along rather than walking as he was helped by sailors on each arm across to the *Sarasota*.

Shortly after the plane blasted into the *Henrico*, one of the gun crews on the *Suffolk*, a nearby APA, spotted a man in the water. Joe Taranto, a member of the gun crew, remembers, "We thought he was a Jap pilot. We were ready to shoot him when he yelled, 'I'm an American GI from the 77th Division.' I think that was the greatest day of my life; we were there to save that GI from dying."

But aboard the *Henrico* many others were not so fortunate. Transdiv 50's commander and the captain of the ship were killed along with twenty-one others from the Navy. Among the Army officers in the wardroom were most of the 305th's top command. The dead included the 305th's commander, Col. Vincent Tanzola, and his executive officer as well as eleven more soldiers.

The *Henrico* was not the only 77th Division transport mauled. Larry Gerevas, a replacement assigned to Company K of the 307th Regiment, sailed from Leyte on the *Telefare*. "Aboard our ship, many of the army troops were assigned various duties. Some assisted the Navy gunners with the 40mm antiaircraft guns and others such as myself stood guard at various stations on the main deck. The purpose was to prevent any Japs from climbing onto the ship.

"During the air attack on April 2, I was on guard near the bow of the ship. At this location were two landing barges secured to a metal support rack about two feet above the deck. Suddenly, a terrific explosion occurred directly above me. Thinking it was a bomb, I dived under a rack holding the barges. Smoking chunks of metal rained down on the area where I had been standing a moment before. Debris was everywhere. Later I learned that a Jap bomber had dived into our ship, sheared off some of the ship's masts, fell on a 40mm gun mount, and then slid into the sea. Three Army men that manned that gun were killed."

Ed Fitzgerald, the first sergeant of Service Company, was aboard the *Monrovia.* "When the kamikazes started to come in, the captain made me chase guys off the deck. We didn't like it below decks. It wasn't comfortable, and we wondered about submarines and if something came busting in there. I was already inside on a ladder going back down when I saw the airplane coming and I knew it would hit. I wasn't that curious that I wanted to stay up there and get a look at the pilot in his white scarf. One sergeant, though, Harry O'Gawa, couldn't resist staying up there. He lost a leg from the explosion." The ship, however, suffered no serious damage.

14

Tennozan

BASED UPON THE SITE OF A GREAT BATTLE IN THE SIXTEENTH century, the Japanese used the name *Tennozan* to mark any critical campaign in subsequent history. They considered the fight for Okinawa worthy of the designation and code-named their massive onslaught against the enemy amphibious forces Operation Ten-Go. From 3–5 April the Japanese raids on the U.S. armada amounted to no more than mosquito bites, but on 6 April, Ten-Go got off the mark as they swarmed over the targets. Endowed with the name of kikusi—floating chrysanthemums—ten massed kamikaze blows employing 355 planes concentrated on the Americans hovering in the seas by the islands. About the same number of conventional bombers also struck.

Minesweepers supported by a pair of destroyers, the *Rodman* and the *Emmons*, engaged in the clearance of a channel between Iheya Retto and the main island. In command of the *Emmons* was Lt. Comdr. Eugene Foss. A Harvard graduate (1934), Foss was a "plank owner," a member of the original

Emmons crew. Said Foss, "On April 6, with a sister ship, *Rodman* number 456—our number was 457—we were providing shore-gun protection along the northwestern coast for some wooden-hulled minesweepers. When they have their gear out, minesweepers cannot maneuver. Shore gunfire did not materialize. But this day, the Japs mounted their first major kamikaze attack. To everybody I knew, this was a totally different philosophy. It was something none of us had any education in. We knew of Marines who would storm anything, but nothing of this definitely suicidal action. But we all realized that these were very dangerous weapons and had heard about them before the Okinawa show. We'd even seen one dive on a light cruiser, coming right out from a combat air patrol.

"There wasn't anything you could do except fire at them. There were no special tactics. We did have the new proximity fuses on our ammo. These had just been issued to the fleet and we were not sure how well they worked. On this fairly mild day, with the weather overcast, around 3:00 P.M. we spotted twenty or thirty of them coming at an altitude of about 3,000 feet. We watched a dozen or so circling overhead, as if they were getting their nerve up. We did have a combat air patrol over us also.

"They started to peel off and head for us, one by one. It didn't work. We had all our guns going and our bursts would show the Corsairs where the enemy was. The *Emmons* gunners got as many as six of them and the Marine fighters dropped at least another half dozen." The *Rodman*, however, was in serious trouble. One plane smashed into the forecastle and a close-in explosion by a splashed plane or bomb ruptured a section of the hull. Sheets of flame darted to the height of the bridge and, temporarily, 456 lost power.

The *Emmons* moved to assist its stricken partner, but soon

realized it now faced its own peril. The *Rodman* was in no condition to offer supporting fire nor were the minesweepers, still frantically trying to retrieve their gear. Foss recalls, "They launched simultaneous attacks, four or five at the same time. As many as five kamikazes slashed through the battery of five-inchers and the spray of 40mm and 20mm cannon fire, to smack into the thin aluminum steel of the *Emmons*. One landed in the wardroom passage and blew up with its gasoline. Another hit the fantail. We had to shut down the engines because we couldn't steer. We were drifting, like a target. But we still had our antiaircraft guns and five-inchers while they came at us from all sides." A third blow also struck aft as a Val [Japanese fighter-bomber] swept away what was still working on the fantail.

"An ensign, assistant gunnery officer Ross Elliot, ordered several people to crouch down on the deck when a plane was coming in for a strafing attack. He draped himself over the men and saved them, but lost his own life." Elliot would receive a posthumous Navy Cross.

On the bridge, Foss tried to shift the steering control. But another kamikaze blasted into the superstructure. The impact shattered the bridge and blew Foss overboard. He found himself, badly burned about the face and hands, temporarily blinded, in the water. The final thrust rammed the starboard bow area. Dead in the water, fires out of control, the crew suffering the horrible wounds of molten metal, burns from searing steam and gasoline-fed fires, the *Emmons* suffered the final indignity of an erroneous 'abandon ship' command. Actually, no one gave the order but word spread that the situation was hopeless. A number of sailors jumped into the water, joining others like Foss hurled there by explosions or who because of the fire in their area had no choice but to take their chances in the sea. The sweepers, *Recruit* and

Ransom, started to rescue those in the water. Two more planes drew beads on the wreckage of the *Emmons* but suddenly shifted their attentions to the pair offering succor. Gunners on the *Recruit* and *Ransom* splashed both.

Remnants of the *Emmons* crew, led by the gunnery officer, Lt. J. J. Griffin—the skipper was gone, the exec dead, and the next in the chain of command badly wounded—struggled to contain the fires and keep the destroyer from sinking. It was a losing effort; she continued to settle ever deeper. Griffin consulted with the few officers still on the *Emmons*. The damage-control news relayed to Griffin left no choice. One main engine was inoperable; there were no means by which to steer. The fire forward could not be controlled. Except for a pair of 20-mm guns the ship was bereft of firepower. They were still sinking and faced an imminent explosion of what remained in the magazines and fuel tanks. Griffin, around 6:00 P.M., some three hours after the first kamikazes appeared, ordered abandon ship. The last man climbed onto a small mine-disposal vessel, the PGM-11, at 8:00 P.M. Subsequently, Admiral Turner directed a destroyer to sink the burning hulk. Sixty-four died and another 71 were injured from a ship's complement of 237. Foss spent many months undergoing skin grafts and other treatments to repair his body.

Meanwhile, in the area of Kerama Retto, combat air patrols scrambled to knock down the enemy aircraft. The relentless kamikazes wreaked havoc in the harbor. To stop the suicide bombers before they reached Kerama Retto, a picket line ringed the Ryukyu chain. In midafternoon of 6 April, the destroyer *Bush* at Picket Station #1 and the *Colhoun* at #2 succumbed to a series of floating chrysanthemums, sinking with more than 100 dead. Combat air patrols had run into so many of the enemy, they could not prevent the attacks.

Destruction of the destroyers *Bush* and *Colhoun* signaled the opening round of kamikaze fury directed at those on picket duty. Jumped by interceptors summoned at the behest of the pickets, the minimally fueled Japanese planes discovered they could not evade the enemy aircraft and then fly onto the strategic targets off the Hagushi beaches and at Kerama Retto. Their meager amount of gasoline would only allow them to focus on those closest at hand, the seaborne sentinels. Furthermore, those in command realized they must destroy or weaken the advance-warning and protection network if the suicide missions were to reach the bigger targets.

With Japanese air and ground forces desperately engaged in the Okinawa campaign, the Imperial Navy threw its last remaining surface power into the Ten-Go game. Out of the naval base at Kure on the Inland Sea steamed the *Yamato*, at 68,000 tons displacement, the largest battleship afloat, and with 18.1-inch guns, more than a match for the mightiest that flew either U.S. or British standards. Their biggest ships fired 14- and 16-inch shells.

The *Yamato* sallied forth on 6 April in the company of the light cruiser *Yahagi* and eight destroyers, designated Task Force II, a puny force considering the massive number of ships available from the American fleet. Worse, the *Yamato* sailed without air cover. The notion that she could navigate the 600 miles to the Okinawa anchorages without discovery, followed by an all-out onslaught from carrier-based planes, could not even be sustained as a fantasy.

In the confused, conflicted, and frustrated direction of Japanese military affairs, some hoped that at least the small task force, as part of Operation Ten-Go, could distract the

American carriers sufficiently to allow the kamikazes of 6 and 7 April to reach their targets. If *Yamato* somehow managed to reach the Okinawa area, it could train its huge turrets on anything in range and, as a last resort, beach itself where it could provide a kind of artillery support for the Japanese ground forces. The operational plans directed that when all ammunition had been expended in this last effort, the ship's crew should try to contact the ground forces and become infantrymen.

Some historians like Morison bluntly describe the *Yamato*'s voyage as designed for a one-way trip with only enough fuel to carry it to the Hagushi roadstead. But George Feifer in *Tennozan* points out that officers on the Combined Fleet staff scrounged enough oil to fill the battleship's bunkers three-quarters full, more than enough for a round-trip. While few held out any hope for survival, enough navy people hoped to give *Yamato* at least a long shot at coming home.

Task Force II had barely cleared the Inland Sea at 5:45 P.M. on 6 April when the U.S. submarine *Threadfin* detected the flotilla. The sub notified VAdm. Marc Mitscher's Task Force 58 some 400 miles off, which included many carriers. Immediately, search planes began to prowl the skies, peering at the sea below for the quarry. At dawn on 7 April, a pilot from the *Essex* sighted the *Yamato* and her companions. Task Force II now endured continuous surveillance from aircraft based on as many as a dozen carriers and which kept safely out of range of antiaircraft fire. The shadow team included flying boats based at Kerama Retto. Mitscher closed the distance to 250 miles and then launched a series of gigantic strikes—the first one sent up 280 dive and torpedo bombers.

Harry Jones, an Avenger pilot, with Torpedo Squadron 17

[VT-17], Carrier Air Group, flying off the *Hornet*, said, "Scuttlebutt on the ship had it that the battleship admirals who outranked the air admirals wanted to shoot it out with the Japanese. But the *Yamato*'s 18-inch guns were bigger than anything we had and the air admirals won out. We would intercept them. We took off from the *Hornet*, seven torpedo bombers with fighters and dive-bombers along with us. The torpedo planes, which had search radar, did the navigation and it was a poor day for flying, rainy, misty, a lot of scud [clouds], not much ceiling. The flight leader from another carrier developed engine trouble and turned the lead over to our air group, bossed by Comdr. E. G. Conrad, a Naval Academy graduate.

"The lead pilot said they ought to be in range, but we couldn't see anything on radar. Conrad said stay on course. One plane radioed that he saw a blip off to starboard about fifty miles out and we turned right. Then we saw them. Holy mackerel! The *Yamato* looked like the Empire State Building plowing through the water, It was really big. We orbited around out of their gun range. They opened up with main batteries, 18-inch guns. What was very surprising to us was there were no Japanese aircraft around even though we were near their home islands.

"The air boss gave us the order of attack. He said, 'Shasta,' meaning those from the *Hornet* 'go in first.' We didn't have too much ceiling. I was at 12,000 feet at most, and usually liked to start at 18,000 feet for a steep approach and then right over the water, drop the torpedo, and then get the hell out of there. Meanwhile, the bombers are supposed to be going down, so we all hit the ship simultaneously. I kept diving toward different puffs of smoke, where shells had already exploded. The first two fighter planes were to strafe destroyers to suppress and draw off the fire. I saw one of our replacement pilots take a direct hit and go down. I went down, dropped my torpedo, and went right across the bow of *Yamato*. The ship was turning, but in our attack we always dropped in a fan shape so no matter which way a ship is turning it's going to get hit. Our group was credited with two torpedo hits among the planes, but the gun camera that showed my angle on the bow didn't credit me with a hit."

The hunters swarmed over the targets while Task Force II responded with fusillades dominated by the *Yamato*'s half dozen 6-inch batteries, 24 5-inch guns, and 150 machine guns. But only nine minutes after the *Yamato* spotted the first wave of attackers, a pair of bombs from Helldivers struck near the mainmast and a few moments later the first torpedo exploded against the thick armor plate of the port bow. Already, the *Yahagi*, victim of a bomb and a torpedo, lay dead in the water, while one of the destroyer screen had slid beneath the sea, bow first, taking most of her crew down with her.

A brief respite ensued as the first attackers retired, but a second strike bore in less than an hour later. The hail of bullets and shell fragments toppled sailors on the supership. Its powerful engines and sleek design enabled it to temporarily dodge torpedoes. To the thick curtain of smaller guns it added its 18.1-inchers, training them low to the water where they exploded great spouts that might destroy aircraft skimming the sea as they prepared to launch their torpedoes.

For the next hour and fifteen minutes, the carrier aircraft, killer bees pouring out of many hives, stung the *Yamato*. Five more torpedoes struck home and the ship began to list. Its commander ordered flooding of several compartments to correct the ship's attitude. The combination of that water, the sea pouring in through the holes created by the torpedoes, and steam escaping from ruptured boilers snuffed out the lives of several hundred sailors. The tactic failed to correct the list and only one screw continued to work. *Yamato* lost speed and any real maneuverability for defense.

Third and fourth strikes pounded away at the crippled behemoth unable to respond to commands or to defend herself. At two in the afternoon the torment of the *Yamato* reached its peak. The assassins, with names like Dauntless, Hellcat, Avenger, and Corsair, drilled her almost at will. It was hopeless. From amid the wreckage on the *Yamato* bridge, the admiral in command, Seiichi Ito, ordered the mission aborted. The ships still able to operate were to pick up men from the sea and from disabled vessels and try to make port. Then Admiral Ito shook hands with some officers on the bridge and locked himself in his quarters. He would go down with the *Yamato*.

With ten torpedo hits and five bomb blasts as well as countless near-miss explosions, the munitions aboard the *Yamato* administered the *coup de grâce*. Deep, subdeck blasts erupted a 6,000-foot-high tongue of fire, and the smoke rose more than four miles as the mightiest battleship in the world expired after two hours of battering. One or two U.S. aircraft, hovering over the battleship, may have been victims of the debris from detonation of *Yamato*'s ordnance. The body counts for the destruction of Task Force II range from 3,700 to 4,250 lost to the Imperial Navy. As many as 3,000 aboard the *Yamato* died. Along with the battleship, the Americans sank the light cruiser *Yahagi* and four destroyers. With the few survivors plucked from the sea, the four surviving destroyers limped away. Mitscher reported his losses at ten planes and twelve airmen.

While the splintered vestiges of the Imperial Navy fled under the onslaught of the carrier-based attack, the 96th Infantry Division rammed up against the first in the series of bulwarks of the Shuri line, the in-depth Okinawa defense. Bob Jackson, with B Company of the 382d, recalled those first days as resembling a tour of an exotic land. "We were in reserve, behind the 381st and 383d making the main attack. We crossed interesting, rather hilly country. The tombs that were to be a big part of the difficult fight ahead were deserted. On breaks we'd inspect them as best we could. We were still in fear of the highly advertised snakes [habu]. My only memory of action in these first days was watching as our company half-ton truck hit a mine and rolled over. There was small damage, but I lost a Japanese bowl I'd found beside the road.

"When the forward regiments ran into resistance, our battalion, led by A Company, was committed and began receiving fire. A small hill had been invested by A Company, from which it was trying to move forward against strong resistance. We in B Company were behind them and could see the mountains where the Japanese had fine artillery emplacements. A Company was mauled pretty badly and had barrage after barrage of artillery thrown at them. This was our first experience with concentrated artillery fire and we were scared!" In previous campaigns, the Japanese had demonstrated a serious ignorance of the most effective use of artillery, limiting themselves to a single shell at a time. On Okinawa, where they possessed ample pieces and ammunition, they showed Jackson they had learned how to use their heavier guns.

"About this time, the Japanese unleashed a previously unknown weapon, a 320mm mortar. It blew a big hole in the ground and frightened us; it sounded like a freight train coming in. But it did little damage to the troops. On this hill I experienced my first abject and shameful fear. We had now relieved A Company and were preparing to move three platoons into position when we came under a severe artillery and mortar barrage. It was awesome. I understand one becomes inured, but that afternoon I tried to dig my way to the center of the earth. When the barrage lifted, I got up, shook the dirt off my fatigues, and went back to work with my platoon. I have never forgotten, however, how I screamed in fear and how hard I shoved myself into the dirt of that Okinawa hillside.

"We had penetrated the outer reaches of the Japanese main line of resistance (MLR) before the largest city, Naha. My company commander assigned my platoon to the left flank of the battalion. I was to occupy a small knoll facing away from the rest of the outfit. Darkness was coming on as I took my messenger to the knoll while the platoon sergeant brought up the squads. The men were about fifty yards behind me as I gave instructions to a squad leader on where to place his BAR and have the men dig in. Suddenly, a Nambu machine gun ripped off a burst of fire. That has the sound of a cliché, but the Nambu was extremely rapid firing and its sound was a frightening rip of noise. I was sloppy and had not thought that the Japanese could have moved so close to our lines.

"At the same time this Japanese unit, probably five or six men, began lobbing knee-mortar shells at us. We used to joke that those shells would have to hit you on the head without a helmet to do any harm. The surprise of the concussive noise and the noise of the machine gun made us drop like tin soldiers. No one was hurt at that time. We were just scattered over an area of about fifty square yards. One of my squad leaders, looking for a site for his BAR, was about twenty-five yards off across a small swale.

"I had jumped into a shallow drainage ditch that ran toward

the enemy line. The squad leader with the BAR and a couple of men occupied a similar ditch on the other side of the swale. We tried to fire at the enemy but the machine gun was well hidden as it searched for us with bursts of fire. I looked for the rest of the platoon and saw them running, helter-skelter across the fields, back toward their previous positions. They were, in the last rays of the sun, a mob returning 'home' with all military discipline gone. I was angry, frustrated, and very frightened.

"Waving and yelling, I tried to get the squad leader to work back to the former company position. He misunderstood and tried to come toward me. The Nambu opened up as he rose to run. He was hit, and I could see, badly. By then there were only the two of us and darkness was coming down fast. Crawling forward in my ditch, I came upon the sergeant, lying on his side, badly wounded, and crying in pain. He was a mess in his middle where the machine-gun burst had almost cut him in two. I had no idea what to do and doubted we'd get help. Every so often the Nambu or a knee mortar would fire. I got my poncho out of my pack, lay it in front of the sergeant, and, with great perseverance on his part, managed to get him onto the poncho. By dragging him a few feet at a time down the ditch I got fairly close to the company line. By this time, something had happened to silence the Nambu and knee mortars—maybe they had just pulled back—and some squads from B Company came out with a stretcher. I went back to the company perimeter, sat down and shook. All night we remained under artillery and mortar fire."

Don Dencker, with Company L of the 383d, reported a similar gradual involvement in the campaign. "Our first encounter with the Japs, except for a few sniper shots, was a heavy shelling from artillery early in the afternoon of April

5. We were still in reserve, but had moved up to about 600 yards of the front lines. Our CO, Captain Fitzpatrick, was seriously wounded trying to drag to safety a man fatally wounded by one of the first shells. This act of bravery cost us a damn good company commander. During the following days we were subjected to numerous artillery and mortar barrages. Our entrenching tools became our lifesavers."

Len Lazarick, with Company K of the 382d, had settled in that first night with the modest luxury of being in reserve. "We didn't take it for granted that we had any guarantee of safety. We did our standard two hours on guard and four hours off vigil on the company perimeter. Although the temperature during the day was comfortably warm, I found the night chilly and stood guard with a blanket draped around my shoulders. We usually dug in three men to a hole and when possible in the shape of the letter Y. The foxhole was deep enough so that from a sitting position, only our heads were exposed while on guard duty during the night. Farther south on Okinawa, we ran into hard ground and often were satisfied by piling loose rocks and coral just high enough to protect a sleeping comrade from ground-level shell or grenade fragments.

"I didn't own an OD jungle sweater until 6 April when I was able to remove one from the pack of a dead GI lying in a ditch beside the road we were marching along. The sweater was a pullover made of lightweight wool. It helped keep me warm during the chilly nights. Before I obtained it I shivered a great deal with only a single blanket. When we moved south, still in reserve, I was assigned to be the point. I don't know to this day what I did wrong to be so honored. It is not a comfortable feeling to be alone, 100 yards ahead of your column, searching for enemy snipers or stragglers."

Company K rifleman Paul Westman said, "The ground

troops met very little opposition at first. We began to hope it would be a walkover. What opposition we did meet served as invaluable experience for untested replacements like myself. Later replacements wouldn't be so lucky. I remember the passwords and countersigns for the first days on Okinawa. They were glass/house; long/lane; forty/thieves; flimsy/skirt, and fair/weather. We were told that the Japanese had difficulty with the letters L and R. When I first heard the cracks of rifle bullets going past, I thought, 'Man, you can get hurt! You don't have a target pit to hide in now.' Close rounds of artillery scared me worse. My mouth would get dry, my legs would go rubbery. I found out they would still function one morning when two shells came very close. The squad leader said, 'Let's get the hell outa here!'—and we did. Two others didn't. Three more shells hit and when we came back, one of the new replacements was lying outside the hole and his clothes were smoking. The other was still in the hole with a shattered leg and other wounds. Litter-bearers took them away. I don't think either one of them got to fire his M1 even once. That was the time I learned that if I paid close attention to S. Sgt. Jeff Brooks, I'd probably last longer."

According to Dick Thom, the S-3 with the 381st Regiment, the preinvasion instructions directed that civilians on Okinawa should be treated as if they were soldiers. "But one day after we landed, we received a brand-new order that said for us to look to the welfare of the civilians we had been killing. At one point I saw fifteen people wearing tan uniforms in a rice paddy. I ordered a tank that was with us to fire on them with machine guns. They were all killed and I found out they had been in the home guard, like Boy Scouts. They had all deserted, but they didn't know enough to discard the uniforms. Nobody knew where the enemy was. Everybody seemed to be standing around and sucking their thumbs. It didn't help that we had a captain who was the CO of a rifle company and couldn't read a map."

On 8 April Bob Jackson, with B Company of the 382d, ate a noontime hot meal brought up from the company kitchens in the rear. It was for him the fourth day of the contact with the enemy. His battalion commander called for a two-platoon attack on Tombstone Ridge, so named for the mausoleum in the distance. "The ground sloped away from our positions to a ditch running across our front," recalled Jackson. "Directly in the middle was a stone bridge. The company commander, [Capt. George R. Gerrans], in textbook fashion, took me, as the leader of the two platoons, to the heights facing the front and pointed out the ditch as the jumping-off point for the attack. It was almost like an exercise at Fort Benning, with the captain even giving me a regulation five-point field order.

"I collected Lt. John Fox of the other attacking platoon and our platoon sergeants for a less formal battle order. I knew Fox only slightly; he was young, from another regiment originally where he had received a battlefield commission on Leyte. Both of us had considerable battlefield experience, but neither knew our men very well. We went down to the ditch, spread out, and in good order. When we were in position there, Lieutenant Fox, with his platoon on my left, informed me he was ready to go. I raised the antenna of my SCR 536 radio, ready to inform company HQ to start the preparatory mortar barrage. It was to precede us as we moved toward Tombstone Ridge.

"I climbed up the side of the ditch, was about seven feet deep, and called the company to start the barrage. When the shiny antenna rose above the ditch, a machine gun opened up from an enfiladed position to our left. It was impossible to see where it came from. But every time I tried to use the radio, bursts of fire skimmed the top of the embankment. It would be suicide to try climbing the steep bank, get over the edge, and into a running position. I scooted down and ordered the men to dig in until I could contact the company for further instructions.

"Exposed as we were to enfilading fire, we'd lose most of our attack group if we tried to complete our move. We had no chance to take the objective. I tried to call in mortar fire by hand signals to the company commander in the position behind us. The captain was unable to read my signals in that deep ditch. I wasn't able to indicate anything but that the fire came from our left. The Japanese apparently moved the machine gun about this time. It fired directly down the ditch into our positions.

"I was wounded twice in this first burst. I had been sitting against the wall of the ditch with my feet stretched out before me, trying to figure what in hell to do. I noticed the nea hole in the middle of my combat boot, turned over anc started to crawl toward the left from which direction the gur seemed to be firing. I was hit again in the upper thigh anc that hurt! My runner, who was digging into the wall of the ditch right next to me, had a perfectly positioned, three-sho group through the top of his helmet.

"The men were panicking with fear; they didn't knov where to fire or how to defend themselves. Neither did I, bu I hauled myself under the stone bridge to Lieutenant Fox' platoon. He had taken a shot in the chest; it gurgled and h was very frightened. I have never felt so helpless! Some o my waving and motions must have gotten through to the CC because mortar fire was laid on and the machine gun was si lenced. The 81mm mortars laid a heavy concentration o smoke around us.

"I figured that if we had to stay there until nightfall, I'

be able to crawl up the side of the ditch nearest the company and wiggle my way up to our positions. However, that wouldn't help those like Fox who were worse off than I. Just then several stretchers, followed by men from the company, came sliding into the ditch. I directed the evacuation and was loaded onto a litter to be carried out. Ever the pessimist, I remember looking over the side of the stretcher as I was hoisted up out of the ditch and searching for a drop place if that machine gun opened up again. I was looking out for Number One! I didn't know that of the approximately sixty men under my command, eighteen had been wounded and two killed.

"Stupidly, after we were evacuated with the help of heavy smoke, the Gung-ho assistant battalion commander ordered me back into that trap to bring in the dead. Several were killed and wounded in this foolish and futile operation. It never made sense to me to endanger fighting troops for the sake of bringing in the dead. My last memory of Okinawa is of lying on a stretcher near the battalion aid station with smoke swirling about and much feverish activity. The battalion surgeon, a good drinking buddy, came over and congratulated me on a 'million-dollar wound.' With a broken metatarsal, infantry duty was over for me!"

In the same area, half a dozen men, including Paul Westman from Company K, sought to scout a ridgeline. "The squad leader, Willard Johnson, had the SCR 300 radio. We were spread out, moving very slow, when the first rounds cracked by. Sergeant Earl Neu hollered, 'Don't bunch up! Take cover!' About then artillery rounds started dropping down the slope, walking our way. Rifle fire seemed to let up and I recall hearing our radio operator calling the company, 'King, King, this is King One. We are receiving artillery fire. Is there friendly fire registered here?' He gave the coordinates and the answer was negative.

"By this time they were on us and Staff Sergeant Neu shouted, 'Back! Go back! Scatter!' I got blast effects from one enough to send me downhill into some coral rock. I could see others heading back and when I picked myself up, I couldn't put weight on my right foot. The leg seemed badly scraped but not broken. Why I didn't draw fire, I can't imagine. I went back, using my M1 as a crutch. It took quite a while to hobble back to the company and the aidman there and he told me to go to the hospital. On the way in an ambulance, a medical officer asked me how I felt. I told him I didn't feel so good after looking around at all those other guys, all shot and burned to hell. All of them were in far worse shape than I. He put his hand on my shoulder and said, 'Soldier, you wouldn't have been able to do your company a bit of good.' "

The 1st Battalion of the 381st, with Thom as operations officer, had continued to march south. By 9 April they faced a natural barrier for the Shuri line, Kakazu Ridge, a steep, 300-foot slope that stretched about 1,000 yards. On the western side it ran down to the sea and to the east it was separated by a cut from another escarpment, the Nishibaru Ridge. A honeycomb of pillboxes, tunnels, and caves, along with an infestation of mortars on the reverse slope, covered every foot of approach with deadly fire. And before they could even attempt to climb the ridge, the troops would be forced to cross a deep gorge, well targeted by the mortar positions, which was part of the Shuri defense.

The first of the Deadeyes [nickname of the 96th division] to batter themselves against Kakazu were from the 383d Regiment, an outfit with Ellis Moore as a radio operator for 1st Battalion Headquarters. Moore admitted his first and then subsequent artillery batterings terrified him. "You just lie there in your hole while they land all around you and wonder where the next one is going to hit, and why it doesn't hit you. The whine of a shell as it passes over and the explosion as it hits are just as nerve-wracking as a shell exploding right next to you. After a while you find yourself ducking every time any shell goes over, even if it's one of ours, and we threw ten shells at them for every one they sent at us."

When the battalion moved up to a hill held by Americans, a wide-eyed Moore observed the results of a banzai charge. "About 150 of them had stormed up that hill toward our guys, and they said it was just like shooting ducks. You had to look or you'd step on them. They were scattered all over the place, so much abandoned equipment, these men with beards no heavier than mine, some with quarter-size holes in their heads; others with half their bodies blown away. A GI stooped down to one, jammed a cigarette into his mouth and muttered, 'Have a cigarette, you yellow son of a bitch. Sorry I don't have time to light it for you.' "

When the line companies of the 383d started their advance on Kakazu they could neither run nor hide. Moore, however, as a radio operator with battalion headquarters, could obtain at least temporary refuge from the terror of artillery in a tomb. "You crawled through on your knees after you removed a stone slab secured in the entrance by a putty substance. The tomb was high enough for us to stand up, with a plot of about six feet by six feet. There were stone shelves covered with iron and clay urns. They evidently died in this family at all ages. The big skulls and bones were in the larger vases and the little ones held remains of what must have been very small children.

"We hauled out the urns to let their occupants get a feel of good fresh air again. With a little further polishing up we had a fairly decent and safe habitat with sleeping room for at least seven. Every tomb along the ridge was broken into sooner or later. It was an unwritten rule that if the tombs offered needed protection it was okay to open them up. But we weren't allowed to mention the raiding of the dead's resting place in our letters." So much for the Japanese belief that American reverence for the dead would preclude their use of the mausoleums.

On 8 April, just before dawn, the 383d made its initial assault on Kakazu. A fearsome downpour of artillery and mortar shells fell upon the defenders and the advance started, led by Able (A) and Charlie (C) Company with Baker (B) in reserve. "There was to be no firing," said Moore, who left the safety of the tomb to occupy a spot at the OP. "They were to get up the hill unnoticed. We just sat there while time dragged by. At about 5:30 Able radioed that they were almost to the top. It looked like it was going to work. Then all hell broke loose. The Japs must have been watching all the time. They struck at just the right moment. Machine guns from both flanks cut Able and Charlie to ribbons. Japs on the top of the ridge looked down at our guys, ten yards below, and threw everything in the book at them—rifle fire, machine-gun fire, hand grenades, satchel charges, even sticks of dynamite. Both Able and Charlie radioed for help. Since Able was farthest up the hill and catching the most hell, Erickson decided to send Baker up behind them. We got a call from Able's CO, Capt. Jack Royster. He asked if he couldn't order a retreat. Said more than half of his company was lost. Erickson replied, 'You've got to hold the ground you've got, Jack, or else all that's happened will be useless. I'm sending Baker up to help you and the two of you ought to be able to reach the top.'

"A few minutes later Royster called again. I've never heard such a pitiful voice. 'Listen, Major,' he pleaded. 'I've been hit and can't see a thing. There are only five men in my company left. There's no sign of Baker Company up here. Will you please give me permission to withdraw what's left of my company?' Erickson replied they were to hold their ground. But where the hell was Baker Company? I got them on the radio and they said they'd no sooner gotten out of their holes than they were pinned down by mortar fire and machine guns. They were trying to advance in short rushes, but the Japs had them in their sights and they were suffering heavy casualties."

All three of the units assigned to charge Kakazu experienced the same disastrous results. Remnants of the trio linked up, but they were a disorganized band desperately seeking self-preservation rather than to overcome the enemy. "Behind these men," says Moore, "was the bulk of their companies, men still pinned down in shallow shell holes, men wounded and crying for help that was to be a long time in coming, and men for whom there would never be any help."

At last convinced that the battalion had all but been destroyed, Erickson finally countenanced a withdrawal. It was about three hours after the abortive assault had begun and the enemy continued to inflict casualties. Litter parties made up mostly from headquarters personnel were shot down while on their errands of succor. Moore, with the battalion staff, had remained at the the observation post. "The Japs had kept their mortar fire out in front of us," says the former communications specialist. "But now, all of a sudden they started dropping in our sector. They were falling like raindrops in a cloudburst. You don't have any warning with these mortars, but we all dove in a trench as the first one hit.

[Floyd] Gore, the battalion commander's orderly, was at one end with me, and four others beyond us. We hugged the ground and I closed my eyes. It must have lasted only five minutes, but I'd swear that 100 rounds hit within a radius of fifteen yards of our hole. The second it stopped, the three officers took off in the direction of the CP with [Lt. Col. Byron] King yelling back to me to stay at the OP.

"Then I heard a groan and became conscious of Gore next to me. He must have received a direct hit from a mortar. His whole side was ripped away and his insides were gushing out with every breath he took. The flesh on his right thigh was peeled down over his knee. While I was trying to comprehend the sight, Gore raised up on his elbows, twisted his head so he could see his body, and then fell flat. He groaned a minute or so longer and then died.

"I was shaking like a leaf as I called the CP and explained I was the only one at the OP and requested permission to return to the CP. King said for me to stay there, that I was safer up there. Another ten minutes and I asked again and this time Captain Young told me to come down. [When I got there] I told him about Gore and that finished King. He was a beat man. He hung his head in his hands and muttered over and over, 'Gore gone, Gore gone.' That night he went back to regiment and that was the last we saw of him."

Those trapped on the slope kept calling for smoke shells to cover their retreat and eventually the artillery expended all it had. The defenders continued to spray the landscape with murderous fire. A supportive strike by Navy planes missed the mark and bombs fell on the hapless GIs. Not until dark of that dreadful day could they escape, slinging makeshift litters with ponchos and shelterhalves on rifles to remove the wounded.

According to Moore, the count of able-bodied soldiers

showed that of the roughly 450 involved in the attack, 128 remained. On the following day, the 383d sent its 2d Battalion into the maw and they, too, were chewed up with horrendous losses and little real estate to show for the investment of men and equipment. The division command now threw the 1st Battalion of the 381st into the battle. Its S-3, Dick Thom, reported, "The 2nd Battalion was on a little knob to our right, west of us. The 3rd Battalion was to the extreme west. General Easley was there with the regimental commander and the regimental S-3. Easley said the 383d Regiment was up on the ridge. 'I want you, Cassidy [Lt. Col. John], to take your battalion in a column of twos on the double, with an attached heavy machine-gun platoon up there. Commit the 3d Battalion when you're ready.'

"The company commanders got the order and we crossed the gulch between us and Kakazu. We went up to the top of a little hill. When we got there, there was an army up there, all right, but it wasn't the 383d Regiment. All hell broke loose. Our men came tumbling down, their rifles falling. I got behind a big rock and saw a light machine gun off to my left chipping away at my rock. I was not happy. We lost half our rifle companies from the battalion. We had two company commanders either killed or wounded, along with a number of lieutenants. By the second or third day in these positions we had only one active officer per company.

"On Okinawa, each battalion had a destroyer or cruiser assigned to it. The ships would fire 5-inch gun shells for illumination—fifty-second flares that burst over the area. We endured a series of counterattacks, and after what must have been the twelfth one on a dark night we pleaded for illumination. The cruiser assigned to us said, 'There's a red alert, possible air attack.' They couldn't give fire and illumination, but, they said, 'We'll give you the baseball scores.'

"Then I got a call from one company commander who was kind of a nasty bastard. He said there are hundreds of Japs in our positions. I sent about fifty of them your way. Their artillery was also coming over. Things didn't look too bright. I thought we were done for. I couldn't think of what to do. I called for the 81mm mortars to fire almost on our positions—we were all in holes that we got into at 7:00 P.M. and never came out of until morning.

"Tech Sergeant Beauford Anderson, who was the section leader for a 60mm mortar team in A Company, had been busy with the mortar and he was down to six rounds and the mortar was no good anymore. They were swamped with Jap soldiers. I saw Anderson pull the pin on a mortar shell, bounce it on a rock to knock out the detent that keeps the shell from going off while you're handling it. Then he heaved it by hand so it would land on its nose and explode. Four out of the six went off and then, although his arm was busted, Anderson took a carbine and went up and down the gorge shooting Japs. He had seemed like just an ordinary soldier, smallish, cheerful, a guy who did his job. He just went ape that night. Later, his company commander put him in for the Medal of Honor and I was a witness. [Thom earned a Bronze Star.]

"They finally pulled us out, but there wasn't too much to pull. We left 700 dead Japs up there but we had 53 fully able enlisted men left from the three rifle companies of our battalion which had attacked Kakazu." Thom blamed much of the carnage upon General Easley. "He was too damn brave, too Gung ho. We were all going to get killed following him."

15

Ie Shima and Beyond

WELL PLEASED BY THE SUCCESS OF THE MARINE CAMPAIGN ON the upper half of the island, even as army divisions to the south cringed under the savage response of the enemy, the brass advanced the schedule for Ie Shima, a mere three and one-half miles off the northwest coast. Its ten square miles, dominated by a large plateau, promised to provide an excellent airfield for the final assault upon Japan. The invasion was set for 16 April and the 77th Division received the assignment.

Intelligence estimated a force of 2,000 defenders, a mix of battle-experienced soldiers who had fought in Manchuria and labor units. The garrison had constructed defensive positions around Mount Iegusugu, a 600-foot-high rocky tower, known as "the Pinnacle" or "the Needle," which overlooked the remainder of the largely flat terrain. From the Pinnacle, excellent fields of fire covered the gentle, southeastern beaches, nominally the prime site for invaders. Because of the strength of these emplacements, nestled in well-concealed and protected caves, the Japanese tried to seduce their foes into the belief that the southeastern beaches were more vulnerable than the steeper shores to the west. To deceive the Americans, the defenders held their fire when recon parties had approached the bait; one U.S. serviceman actually strolled a few yards surveying the area without drawing a single round. The well-disciplined Japanese soldiers hid themselves from the prying eyes of observation planes that flew as low as 100 feet over the site. On the other hand, anyone attempting to gather information about the other beaches quickly came under fire, as if these places were where the enemy could expect intense opposition.

In spite of all of the guile and camouflage, the 77th Division brass spotted the trap. The plans specified landings on the south and southwest coasts that employed the 305th and 306th Regiments supported by field artillery, including one unit set up on a sandy islet four miles off Ie. The beach choices dismayed those charged with supply because high, jagged coral reefs limited the use of landing craft. Division commander Maj. Gen. Andrew Bruce's staff believed that a quick breakthrough would enable them to open up easier access, but the Americans committed one serious blunder: when aerial inspection was unable to find Japanese soldiers, they undercounted the size of hostile forces. Bruce advised the Tenth Army commander, Gen. Simon Bolivar Buckner on 6 April: ". . . original estimate of enemy is considerably reduced. It is planned to take entire division to target area; secure island quickly with minimum forces, less heavy equipment."

During the three-day period prior to the debarkation of the GIs on "W day," naval guns and aircraft furiously bombarded Ie Shima. A cloud of smoke and dust soon enveloped Mount Iegusugu until it faded from sight. And when the Liberty Division soldiers headed for the beach, it seemed almost a repeat of Love Day. Bruce noted, "Our good fortune continued because we landed apparently where the Japs did not expect us. Only scattered light resistance was met during the first hour or so."

"Light resistance," while gratifying to upper echelons, still means casualties, and those upon whom injury is inflicted can find little solace in the term. Buckner Creel, a company commander in the 306th Regiment, described the landing for his outfit as "rather uneventful, although the amtracs on either side of mine in the first wave hit aerial bombs planted in the ground. One was blown upside down; the other lost a track." These incidents aside, Creel and companions made swift initial progress. "We swept over the airfield with virtually no opposition."

Promoted to executive officer of Company C, in the 706th Tank Battalion, William Siegel commanded a tank that first day of the invasion. "My tank had no sooner come ashore than I was immediately ordered to rescue an infantry platoon pinned down by Jap small-arms fire on a plain about 300–400 yards from the beach. We were able to bring this unit out under extreme small-arms fire with no casualties by backing the tank up and the infantrymen using us for cover."

Larry Gerevas, a newcomer to Company K, 307th Regiment while it recovered from Leyte, now found himself on a landing boat headed for Ie Shima. "There was no enemy fire as we pulled into this small cove. The beach was surrounded on three sides by a steep, crescent-shaped slope rising about thirty feet to the island's plateau. We dug in as well as we could in the coral sand. That night, we repelled a banzai attack. An old man was killed while trying to spear one of our men. Heavy explosions shook the ground during the night, caving in foxholes dug in the coral sand slope. We thought it was Jap artillery, but it was the Navy underwater demolition team, blasting the coral reef in the cove to open the way for supply ships."

Joe Budge, a Scotland-born Hawaiian sugar plantation technician, now a sergeant replacement in a mortar section with Company D of the 305th, boarded an amtrac for the trip to the beach. "Most impressive of all was the rocket ship, an LST with banks of rockets fired in waves from its deck, a fearsome sight and even more fearsome to hear . . . roaring and screaming of rockets and a thunderous echo from the shore, which disappeared under a gray blanket of smoke sparkling with red flashes. Someone wondered out loud if anyone could live through that and a sergeant said not to worry, there would be plenty left. 'Right now,' he said, 'they will be running around a jibber-jabbering to themselves and a-sharpening their swords.' He asked me if I was scared and I said not yet. He said, 'Well, you better sceered [*sic*] and stay sceered. That way you will react quicker. Adrenaline or something.' Someone had asked him what the island looked like as an objective for infantry. He peered at it, noting that it was a flat plain, dominated by a pyramidal-like hill, militarily uninviting. He grunted and obviously with unfond memories of the South Pacific found something good to say. 'Vaal, anyway, there ain't no goddamn palm trees on it.'

"At the moment, I was more worried about our mode of transport than the Japanese, so I unbuckled my ammunition belt, which meant that if it came to swimming in a hurry, I could shrug off all my equipment and retain my rifle, with which we had been trained to swim. One soldier was crossing himself and muttering prayers. Presently, the man beside the driver of our conveyance winked at me through a small hatchway and then slammed it shut. We roared down the ramp and bobbed reluctantly up to the surface, then roared across a submerged sandbar to the accompaniment of a few pillars of water that suddenly appeared near us, without apparent cause. As soon as the tractor heaved itself up on the beach, it dropped its rear ramp and we debarked to run as fast as we could through scrub bushes into the open that lay beyond. The riflemen among us pushed on while we set down the mortars and waited for further orders. A few yards away lay another amtrac, fitted with a turret like a tank, but which now lay upside down with a huge hole in its bottom. Someone asked about the crew but the rest of us just looked at the smoking, shattered hulk and said nothing.

"A certain amount of small arms fire passed overhead and we could hear our own infantry also at work. One could sometimes tell what was happening [from the sound] . . . the chatter of a Nip machine gun getting more and more erratic as the boys closed in on it, from the slow thump-thump-thump of a BAR, and a spattering of our own rifle fire. Then might come the thud and whine of a U.S. hand grenade; the whine being the flying fragments, and the Nip gun would cease forever. Sometimes there was no whine, which meant the grenade had been thrown into a pillbox.

"A jeep came down, this one fitted with brackets to hold litters. There were four litters, all occupied. It stopped by us and one of us recognized a friend and walked over to see him. There was a tremendous explosion under the jeep and the spare tire went humming over our heads. A few pieces of metal remained of the jeep and nothing of the men except for the GI who had been walking toward it. Now, he was on the ground, crawling frantically away from the site of the explosion, dragging a leg, until somebody got to him and made him lie still. 'If that was a mine, it was the damndest mine I ever saw,' said someone. We found plenty of them, large sea mines or airplane bombs, sticking up through the ground, with a rubber tubelike fuse visible above the surface."

Dick Forse was a gunner on an M8, self-propelled 75mm gun. After arriving on the beach, Forse climbed up to remove waterproof tape from around the turret. "I heard a machine gun and couldn't tell whether it was a U.S. or Japanese one. But I dropped down on my hands and knees. I tried a second time to strip off the tape and when the machine gun went off, I knew it was a Japanese one because of its rapid rate. I tried a third time to get to the tape but that machine gun opened up again and I gave up for the moment.

"We had another M8 coming in from the sea and I tried to signal them there was a machine gun firing at this beach. I saw spouts of water around the M8 but they weren't paying any attention. They were lucky, because that gunner must have run off. Lieutenant Jesse Gershberg, our platoon leader, and two others went back for orders. A machine gun opened up, hit a nearby pine tree and a piece struck Gershberg in the forehead. But he stayed with us.

"We started up again and found we were all by ourselves. There were no targets and I didn't know what we were doing. Then we came across a bunch of guys from our company and they warned us to go between the tape [put down to indicate a safe path through mined areas]. It was nerve-wracking; there were so many of them, aerial bombs buried in the ground, and the pressure of a finger could set them off. But you could see where the mines were even though they tried to camouflage the spot. They would plant grass around them but it died, turning yellow, while in the safe spots, the grass was really green.

"Gershberg learned that the road up ahead wasn't secured. We entered a field where there were a bunch of Americans moving toward a woods. I watched guys creep along, like they were reluctant to move out. Then one would get up, run, and then drop. Boom! I thought, boy these Japs are accurate with their mortars. I saw what I thought was a knapsack, but it was half a body; he must have triggered one of the mines. We settled in for the night and it was peaceful for a while and then there was an explosion. They were attacking with satchel charges and grenades. I heard a clang against the side of the tank. It must have been a grenade. In the morning I found a bone, a human knee bone. It must have come from a Jap who ran at the tank and blew himself up with one of the satchel charges."

On 17 April, the 77th welcomed Ernie Pyle, who had chafed at the relative absence of action with the Marines on Okinawa. Pyle once explained the lure of the battlefield. "The front does get into your blood and you miss it and want to be back. Life up there is very simple, very uncomplicated, devoid of all the jealousy and meanness that float around a headquarters, and time passes so fast it's unbelievable. [I tried] not to take any foolish chances but there's no way to play it completely safe and still do your job."

Pyle began his tour on Ie Shima with the 305th Regiment, led by Lt. Col. Joseph Coolidge, who wrote: "Every man in the outfit anticipated this visit with pleasure and pride and with the hopes of meeting this great little fellow who had portrayed the lot of the doughboy in Europe with such moving simplicity. Now we would have our chance to show him that fighting in the Pacific was just as rough and dirty, and a lot more unglamorous than that in civilized Europe."

The correspondent joined a group at an observation post overlooking a plain that led to a village at the foot of the Needle. According to Coolidge, two or three other reporters, "acting like general aides," accompanied Pyle. The regimental commander noted that when the other reporters stood up to get a better view, the defenders apparently noticed the activity and began dropping mortar shells. Those who had come with Pyle "had seen enough and left us. Ernie remained in his corner until the final action of the day."

On the following day, Pyle visited with General Bruce at the 305th command post. After scrawling autographs for several GIs, Pyle accepted a ride with Coolidge—bound for an observation post according to Bruce, although Coolidge claimed their destination was division headquarters. Five men packed into the jeep, a driver, two members of the regimental staff plus Coolidge and Pyle. "Our route," reported Coolidge, "lay well within the area we had already 'secured'; it paralleled a coral cliff about 300 yards to our left. We fell in behind three trucks and another jeep [with military police]. Just ahead lay a road or cart trail junction. On either side, two infantry battalions had bivouacked the night before and were packing up after breakfast, getting ready to move up to the fighting. Just as we reached the road junction, a burst of machine gun fire exploded around us; our jeep with two flat tires stopped quickly, and we in turn exploded from the jeep to the ditch on either side of the road.

"Ernie and I, on the right side of the jeep, landed in the ditch away from the line of fire; the others, we hoped, had found shelter on the left side of the road. I had seen Barnes, our driver jumping to the left. Ernie and I were quite safe; the ditch dropped off three feet from the side of the road. The jeep fortunately had taken the brunt of the burst, two flat tires, a jagged hole in the bumper, and a hole in the radiator. Ernie reported he was safe.

"I told him to keep down while I checked the rest of the party; I raised my head and called each man in turn. They all reported that they were safe in the sheltering ditch. Then another burst from that machine gun. One shot kicked dust in my face, but ricocheted over my head. I ducked and turned to Ernie. He was lying on his back; his hands resting on his chest were holding a knitted arctic cap which he was known to carry at all times. His face was composed. It must have taken an appreciable time for me to realize that he had been hit; no blood flowed, and only after I looked at him more closely did I see the hole through each temple. His bullet had not ricocheted. A platoon was dispatched to search out the machine gunner, but hidden in the coral crevices that honeycombed the entire island, that Jap might well have escaped for another day. A tank was sent in to pick up Ernie's body.

"The ironic element to the story is that the two battalions on either side of the road knew only, that machine-gun fire had hit quite close to them. The men felt no danger nor did they know the tragic loss of this fine Little Man [*sic*]. The machine gunner must have located himself well back in the curve so that his line of fire was limited to the road junction and he patiently awaited a vehicle carrying personnel, a far more valuable target than the lumbering two-and-a-half-ton truck that preceded our jeep."

Coolidge's account implied that the area and road seemed relatively inactive and Bruce remarked, "Many vehicles had been over [the road] and we all thought [it] was safe." But to the infantrymen near the site, danger remained a constant. Joe Budge with his mortar section recalls, "That night I kept really far down in my foxhole for two reasons. One was that a U.S. machine gun was firing protectively very close over my head. Another was that a Japanese heavy machine gun was chipping dirt off the lip of it all night." When morning came, Budge observed a jeep with an antenna—a sign of a radio and personnel of some importance—run along a road the troops knew was covered by enemy fire and clearly visible to spotters on the Pinnacle. Budge saw the occupants of the jeep fling themselves into the roadside ditch and then watched as one lifted his head for a peek at the action. "The gun fired a short burst and the man was dead." Only later did the sergeant learn that the victim was Pyle.

When Bruce learned in a series of somewhat garbled messages of Pyle's death, he immediately sent a message to Tenth Army headquarters, "Regretfully report Ernie Pyle who so materially aided in building morale for troops killed by surprise Jap mg fire while standing beside regimental commander of foot troops, 77th Division, Lt. Col. Coolidge, on outskirts Ie Shima town about 10:15 today." Later, with facts in hand, he corrected the description that placed Pyle upright when he died. When the GIs hastily erected a crude memorial, Bruce decreed an inscription, AT THIS SPOT, THE 77TH INFANTRY DIVISION LOST A BUDDY ERNIE PYLE, 18 APRIL 1945. The body was at first interred in a cemetery for Liberty Division dead on Ie Shima and later transferred to the Punchbowl military graveyard on Oahu.

Budge recalled that on the day the machine gun cut Pyle down, he moved along the shore as the troops encircled the town. A brigadier general, the assistant division commander [Edwin H. Randle], was strutting around the beach with a walking stick, a habit he had picked up from the British in Libya. He encountered a little yellow sparrow of a soldier using a mine detector on the beach, but with a bad case of the shakes.

"Son, where is your officer?" inquired Randle.

"Dead, sir," stammered the GI.

"Then where is your NCO?"

"Dead, sir."

"Where is the rest of the bomb disposal squad?"

"Sir, I *am* the bomb disposal squad."

Budge reported that the general gulped and said very gently, "Son, get on that landing barge and come back to the ship with me." According to the mortar section sergeant, booby-trapped aircraft bombs planted as mines had wiped out the disposal experts.

Larry Gerevas and Company K of the 307th left the comparatively quiet beach area and marched along a dirt road above the beach. "Within minutes machine-gun bullets were cracking all around us and we ran for cover. No one was hit and it seemed the firing came from a great distance. There were a lot of trees and brush at the sides of the road so we took advantage of this cover as we continued on our way. We all knew for sure that our movements were being observed by the Japs on the Pinnacle.

"Later, as we tried to climb over a saddle on a small ridge, mortars began falling on the only path. The mortars landed every thirty seconds. As soon as one hit, the platoon leader would point to one of us and tell us, 'Go!' The path was very slippery from the rains and when it was my turn, I started to run. About halfway there, I fell and started sliding down the slope. My rifle flew out of my hands and I knew it was only a matter of seconds before the next mortar shell exploded. There wasn't time to retrieve my rifle. I dug my fingers into the muddy path and pulled myself over the hill just before the next mortar blast.

"On the other side of the hill I expected to find the rest of my platoon, but there was nobody in sight. Here I was, without my rifle and alone. I knew that I had to find my group quickly. Nearby I found a group of tombs. I decided to hide in one for a while until I could make a plan. I decided to retrace my steps to see in which direction the others went after they came over the hill. As I was doing this, I saw some medics placing a wounded man in an ambulance. I ran over and asked for the rifle of the wounded man. They handed me the weapon and I found my platoon."

Gerevas and his companions dug in on Ie Shima. "One man in our platoon was nearly frozen with fear. He was really dangerous to everyone around him. We wouldn't let him have grenades during the night because he would throw them anywhere without thinking. Usually two shared a foxhole, but nobody wanted to be with him. That night the Japs attacked our position and we managed to kill them or drive them off. During the attack there was a lot of gunfire and grenades. When things quieted, we could hear a baby crying. We continued to throw grenades toward the sound until it stopped. The next morning we found dead Jap soldiers and women who carried spears. One of them had a baby strapped to her back. I don't think I will ever forget the sound of that crying baby.

"The really frightened guy survived the night. The following day we had to run across an open area under sniper fire to reach wooded cover. After we arrived there, grenades started falling around us. Many were duds. The scared GI was sitting with his legs spread and one of the grenades landed between his legs. He didn't move—just sat there and stared at the grenade. He was paralyzed. Thank God it was a dud. All of us were afraid, but we all felt sorry for this man who was filled with terror every moment."

On 19 April the big push for Ie Shima town and the Pinnacle started. Elements from all three regiments united in an effort to capture the town and participated in the final bloody effort to eliminate the tenacious defenders hunkered down in the deep bunkerage of Mount Iegusugu. Backed by artillery, the 305th initially gained some ground in Ie town, but a buzzsaw of machine gun and mortar fire drove the attackers back from a hill that overlooked the town. The same deadly reception met infantrymen seeking to enter the town, where defenders hid themselves in the rubble of concrete created by incessant bombardment. Tanks and self-propelled guns halted for fear of the abundant mines. Engineers could not clear these obstacles because any open space lay exposed to withering scythes of bullets.

Among those advancing on the objectives were Gerevas and his buddies. "As we reached the foot of Iegusugu Mountain, an American tank and some infantry came into an opening about 150 yards below us and immediately started firing at us, thinking we were Japs. Our squad leader frantically removed a bright orange banner from his pack and held it up. The firing from the tank and the infantry stopped. This was the closest I came to being killed by friendly fire."

On 20 April, two battalions of the 307th pressed forward in spite of intense fusillades from above them to finally occupy a major objective, the town's government house atop a hill. Their triumph proved short-lived. A battalion of the 305th that had seized a flanking hill withdrew without notifying the GIs around government house. The enemy swarmed back onto the position vacated by the men of the 305th and rained fire down upon the 307th's troops. Running low on ammunition and now highly vulnerable, the infantrymen pulled back.

The 706th Tank Battalion added its might to the battle. William Siegel in Company C remembered, "Our tank was disabled and set on fire by a satchel charge. My crew and I were forced to abandon it and wound up in a close-quarter fight with three of the enemy. Corporal Kenneth Rogers was killed in this action, but we were rescued by another unit from my platoon."

Joe Budge, as a mortar sergeant with the 305th, endured prolonged terror. "Heavy artillery or mortar fire can be seen in any war movie, but it is usually toned down because nobody would believe the size of the explosion one is expected to live through. Sometimes you can hear them coming. Usually there is too much other uproar going on, as in this case. These shells kept making great thunderous explosions in our midst, and flat on the ground—as flat as the human form can get when frightened—we felt the ground viciously kick us in the belly. Things flew around, helmets, bits of rock, bushes, branches, sometimes bits of soldiers. There was nothing to be done except to lie there and try to be ready to receive the horde of nasty men with bayonets and swords who were likely to show up the moment the barrage stopped.

"Then the rifle company we were supporting told us to pull back and we went with it. I grabbed the base plate of one of the mortars and proceeded to walk out of that hellfire spot toward a ruined building in a field. A standard Japanese reaction the moment they saw anyone retreating, was to pour on the fire. This time was no exception. Unfortunately, when we pulled back, so did another rifle company, leaving a gap at the edge of the town into which the Nips poured some infantry. Every Jap, weapon in or out of range, opened up, mostly mortars, machine guns, and rifles, but including one small field gun.

"The forty-pound mortar base plate jumped energetically and a bullet screamed off it. With considerable relief, and after resisting a strong temptation to run, I reached the ruins and lay down in a sunken road. I felt comparatively safe until a jerry can lying by my feet jumped up with a clang and exhibited a neat bullet hole. One forgets that bullets have a dropping trajectory. We set up the mortars to be ready for any Nip attack, which the book would have it should come at any moment. But they were too smart to charge us across a wide-open field in daylight.

"Our battalion commander had been promoted to fill one of many vacancies from the slaughter of the regimental staff on the *Henrico*. We had inherited a major who carried no respect from the troops. He showed up with his radio operator. The latter squatted on the ground with his set. The major walked round and round him, actually wringing his hands and wailing out loud, 'What should I do? What should I do?'

"The radio operator's head, like an owl's, swiveled about watching him in amazement. If the troops had respected the major this might have become a bad situation, the nervous collapse of a battalion commander at a bad moment. But the men had no expectations of anything better because of incidents with him on Guam.

"An old sergeant—or maybe he just looked old and tired—said, 'Oh, shit!' Then he calmly started giving orders. Other noncoms followed suit—there were no other officers around. Within minutes a call came over the radio for the major to report to the beach. Major Eugene Cook, a fine officer, took his place. We reorganized." Budge and his mates remained for the moment removed from the worst of the fray. "A few Nips came our way but they seemed to be stragglers. When we shot at them or threw grenades quite often there'd be a pause for a few seconds and then an explosion of a Nip grenade and a body would fly into the air. They were blowing themselves up, being afraid of capture and incapable of figuring out a more profitable method of committing suicide, such as taking one or more of us with them.

"Throughout the night continual heavy action continued in the town around the Pinnacle. There was one particular U.S. machine gun that seemed to be firing all night. It must have used up several barrels and thousands of rounds of ammunition. One could see the constant stream of cherry red tracer bullets encountering some target at quite close range, and disappearing or ricocheting off into the night. From the opposite direction came an equally constant stream of yellower Japanese tracers. We discovered later this fight ended in the CP of the 3d Battalion with clerks, cooks, and the battalion commander in hand-to-hand combat. The stubborn machine gunner, Pfc. Martin May, earned a posthumous Medal of Honor."

The noose around Iegusugu tightened as the American forces enveloped the base. For Buckner Creel, with G Company of the 306th, the assignment was the northern slope of the Pinnacle. At 2:30 on the afternoon of the twentieth, the troops jumped off, preceded by a concentration of shells from the 304th in addition to the rounds that tanks and self-propelled howitzers could toss onto the Pinnacle. Company C of the 306th led off, sprinting, falling, rising, and then running again across 200 yards of open, fire-swept ground. Rushing forward in the tracks of C Company and on its flanks came the others in the assault, including Creel with G Company.

Earl Miller, the replacement machine gunner with G Company, recalled the final push up Mount Iegusugu. "It was a volcanic hill with caves three stories deep. Also a field gun on tracks behind sliding doors—all of this looking right down our throats! On the morning of our assault, we charged through a mine field and barbed wire on the run, stepping in the tracks of the man in front. We all made it to the base of the hill. It was the first time I had heard bullets snap and crack around my ears. Right after we charged through the minefield, and fell behind a big rock to catch our breath, I saw my first case of battle fatigue. ——— was not hit, but he could not move. The medics gave him a shot and sent him to the rear."

While an occasional soldier flinched, as Miller saw, the assault brigades reached the steep slopes where the entrenched foe could only be routed with bayonets, flamethrowers, satchel charges, and grenades. An observer from the War Department in Washington marveled, "It was the most remarkable thing I have ever seen. The attack looked like a Fort Benning demonstration. Why, I saw troops go through enemy mortar concentrations and machine-gun fire that should have pinned them down. But instead they poured across that field and took the mountain against really tough opposition without even slowing down."

Over a period of three days, units from all three regiments fought, bled, and died on the slopes, taking ground, retreating in the face of devastating onslaughts and counterattacks, and then regrouping to climb ever higher. Even after the GIs gained the northern slopes of the 600-foot tower, groups of well-concealed, determined resisters remained. "We were 'mopping up,' " recalled Creel, "and destroying pillboxes. We made attempts with a Japanese language interpreter to get them to come out. Rarely would they do it. On one particular occasion, we had tried to get an unknown number of Japanese soldiers to come out but to no avail. So I gave the order to blow it. An engineer demo man "capped and fused" a satchel charge, lit it, and threw it into the emplacement. We waited and nothing happened. We figured it was a dud so we threw another one in. Nothing happened; a third satchel charge followed—nothing.

"I got hold of the engineer platoon leader, lst Lt. Charles E. Sears, who was part of my landing team. Together we figured out that the Japanese must be pulling out the flaming fuses on the charges as they came in. Sears got a satchel charge and he and his demo man rigged it up with about ten to fifteen fuses, all different lengths. The last five to be lit were capped and live. When all the fuses were lit and spurting fire, he heaved the satchel into the open door of the emplacement. We got down behind the berm and could picture the Japanese furiously pulling out the fuses, wondering which one was live. A tremendous explosion shook all of us. All the ammo in there as well as the three earlier satchel charges went up at once in a sympathetic detonation."

Company K of the 307th approached a clearing on the third day of the operation. Gerevas recalls an Okinawan woman accompanied by two small boys. "When they saw us they ran as fast as they could to escape. We caught the woman, but the little boys were too quick and got away. However, as soon as they were far enough off to feel safe, they stopped and watched to see what we were going to do with their mother. I was holding her by her arm as we walked along a dirt road. Suddenly, she tried to pull away and kick at a wire that ran across the road. Another soldier grabbed her other arm and we lifted her over the wire. We examined the wire and saw that it stretched from a stake on one side of the road to a 500-pound bomb on the other. When we continued down the road we spotted three more of these booby traps and lifted the woman over each. The small boys kept us in sight. When they saw we were not harming their mother, they came up. Later we turned all three over to a group collecting civilians. They were loaded on a truck and driven away."

A few days later, Gerevas's unit was ordered to secure a small hamlet. "The day before, a squad from another company had tried to enter the village and nearly all were killed or wounded. My squad was now picked for this attempt and I was made the scout. Up to that moment, I thought I had been very lucky, but now I felt my luck had run out. The scout leads and is at least twenty yards in front of the others. He is the bait for a sniper and usually the first to be hit. If the scout is wounded, the rest of the squad might retreat and abandon him to the enemy. I know that's not what it is like in the movies and it is what I saw happen in real combat.

"I knew someone had to do the job and it was my turn. We moved through the streets, expecting to be machine gunned at any moment. When we had walked through the entire place, we turned and came back. Not a single shot was fired. The Japs had left during the night.

"During the last week of April, we dug in as we had every night since we arrived on Ie Shima. Two of us would dig one foxhole. We would sit, facing each other. One person would sleep for an hour while the other kept watch, alternating throughout the night. About midnight we were attacked by a small group of Jap soldiers while I was sleeping. The firing of the rifles awakened me with a start. I sat up quickly. My head came up alongside the muzzle of my foxhole companion's rapidly firing automatic rifle. My head felt as if it had exploded. I thought that I had been shot. The muzzle blast caused concussion deafness in both of my ears. Still, I was able to grab my rifle and fire at the gray shadows around us. Soon they were either dead or driven off. When morning arrived, my hearing had not returned. No one knew of any aid station nearby, so I had no choice but to stay with my unit until we returned to the ship. It was especially frightening to continue in combat without being able to hear. But I had no other option."

On the third day, a small patrol of GIs with mountain climbing experience scaled the last 50-foot cliff guarding the peak. Although snipers peppered the area, one man waved an American flag from the summit, while others below tried to bring up a flagpole for a replica of the Mount Suribachi scene on Iwo Jima. Intense fire forced the GIs to abandon the project. Still, a day later, two U.S. banners waved atop the Ie Shima peak. To the troops, Bruce issued General Order 56: "Ie Shima is captured. Thank you, tough guys." Not until 27 April, when the last substantial U.S. forces boarded ships, leaving behind a small garrison, could the battle for Ie Shima be regarded as actually finished. Sandwiched between the relatively easy landing and the final few days eliminating small pockets of defenders had been six days of fierce combat that Bruce compared with other bitter battles like Iwo Jima.

The Americans estimated about 4,800 dead enemy, including as many as 1,500 civilians who put on Japanese uniforms and bore arms. As Creel's anecdote indicated, even women served the emperor on Ie Shima. The division's 239 KIA, 897 WIA, and 19 MIA nearly equaled the 1,143 casualties for Guam, a campaign that lasted three times as long. In comparison, Iwo Jima required twenty-four days to subdue, with 24,000 Marine casualties, including 1,600 classified as "combat fatigue," while the Japanese dead totaled well over 20,000. Navy losses at Iwo Jima ran around 2,700 killed, wounded, and missing.

From the Ie Shima beaches, the GIs of the 77th Division could observe war-wracked Okinawa. Joe Budge saw "constant artillery fire and flames. One could see the shells red-hot from the guns soaring off toward the front, losing their color as they went. It did not look very inviting and from what we heard, it was turning into a World War I type of operation."

Indeed, with the 96th Division so badly battered, the Tenth Army summoned the 27th Infantry Division from its reserve status and tossed it into the fight. This was not an infusion of a full-strength, combat-ready outfit. The 27th's ranks remained badly depleted after Peleliu and the veterans were combat weary. However, initially the division achieved gains that helped bring the Americans beyond Kakazu Ridge. But then the 27th's advance bogged down, to the intense frustration of General Buckner.

Across the island, the 7th Division committed itself to another natural defensive fortress, Kochi Ridge. Platoon leader Gage Rodman, preparing to send out a patrol, headed forward to deliver the orders to one of his squads. "About that time, we began receiving mortar fire. Trying to move only in the intervals between bursts, I was running forward toward an irrigation ditch. As I hurled myself forward to land lengthwise, a mortar shell exploded against the side of the ditch close to me. My eye caught a flash of black falling, which I suspect was the mortar shell. The next thing I knew, I was sitting on the ground instead of running forward. I knew I was hit but the only blood I could see was on my leg. Then I caught sight of what seemed like several yards of pink tubing on the front of my trousers."

A nearby medic, after bandaging another wounded soldier, injected Rodman with morphine while one of his squad leaders, using a first-aid dressing, covered Rodman's exposed intestines. He was evacuated and at the 102d Portable Surgical Hospital, surgeons removed the majority of the shell fragments and manufactured a colostomy to replace his severed bowel.

The 7th Division assault on Kochi Ridge stalled. Tenth Army gave up on the 27th Division and shifted it north to replace the lst and 6th Marine Divisions in basically occupation duty. The renewed assaults slowly forced the Japanese backward but the flow of GI blood quickened.

16

Liberations and Victory

WITH THE RHINE AND THEN THE RIVER MAIN CROSSED, THE ability of the Germans to mount organized large-scale resistance collapsed. Pfc. Harry Herder Jr., an over-six-foot infantry replacement, had volunteered for special assignment, and after a physical examination and an interview, was assigned to the 5th Ranger Battalion. The need for foot soldiers, which bent the color line enough for 2,500 black volunteers to serve in provisional rifle platoons, also forced the Rangers to accept recruits without the previously required credentials or training. When his new company commander spotted Herder wearing eyeglasses, he almost booted him out. Ranger Harold Stover, a post–D day replacement himself, but a veteran of combat, tutored Herder in tactics with a four-day crash course. "He worked me over on the bazooka until I knew it well. He would accept nothing but complete understanding. Stover taught me that when firing at a tank to aim at the seam between the body of the tank and the turret, in order to weld the turret to the body.

"I remember once when we were working on a German pillbox, I loaded Stover up, hit him on the helmet to let him know all was ready, and he rose to one knee and fired. The round skipped in front of the bunker and into the port the machine gun was firing out of and exploded against the backside wall. Stover was mad at himself, had me load him up again quickly and fired again. The second round went right in the port. It wasn't necessary any longer, but Stover just had to know that he could do it."

The 5th Ranger Battalion reached the Rhine in time for Herder to cross the Ludendorff span in a truck. "Our outfit hooked up with a tank destroyer outfit and we were in a hurry. We blew across the landscape of eastern Germany with little opposition. We eventually drove up some gentle valley where there were trees on either side, when we made a sharp left turn, so sharp that those of us on top of the vehicles were grabbing things to keep from falling off. By the time we regained our balance, there it was; a great high barbed-wire fence at least ten feet high, maybe more. Between us and the fence running parallel to the fence was a dirt road and beyond the fence two more layers of barbed wire. The barbed wire in those fences was laced in a fine mesh, so fine, no one was going to get through it.

"Our tank destroyers slowed down, but did not stop. They blew straight at and through the barbed wire. Those of us riding the top scurried quickly to get behind the turret while those vehicles just continued to charge. At least one of those fences was hot with electricity, but they shorted out when it hit the damp ground. When we broke through the first of those fences, we got a clue, the first, as to what we had come upon, but had no real comprehension at all of what was to assault our senses for the next hours, the next days.

"I was very much on the alert. The tanker on our vehicle

assigned to the machine gun was on that weapon and ready to use it. Those of us riding were ready to bail off and hit the ground on the run. As an assistant bazooka man I had a sack with ten bazooka rounds hung over my shoulder. I had an M1 Garand and some bandoliers of ammo for that; some grenades hanging one place and another; a fully loaded cartridge belt.

"I remember scouting the area in front of us. Over to the left, just inside the fence, were some major buildings and next to one of those was a monster chimney, monstrous both in diameter and in height. Now black smoke was pouring out if it, and blowing away from us, but we could still smell it. An ugly horrible smell. A vicious smell."

The tank destroyer columns performed a standard series of wheel maneuvers that enabled them to present a single front. Meanwhile the Rangers dismounted and spread out along the same line. "None of us in the lower ranks knew what it was we were up to or where we were, but we fully expected a firefight with German troops whose camp we had just stormed and I thought would be angry. It turned out there were no German troops present. Slowly, as we formed up, a ragged group of human beings started to creep out of and from between the buildings in front of us. These human beings, timidly, slowly, deliberately showing their hands, all wore a sort of uniform, or bits and pieces of a uniform, made from horribly coarse cloth, striped, the stripes running vertically, alternating a dull dark gray and a darkish blue a half inch or maybe more wide. Some of those human beings had pants made of the material, some had shirt/jackets, and some had hats. Some had only one piece of uniform. They stood there, making me feel foolish with all of that firepower hanging on me. I certainly wouldn't be needing it with these folks."

While the GIs lowered their weapons, their officers and top noncoms entered one of the buildings. The two groups outside cautiously inched toward each other. "Some of them spoke English and asked, 'Are you American?' We said we were and the reaction of the whole mass was immediate; simultaneously on their faces were relaxation, ease, joy, and they all began chattering to us in a babble of tongues. It was then that the smell of the place started to get to me. We could only rarely take a shower and our uniforms were never fresh or clean. We had been blowing around Germany for some time and we were all a little raunchy in the odor department. I was probably more than just a little gamey and would not have noticed the other guys in the company because they were in about the same state as I. Our noses, rebelling against the surroundings they were constantly subjected to, were not functioning anywhere near normally. But now there was a new odor, thick and hanging, and it assaulted the senses."

The platoon sergeant issued orders for the men to guard holes in the fencing and to allow no one to pass through. Herder and a friend, Bill Justis, at one post were instructed to inspect a nearby four-story tower. Inside they found bunks for sleeping and a platform with a table rigged to accommodate a machine gun. From their perch they could see that similar towers ringed the encampment. "None of us knew what we were encountering. We were both too young to have any meaningful way of understanding the thing going on in Germany. Our first thought was that we were at a prisoner of war camp and all the people in strange uniforms were the troops who had been captured by the German Army. That made a little sense, but where were the German guards? Why the strange uniforms? Why were we keeping them in there? Bill Justis and I, standing on top of the tower, did not know we were at Buchenwald. We had to wait another hour or so to find out that this place had the name and what a 'Buchenwald' was."

Relieved of their station, Herder and Justis piled onto the back of a truck that carried them past a string of buildings with a few barred windows and then along a well-tended road, "through a manicured area of good houses—no, better than good. We didn't know it then, but the best of them was the home of Ilse Koch. Her husband was the camp commander and from what we later heard the two of them deserved each other."

Even as the Americans were moving into some barracks for guards, they saw a long truck convoy entering, a U.S. Army field hospital. "Sergeant [Adrian] Blowers told us that some of the prisoners spoke English. Then he got even quieter, looked at the ground for a moment, raised his eyes, and looking over our heads began very softly—we could barely hear him. He told us this is what was called a 'concentration camp,' that we were about to see things we were in no way prepared for. He told us to look, to look as long as our stomachs lasted, and then to get out of there for a walk in the woods. I had never known Sergeant Blowers to be like this. The man had seen everything that I could imagine could be seen and this place was having this effect on him. I didn't understand. I didn't know what a concentration camp was or could be."

With two other Rangers, Herder began the explorations. They passed a gate with a sign the Nazis hung over a number of camps, which Herder could translate into WORK WILL MAKE YOU FREE. "We were slightly apprehensive of what we might see. Our antennae were up. We had been teased by bits of information and we wanted to know more. The lane we were walking on bent to the right as we cleared the building. We had barely made the turn and there it was.

"The bodies of human beings were stacked like cordwood. All of them were dead. All of them stripped. The inspection I made of the pile was not very close, but the corpses seemed to be all male. The stack was about five feet high, maybe a little more. I could see over the top. They extended down a slight hill for fifty to seventy-five feet. Human bodies, neatly stacked, naked, ready for disposal. The arms and legs were neatly arranged, but an occasional limb dangled oddly. The bodies we could see were all face up. There was an aisle, then another stack, and another aisle, and more stacks. The Lord only knows how many there were.

"Just looking at these bodies made one believe they had been starved to death. They appeared to be skin covering bones and nothing more. The eyes on some were closed, on others open. Bill, Tim [Daly], and I grew very quiet. I think my only comment was 'Jesus Christ.' I have since seen the movie made about Buchenwald. The stack of bodies is vividly displayed just as I saw it, but it is not the same. The black-and-white film did not depict the dirty gray-green color of those bodies, and what it could not possibly capture was the odor, the smell, the stink.

"The three of us looked and we walked down the edge of those stacks. I know I didn't count them—it wouldn't have mattered. We looked and said not a word. A group of guys from the company noticed us and said, 'Wait till you see in there.' They pointed to a long building, about two stories high and butted up tightly to the chimney. It had two barnlike doors on either end and they were open. We walked back to the building where we found others from our company, along with some of the prisoners, milling around between the bodies and the building. We moved gently through those people, through the doors, and felt the warmth immediately.

"Not far from the doors and parallel to the front of the building, there was a brick wall, solid to the top of the building. In the wall were small openings fitted with iron doors. Those doors were a little more than two feet wide and about two and a half feet high. The tops had curved shapes much like the entrances to churches. Those iron doors were in sets, three high. (My memory might be wrong about the exact number but there were many.) Most of the doors were closed, but down near the middle a few stood open. Heavy metal trays had been pulled out of those openings, and on those trays were partially burned bodies. On one tray was a skull partially burned through, with a hole in the top; other trays held partially disintegrated arms and legs. It appeared that those trays could hold three bodies at a time. And the odor, my God, the odor!

"I had enough. I couldn't take it anymore. I left the building with Bill and Tim close behind me. As we passed out the door, someone from the company said, 'The crematorium.' Until then I had no idea what a crematorium was. It dawned on me much later that the number of bodies which could be burned at one time, three bodies to a tray, at least thirty trays, and the Germans still couldn't keep up. The bodies on the stacks outside were growing at a faster rate than they could be burned." Ranger leaders shut down the furnaces.

A newly freed inmate led Herder and others to the inmates' quarters, large barnlike structures packed with five- and six-tier-high cots. "The bunks were much too short even for short people," noted Herder. "Just inside the door were people on the lower bunks so close to death they didn't have the strength to rise. They were literally skeletons covered with skin. There appeared to be no substance to them. The next day when the press arrived, one of the photographers for *Life* magazine had one of the really bad ones propped up against the door frame in the daylight. He took the photograph, but out of sight, in the darkness of the building, behind the man, were the people propping him up." Most of those still alive at Buchenwald, Herder learned, were political prisoners; most of the Jews had either died or been marched away.

Blowers informed the Rangers about Ilse Koch, who favored jodhpurs, boots, and a riding crop. "He told us this story about her. Once she ordered all the Jewish prisoners stripped and lined up. She marched down the rows of them and as she saw a tattoo she liked she would touch it with her riding crop. The guards would take the man away immediately to a camp hospital where the doctors would remove the patch of skin with the tattoo, have it tanned, and with others, patched together to make lamp shades. There were three of those lamp shades."

Herder learned that the German guards had packed up and moved out several hours before the Americans arrived. "George [Patton] had assigned us to this place for four days, ostensibly to keep the now free prisoners off the roads he needed to supply his troops, who were racing through Germany. The full explanation was given to the prisoners and there was no problem. George had assigned a whole field hospital to the place along with a big kitchen unit. He eventually sent in an engineering outfit with bulldozers to dig a mass grave for those bodies. We were doing everything we possibly could for the prisoners.

"While we were sipping coffee after breakfast, a great commotion broke out down at the gate and it grabbed our attention. A bright shiny jeep came through the gate with this fellow standing in front of the passenger seat, holding onto the windshield. His helmet was gleaming and elaborately decorated, his uniform spic and span, his pistol belt highly polished and oddly shaped, and, by God, there he was; it was George himself, and he was touring this place. From time to time the jeep would stop and he would ask questions. In front of the crematorium, the jeep stopped and he alighted, walked inside, was out of sight some minutes, appearing again with a very stiff back. Into the jeep again and he was all over the place in just a few minutes. He passed us on the way out and it was obvious he was some kind of mad. Damn, he looked mad, about as mad as I had ever seen anyone look. The jeep sped back out the gate and on down the road."

A flood of visitors from other units and the press washed over the camp. "It was an exhibition, God help us," said Herder. "Those people in the stacks were dead; they were gone. Nothing could really hurt them further, but it hurt me that they were now on exhibition. Some of our guys had been disgusted by a bunch of nurses or WACs in their Class A uniforms taking pictures of the naked dead. It was not the display of genitals that shook some of us up; it was the final indignity, the exhibition." He was further appalled when he inspected a building in which physicians who experimented upon inmates stored organs harvested from their victims.

One day, a band of prisoners, with the connivance of a GI, sneaked through a hole in the fence. They returned leading an individual, a rope around his neck. While in the nearby town of Weimar, they had recognized one of their former guards. In a Buchenwald cell, they interrogated their captive. Herder observed the proceedings, saw tears roll down the man's cheeks and then left. Later he and some others returned to the scene. "The hands of the German were untied, and he held a stout piece of rope. He was being given instructions and as we watched, it wasn't long before we realized he was being told how to tie a noose. The German guard was corrected three or four times, and had to undo some of his work to redo it correctly. When he was finished, he had a very proper hangman's noose, thirteen turns of the rope and all. A table was brought to the center of the room and placed under a very strong-looking electrical fixture. The guard was assisted onto the table and instructed to fix the rope to the light fixture. Finishing that, he was to put all of his weight on the rope and lift his feet. The fixture held. The guard was told to place the noose over his head, around his neck, and to draw the noose fairly snug. Then he was told to place his hands behind his back and his wrists were tied together. The table was moved and he barely stood on its edge. He couldn't see that; his eyes were unhooded and open, but the noose kept him from looking down. He was talked to some more and then he jumped. He was caught before all of his weight was on the rope and they set him back on the table. The next time he stepped gently off the end and the table was quickly slid away from him and out of his reach and he dangled there. He slowly strangled. His face went through a variety of colors before he hung still. My stomach did not want to hold food any longer. I turned and walked away; the rest of our guys following me. The Buchenwald prisoners stayed on to view their handiwork.

"Here we were, five or six of us, fully armed with semiautomatic rifles and we did not make the Buchenwald prisoners stop. In one way, we sanctioned the event; it was murder. The prisoners never touched the rope after it was placed in the German's hands, unfastened. They did not tie the noose nor did they fix it to the ceiling. They did not place the rope around the man's neck. They did not pull the table out from under him [until after he stepped off]. In one sense they had not committed murder, rather the German had committed suicide.

"I [and my companions] had the ability and means to stop the whole thing, but did not. Ever since that day I have been convincing myself that I understood why the Buchenwald prisoners did what they did. I had witnessed their agonies. I had wondered how human beings could treat other humans beings as the prisoners at Buchenwald had been treated. I felt I knew why the prisoners did what they did—so I did not stop them. I could have stopped the whole action, and I did not. I have had that under my hat for the past [fifty-three] years. Now I have written it. I have acknowledged it. Maybe it will go away. There are so many things from that week I wish would go away, be scrubbed from my memory. When we returned to the barracks we did not tell anyone what we had witnessed." A few days later the Rangers pulled out of the camp, bearing with them images that obviously have haunted some for their entire lives.

According to Bradley, when the Third Army overran the first death camp at Ohrdruf, Patton insisted his colleagues view it. "You'll never believe how bastardly these Krauts can be," he said, "until you've seen this pesthole yourself." Subsequently, he forced townspeople to march through the installation. Afterward, the mayor of nearby Gotha and his wife hanged themselves.

Carl Ulsaker, as a company commander in the 95th Division, moved into the outskirts of Dortmund. "The area through which we passed consisted of a maze of steel mills and factories that had been bombed into twisted ruins by heavy air raids. The devastation wrought by these raids had even altered the landscape so that I found it difficult to navigate. Roads had been obliterated and man-made objects so badly destroyed that they were unrecognizable."

Except for a roadblock that required a tank to discourage the Germans who manned it, the Americans met no opposition. In the stygian darkness of a rain-sodden night, they marched down a broad boulevard to the central square of the eighth-largest German city. "We moved in silence," recalled Ulsaker, "calling for no supporting fire to precede us. Somewhere in the distance off to our right, occasional volleys of artillery fired by some unknown unit lit up the horizon like summer heat lightning. We met no enemy, the Germans apparently having the good sense to seek shelter in such unpleasant weather."

On the following day the GIs marched toward the Ruhr River, again with no sign of the foe. "One of my flank guards emerged from some bushes on the right side of the road with information that just beyond a patch of woods on the other side of the bushes he had come upon a military encampment with several hundred German soldiers drawn up in parade ground formation with weapons neatly stacked. Noting that they obviously were not prepared to fight, he had approached the commander, a colonel who stood in front of his troops. The latter informed my scout he was prepared to surrender his entire command, but would do so only to an officer of his equivalent rank. Taking a squad and a machine-gun crew with me, I accompanied the flank guard to the German camp. I approached the colonel, who saluted and restated his proposition.

" 'Colonel,' " I said, " 'I'm the senior officer in our advance guard; no officer of your rank will be along for hours. I'm in a hurry. You can either surrender to me or take the consequences.' I pointed toward my machine gun and rifle squads, who had taken a position on the bank overlooking the scene.

" '*Ja, Herr Hauptman*, I surrender to you,' " he responded wisely. Whereupon I designated two men to escort the new POWs to the rear and two more to guard the weapons piled on the parade ground." Ulsaker resumed the march toward the objective by the Ruhr River. Impatient to finish the mission, he joined an advance party as it entered some woods. "Suddenly a whistle blew and about a platoon of German infantrymen popped up from concealed foxholes all around us. A lieutenant walked over and said, 'I surrender my command.'

" 'I accept,' I responded with relief, embarrassed at having nearly been caught in a clever ambush, then added, 'Why did you surrender? You had us surprised.'

" 'I know,' he answered, 'but the Americans are there just across the river,' pointed toward the Ruhr, now visible in the distance. 'We are caught here in a vise. The situation is impossible for us.' I found this characteristic of the Germans. They were excellent tacticians and would fight hard until the situation became hopeless. Then they either retreated or surrendered."

Two days later, 12 April, the day President Franklin D. Roosevelt died, the battalion commander formed the outfit to announce the news and have a moment of prayer for the late commander in chief. That day also ended combat for Ulsaker and his people. With the Ruhr pocket closed, the front was now 150 miles away, where Americans in the west and Soviets in the east were closing on the Elbe River.

In the air, Cary Salter, with the 354th Fighter Group, patrolled the skies protecting the spearheads of Patton's Third Army. Ordinarily, few if any German aircraft attempted to interfere, but on 2 April, a coterie of Luftwaffe rose to challenge the Americans. "I was the wingman for Andy Ritchey and I saw four 190s below. I gave him a little space to go after them when I saw eight more. I called out, 'Watch out, Andy, the whole damn Luftwaffe is down there.' We were coming down on 'em, maybe 400 miles an hour. I got some hits on one and then he bailed out. I was coming head-on another, but I ran over him and had to pull up. Meanwhile Ritchey shot down three 190s. On the way home I came on an ME 109 and shot it down. I later heard Patton said we should have gotten a Medal of Honor for protecting his people."

On 4 April he took off from a strip at Wiesbaden for the first fighter mission to originate east of the Rhine. "This was an armed recon mission where we would search out and attack targets such as trains, motor transport, or anything supporting the war effort, while always looking for enemy aircraft. We had not gone very far when we came to an area of a good bit of ground fighting. This was not what we were looking for; this was what P-47s worked on. One of our fellows ahead was hit and killed. I don't know if he was shot down by our own forces or the Germans. About the same time, tracers were coming by me from off my left wing. I heard a loud WHAP! and hardly felt anything. One bullet went into the left side just a foot or two behind my seat. It hit my radio and put it out of commission and all of my maps had come out of place, out of reach." Salter turned around and headed in the general direction from which he took off. He eventually found his home field and when the mechanics inspected the damage, they diagnosed the pieces of the spent bullet as most likely from an American .50 caliber.

Salter said he was surprised to learn that some flyers dreaded missions and wondered whether they could strafe enemy soldiers who were caught in the open. "The enemy was the enemy and if we didn't kill him, he would kill us. We knew we were killing people when we shot down planes. I don't know any of our guys who lost sleep over it. On the other hand, we never shot at a pilot in a parachute, although three times I could have."

Bill Kunz, with the artillery for the 3d Division, crossed the Main River near Schweinfurt, the ball-bearing center where the Eighth Air Force lost so many planes early in the war, but now was in shambles. Flanked by old comrades from the 45th and 36th Divisions, the 3d advanced upon Nürnberg, still girded by numerous 88s and antiaircraft weapons now leveled as ground fire. "We entered Nürnberg April 21," said Kunz. "The city was flattened by combined Air Force and artillery action. Still, resistance was heavy. A lot of it, Hitler Youth and other civilians using individual rifle fire and *Panzerfausts* (one-shot bazookas).

"Our section was about one-third in the city and laying wire from the OP over heaps of rubble. I needed a length of line and spotting a Kraut line I cut into it. It turned out to be electrical and live! It knocked me right off my rubble pile into the street. A few blocks away the OP was under sniper fire. It was located in a relatively high building remnant and had taken a casualty from rifle fire some distance away. One of the infantry squads had entered the building and fired into the upper floor. The 'enemy' turned out to be children—fully armed—none older than possibly twelve or fourteen. Two were girls, fanatical, ready to die for the Führer. On the other hand, many of the older men, pressed into service, were happy to surrender."

Stan Newman, a late replacement for the 162d Fighter Squadron, flew mostly recon missions. As a wingman it was his job to watch for enemy planes. "We flew in conjunction with the French who had Spitfires," said Newman. "The P-51 looked like an ME-109 and I had a friend shot down by a Spitfire. One time when some Spitfires came after us I rocked my wings up so they could see the big airscoop of a P-51. At the battle for Nürnberg, I spotted an ME-262 [German jet fighter]. I dove on him and had never flown a P-51 that fast. But just before I got within range he went—pssst, and was gone. I saw black puffs and thought it was flak. But there was another one of them up above and I'd taken the bait. Luckily, I could outturn him with a P-51.

"As we moved east, we picked up our tent city, moved to Mainz, then Wiesbaden, a German fighter strip with wrecked 109s and 190s all over the place, and finally a permanent Luftwaffe base near Nürnberg. This was luxury; flush toilets, hot water, two pilots to a room, and displaced Ukrainian girls as maids. Actually, we hardly ever saw the Luftwaffe in the air. But on one of the last days of the war, when we were flying at lower altitude than usual, we got bounced by FW 190s. Each of us shot one down. Mine put his gear down and rocked his wings to show he was going to surrender and he landed at our base. They surrounded him like he was Lindbergh at Le Bourget. I then flew another mission and came across this two-engine plane. I got him pointed west and he landed at our airfield when it was almost dark. It was a high-ranking German officer with his wife, daughter, dog, and an aide. I got a souvenir .25-caliber pistol."

Captain Charles MacDonald, wounded in mid-January with I Company of the 2d Division's 23d Infantry Regiment, returned the first week of March to a new command, G Company. He crossed the Rhine in boats uneventfully. The division was part of a combined operation of the U.S. Ninth and First Armies that snared 317,000 prisoners in the Ruhr

Pocket. Said MacDonald, "As infantrymen we would have many another anxious moment in the war, but never again would we face a cohesive enemy front."

MacDonald's people pressed on against sporadic resistance, crossing the old German border with the Sudetenland, first annexed by Hitler and then Czechoslovakia proper. The stream of surrendering enemy swelled to flood stage. "As our column advanced down one side of the highway, a ragged column of Germans in horse-drawn wagons, dilapidated German Army vehicles, civilian automobiles, bicycles, and on foot met us coming down the other side. Some had their families with them. All had thrown away their weapons. . . . The Germans were running from the Russians to surrender to the Americans.

"The traffic became almost a hopeless mass of milling people. Regiment would take no more POWs—division said their POW cages were overflowing and would accept no more from regiment." His colonel invited MacDonald to ride with him into Pilsen, amid a deliriously joyful celebration. "The news came by radio that the war was over. There was no defining our joy. Sergeant Quinn brought out the treasured keg of cognac. The next day, May 8, would be V-E Day."

Tony Vaccaro, as a member of the intelligence team with the 83d Division, met up with Soviet troops. "Actually we crossed the Elbe River near Barby, north of Torgau. There were no Russians, because at that point the river turns a bit north. We had gone farther than any other American division. We were not supposed to cross, but General Macon [the division commander] was a good friend of Patton's who told him that he could continue. The Russians fired on us but most of them were drunk, they had no uniforms or helmets. They'd been told the Americans would not be on this side of the Elbe so I don't blame them. Only after about four or five days of sporadic shooting at us—we didn't return fire—did we get together, around 7 May.

"That night I went with a patrol to get information and we left at one o'clock with our faces painted black. Beyond a town called Zerf on the east side of the Elbe, we didn't meet any Germans. We could almost have walked to Berlin. The Germans were all hiding themselves. We found not much information other than some tanks knocked out by the Air Force. We came back about about 5:00 A.M., went to sleep. About eight or nine someone shook me, 'Wake up, Mike, the war is over.' It was 8 May."

For many of the American POWs liberation preceded V-E Day. After the Germans repulsed Task Force Baum they shut down the camp and marched the prisoners off. Alan Jones, his feet in wretched shape, remembered, "We reached Nürberg on 5 April. It had been badly bombed and the citizens spit on us and yelled epithets. We looked up and saw B-17s filling the horizon. The last ones in the group dropped a stick near us, killing the captain of our guards, wounding fifty or sixty American prisoners, including Colonel Cavender who was with us. During the march we traveled mostly at night because fighter planes patrolled the skies like police. We organized ourselves into syndicates of two and three to divide responsibilities. Just before daybreak one man would get us sleeping space in a barn, another would look for food to steal, and a third might try to pick up material that could be fashioned into weapons for use during an escape try.

"Our chance came between Nürnberg and the Danube. We were in a barnyard and the air force man and I noticed there were no guards around. We nodded to one another and then hid in a ditch. When the others moved out, we beat it, going east one day, then south and west to outguess the Germans. We became very hungry and knocked on a farmhouse door. The woman let us in, fed us bread, jam, and milk. There was a German staff sergeant, recuperating from the Russian front there. We all talked in English, and I still had on my lieutenant's bars and insignia, but nobody tried to turn us in. When we left, they gave us each half a loaf of bread.

"Still trying to reach our own lines, we heard artillery far off to the west. Late at night we reached a little town, jammed with SS troops. Before we could pass through, they caught us. We were marched about two miles and met the same column from which we escaped. The guards simply accepted us, stuck us back in line and off we went.

"On 2 May, we came to a place with signs in German that said, in effect, this is a restricted town. Any German who remains four hours must turn in his weapon to the provost. Our senior officers told us it can't be much farther. But some like me said, 'To hell with it. We're not going on.' We sat down on the curb. I wasn't there for more than a few hours when I looked up and there was a young kid, carrying an M1, chewing gum. Then I saw more and more of our kind of steel helmets. They rounded us all up. We looked more like displaced persons than officers. They threw some K rations to us and two-and-a-half-ton trucks carried us off to a regimental field hospital. I washed for the first time in months. The GIs who found us went off to a bitter fight with those SS troops who had picked us up. Seventeen days later, I was aboard a steamer, bound for the U.S."

Lyle Bouck, held in a riding stable after being seized with the remnants of the task force, received two pieces of sausage and a chunk of bread before a brief train ride. From there he went on the road, through Nürnberg, escaping the

B-17s that clobbered the column, with Alan Jones. With Matthew Reid, a captive from the 99th division, he sought to escape as they approached the Danube. Caught again, Bouck was incarcerated at Moosburg with thousands of others until 29 April, when elements of the 14th Armored, which had freed Abe Baum, brought his release.

At the end of March, John Collins, captured in the Ardennes, and POW companions were laboring at a brick factory. After an air raid on the railroad next to their camp, Collins watched "Jerries whipping some prisoners dressed in stripes and I mean whipping them! We were standing by the fence and yelled at the guards, but they ignored us. In one of the bombings, the planes dropped leaflets stating they intended to bomb the place off the map. Four of us decided we couldn't take any more of this and formed an escape plan. Very simple—wait until dark, enter the big crater by the fence, and crawl through, digging if required. Sometimes the guards walked the path between the fences, but we would take our chances. During the bombing, the smoke was so thick you could not see a damn thing."

On 1 April at 9:30 P.M. they made their break. "We made it through some small brush and into the city streets, where we separated as planned. Sergeant Vernon Hunt, who spoke four or five German dialects plus some Polish and Italian, and myself, English only, took one side of the street. Corporal Thomas Keneshea, a nice kid who could steal the Jerries blind, and T/4 Elmer George, almost deaf in one ear from concussion, but who seemed not to know what fear was, went down the other side. We had almost gotten through town when we heard marching troops and ducked into a doorway. They came down the street, a light flashed, and a lot of yelling started. A German came out of the door where we were to see what the commotion was about. He and Hunt had quite a conversation. Hunt told him we were kriegies, and we were going home. The fellow did not question us and I kept my mouth shut."

Three days later, they were caught while attempting to cross a bridge. "The commander in charge asked this guard why he did not put us in the canal like they did the airman. They were Volksturm—civilian guards. They seated us against the wall, everyone returned to their posts except for seven or eight sleeping on the floor. Hunt and I stayed awake, placing lice on our knees and flipping them on the sleeping guards."

He and Hunt were taken to Stalag XI B. The guard who accompanied them gave them his food as he put them aboard the train to the camp, inhabited mostly by French and British POWs. On 11 April, Collins noted, "We were unofficially liberated. All the guards left their posts and the gates were torn off their hinges." Rather than flee, the captives waited for Allied troops.

On 13 April, the senior British officer at the stalag sent around a message stating that President Franklin Delano Roosevelt had died and that the British wanted to share in the grief of the Americans. On 16 April the "Irish army" [Irish members of the British forces] liberated Collins. "Men who have gone through hell for many months, in some cases years, are like wild men. Grown men crying and giving thanks to their God." The Britons included Collins and any other Americans in the evacuation, flying them to an RAF base in England. "The English have treated us royally, feeding us one meal a day, a continuous meal from the time we arise till we leave." Collins was designated a malnutrition case, having lost just about one-third of his original 150 pounds.

Frank Raila also finally engineered his own freedom. Toward the beginning of April he was in a group of prisoners that included both Americans and Britons. Temporarily, they were held in a soccer field, surrounded by a low barbed-wire fence. Raila fell into conversation with two Welshmen and they were game for an escape try. "The guards were patrolling, but some of the Brits stopped them and offered cigarettes along with conversation. While they were distracted, it gave us time to slip away. We went separately, crawling under the wire, then running. We had planned to meet under a haystack we'd seen at dusk, but couldn't find it. We hid ourselves as best we could and when the sun came up, the haystack was only about fifty feet away. There was a large woods nearby, and we slept there the first day.

"At night we saw in the distance the glow from Leipzig being bombed. We headed in a direction that kept it on our right. Then we heard voices. They were eight to ten Russian slave laborers. At first we were scared of each other, but then they hugged us. They had made a homemade brew, a kind of vodka. Everyone was stewed, some lay on the ground puking. They shared some food with us, potatoes, and then they stole a rabbit and cooked it. I ate pieces of the head, eyeballs, tongue, even the brains. It was the first protein I had since being captured. We stayed with them several days. They told us the Germans were shooting anyone they found on the roads. Then a couple of the Russians ran into an American patrol. We approached them and they trained the .50s on the half-tracks at us. Once they realized we were escaped prisoners, I took off my overcoat and threw it to the slave laborers. The GIs also tossed them some Spam."

Shortly thereafter, Raila flew to Camp Lucky Strike. He quickly learned that overeating after a starvation diet adds complications. "One guy who stuffed himself with donuts died." He also found the interrogators suspicious of his claim of having escaped. Within a month, however, Raila shipped out for the States.

Spring brought a boost to the morale of Pfc. Phil Hannon at the stalag outside of Bad Orb. "The Germans were less strict in taking the correct count and were not insisting on our saluting them. On March 30, one of the older German guards remarked to me, 'Pretty soon,' and raised his hands in the air indicating he would soon be the prisoner." Easter Sunday, 1 April, the sounds of small-arms fire and even the smells of war, said Hannon, reached Bad Orb. "We couldn't see the fighting. But none of us were in a hurry to go looking for it. We had lived this long and didn't want a stray bullet to get us. That day, most of the Germans melted away and by evening, there were no Germans around. The following morning, three American tanks rode over the gates of the camp and we were liberated!"

An outbreak of spinal meningitis early in March placed Ed Uzemack and others in a stalag near Bad Orb under quarantine. By the middle of the month, the sound of American artillery fire could be heard. "Liberation fever was mounting. Because of the quarantine, the Germans made no effort to move the prisoners to another camp. Bets were freely made the men would be free by Easter Sunday." On that holiday, Uzemack jotted in his diary, "Our boys may come up tonight. The men are all excited—now they are tearing the wire off the windows. We are sure to be liberated tomorrow—Happy Easter." Uzemack roused himself at 2:00 A.M. to work in the kitchen and see freedom arrive. An inmate MP draped a white flag on the clock towers. And at 8:12 A.M. Uzemack scrawled, "The first American recon car rolls into the camp. Holy Smokes!"

In Stalag Luft II near the Polish border, late in January 1945, Lu Cox and his fellow airmen inmates heard the heavy artillery from the advancing Soviet forces. Within a week, Cox walked at the head of a column of 1,800 officers and enlisted men marching south through a driving snowstorm to evade the oncoming Red troops. "It was so cold that our bread and margarine froze. Our clothes froze. Worst of all our shoes froze. To start up again after a ten- or fifteen-minute rest was sheer agony. I felt as though I was wearing iron shoes with loose gravel inside. My shoes had frozen so solidly that both of them broke in half at the balls of my feet." The men drew some consolation from the poor shape of the guards, some of whom had discarded helmets, packs, and rifles. A number simply deserted. It was a mini death march for the kriegies. Men collapsed from unhealed wounds, hunger, and disease. They either froze to death where they fell or else guards murdered them. Occasionally, prisoners carried a sick comrade to the door of a house and after knocking, left him, hoping for mercy from the inhabitants.

The torturous hike covered 100 miles. Cox saw a vast caravan of German refugees, old men and women, small children and babies, in farm wagons pulled by oxen or on foot, fleeing the Soviet advance. At the end of the nearly six-day journey, the prisoners entered a huge camp with 100,000 Allied soldiers and airmen. Only after pleas for help was minimal medical treatment given, but still a diet "unfit for pigs to eat" and a lack of medicine left men prone to dangerous, even fatal bouts of pneumonia, flu, dysentery, frostbite, and festering wounds. Release through the appearance of U.S. troops was too late to save many of the afflicted.

David Jones remembered that late in the war, the guards, increasingly jumpy, killed and wounded prisoners on the slightest pretext. In January 1945, as Soviet armies approached Stalag III, with twelve to eighteen inches of snow on the ground, word the prisoners would be shifted west circulated. "People had collected all kinds of junk with them. I had the money. When people came in you took everything from them and I had money buried all over the damn compound. When it came time to retrieve it, the ground was frozen. We were having people heat pots of water and I poured it in the area and maybe twenty minutes later you could dig. I recovered lots of the money and passed it out to various people." Evacuated to Moosburg in the vicinity of Munich, Jones survived a death march where prisoners and guards fell by the wayside. But the 3d Army freed him and his comrades.

Jim Mills, part of the Slaughterhouse-five contingent at Dresden, remained a prisoner until the final week of the war. The artillery noise boomed from the east, Russian forces surging ever deeper into Germany. On 7 May, the guards led them out to the road with the objective of surrendering themselves and their captives to American troops. German civilians, soldiers, and POWs clogged the highway. Suddenly, out of the sky a flight of a dozen Soviet planes peeled off and started to strafe the refugees. Mills saw one of the aircraft coming in his direction. He spotted an earthen ramp to a hayloft that might provide some protection.

"I had just gotten to the edge of it when the plane started firing its machine guns. Shells were hitting the ground all around me, then up the side of the barn. The plane banked right, hit a cow in the hind end." That threat passed and Mills started down the road again. Another plane dove and released a bomb. "The screaming and whistling noises got even louder, we knew it was coming right down on us." He crouched in a small stream, with a woman, a child, one German soldier, and two prisoners. Showered with dirt and debris from the blast, they escaped injury.

The area was overrun by Soviet troops. "We saw Russians

carrying buckets of beer in each hand. The Russian soldiers indicated that if we wanted anything we should simply take it." Mills heard reports of rape and suicides. "Women would stop you on the street and want two fellows to spend the night. The Russians would not bother them if a fellow was present."

Slave laborers who picked up abandoned machine guns amused themselves with random bursts. Some British prisoners arranged for a train to haul POWs to their own forces. Mills, other prisoners, slave laborers and their female friends piled on. But the engine soon shunted off to a sidetrack. The famished prisoners stole some chickens and that aroused a mob of angry farmers. A Soviet officer quieted them, then secured some larger animals to feed the train passengers. "Our group was given a bull. One of our people had a pistol and shot the animal five times in the head. It got real mad, but finally staggered and fell. In a matter of minutes the bull was cut up and shared. The meat was still warm, when I got my piece [raw]." Mills gave up on the train and started walking. He reached Pilsen and from there was directed to American troops. It was well after the last shots had been fired.

17

Penultimate Actions

CESSATION OF FIGHTING IN EUROPE MEANT NOTHING TO THOSE embroiled in the final confrontations with the Japanese on Okinawa and in the Philippines. As platoon leader with G Company of the 1st Marine Regiment, during the first week of May, Bob Craig and his men were on a reserve status on Okinawa when the Japanese opened a counteroffensive. It began with a predawn seaborne expedition that sought to place Japanese soldiers behind the Marine lines. Leathernecks on G's right flank dealt with the threat. "We knew something was going on," says Craig, "because Navy star shells and land-based flares lit up that area all night long.

"The next morning, Jim Paulus, the company exec, came up from the CP to see how things were. He looked over our left flank and saw a little smoke coming up from down below. He said to me, 'I think some gook is cooking chow down there.' I replied I didn't think so; it was probably some timbers in the cave still smoldering from yesterday's burnout by the tanks, but that I'd check it out."

Craig approached the area from his ridge position. "As I looked over the edge, I saw a Jap at the entrance to the cave. At the same time he looked right up at me. I quickly pulled a hand grenade from my pocket, yanked out the safety pin, released the activator handle, counted a fast one-two, and dropped it. It had hardly left my hand before it went off. After the handle flew off, only three seconds elapsed before the grenade exploded. Of course the Jap had ducked back into the cave when he saw me, but my concern was the apparently fast fuse.

"Jim Paulus and I immediately went back to the command CP to check the supply of grenades. We found that they had sent up a new model with three-second fuses, instead of the original five-second models we had been using. No one had advised us concerning the new model and I would have been killed if I had held onto it for the time we had been trained to do with the five-second model. The reason for holding on was to avoid giving the Jap time enough to pick up the grenade and throw it back as they had done earlier in the war. I warned all my men to check the fuse model numbers on what they had and any new ones they got."

"About ten o'clock that night, I saw a smoke screen thrown up on Hill 60 [in front of Craig's position on Hill Nan]. I used the phone to call for an emergency barrage because it looked like the Japs were either going to make a night attack or were making troop movements behind the smoke screen. Within less than one minute the first of thirty rounds came over and appeared to burst right overhead, not in the draw where they were supposed to fall. I thought the FO had made a miscalculation in laying in the target because the rest of the rounds burst in similar fashion.

"No attack came and the next morning I got with the FO

to find out what had happened. He explained that the shells had proximity fuses that caused them to explode so many feet above the ground, throwing shrapnel into anything or anyone below. We had suffered no injuries or death from this event, solely because howitzers fire at high-angle trajectories. The shells we thought were landing among us actually burst as they came down on the forward slope of Hill Nan. It was another near miss for my platoon." Like the shorter-timed grenades, the incident illustrates the dangerous short-circuits of information and coordination that confound the vast enterprise of war.

Craig's 3d platoon jumped off around 10:00 A.M. seeking to make its way past Hill 60. "We didn't get very far before a counterattack by Jap mortars stopped us in our tracks. The 1st platoon then tried to relieve the pressure on us, but it, too, was hit by Jap mortars. Only fourteen escaped without injury. [Forty-nine officers and enlisted men ordinarily make up a Marine infantry platoon but the number available by this time was somewhat less.]"

Those in command committed the 2d platoon of G Company, but everyone was forced to fall back, and needed tank and heavy machine guns even to accomplish a successful retreat. The second day of the battle produced similar results, large numbers of casualties and a retreat back to the foxholes from which the attack was originally launched. At midnight, the Japanese tried to overrun the position. "When this battle started," says Craig, "I was off watch trying to get some badly needed sleep. My runner Lecklightner and another rifleman were on watch—we were using three men in a foxhole to avoid what had happened earlier on Hill Nan. Leck later told me he couldn't arouse me, presumably because I was so exhausted, but I didn't believe him and reamed him out. I have no recollection of that night, and, thank God, those two with the rest of the platoon stopped the counterattack.

"About 4:00 A.M., when it was over, I came to, probably because the sudden silence prodded my inner senses. I saw dead Japs all over our area, maybe eighteen or twenty. As a matter of security, Leck and I ventured out of our foxhole to check them out and make sure none were faking dead. Sure enough, one was lying on his side, still holding onto his rifle. When I kicked the bottom of his foot he flinched, then tried to rise up and shoot me. The slugs from my Tommy gun knocked him back down."

The Marines renewed their drive and the battalion with G Company advanced southeast toward Dakeshi and Wanna Ridges, natural ramparts that guarded the town of Shuri and the anchor of the defenses bearing its name. Craig became pinned down by a Nambu machine gun in a large shell hole, half full of water. With him were Leck and a wounded marine. "I concluded we were going to be there for a while because there was no cover and we would not leave the wounded man there by himself. One of our tanks appeared and I attracted his attention. The tank commander told me he would drive the tank right over our hole, open up the escape hatch in its bottom, and take the wounded man up inside. He did this and then Leck and I crawled out on the side of the tank where we were not exposed to Jap fire. We walked back to a little knoll with the tank and waited for a corpsman and stretcher-bearers. I could see bullets bouncing off the side of the tank. I hoped there was no antitank gun nearby because the tank just sat there protecting us."

After four days, the strategists determined the position of the 2d Battalion untenable and under cover of darkness the Marines retreated. "The happy surprise for us," says Craig, "was that we continued to march back to a rest area. For the next four days we got some cooked meals, daily showers, and brand-new clothing. We had been wearing the same uniforms for forty-four days and mine just about stood up by itself. We also received replacements for the three platoons, and, in addition, two new platoon leaders. But the slot of executive officer was not filled, which indicated a shortage of experienced officers."

Jim Moll, an acting platoon sergeant in A Company of the 7th Marine Regiment, and his unit had been pinned down by artillery a day or so after they relieved the 27th Division soldiers. "I told Sgt. Vern Smith, acting as platoon guide, we were all going to be dead ducks unless we did something soon. With deadly fire coming in from behind us, the only way out would be with a few tanks to cover our rear. I told Smitty that whoever tried to get back to headquarters had a very slim chance because he had to run along the ridge we were on, run down through the draw, and climb the only footpath up to the higher ridge. I told Smitty I would go, but he insisted it would be better if I stayed with the platoon. He took off his pack to lighten the load and shook hands with me. A few minutes later, word came back to me that Smitty was killed.

"I dropped my pack and took off. When I got to the spot where Smitty was hit, they opened up on me with heavy machine guns and mortar fire. I dove into a small, shallow hole that left my feet and legs exposed. I felt two bullets hit my left shoe, but no pain. A few seconds later, a mortar exploded next to the hole. The blast knocked the stock off my weapon and me cold. When I came to, I jumped up and kept running until they tackled me. The bullets had passed right through the heel of my shoe but barely nicked me. Later, just before dusk, the Marines dropped smoke shells and got everyone off the ridge.

"That evening, we could see the Japs building up a heavy concentration of troops on a ridge about 200 to 300 yards in front of us. I had never seen such a massing of Jap troops and I was concerned because we had no protection on our right flank. I had to send a man back to bring me a telephone so I could get some artillery support. Our machine gunners wanted to open up on the Japs, but I knew then all hell would break loose. I had them hold back until I got the phone. The Japs started to blast hell out of us with their artillery and I finally contacted the 11th Marine Artillery. Unfortunately, I had no map to pinpoint our position. The Marine at the other end said they would fire three rounds and I should let him know where they landed. But with all of the Jap shells I couldn't hear anything at first. Then during a short pause in the action, I thought I heard the three more rounds they fired way off in the distance. After about a dozen more tries, shells began landing between us and the enemy. I told them to start at that point and work their way outward on a path about 400 yards wide. I never witnessed such a masterly display of artillery. They literally blew the Japs off the hill."

On 11 May, Gen. Lemuel Shepherd, CG of the 6th Marine Division, signaled for the tanks to lead the way as the 22d Marine Regiment led off the assault. Exposed to enemy artillery for a distance of 3,000 yards of level ground, the Marines slogged on through the mud until they reached the Asato River estuary, which lay in front of the city of Naha. The assault teams paid heavily; the spearhead Company C of the 22d lost 35 killed and another 68 wounded from the original 256-man contingent.

Instead of focusing upon the town, the strategists concentrated on Sugar Loaf Hill, a citadel of well-armed, well-dug-in Japanese troops who could count on additional firepower from comrades dug in on two lesser neighboring slopes. For five days, men from the 6th Marine Division battled to reach the heights of Sugar Loaf. Captain Martin "Stormy" Sexton, from K Company of the 4th Marine Regiment, said, "When we encountered the Japanese MLR [main line of resistance] it was vicious, hand-to-hand combat. And to aggravate the situation, the heaviest fighting coincided with the rainy season."

Harry Manion had a front-row seat to observe the butchery. "Moving forward was slow; the infantry were catching all kind of hell from the deeply dug-in enemy. The caves were a big problem. We used everything we had against them, white phosphorus, bulldozers, flamethrowers and any other available ordnance. Throw in a smoke grenade and watch for where the smoke comes out the air openings. Pump in gasoline and bang. Some caves had many levels and complex entrances. There were no simple solutions, but we continued to underestimate the Oriental fighter. He can dig."

In the center of the American offense the 77th Division stood alongside the 1st Marine Division. While other Army units frequently expressed resentment toward the leathernecks, the Statue of Liberty Division troops believed they were respected by the Marines. Buckner Creel of the 77th notes that on Guam, they served operationally under the III Marine Amphibious corps. "We had no unforeseen problems and unlike the fiasco on Saipan, things went easily. The III Phib commander, Maj. Gen. Roy Geiger, was a much smoother commander than Howling Mad Smith. Furthermore, our general, Andrew D. Bruce, was respected in all circles. After Guam we were known as the only division that could get along with the Marines. We did not always agree with their tactics. They seemed to use more 'frontal' assaults than we. We preferred fire and maneuver [a tactic scorned by Patton]. In their defense, many situations in the Pacific, frontal assault was the only possible thing to do."

The enemy occupied the high ground in the form of hills called Chocolate Drop and Wart, and the Japanese soldiers protected by a deep trench pumped bullets at the oncoming infantrymen. The GIs fell back more than once. Buckner Creel attempted to rally and direct his men. "While running across an open area, I would be chased by a Nambu machine gun that failed to 'lead' me correctly. The third time I crossed, he managed to shoot the heel off my combat boot." Along with Creel's G Company, E and F from the 2d Battalion had also absorbed brutal blows. "In spite of the heroics of the soldiers in G Company," says Creel, "we were now down to two officers and forty men. They formed the battalion into a 'provisional company' by consolidating E, F, and G. We had a total of only seventy-nine effectives. The World War II strength of a rifle company was 6 officers and 196 men ordinarily, more than 200 total. There should have been 600 troops. I was designated the company commander, although the COs of E and F were senior to me in rank." [The 3d Battalion of the 306th, in no better condition than the 2d, also formed into a provisional unit and with Creel's group composed a single makeshift battalion.]

The ordeal reduced the effective fighting force even below the number seemingly available to fight. "I don't recall any men who broke and ran," said Creel. "But it is an axiom of combat that it is probably better to wound your enemy than kill him. Because it will take two or more people off the battlefield removing the injured soldier. We did have some problems then getting back people who had assisted the wounded to the rear. They would be gone for a day or so, sometimes because they could not physically return, but sometimes because they dawdled."

At Flattop Hill, Company K, with Larry Gerevas, was shattered by a series of futile attempts to wade through an avalanche of grenades, mortar rounds, and bullets. "I could see the squad leader and I was listening to his instructions. Suddenly, he seemed to explode. The upper part of his torso was gone. A moment later his helmet fell from above and rolled down the hill. A mortar round had made a direct hit on him. We were all sickened to see what was left of him." When the last officer on his feet fell dead with a bullet through his forehead, Gerevas said he and his buddies felt this was an impossible mission.

"An officer from another unit came up the hill to us and ordered us to go over the top. He looked like he had just come from some rear area because he was so clean and neatly dressed. We had lost nearly our whole company in this suicidal, frontal attack and weren't about to go to a certain death for this guy. We all refused. He became very angry and demanded that we follow his orders or we would all face a court-martial. We told him to go to hell. The threat of being court-martialled didn't sound very frightening to any of us at this point. As he stood there, looking at this motley group of weary, unshaven, determined, armed men, he must have realized how hollow his threats were. He turned away, went down to the base of the hill and left the area. A short time later we were pulled off the hill and sent to the rear. It was May 17 and in two days we had lost nearly 85 percent of our company."

The torrents of blood gushing from the 77th Division prompted a distraught Sgt. Alfred Junkin, who assumed command of a unit, to write 77th division commander, Gen. Andrew Bruce. "I believe it is proper to report to you directly on my actions as 1st Platoon, C Company leader from 6 A.M. May 17 until 12 noon May 18 due to the fact that Lt.

Lusk was KIA shortly after our objective was taken. Also, I understand Lt. Campbell and Sgt. Stanick since have both been KIA so I am not aware as to who is in command of C Company."

Junkin recounted some of the fight. "The Japs began to pop up on our right flank and we shot them down like ducks. Then all hell broke loose with intense mortar and MG fire punctuated by accurate sniper fire. Sergeant Chambers spotted a Nip AA gun on a knoll seventy-five yards away and blasted the crew. Sergeant Kelly was superb in encouraging thirty replacements to dig in deep and pick off Nip targets. I was one of the first to be hit, a mortar fragment punctured my cheek. . . . During the next half hour [Private first class] McCauley and Sergeant Kelly were KIA. We were getting no effective supporting artillery or mortar fire on our right flank and I dropped back to the platoon CP twenty-five yards to report to Lieutenant Lusk. I found him dead in his foxhole from a direct mortar hit."

Junkin described the slight shifts in position he directed in order to protect his diminishing forces. While he praised the mortar work of nearby E Company, he remarked that "our own artillery dropped several shells in our area" but then praised the work of some other big guns and the tanks. "I was up and down the line, trying to encourage our new men to hold fast, by pointing out troops far below who were trying to pass through us and telling them that water and ammo would be brought in at night and the wounded taken out.

"As night came, H Company withdrew their heavy machine guns, leaving our left flank exposed. By now there was no one left on the ridge except twenty men of C Company. . . . We drew a tight line, shifted the wounded so there was not more than one in each hole. Sergeant [Victor] Winschuh set up his light machine gun in the center facing the crest of the ridge. There was nothing we could do except crack down on targets as they came up within twenty or thirty yards, and pray. We did plenty of both.

"A grenade fell into the foxhole next to the CP that Del Rosso and I shared. I pulled out [Pvt. Andrew] Mezines but could not save [Pvt. Arlo] Mellberg. Our thirty replacements showed great courage, but were too new to the job. One of them saw two Japs who got Mellberg thirty feet away. His finger froze on the trigger. Another saw a Nip standing on the horizon and shouted wildly at others to shoot the man, but he had his own rifle in his hand. Another sees Nips a few yards from his hole, aims, and fires and . . . empty rifle. In the excitement he had emptied his magazine and forgotten to reload.

". . . I ask nothing for myself but I would like to see every one of my men on the line that night receive a citation. When 20 men stave off a Jap regiment, it is certainly beyond the call of duty." Junkin seized the opportunity to call for promotions for several whom he felt deserved recognition that was denied because of turnovers in commanders. The sergeant then expressed his deep misgivings over the exigencies of the war. "The record speaks for itself . . . [the victory] belongs to the 77th and especially C Company, but I deplore the necessity for taking green recruits who hardly know how to load a rifle into combat. . . . I know you [Gene Bruce] have the interest of the men in our battalion at heart and believe you will agree that these teenage youngsters fight with great courage, but are just too green and inexperienced to do the job." Junkin himself received the Distinguished Service Cross. Several men earned Silver or Bronze Stars and the entire platoon was given a Presidential Unit Citation.

The flow of replacements for the GIs included OCS graduate Si Seibert, assigned to the 382d Regiment of the 96th. His initial fears of acquitting himself satisfactorily vanished with a small success in an attack. After accepting compliments from company commander Capt. Cledith Bourdeau, Seibert said he felt relieved. "My first firefight had gone better than I dared hope. It appeared that I had been accepted by the troops. In fact, I got the impression that the men were hungry for leadership, they willingly gave their loyalty and confidence to each officer placed over them until such time as he might prove himself inept, or for some other reason unacceptable. As a result, the men had accepted me with far less reserve than I had anticipated."

Much of the euphoria that gripped him earlier disappeared the following day. "Just as we were looking for a night position, there was a flurry of shots to our front. I watched in horror as one of my soldiers fell to the ground. It was obvious from the way he fell that he was dead. It was a traumatic thing for me. He was the first of my men to be killed and it was the first time that I felt responsible for the death of someone. I didn't even know his name. Suddenly, I was aware of a strange dichotomy in my thinking in combat. Killing the enemy did not bother me, though I took no pleasure or pride in it. There was no sense of responsibility for the enemy's death; it was simply the job to be done. On the other hand, the death of one of my men, although I was not directly responsible for it, placed a heavy burden on me; I could never, and have never, gotten over that feeling. I actually cried a little when that first man was killed, but soon got myself in hand. Nobody noticed.

"It is a feeling I have never ceased to have in combat [Seibert served in Korea and Vietnam]. Where had I erred that this individual was killed? Was my plan or my leadership lacking? This is probably healthy if you do not let it overwhelm you. As a result, you analyze plans, orders or leadership more carefully in order to make the best possible decision. I did not go into a deep depression or permit it to disturb me to the point that I couldn't think of anything else, but it was a difficult thing to accept."

However awful the losses inflicted on the Americans, the military resources of the Japanese eroded with each attack. The mighty waves of kamikazes that peaked during April and early May dropped off sharply as the third month of Operation Iceberg approached. But even on a lesser scale they rocked the picket ships. On 27 May, the destroyers assigned to Picket Station #5 were the *Braine* and the *Anthony*. Clyde Van Arsdall, the *Anthony* skipper, a 1934 USNA graduate, commanded a veteran, well-trained crew. "We had had our first opportunity to talk to people who had actually been under kamikaze attack right before Iwo Jima," recalled Van Arsdall. "There was no consensus as to what to do under these attacks. Everybody seemed to have their own ideas. There was a bit of an argument, whether you should go at high speeds or lower ones where you had better control of the battery [antiaircraft guns]. I was one who joined the 'speed demons.' If there was an attack imminent, we were at twenty-five knots or better. We tried to keep incoming planes on our beam to allow the maximum number of guns clear shooting. Once a fellow started in, we would then maneuver hard right or hard left to get into a turn. The idea was that when a guy made his decision to come at us in a certain way and we got into a turn, he couldn't keep up with it so we received some extra shooting time while he maneuvered either astern or on the quarter." He concluded, "Keep the guns ready and shoot like hell."

The *Anthony* had started its picket station screen duty with some success against several nighttime prowlers. When the *Braine* relieved another destroyer and became *Anthony*'s partner, about daylight, radar picked up four planes coming from the north. "It was accepted," says Van Arsdall, "that if the picket station was attacked, it was every man for himself, with number one, don't have a collision with anybody. We immediately ordered General Quarters. There was a solid overcast, my guess is 2,000–3,000 yards. Horizontal visibility was very good, there was no sea. *Braine* was clear, the LCI gunboats [accompanying them to add firepower] were out maybe 4,000 yards and we began to open up a bit on *Braine* and build up some speed.

"Combat kept reporting, 'They're coming straight in toward the picket station,' followed shortly by, 'it looks like they're breaking into two groups.' " The enemy aircraft followed a course to take them directly over the pair of destroyers as the distance between the ships spread to 2,500 to 3,000 yards, as they traveled roughly in the same direction. *Anthony*'s combat intelligence now advised two planes were headed for it while the others would be on the starboard. Fire-control radar began tracking the nearest ones.

The planes passed over the picket station and then Van Arsdall received word they had turned and fire control had a solution. "I couldn't see them through the overcast," remembered Van Arsdall, "but I immediately gave the 'Commence Firing.' *Anthony* opened up with its forward guns, the main battery. I started turning to get our after guns cleared. Things started to happen very fast. I heard a report, 'we're on target,' and wanting to get the planes on our broadside, turned left. About that time, a plane, on fire and smoking, came through the overcast, it went on down and splashed. A second plane headed directly toward us. I tried to keep him on the starboard beam. There was so little time left the maneuvers of the ship didn't mean anything. Our 40mms and

20mms opened up and there was really a blanket of fire going out.

"This joker came right on in. I couldn't do any more maneuvering he was so close. But he was right where we wanted him, all the guns could bear on him. Some chips flew off, but he kept coming. He actually passed over the ship, not many feet above the Number 1 stack. All of us thought he would crash into us, but he did not nose over that much. As he passed, I went to the wing of the bridge so I could watch him there. He had pulled up, just a bit to climb and turn to his left. He did a beautiful job because pieces were coming off his aircraft.

"It looked like he was in control, because he did a nice climbing left and never came out except to then put his nose down, crashing into *Braine* probably 2,500 yards from us. There was a lot of yelling and shouting, but from it I got the idea that *Braine* had been hit probably thirty seconds before this plane came down. Two kamikazes had crashed her in succession. Those who were watching said the Number 2 stack on *Braine* just disappeared. I don't know whether that was the one that came over us or the other. She was hit twice. One struck a little to the starboard of the center at the bridge, demolished the bridge, and went down into the wardroom country. A tremendous mess of the ship there and caused everyone forward of amidships on the bridge level to abandon ship.

"The second hit destroyed a fireroom, did serious damage in the engine room, and from my vantage point, the whole topside from the bridge to the afterstack was a mess. The two ships were on almost opposite courses, well clear of each other. *Braine* still was underway. What happened to the fourth plane is conjecture so far as I am concerned. I never saw it. Some on our bridge told me it had gone into the water between the two ships. We could see people from the bridge level of *Braine* jumping over the side into the water and we saw people on the ship rolling wounded off the deck, which was on fire, into the water. Many of the crew ended up in the water. Gunboats picked up some and so did we."

After a brief respite, *Anthony* returned to picket duty and on 7 June fought off kamikazes. At dusk, a pair of Vals streaked toward the destroyer, coming in low enough to the water that they escaped interception by a combat air patrol. Pete Boyd, chief engineer for the destroyer, recalled, "When the bridge detected bogeys and sounded the GQ alarm, they also immediately rang up Flank Speed on the engine-room telegraph. This was our signal to bring up engine revolutions to maximum speed." Boyd noted that in the superheated din of the engine room in order to converse one couldn't just shout or yell. "You put your mouth close to the other guy's ear and scream. He may answer with sign language, and lip reading is almost a necessity."

Those down below could see nothing of what was happening on the surface. "In the engine control room," said Boyd, "there were two 'talkers,' ratings who wore sound-powered telephones. The first talker was on the circuit that included the topside stations. This was our only contact with the outside world. The second talker was on the circuit with all of the machinery spaces. He would repeat for them the information from the first talker. We'd get the word, 'Bogeys sighted, bearing 200 degrees, 8,000 yards.' We'd wait. Then BAM! BAM! BAM! Our main battery, the 5-inch guns would be firing. Then the report, 'He's coming our way!' and the 40s would start, FWUMP! FWUMP! FWUMP! FWUMP! Then we'd hear the 20s—tatatatatatat. By this time the first talker usually had frozen. All we could learn from him was through reading his facial expressions. The other talker would then report, 'I think he's gonna hit us,' or 'He missed us.' Only after securing from General Quarters could the machinery-space personnel emerge and learn from topside observers what had happened."

Boyd recalled the 7 June incident with the 5-inch main battery firing and then "a good report that the first plane had been splashed at about 2,000 yards. The news on the second wasn't as good. As the ship's speed rapidly increased, the bridge was maneuvering erratically, hard left, hard right, hard left. By now the 5-inchers, the 40s, and 20s were firing everything they could. The entire ship pitched greatly as the helmsman steered an evasive pattern.

"The FWUMP FWUMP FWUMP of our 40s and the tatatatat of our 20s told us down below that the number-two Bogey was almost on us. The ship was turning hard right, then a tremendous WHAM! A very strong smell of gasoline and some smoke followed in about two seconds. The forward repair party hollered that the bow was on fire and they couldn't get pressure on the forward firemain. The vessel at very high speed turned in the other direction. As it lurched a large shower of water came down from the hatch above the chief machinist and me, dousing us completely. My immediate reaction was the firemain had been hit. I started to discuss it with the chief—screaming at him—the location of the firemain and what to relay to the repair party. Then I saw his lips and hands. He screamed back, 'Does that taste like saltwater to you?' We both screamed 'Soap!' It was the laundry line that had ruptured."

The last week of May, Gen. Lemuel Shepherd ordered Tony Walker's Recon Company to sneak into Naha, the city on the western end of the Shuri line. Walker set up a base camp on the banks of the Asato Gawa River and a quartet of four-man teams crossed the stream to appraise the enemy strength. The interlopers bumped into Japanese patrols, exchanged a few rounds, but all of the GIs returned safely with the information that the city was not heavily defended.

On 28 May, Recon Company spearheaded an attack into Naha. "A Jap machine gun was firing through a break in one of the concrete walls surrounding most of the houses," recalled Walker. "Fuller Curtis with his squad had worked their way next to the wall. On order, each man pulled out a grenade and threw it. Then the squad all together went over the wall. When I got there, they proudly gave me a samurai sword, covered with bits and pieces of a Jap officer."

Recon settled in for what Harry Manion, one of Walker's sergeants, called "fun and a nightmare" amid the ruins. "After we cleaned out the university, bank, and other smaller buildings we found millions of yen and Japanese war bonds. Night brought in heavy artillery fire from large caves on the Oroku side of the Naha River. One time, one of our men was waving to a Marine fighter pilot coming in. The pilot shot at our man and killed him with a .50-caliber round. This was the second time Marine pilots fired at Marines on the ground. After that incident I always had a little suspicion about our air close-support Marines. We fired at him, but to no avail. Gone back to the carrier and a hot bath.

"About this time, dead at night, raining like only war can produce, we received a group of replacement Marines. Wet and miserable as Marines should be on their first night. We started switching older men with new men. The new Marines were fresh out of boot camp. Ten-day home leave and over they came. Training started in our platoon. Lessons: Don't go anywhere alone. Don't go into caves. No souvenir hunting. The next day I saw two of these Marines coming back from a souvenir search. A group of us were on a roof and I grabbed an M1 and fired three or four rounds at the feet of the Marines. They stopped, then came forward into the platoon position. Chew-out time. I believe one later shot off one of his toes." The following day, Manion spied two more recent arrivals investigating a cave. He raced after them, badly cut his head on the cave ceiling while ordering them out. Commented Manion, "It was chew-out time again."

Shepherd now outwitted the defenders on the Oroku Peninsula with a seaborne assault that brought tanks and leathernecks ashore on the western point of the coast rather than striking at the base of Oroku as the Japanese commander expected. The 4th and 29th Marine Regiments began to push the foe backward. Walker's forces participated, first by seizing the island of Ono-Yama in the Kokuba estuary, and then later wading out 600 yards to capture an offshore patch, Senaga Shima, disposing of a few enemy soldiers and finding many deep caves with some large artillery pieces. Meanwhile, the 22d Regiment, hitherto in reserve, entered the fray, applying pressure from the east, squeezing a dwindling pocket of resistance. With his position hopeless, his men either being cut to pieces or, in the first instance on Okinawa, surrendering in a large group (159), Admiral Ota committed suicide. By 15 June nothing remained of the Oroku defense.

Si Seibert recounted an incident in which the demands of higher-echelon officers became unacceptable. "We neared a formidable escarpment made of the Yuza-Dake and Yaeju-Dake hills. The north side was steep, about 150 feet in height. The 383d fought for Yuza-Dake and was so badly mauled that our 382d was ordered to relieve two of its battalions. Our 2d Battalion took over for their 2d [Lt. Bob Muehrcke's organization] and, initially attached to the 383d, was to attack in a narrow zone to gain a foothold on the escarpment. Leading the assault was F Company, with my platoon providing the point."

At first, the advance went well and Seibert's unit gained the top of the escarpment. But as they slipped to one side to permit the remainder of the company to join them, intensive small-arms fire cracked down on them. With one soldier killed and another wounded, the platoon scrunched down behind the ridge line. Seibert peeked over the top to see a completely open field to the front, one pockmarked with bunkers, foxholes, and spider holes undoubtedly occupied by enemy soldiers prepared to spray the area with deadly results.

He consulted with his company commander, Cledith Bourdeau, who said that because of other exigencies no artillery could be brought to bear. The infantrymen would have to charge forward with only the minor aid of 60mm mortars. "The machine gun positions," said Seibert, "seemed poorly constructed. I called for rifle grenades, but there were only three and one grenade launcher. It had been so long since the men had used them, they had gradually stopped carrying the weapon. I had failed to check this out since I assumed command and now my neglect was to be costly. None of the men left had even fired rifle grenades so I became the grenadier. Because there were no launcher sights, I used the field experience of putting my foot in the rifle sling and measuring the angle with my eye. Surprisingly, I did pretty well. The first round fell short and did no damage, but the second and third destroyed two positions.

"As I was sighting the second round, however, the platoon medic came up behind me and looked over my helmet. There was an instant report from a sniper rifle and the medic fell. He had been shot squarely between the eyes and lived only a few minutes, dying before he could be evacuated. It was obvious what the platoon was up against. I called again for supporting fire. Bourdeau told me none was available, but we had to keep moving to permit the remainder of the company and battalion to get into position. I told him it was suicide to take the platoon into that fire. I asked if there were any tanks. He said no. Finally, Bourdeau came up and looked over the situation. As I pointed out the enemy positions that permitted the Japs to cover the area in a crossfire, his radio operator looked over his shoulder. There was a characteristic report and the man fell dead. A sniper round had struck him, too, squarely between the eyes.

"Bourdeau agreed it was suicidal to continue. He went back to talk to Lieutenant Colonel Sterner, the battalion CO. He called shortly, ordering me to move out, regardless of the odds. I argued, telling him that I would not feel right if I took my platoon into certain death. Finally, he said, 'I'm giving you a direct order, Si.' 'I know you are, Cledith, but I can't obey it. We have to have some support.' There was silence on the radio. Suddenly, Bourdeau appeared, 'Dammit, Si, move out! That's a direct order. You know what it means if you fail to follow orders in the face of enemy fire.' "

Seibert acknowledged his responsibility but refused to order his platoon to advance without support. Colonel Sterner arrived and inquired of Bourdeau why the delay. The company commander explained his subordinate's reluctance. Seibert pleaded his case. "Look at those positions, Colonel. They have us in a crossfire. We have already lost three men. It is suicide to move out there until we knock out some of those positions. We need artillery or tanks." And as the lieutenant pointed out the foe's emplacements, hostile rounds whizzed overhead.

Sterner responded, "I see what you mean, but we have to get this hill and move on. Move out!" Seibert yelled to his platoon sergeant to get the GIs going and personally started to lead the advance as some of his men started to follow. But no sooner did they poke their heads over the ridge than the enemy drove them to cover with a withering slash of bullets. Seibert told Sterner, "I can't take this platoon out there. You have to get us some support."

Grim-faced, Sterner, as Seibert remembers it, said, "You have violated a lawful order in the face of the enemy. You will have to face the consequences after this campaign is over."

"I realize that," answered Seibert. "Am I relieved of my platoon?

"No, you will continue to command. Now let's see what can be done."

As they discussed their limited options, a single tank suddenly clanked into view. Sterner and Bourdeau immediately informed the platoon leader that the tank now was attached to his platoon. Seibert explained his predicament to the tank commander, who maneuvered into a position where he could hit the enemy machine-gun positions while foot soldiers hugged his sides for protection and added their firepower.

"After he had destroyed several bunkers, he stopped. I got up on the tank deck, while drawing small-arms fire, to communicate with him. He opened a pistol port while the tank remained buttoned up. There were two more bunkers I wanted him to destroy. If they were neutralized, my platoon could take care of the foxholes and the rest of the resistance. As I was talking to him, the tank gunner spotted something and fired. My ear was about an inch from the barrel of the weapon. The concussion knocked me off the tank deck and it was five days before the ringing stopped in my ears and I could hear again. In fact, my hearing was permanently damaged, resulting in partial deafness.

"Otherwise, however, I was not hurt. The tank knocked out the two targets I had indicated. My platoon moved out, passed ahead of the tank, and swept over the area. A quick survey of the Jap defensive positions revealed it was a nest of tunnels and pillboxes completely covered by machine-gun fire on the reverse slope of the small ridge behind which we had taken cover. Had we charged over without the tank, we would have been taken in the back by those machine guns. I was glad I had stood fast to protect my platoon. They would have been wiped out if I had not refused to move out without support. But I also knew the seriousness of having disobeyed an order in combat. For the next month I lived with the dread of what would happen when the campaign ended." When the war did end, Seibert escaped with only a reprimand.

Although the enemy fought hard, the Americans squeezed the remaining defenders into ever smaller parcels of land and forced them out of their protected enclaves. George Brooks remembered a terrible scene as the last of the enemy yielded their places on the Yaeju-Dake escarpment. "There was no escape for them. We had blocked them off. The heavy-weapons company had set up their water-cooled machine guns and it seemed as if they would never stop shooting. Some of them were laughing and chortling all the while they were killing anything that moved within their field of fire. I was disgusted with their glee. It turned me off."

The 1st Division's 7th Marine Regiment was a pitiful semblance of its once-robust fighting force. Jim Moll in A Company recalls, "As we moved farther and farther south toward Kunishi Ridge, we were losing more and more men until finally we had to consolidate the rifle platoons from the entire company into a single platoon with Lt. Tom Cook as the leader and myself as platoon sergeant.

"It was about a month since I had the concussion and each day since, my physical condition was going downhill fast. I had just about run out of gas, losing my equilibrium and falling down a lot. Every bone in my body ached. I was becoming short of breath and had no more energy or endurance left. I told Cook that I thought I should turn myself in to sick bay for a few days. Maybe with some medication and a shot of something that would knock me out for a few days it would do the trick. Cook asked me to hang on a little longer and I agreed."

Don Farquhar, as a platoon leader during the march south beyond the Shuri line, says, "There were no major battles, only small firefights along the way. The rains were over and we moved fast. The most interesting thing was almost all our supply had to come by air. The landscape was dotted with parachutes of different colors. But at Kunishi Ridge, as we had found earlier on Okinawa, was one more ridgeline with no room to maneuver by means of an end run."

Although his 1st Battalion of the 7th Marine Division had absorbed 125 dead and wounded in a single day at Dakeshi Ridge, Charles Owens, the kid who joined the Marines at age fourteen, says, "The battle for Kunishi Ridge was the hardest fighting I saw. The regiment took heavy casualties because of fire coming from the front and flanks while trying to go over a long open area. Colonel Edward Snedeker, the regimental commander, knew he had to do something desperate and he did. On the night of June 12, he had two companies, C and F, jump off at night. This had never been done before. We thought someone had gone nuts.

"The two companies got on Kunishi Ridge okay," said Owens. "However, at daylight, the shit hit the fan. The remaining rifle companies tried to cross the open area three times to join those already on the ridge. Because of heavy losses we had to stop, although C and F needed water, ammo, and medical help."

The 1st Tank Battalion made arrangements to bring reinforcements, carry supplies, and remove wounded. Tank commander Bob Neiman explained, "The men up on Kunishi Ridge were surrounded by thousands of enemy soldiers and the Japs were mortaring, machine gunning, and grenading them. They had to have reinforcements. In the past, Marine tanks occasionally carried men into battle, but this was more significant in the outcome of the fighting than at any previous time.

"Each Sherman normally carries a crew of five, but needs only one man to drive it and a tank commander to guide it. If we removed the gunner, loader, and assistant loader, there was room for at least three men and if the ammo was removed that made room for a fourth man. On a short trip you could squeeze in a fifth Marine. Our tanks went to the designated infantry battalion where the Marine riflemen climbed in with the two-man crews and the reduced loads of ammo. The supplies for the infantry were strapped on the backs of the tanks. We began crossing the rice paddies and climbing up Kunishi Ridge, single file, like a line of ants.

"When the tanks reached the Marine positions on Kunishi, they opened the escape hatches and the riflemen crawled out through the bottom of the tank. Someone would scrape off all the ammo and other supplies from the top of the engine compartment. Marine wounded then got inside the tank or if too badly hurt they were strapped on the back along with the dead. The tanks then backed down through the valley until they could disgorge their cargo in safety. Another group of riflemen then boarded the tanks for the trip. This continued for two days."

Neiman's description fits that of the foot soldier passengers except in one respect. From their accounts, it appears that the tank commanders expected the riflemen to exit through the top of the tank. Jim Moll, the platoon sergeant in Company A of the 7th Regiment, says, "I think there were only four of us with the driver and commander. We went like hell through the shellfire and as we neared our destination we heard small arms fire hitting the tank. Finally, the tank stopped and the officer said that was where we got out.

"He opened the door on the turret and as I started to climb out, machine-gun bullets were hitting the door. One ricocheted off my helmet. I dropped down and asked if there were another exit. He told us about the trapdoor in the floor. Also, earlier, when I stuck my head out the turret opening, I noticed the tank was still out in the open and we'd have no kind of cover. I asked him to move in closer to the base of a vertical ridge. Reluctantly, he moved a little closer to it. One by one we stripped off our packs, canteens, etc., so we could squeeze out the trapdoor. Soon as our bodies were out of the tank, they pushed out our gear. Then we crawled out from under the tank and ran like hell to the base of this high, vertical ridge. As I was crawling out from under our tank, I saw another one nearby and the first Marine who got halfway out the turret was killed by machine-gun fire. After that, they also began to leave from the bottom."

Earl Rice received the privilege of one of these tank rides to the battlefield. "Lieutenant Cook, the other guys, and I had never been in a tank before. I could hear the bullets bouncing off the sides. I was standing beside the ladder when the tank commander ordered me to go up out the hatch. I realized the odds were against me getting out alive. Lieutenant Cook asked if there were a way out below and the tank commander said yes. Cook said that's the way we would go.

"After we left the tank, we tried to take the pinnacle of our hill. My good buddy and former squad leader, Pop Wilson, was hit in the throat by a dum dum bullet. Others were either hit or scattered back down the hill. The corpsman stayed with Pop until he passed away. I was upset, stood on the top of the hill and yelled, 'You yellow bastards! Get up here!' There was a surprised look on Lieutenant Cook's face and they all came back up. There was a Marine there, a replacement about my age who'd cracked up. Lieutenant Cook told me, 'You two take Pop back and stay there.' I protested that there wasn't anything wrong with me. I just got angry. He said, 'The less people we got up here, the more chance we'll be relieved.' We carried Wilson back and put him on a pile. The pile was over five feet, at least up to my shoulders if not higher. It was a helluva feeling to put that guy on there.

"Two Marines there told me to give them Wilson's wallet, watch, and ring. They'd see that these did not arrive before the family got the telegram about him. I found out what slimeballs they were when, a year later, someone wrote me that Wilson's family had taken out an ad in a Marine magazine asking if anyone might know where Wilson's belongings were. I did send them the rifle he took off a Jap whom he killed.

"There was a sergeant there when we brought in Wilson, a guy who looked like a poster for the Marines, but I never saw him in any bit of combat. He was giving out supplies. He says to me, 'Get back up there.' I says Lieutenant Cook told me to stay here. He says, 'You get back up there; that's an order.' He made me take the kid back with me. Cook was very angry when we came back, but he couldn't do anything about it at the time."

Charles Owens rode up onto Kunishi Ridge in the belly of a tank like the others. "The only way off was to be killed or wounded. Myself and a buddy, Jim Wolff, were put on a working party, to load the dead on trailers pulled by tanks. The bodies were wrapped in ponchos and the pile covered with a parachute. Before we finished, most of the working party had left. Wolff and I got all of the dead on the trailers. The smell was on us for a month. It was like being on an outpost. Our supplies were dropped by parachutes from planes. We could get hit in the head because the containers would come open and cases of ammo and food fall to the ground. We just knew we were going to die on this ridge. There was no sleep. The replacements who reached us were either old or very young and not very well trained. Before you got to know them, they were dead."

Jim Moll spent nearly a week on Kunishi Ridge. "We had very little protective coverage and many casualties from grenades dropped down on us. We finally found what we thought was a way to the top and I took a squad up one morning, climbed the cliff, which I never thought I'd make in my condition. Up there, we received lots of sniper fire and our squad leader, kneeling next to me, had his whole jaw shot off. I guess they were using dum dum bullets.

"I cannot remember how the hell we got back to our platoon that night, but I know that Earl Rice carried the squad leader back to where we had climbed up that cliff. A few days later, I woke up in the field hospital. Our company was taken off the lines. I missed about two days of the whole damn battle and it bothers me even today."

Earl Rice stuck it out. "I think I became a man on Kunishi Ridge because Lieutenant Cook treated me like one. He made me a squad leader with a corporal under me. I had been the biggest shitbird in the company and he talked of me being a sergeant. I felt like I was thirty-five. I learned what discipline and responsibility were all about. When they wanted to organize petitions to leave the hill and asked me to sign, I refused.

"Later, a fellow named Birch, thirty-eight, thirty-nine years old, a replacement who had something like nine kids, because of his family, was supposed to leave the ridge. But a damn knee mortar landed in his hole. We cried for his wife and kids. There's no way an old man should have died that way.

"At this point, with all the people killed and wounded, I am only two or three men away from being platoon leader. Lieutenant Farquhar took over the company. The corporal in my squad said for us to move to the rear. As I turned around, Lieutenant Farquhar put a Tommy gun in my face and said get back. That really upset me. I may have been a screwup but I was not a coward and I thought the order to move back was his order. Subsequently, Farquhar sent me out on a few skirmishes.

"Then, June 18 Lieutenant Farquhar told us we would be relieved the next morning. That night we were pretty high up on the pinnacle with Burns and me on the flank in a hole. Arky and a new guy were in the nearest hole. I knew that during the night, the Japs would make their move. I had sixteen hand grenades around my hole plus my weapon and Burns's. After an hour or so into my watch during the night, I called over to Arky and got no answer.

I called a second time. Still no answer; they were both napping. I rolled a hand grenade over, seven or eight feet from their hole and when it went off that woke them up. 'Man alive,' I yelled, 'Didn't you see them?'

"I didn't have to worry any more about them being awake during the night. Then the Japs started moving down on us. I threw about a dozen grenades all over the area. I heard some hollering and knew I hit somebody. The rest of the night there was very little sleep. The booming of the grenades kept everyone up.

"At the crack of dawn, I looked out the front for Japs, but didn't see anybody. All at once I hear someone coming over the top. It was a bunch of 2d Division Marines, in fresh uniforms. I started to prowl around, seeing what I got during the night—always the souvenir hunter. One of the 2d Marine Division guys, just coming in, got shot. I went back to my hole quick." The relieving troops belonged to the reinforced 8th Regimental Combat Team of the 2d Marine Division, in reserve from the time of a Love Day feint at the Minatoga beaches until finally capturing two small nearby islands against minimal opposition. Rice recalls his departure from Kunishi. "I wasn't moving too fast, but when I reached the place where that Marine had been hit, I did a 100-yard dash. We came off the Ridge of Death to hot food, showers—we hadn't showered from May 8 to June 18. I didn't realize until we were off the line for a few days that I had been hit, that I had shrapnel in my face. I knew I had a hole in my hand and in back; both had turned green. They put methiolate on my back, hand, and face. But the wounds stayed green."

On 18 June, as the defenders of Kunishi Ridge fell back in disarray, the Americans on the left flank of the 1st Marine leathernecks completed their mission. Bob Muehrcke and another platoon leader, Lt. Bill Frothinger, the two surviving officers of Company F, walked off the Yuza-Dake escarpment leading the handful of twenty-one GIs still on their feet. Says Muehrcke, "The men hadn't washed or shaved for the past thirty-nine days. They were exhausted, filthy dirty, their combat fatigues were coated with blood, either from their buddies or from their own bodies. All but one were wounded at least once. They were a pitiful sight, but they were alive and very proud men as they walked off the Okinawa escarpment to the reserve area. The sun was shining brightly, but they still received heavy enemy fire."

By the third week of June, the remaining defenders, their ammunition depleted, without food or water, had been squeezed into a tiny enclave. The imminent demise of the enemy resistance brought General Buckner to a forward observation post. A shell exploded nearby and drove a piece of coral into his chest, killing him. The authorities attributed the death to enemy fire, but some Americans thought it another case of friendly fire. One day after Buckner fell, Gen. Claudius Easley, the assistant commander of the 96th, known for his predilection to hang about the front lines, while pointing out the site of an enemy machine gun that had wounded his aide, took two bullets from that weapon in the forehead. Within twenty-four hours, and victory only a few days off, death in combat had claimed two general officers.

The two top Japanese generals, offered an opportunity to surrender, declined, and obedient to the Bushido code, chose the rite of *seppuku*, self-disembowelment. For several weeks, GIs flushed holdouts from caves, but, altogether, their dead numbered 110,071 with 7,401 captured. American dead soldiers, marines, and navy personnel added up to 12,520. Wounded totaled 36,631 and nonbattle casualties were more than 26,000. The Japanese lost 7,700 planes compared to 763 American aircraft downed or destroyed. But the kamikazes sank 36 ships and damaged another 368. Few campaigns could match the savagery and destruction of Okinawa.

18

Endgame in the Philippines

FOLLOWING THE FALL OF MANILA, THE GIS PURSUED THE slowly retreating enemy into a countryside hospitable to concealment, ambush, and nature-made redoubts. While the three Japanese armies of Luzon could no longer support one another or exchange men and equipment, they fought on, determined to exact as much of a blood penalty as they could before succumbing to the superior forces arrayed against them. The U.S. 6th and 43d Divisions and units from the 2d Cavalry Brigade drove the enemy soldiers concentrated to the east and northeast of Manila. Again, despite the guerrillas able to sift through the countryside, intelligence underestimated those still contesting the turf. As the commander of the 3d Battalion, Maj. Arndt Mueller of the 63d regiment, 6th Division, grappled with the enemy forces along the Shimbu line in the mountainous area east of Manila. On the maps, "Hill 400" and "Hill Z" denoted the critical territory assigned to his outfit. Mueller surveyed the terrain from an observation plane, compiled data on the phases of the moon and its hours of illumination, and plotted a night attack. "The battalion, contrary to most units in the Pacific War," said Mueller, "had experience in night operations on Luzon. The troops to carry out a night attack under the circumstances possessed confidence born of experience to accomplish the mission."

Mueller commandeered as much tracer ammunition as he could for aid in directing effective fire during the dark. "We also had a standing operating procedure that on a deep operation such as this, the riflemen of units in reserve carried mortar ammunition that they dropped by platoon or company piles when they went into action. You'd be surprised how much three hundred men can carry, especially if it might mean their lives! Another item covered individual equipment. No letters, diaries, or items showing unit identification. No mess kits, which were always a source of rattles. Canteens and canteen cups muffled. Any shiny helmets dulled—mud, usually. Faces blackened, provided we could find the material. In those days camouflage grease sticks were not an item of issue. Grenades carefully secured to prevent sounds and accidental detonation. We probably issued a day's ration with the precaution they might have to make it last for two days. Usually we included one emergency ration, a large, highly concentrated chocolate-type bar. Personal items were limited to a change of underwear and socks, a poncho, a towel usually draped around the neck, shaving equipment, soap, toothbrush, and dentifrice."

The troops moved out as daylight faded into a darkness pierced only by a bright moon. "The ghostly, silent movement of those soldiers sent chills up my back. How confident they were! How calm they appeared to be! But I knew every nerve fiber in their bodies was tingling, supercharged with anticipation, alert for enemy action. Before we departed, Dwight Dickson, the regimental operations staff officer, saw us off and gave me a chew of tobacco for luck. I did not smoke or use any form of tobacco at the time, but the shot of nicotine in my unadjusted system charged up my tired body, which had not had very much sleep in the preceding thirty-six hours."

A brief firefight broke out on one flank and the troops started to turn toward the direction of the shooting and away from the path to the objective. But because Mueller with the command group was right behind the infantrymen, he was able to redirect them to the proper direction. As the columns pushed ahead, leaving behind the cries of Japanese wounded—no Americans had been hit—the radio operator informed Mueller of a code transmission that called for him to plug into the telephone line. "Bad news! The column had been broken because one of the connecting files had fallen asleep during the engagement with the Japanese outpost. Some soldiers are very adaptable to the situation. Evidently the connecting file was one who could fall asleep easily." Mueller impatiently waited for the stragglers and then the advance continued.

"The moon still shone brightly. Nervously the formation slowly crept forward. But the discipline held. No soldiers saw ghosts; none fired at phantoms. When troops are advancing in darkness across unfamiliar terrain in the presence of suspected enemy forces, it is not uncommon for them to begin firing at imaginary figures; even veterans are sometimes subject to an attack of nerves. The unforeseen, however, suddenly halted progress. The brush at the foot of Hill 400 was a tangle of undergrowth, as much as ten feet high and full of long thorns. Passage required a time-consuming labor."

The deployment of Mueller's battalion at the moment placed I and K Companies in the vanguard with L bringing up the rear. Suddenly, a group of Japanese soldiers marched along a road from the north. Machine guns from I Company scattered them. Mueller had hardly digested the news when K Company saw more enemy swarming up the slope between them and Company L. Mueller could only speculate that these defenders came from well-concealed caves in the bush or a dry stream bed. Because of concern for the whereabouts of L Company, Mueller ordered K Company to keep its fire below the crest of the slope. As the GIs poured devastating fire on the climbing interlopers, Japanese soldiers gained the top and stood upright for a few moments. Suddenly, the hitherto invisible L Company soldiers opened up. "A storm of fire swept the Japanese from the crest. They had approached within hand-grenade range and suffered a barrage of fragmentation and white-phosphorus grenades for their pains. Several unfortunates came running off the hill in flames. The K Company troops cheered when they saw the results. The action had been short, furious, and now over, we had no casualties yet reported."

But the defenders now knew of the threat from Mueller's forces. "Our time to suffer had come. A thunderstorm of mortar fire pelted K Company. I sought refuge between two K Company soldiers snuggled up against the bank of the dry stream we occupied. After what seemed like an eternity, the firing ceased. I lay quietly for a few minutes to make sure that the firing definitely had ceased. One of the oldest mortarmen tricks was to suspend firing for a few minutes to deceive their targets into believing that the firing had terminated and then blast off again hoping to catch targets in a vulnerable posture.

"Convinced that the mortar fire had terminated, I gingerly got to my feet. Cries of 'Medic' and the groans of the wounded dominated the air. I paused, listening intently for any more sounds of mortar 'thumps' signaling the discharge of shells from their tubes. Then I spoke to my two K Company comrades, still embracing Mother Earth, advising them I thought the fire had ended. I got no response. I noticed that both were bloodied. I turned them over and checked their pulses; both dead. My God! Both dead, one on each side of me. I was shocked and unnerved."

From his command post, now shifted to another small hill, Mueller noticed that short rounds from his supporting mortar fire beat down the thorny underbrush that blocked his infantrymen. He arranged for a walking bombardment of the obstacle and a corridor up Hill 400 opened. Driven to cover by a barrage directed at the command post by the Japanese, Mueller never saw his men scale the heights of Hill 400 and establish a strong defensive position.

The enemy responded, infantrymen attacking, backed by intensive artillery and mortar fire. Mueller credits the U.S. 81mm mortarmen for preventing the enemy overrunning the GIs atop Hill 400. "Their actions were without a doubt one of the most heroic and dedicated unit actions I observed during the war. They suffered severely for their self-sacrificing devotion to duty. Among the casualties was their platoon leader, Lt. J. H. Childs. I saw him as he was carried to our location. Ugly steel shards of a 150-mm shell had penetrated his body. When the shelling ceased, the evacuation of wounded began after dark. I remember saying to my comrades there was no doubt in my mind that Childs's wounds were fatal. But he survived, although he spent the rest of his life in a wheelchair."

Mueller also observed the opposite end of the courage-cowardice spectrum. A captain in command of an independent but supporting 42mm mortar company pulled out with his men and weapons as soon as the enemy shelling allowed.

Outraged, Mueller described to his regimental commander what had happened and wanted to prefer charges against the offending officer. He learned that because the officer was not attached to Mueller's outfit, but officially only designated as support, he had the prerogative to locate where he saw fit.

A day later when the same captain reported in for another support mission, Mueller borrowed a carbine and led the captain forward to orient him about coming operations.

"Be sure your weapon is locked and loaded because there might be some Japs lurking around," Mueller advised the mortar commander, and then escorted him through the GI positions.

They headed out for some 500 yards and then reached a point where Mueller suggested they crawl under a hut on stilts to conceal themselves while they looked over the terrain around them. "I turned to him, 'Why did you run out on us during the shelling?' "

The officer answered, "I talked to the Lord and told him that I was going to pull out to save my troops from that awful shelling. I asked him to give me a sign if that was the wrong thing to do."

"What was his answer?" inquired Mueller.

"When I ask him to give me a sign he always answers very soon. I waited for some time and then asked him again for a sign if I was doing the wrong thing. But there was no sign, so I knew that it was the right thing to do."

"Well," said Mueller, "I also talked to the Lord. I said to him 'Lord, what shall I do to that officer who ran out on us when we needed him so urgently?' And the Lord answered, 'Take him out and show him the promised land.' I knew what the Lord meant. He meant for me to take you here and show you the land where we have never set foot. And that is the land between here and Hill Z over there, including the hill itself. Where do you think our front line is?'

" 'Aren't we on our front line?' he asked.

"Do you see any sign of our troops? We left our front line when we passed through those machine gunners back there. This here is Jap country. Do you know what we are going to do if the Japs attack us? We are going to fight to the death, you and I, if we have to. And you are not going to turn around and run. Do I make myself clear?'

" 'Yes sir,' stammered the captain, visibly disturbed."

Mueller completed his lesson with an explanation of what he expected the captain to do on his next mission, but on his return to the American lines Mueller related his conversation to the regimental commander. He told him he did not want "this nutty officer and his unreliable outfit in support." Mueller never heard of or saw the officer again.

According to Mueller, the crest of Hill 400 resembled a moonscape. "The entire top was dug up. Because the force had been reduced to about sixty fighters [the Japanese had all but abandoned efforts to reclaim the position] there were plenty of empty foxholes, all very deep because of deadly 150mm mortar fire and some direct-fire 77s from Hill Z. A very wide field of barbed wire and mines surrounded the entire position. 'We're wired in like a prison camp,' said one inhabitant. There were both light and water-cooled heavy machine guns, a couple of 60mm mortars. Ammunition of all types was stockpiled in great quantities in the extra foxholes.

"The stench of decaying flesh was unbearable, quite like that of hundreds of bodies on Lone Tree Hill, our first battle in New Guinea. There were innumerable bodies tangled in the barbed-wire barrier, the result of numerous attempts by the Japanese to retake the hill. There were probably more bodies at the bottom of the hill. Our enemy was not known to spend much time and effort to recover their dead. Eating a meal out of canned rations became a real problem because of the voracious appetite of the flies [attracted to the decomposing dead]. Because of these extremely harsh conditions, we frequently rotated troops on the hill. Morale remained surprisingly high. Soldiers seemed to regard it as a badge of honor to have served on 'Hell's Hill.' "

Grit and courage notwithstanding, Mueller also dealt with breakdowns from the stress of combat. Subsequent to the action on Hill 400, Mueller investigated a company bogged down in an attack on the town of San Isidro. At the battlefield he noticed a young enlisted man casually leaning against the bank of a ditch and then saw a lieutenant who led a platoon. "I knew him well because he was one of our old-timers who had trained with us in the States and served in all campaigns up to this point. The lieutenant did not seem to be aware of my presence. He was bent over praying a rosary. I watched him for a while because I did not want to disturb him during his prayers and maybe it would do some good. But there seemed to be no end to his prayers.

"I looked questioningly at the young soldier. He shrugged, threw up his hands and said, 'That's the way it always is. That's why we never get anything done!' " Mueller questioned the officer and, unhappy with his vague responses, sought out the company commander. "I instructed him to execute a left hook through the wooded area to strike San Isidro from the north. After adding some detail, I asked if he had any questions. The captain turned to the first sergeant, 'You heard the battalion commander; do you have any questions?' When the first sergeant replied in the negative, the captain said, 'See to it that the instructions are carried out.' This was most unusual; company commanders ordinarily issued orders personally to platoon leaders. I left the captain to track down the first sergeant and his party and asked, 'How long has this been going on?'

"Someone replied, 'For some time. The captain is not well.'

"I had noticed that the captain's hand was trembling and his arm twitching. He jammed his hand into his pocket and tried to keep his arm rigid. He was also one of our old-timers, in training, Stateside maneuvers, New Guinea, and the battles on Luzon. I dreaded the duty I had to perform—I hated it; but the battlefield is a harsh taskmaster, unrelenting, unforgiving. Infantry soldiers deserve the best leadership; their lives and bodies are daily on the line when they are in combat. What matters is what you do today—not what you did in the past.

"With deep regret, I had to order both those old-timers, the captain and the lieutenant, to battalion headquarters, leaving the company in charge of the senior officer present. Despite the personnel changes, the company drove the Japanese intruders out of San Isidro the same day."

The 169th Regiment of the 43d Division traveled to the Ipo Dam area, which featured limestone palisades several hundred feet high and was honeycombed with caves harboring Japanese soldiers. "More replacements came in at about 2100 hours," remembered John Higgins. "Each of the rifle companies sent a guide down to the CP area to pick up its replacements, with about twelve to fifteen for each company. The next morning we had to move out two or three of the replacements through medical channels since they were killed that night during a Jap attack. At a staff meeting I strongly recommended that any time replacements came up in the dark, they remain at the battalion CP site until daylight to enable them to at least see the sergeants and officers in their new unit. Also, they would get some idea of what was happening. The CO agreed and it became SOP."

Curtis Banker, the gun crew member of Cannon Company in the 103d Regiment of the 43d Division, rode out a number of engagements in his M7, self-propelled 105mm piece. "Some of the time we did direct fire into caves and at night there were fire missions for harassment or to help stop banzai attacks. The terrain to the north, around the summer capital [Baguio], was very mountainous and easily defended. The weather there was better than New Guinea and we could get some fresh food on Luzon. I had jungle rot, malaria, and yellow jaundice. The first thirty-eight days of combat on Luzon cost the 103d 172 killed in action, 1 missing, and 551 wounded.

"I had been wounded near San Fabian; two of my fingers were severed near the first joint and sewed back on. Combat fatigue was diagnosed by the doctor after I was recuperating from yellow jaundice. I was transferred from a Manila field hospital to a unit on Leyte by air. I requested to be returned to my unit, which was advancing on Ipo Dam. Instead, I was sent to a replacement company in Manila. I threatened to go AWOL and they allowed me to rejoin my company. I traveled by train and then many miles on foot. I was not that fatigued before I went to the hospital but I sure was afterward."

Arden Kurtz, a mortarman posted to a machine-gun crew after losses near the Clark Field shootouts, recalled his company was picked for reconnaissance [43d] as the division approached the Ipo Dam area. "We went across this flat area and about 500 yards ahead of us are some cliffs. They're looking right down our throats and, boy, they started to pour it on us. Boy, everybody tried to get their whole body into that helmet. I had some shrapnel bounce off my helmet.

They had the whole company pinned down. We couldn't move.

"They called in an air strike for us and there must have been thirty or forty planes. They'd come in real low, right over our heads. Boy, were they noisy. The planes hit them with rockets, napalm, bombs, machine guns, and really softened them up. Just before the planes left, we started moving up. When our regiment got through the cliffs to the other side, we stopped and dug in to consolidate our position."

Tom Howard's tank platoon from the 754th Tank Battalion, attached to the 103d Infantry Regiment, maneuvered to positions for firing at caves carved into the mountains. "The caves are all on the reverse side of the mountains," noted Howard. "You can move up, but when you pass, they open on you from your rear. The tank turrets must be traversed 180 degrees to face the rear. You have to be extremely careful when you fire back toward your own lines. Maybe there is method to their madness. Once you get in, you have to fight your way out."

Ordinarily, the tankers lived a bit more comfortably than the foot sloggers. The armor sometimes set up its perimeter at a barrio, enabling the crews to commandeer a few houses where they could maintain good observation and sleep indoors. Even when out in the field, the kitchens could advance and set up shop in the center of a circle of tanks. Occasionally, Howard and the others, granted passes, visited Manila.

"We learned to live off the land," said Howard. "We fixed fish by drying, we boiled then dried sugar cane syrup that we had squeezed and made sugar bar candy. We boiled and dried peanuts from wild plants. We gathered sweet potatoes—camotes—and fixed them by cooking into a paste, then drying it. Our mixtures could later be diluted in hot water and prepared like soup. By using bows and arrows, we killed wild chickens and cockatoo birds for meat." Obliging Filipinos even taught the Americans how to capture monkeys, turning them into useful pets. "We fed them the fruit from trees and berries from plants first. If they were poisonous the monkey would not eat them."

The Japanese slowly fell back into northern Luzon and the summer capital of Baguio in the mountains. Among those pressing the shrinking forces of Yamashita's Shobu Group were the 25th, 32d, 37th Divisions and the 1st Cavalry Division. Emil Matula, the first sergeant of D Company for the 25th Division's 35th Infantry Regiment, had remained in a field hospital for twenty days because of the sniper's bullet that penetrated his upper jawbone and sinus area. Discharged back to duty, Matula returned to his company and learned he had been awarded a field commission and transferred to Company G in the 2d Battalion as a platoon leader. The I Corps command expected the 25th in tandem with the 32d to carve a wide swatch up the middle of Luzon, exploiting the two-lane gravel road known as Route 5. Matula's 35th Regiment, blessed by exceptionally heavy air, artillery, and mortar support, and confronted at first by poorly organized Japanese defenders—a rarity—stepped out faster than its brothers, the 27th and 161st Regiments of the 25th Division. But by the end of March, all three encountered ever-stiffening resistance.

While fighting toward the final redoubts of the Yamashita Shobu Group, Matula directed his platoon as it captured one of the endless hills and killed twenty of the enemy. "We received orders from battalion to turn over the defense of the hill. During the night, the Japs ran the platoon of guerrillas off, capturing a machine gun from them and used it against the 2d Battalion CP. My platoon had to take the hill back.

We turned the defense over to the same guerrillas after killing another twenty Japs and recapturing our own equipment. That night the same thing happened again and I lost my platoon sergeant to a sniper. After that I refused to allow the guerrillas on the hill again."

Others held the irregulars in much higher regard. In the southern half of Luzon, the 11th Airborne counted on the guerrillas to supplement their limited numbers. The 11th's Joe Swing wrote, "The only thing that keeps my lines open and allows me to spread so thin is the fact that I have organized 5,000 guerrillas and have them attached to all the infantry, artillery, and engineer units. Even have a picked company at hdqrs. They call themselves G.S.O.G. (General Swing's Own Guerrillas). Let them wear the 11th AB shoulder patch over their left breasts. They are proud as punch and really fight. Put artillery forward observers with them, give them all the captured Jap machine guns and mortars and they keep on pushing and making the Japs like it."

On the Villa Verde Trail, Bob Teeples, a former Alamo Scout and an acting platoon leader while still first sergeant of Company L, 128th Regiment of the 32d Division, led a reconnaissance patrol. "I sent out the two scouts and I followed behind them. In turn, behind me came the BAR man, his assistant, the other members of the patrol, and a corporal known as Jim Snyder. As we moved out, the wetness of the red clay from the foxholes made our uniforms glisten against the green foliage, like walking bull's-eyes.

"We had barely started onto the plateau we were supposed to reconnoiter when we came to a mound of fresh-dug earth. It was still smoldering and I warned the scouts to keep a sharp lookout as the Japs had undoubtedly just buried one of the victims of our artillery barrage. As the BAR man's assistant climbed onto the plateau, a shot rang out and he fell back over the edge. Almost immediately another shot and the BAR man grabbed his throat and ran forward toward me. As he ran, he began to cry, fell down on his knees, onto his face, and lay still. By this time the two scouts and I were flat on the ground as a Japanese machine gun had opened up on us from the high ground to our left. I crawled to the BAR man and felt for his pulse, but he was gone. I thought back to a couple of nights before when he had proudly showed me a pictures of his wife and their one-year-old son. Now another machine gun started to fire on us from a position on our right flank and the twigs and branches were snapping all around us. The sound of the bullets over my head reminded me of a group of wires being rattled together. The Japs started to drop occasional mortar rounds. I realized we would have to withdraw.

"I motioned for my scouts to come back, and I tried to keep firing toward the Jap position to keep the scouts covered as they made their way back past me and over the edge of the plateau. A bullet ricocheted off the helmet of the first scout, but otherwise they made it back safely. I tried to drag the BAR man's body toward the edge of the plateau, but his ammunition harness kept catching in the brush. I managed to drag him back almost to the edge, when all of a sudden it felt like someone hit me in the head with a sledgehammer. The first thing I saw when I regained consciousness was a light flashing on and off. As my mind became more clear, I realized I was in a tent, apparently the rear aid station."

Jim DeLoach, a company commander for the 32d Division from the New Guinea days, believed the division and his regiment suffered from a number of poor commanders and he was less than enthusiastic about the policies of the general staff. In particular he disparages "the American system for leaving an outfit, particularly its troops in, until either the million-dollar wound, the ultimate, KIA, and the lucky, of which I am one." On the Villa Verde Trail, DeLoach noted, "While other divisions got to Manila and points of interest to the press, the 32d drew the losing hand, leading to nothing more than one hill after another. We were MacArthur's tactic of skipping around and leaving behind Jap forces to be cleaned up later. Worked splendidly when it came to islands, but in our case, simply set us up for small Jap groups to slip in and blow us up—charges of picric acid were their specialty.

"We were pulled out of the line for what was to be a rest and regrouping. We were at a small village and then were moved to take part in securing Balete Pass. The men expected a short rest and now faced with another assignment were, at best, pretty upset. We pulled through, but took some heavy casualties at the pass."

By the time the 32d Division finally cleared the Villa Verde Trail, over a nearly four-week period, it counted almost 3,000 combat killed and wounded with an additional 6,000 men withdrawn from the lines because of sickness or psychoneurotic problems. DeLoach himself would be fighting small pockets of the foe right up to the moment of V-J Day.

Aside from the forces directly under Yamashita on Luzon, almost all of the surviving 102,000 Japanese troops in the central and southern Philippines occupied four islands, Negros, Cebu, Panay, and Mindanao, with a small detachment on Palawan. The combat-effective men, exclusive of service, navy and air force personnel, numbered about 35,000 scattered over the four sites. Whatever the makeup, the defenders could expect no help from the beleaguered Yamashita or from home and faced declining amounts of ammunition, artillery, and eventually, food. The generals understood they could not expect to defeat the Americans. Their sole duty was to delay and inflict losses that might allow a peace with honor.

The campaign beyond Luzon opened at the end of February with the 186th Regimental Combat Team from the 41st Division clearing out an area on Palawan. Lying between the South China Sea and the Sulu Sea, Palawan seemed ideal for airbases that could support assaults both on the southernmost Philippines and the former Dutch East Indies. Unfortunately, the soil composition and compaction defied the best efforts of engineers and delayed immediate exploitation of Palawan.

Mindanao, the second biggest and most southern of the Philippines, drew the next card from MacArthur's strategic deck. Under Col. Wendell Fertig, the Mindanao guerrillas operated with increasing boldness. They even controlled an airstrip at Dipolog for supply operations on the north coast of the Zamboanga Peninsula, a 145-mile-long neck of land on the western end of Mindanao. Two days before an amphibious assault, Marine fighter-bombers, protected by guerrillas and troops from the 24th Division, began operations at the Dipolog site.

Fertig assured General Eichelberger and the Eighth Army that landings near Zamboanga City would be unopposed. Underwater demolition teams and guerrillas sanitized the beaches of mines without interference, but taking no chances, a preinvasion bombardment pounded sparse enemy artillery positions. When the troops of the 41st Division stepped onto the Zamboanga shores some met little or no fire while others quickly took casualties.

To conquer the eastern part of Mindanao, occupied by a mélange of 55,000 soldiers and armed civilians loyal to the Imperial Empire, the 24th and the 31st Divisions in the third week of April landed 100 miles from the main objective, Davao, a port across the waist of the island. The Japanese apparently expected the approach to be from the Davao side and the bulk of their defenses were oriented in that direction. The Americans, aided by guerrilla intelligence and operations that ensured an absence of hostile forces, moved rapidly in the first weeks.

Han Rants, the 34th Infantry wire-section chief whose terrifying experiences during the battle for Zig Zag Pass he says converted him into a devout Christian, left Mindoro after a period of R&R for Mindanao. "We had been warned there were Moslem tribes—Moros—there and there were Huks who actually held communist-type beliefs and they hated any outsider, not just the Japanese. Fortunately for us, we found that they hated the Japanese much more."

The march to Davao took Rants and his buddies through the interior, largely uncharted section of the island. "As we crossed the center of the island and got on the Davao side, still some fifty miles away from the city, resistance got heavier and heavier. Where they had blown bridges, they would set up machine guns across streams or rivers so that as we crossed they could pick us off in the water. As we came to these streams it took a long time to send out scouts and patrols, get the area cleared, so we could ford the stream and keep on going."

Even though it must have been obvious that Imperial Japan had been defeated, a few local people still cast their lot against the Americans. Rants recounted that some Filipino traders approached the battalion and said they could lead the GIs to an enemy encampment. "My good buddy from L Company, David Flaherty, had been wounded in each campaign we had and he was one of the best line sergeants in the battalion. Flaherty was picked to lead some fifty-four men who went with these Filipinos because we felt we could trust them. But when Flaherty came out, he was one of only five left alive. Those Filipinos had led them to an area the Japanese had laced with crossfire from higher positions. Flaherty was awarded the Distinguished Service Cross because of extremely heroic action he took trying to save the group. He became a nervous wreck for life. He was in college with me some years after the war and he just couldn't stay in class. He dropped out and I lost track of him." The strategy and tactics of the Japanese failed to halt the advances but succeeded in drawing considerable blood. A number of men who had been with Rants from the beginning went down with serious wounds as his battalion struggled toward Davao.

Battalion surgeon Phil Hostetter accompanied the 19th Regiment of the 24th Division to Mindanao, and his duties covered the spectrum of medical therapy from continuing to teach first aid, sanitation, psychology, and, of course, treatment of horribly wounded men. "We received fifteen recruits fresh from the States in the medical detachment. I decided to have a class in giving blood plasma. None of the men had ever done it." Hostetter divided them into pairs, but while he would not require them to use a needle on each other, he suggested they learn by doing. "I heard, 'By God, no one is going to stick me.' I said, 'This is the way to do it, as I put a rubber band around the arm of one fellow. I inserted a hypodermic needle and drew back a little blood. Now you do it to me.' The venipuncture had not phased him, but I thought he might go into shock with that order. He may have imagined what would happen if I lost an arm or even if he messed it up. I did not expect him to be good the first time, but he did a fine job. Everyone in the group then performed the exercise with success and felt confident."

Back on the trails with the troops, Hostetter became briefly pinned down in an exchange of gunfire. When it subsided, one soldier could only drag himself on his elbows. "My legs won't work," he cried out to Hostetter, whom the soldiers recognized although he wore no insignia. The doctor recalls telling the man, "I am going to fix your legs and you will be all right." Hostetter flexed one thigh against the GI's body and then the other. Then he declared, "Now you can walk." The soldier stood up and walked back, his hysterical paralysis cured.

An epidemic of diarrhea, "the worst I had encountered," according to Hostetter, devastated the battalion. In spite of his efforts to treat the troops with sulfaguanidine tablets, they continued to weaken. "At the same time the battalion commander told me he had located some enemies, but was not able to clear them out because he didn't have enough men. Everyone knew the only honorable way a soldier could be relieved of duty was through the medical department, me in this area. I knew almost every man was affected by the epidemic, yet we were required to keep fighting. Men kept coming to me in their weakened condition believing they could never make another patrol, and I had to send them out anyway. I decided a man whose temperature was less than 101 degrees would stay on duty.

"I sent the regimental surgeon a message saying the battalion was in very bad health because of gastroenteritis, and could not carry out its mission for long. He spoke to the regimental commander and the battalion was immediately replaced by another. With no excessive demands on their strength, the men recovered within a few days."

Men rarely died of the GIs, as the disease was known, but around Hostetter, even at this late date in the war, the maiming and killing continued unabated. " 'Medic!' someone shouted. I ran over to where a soldier writhed on the ground. His abdominal wall was blown away, exposing the loops of intestines. He must have been hit by a grenade or land mine." As Hostetter approached him, the injured man, "functionally decerebrated or unable to think" from extreme shock, tore at his own insides. "We put him on a litter. Someone restrained his hands while I wrapped a large towel from our medical supplies around the abdomen. I cut perforations in the ends of the towel with the pocket knife I always carried, and laced it tightly together with a roll of bandages. This served to hold in the intestines, prevent further loss of fluid, and restore blood pressure. We gave him a Syrette of morphine, started blood plasma, and moved him toward the nearest hospital. He may have lived. I never knew because I hardly ever heard what happened to such patients." At other times, Hostetter saw his patients die before they could be evacuated, or in other instances, the explosions and gunfire snuffed out their lives before he could even start treatment. And his medical unit was not immune from injury as several close associates, seeking to succor the wounded, lost their own lives.

On 1 July, Eichelberger declared the eastern Mindanao operation ended. Nevertheless, armed Japanese continued to sporadically combat elements from the 24th, 31st, 40th, and 41st Divisions, supported by the guerrillas. Rather than leave their garrisons to wither in isolation, MacArthur similarly directed operations against smaller islands like Panay, Cebu, and Negros. Each one of these wiped out the occupying Japanese forces, but liberation exacted tolls in lives and bodies.

In northern Luzon, Yamashita still counted 50,000 troops at his disposal. But they occupied an ever-shrinking area of mountainous jungle, and malnutrition stalked them as fiercely as it had the defenders three years before on Bataan. Combat on land petered out. It had become a war of attrition with the last chapter the scheduled invasion of Japan itself. There were no large battles like those that occurred during the early days of the Luzon invasion and within Manila. Instead, small groups of men participated in deadly exchanges, with the defenders being forced ever deeper into the mountains, bereft of overall command and control, increasingly short of ammunition and food. After victory in Europe, the American forces could expect an influx of reinforcements. By June 1945, thousands of soldiers had begun redeployment from Germany to duty in the Pacific.

19

The Bomb and the End

FREDERICK L. ASHWORTH, WHO ATTENDED DARTMOUTH FOR A year before entering the U.S. Naval Academy in 1929, inspired by both Lindbergh and an elder brother, opted for flight training. As a prewar dive-bomber pilot he was advised to attend an advanced school if he hoped to make the service a career. On a whim, he chose aviation ordnance, a decision that profoundly put him on stage for the debut of the most dramatic weapon of the twentieth century.

Ashworth assumed command of Torpedo Squadron 11 after Pearl Harbor and became part of the Cactus Air Force on Guadalcanal during the height of activity around the Slot. He flew many missions, scored some hits on ships, and after a tour as an air officer on the staff of Adm. Richmond Kelly Turner, was assigned to the Naval Proving Grounds in Dahlgren, Virginia. That last post, plus his education in ordnance engineering and experience with various bombing operations, recommended him for the Manhattan Project—development of the atomic bomb under Army auspices. He took up residence at Los Alamos, New Mexico, on Thanksgiving Day 1944.

While Ashworth did not receive a crash course in nuclear physics, he had a desk in the office of Capt. William Parsons, a 1922 Annapolis graduate and chosen by the Manhattan boss, Gen. Leslie Groves, to direct the project's ordnance division. "I was able to listen in on many important technical discussions between the captain and his associates in the laboratory. I was permitted to attend the so-called colloquia that were held each week to discuss the week's technical problems and develop fixes for them. I wasn't able to absorb much of what went on, but it was fascinating to watch Oppenheimer [J. Robert, chief of the civilian scientists involved] lead these meetings. When a problem was raised and seemed to get bogged down trying to find a solution, Oppenheimer would get out of his chair, go to the blackboard. He would ask if this had been tried, and he would proceed to formulate a procedure with sketches and equations that he thought would do the trick. More often than not, the reaction would be, no, I haven't thought of that. Oppenheimer was definitely the technical leader of the laboratory. These colloquia would always be attended by the top scientific people in the lab. I recall seeing Niels Bohr, Wigner, Weisskop, Hans Bethe, Rabi—if my memory serves me, there were six Nobel laureates at the laboratory during the bomb research and development."

Ashworth brought to the table the practical experience of someone who had actually dropped bombs. He explained, "I am sure that he [General Groves] was looking ahead to the day when the bombs would be put in operation against the enemy, whether Germany or Japan. Germany was certainly contemplated as a target, but she was defeated before the bomb would be ready. Groves was certain that he would require a member of the crew on the bomb-carrying aircraft who had at least a general background on the bomb's technical characteristics, so that proper decisions could be made should they be required. Groves always wanted spares for everything. I would be Parson's spare.

"The aircraft crews that would man these aircraft in the combat operations simply did not have and never were exposed to the technical aspects that would be required for the job as he, General Groves, saw it. Up until the night of the preflight briefing for the Hiroshima operation, no one in the 509th Bomb Group had any knowledge of the ultimate mission of the group, except Paul Tibbets, a thirty-year-old Army Air Corps colonel in command of the bomb group, and he had very little if any technical knowledge of the bomb design and how it worked." (Tibbets flew the first mission of B-17s against Rouen by the Eighth Air Force in August 1942.)

The first workable design for a nuclear bomb used uranium in the form of U-235, produced from its sire, U-238. It was the fissionable material for "Little Boy," which would be exploded over Hiroshima. For the second device, "Fat Man," the scientists intended to employ plutonium. Ashworth recalled that the successful explosive system for the plutonium bomb depended upon a spherical shape, hence the nickname "Fat Man," but notoriously a poor ballistic shape. The question was how to wrap this package into an efficient ballistic form. "Some of the ancillary equipment that went into making this into a bomb—fuses, batteries, capacitors to provide the voltage to the detonators and the like—it was decided was to be mounted on opposite sides of the sphere. The elongated shape suggests that a spheroid shape was the best that could be done. Clearly some sort of a stabilizing tail structure would be required. Fins seemed to be a logical place to start. Wind-tunnel tests showed that the arrangement might work, but experimental drops from a B-29 were all unstable. Next, a large box tail was attached to the after end of the spheroid and test drops made to determine if this would improve the ballistics. Some improvement, but still not acceptable [for] uniform flight. I believe it was Parsons who suggested baffles placed in the box to create the effect of a parachute, which was adopted as the final form of the tail."

Although the role of Navy experts in the Manhattan Project is rarely mentioned, Ashworth credited his immediate boss, Captain Parsons, with having contributed considerably to the technique of implosion worked out with John von Neumann. "I have always believed firmly that without Parsons's drive and capability the bombs would never have been out of the laboratory in the timely fashion that they were." While Ashworth could add little expertise to the actual building of the bomb, he supervised much of the in-flight testing of components carried out at Wendover Field in Utah. He also was charged with recruiting military personnel whose knowledge could contribute to the work.

After Groves gained the highest priority in the military for procurement of people and supplies, Hap Arnold, chief of staff of the Army Air Corps, created the code name "Silverplate" and directed that any time a responsible official used the code word, that person's needs would have the top priority over any programs. According to Ashworth, the Air Corps accepted the dictum, but the remainder of the Army treated it with less respect. "Some of the men were the most experienced and senior enlisted ratings in the Army. Needless to say, pulling them out of the Army for this assignment became subject to a high degree of inertia. I would go to Washington to extract these people from the Army. The magic code word 'Silverplate' would help but there was a lot of foot dragging by the Army Ordnance Corps, mostly when it came to the assignment of the highly qualified men we needed. It was fun for me, a Navy commander, to roam the halls of the Pentagon and try to force compliance of the orders they knew they would have to obey.

"In February 1945," said Ashworth, "I was designated to carry a top-secret letter to Guam and hand it personally to Admiral Nimitz. This letter would inform him for the first time that there was under development an atomic bomb, which would be available to him in the Pacific about the first of August 1945. This letter, although I am sure it was written by General Groves, was addressed, 'Dear Nimitz' and signed 'King' [Admiral Ernest J.]. It informed Nimitz that the explosive yield of the bomb would be about 8,000 tons of TNT equivalent, and that support of his command would be required. He was authorized to inform only one officer on his staff. If he had any questions, the bearer of the letter would be able to answer them. It directed Admiral Nimitz to give me what support I might need in selecting a site for the operation.

"I traveled from Washington direct to Guam wearing the ordinary cotton khaki uniform of that period. I carried the letter in a money belt around my waist next to my skin. When I arrived on Guam I went directly to the headquarters of Admiral Nimitz and told his aide I had an important letter to deliver to the admiral. He said okay, he would carry it in. I said that wasn't okay. I was required to hand the letter directly to the admiral. With some reluctance he went into the office to find out if the admiral would see me, coming out in a moment with word I could go in. The aide followed me. I told Admiral Nimitz that I had been ordered to hand the letter direct to him and that no one else could be present.

Admiral Nimitz told the aide to leave and I proceeded to break out the letter.

"I opened my uniform jacket, unbuttoned my shirt enough to extract the money belt, all to the amusement of the admiral. After the long trip, the money belt was a bit the worse for wear and its contents a little stained and damp from sweat. However, it was in good enough shape for the admiral to open and read it. When he had finished, he rang for the chief of staff, Adm. [Charles] 'Soc' MacMorris, and handed him the letter to read. Then he told me to tell Admiral King he could not provide the services he knew would be required by this project without his operations officer, Capt. Tom Hill, being aware of the program as well. He pointed out to me that it was now only February and didn't they know back there that he had a lot of war to fight before August. Why couldn't he have the bomb now? I described briefly the status of the development of the weapons and told him August first was selected by General Groves as the first realistic date the bomb would be ready for delivery in his theater of operations. He turned in his chair and looked out the window for several seconds, turned, and said, 'Thank you, Commander. I guess that I was born just about twenty years too soon.' I felt he had sensed the magnitude of the thing. Perhaps he also saw that the bomb might have a possibility to end the war."

Ashworth had the responsibility to explore the area for the space to be used by the 509th Bomb Group and the Los Alamos scientists and engineers accompanying the atomic bomb when it went to war. "The selection of the island was easy," said Ashworth. "Guam was too far south, Saipan was farthest north [closest to Japan], but did not have the air operations facilities that were available on Tinian." The Air Corps commander on Tinian, Brigadier General Frederick

Kimble, apprised that the project held Silverplate status, suggested the site used for B-29 operations.

Those involved at Tinian attempted to maintain strict security. When the chief engineer, Elmer E. Kirkpatrick, an Army colonel who directed a Navy SeaBee battalion to construct facilities for the A-Bomb project, began to run short of concrete he informed Nimitz's operations officer Tom Hill. Immediately, Hill sent a message to an organization that possessed the materials, saying, "You will deliver to Colonel Kirkpatrick [———bags of cement]. This is a project of which you have not been informed and will not be informed."

To accommodate the nuclear devices, the engineers modified the B-29 bomb bays. Ashworth recalled that when Sheldon Dike, a young aeronautical engineer, described to Boeing experts the dimensions of Little Boy as being about eight feet in length with a twenty-two-inch diameter, and its weight of 10,000 pounds, they looked at him as if he were deranged, saying it was impossible to pack that much weight in such a small package. They were unaware that the uranium, which was heavier than lead, packed around the explosive material, plus the special armor steel and the other components, could add up to five tons. Standard ordnance ordinarily ranged up to 2,000 pounds maximum for a single item. However, the Air Force had experimented with larger packages.

The 509th Bomb Group under Paul Tibbets practiced for the mission both at Wendover Field and Batista Field in Cuba. George "Bob" Caron, a Brooklyn, New York, native who had attended a technical high school and then worked as a draftsman and mechanical designer, had enlisted in the Air Corps in the autumn of 1942. Eventually he was assigned to power turret school and then became an instructor on the systems. Caron met Paul Tibbets while engaged in test work with the first B-29s. When Tibbets assumed command of the 509th Bomb Group he asked Caron to join him. Caron applied for a transfer, but his commander refused to release him.

"In a telegram," said Caron, "I told Tibbets, 'I tried to get out of instructing, but I was told I was frozen.' He sent me another telegram back, saying, 'Just sit tight, we'll take care of the being frozen business. I'll have orders through for you as soon as I can.' " Apparently Silverplate again demonstrated its power, for Caron soon reported to Tibbets at Wendover.

Caron recalled that Tibbets informed him, "We are on a highly secret deal, Bob, and I can't tell you a thing about it. You only need to know what you are supposed to know. We are selecting the people we think can keep their mouths shut, and security is going to be very high. I can't tell you what it's going to be, but we are going overseas and we are going to end this war. That's all I can tell you."

According to Caron, "We knew some of the men [in the 509th] weren't military people even though they were wearing khaki clothes. We knew it was highly secretive, nobody seemed to know anything, or at least they wouldn't say much. I understand the reason for a lot of the fellows just simply disappearing, stealing away in the night, was [that] they talked a little too much. They were shipped out and we didn't see any more of them. I understand a couple of 'em had gone on a pass to Salt Lake City and got a little too talkative over a few beers. They were gone; they just packed their bedrolls, bedouin tents, and slipped away in the night.

"You didn't know whether the guy sitting next to you was an FBI man or somebody checking on security. My mother told me that within a few weeks' time there were two groups of well-dressed young men who came to the house. One of them was from Brooklyn Technical Alumni Association, wanting to know how I was doing. They were coming out with a manual, and so forth. And she says, 'The Brooklyn Technical Alumni Association? Isn't that just a high school?' [There were] two well-dressed young men coming out for this interview, but she didn't say anything. Another one who came out was supposed to be an insurance investigator asking all kinds of questions. She said she was wondering what the hell was happening.

"We formed our crews and Captain [Robert] Lewis was airplane commander for ours. It was my understanding that this was Colonel Tibbets's crew, but as group commander he wasn't supposed to have a crew. Captain Lewis would be the copilot for Colonel Tibbets, who would be airplane commander for this special deal. At Wendover we did a lot of high flying, dropping a single bomb. There was a lot of flying, but there wasn't really much for me to do." Caron worked in the B-29 tail, originally equipped with a pair of .50 calibers and a 20mm cannon. The arrangement was clumsy and ineffective. The cannon disappeared.

Caron reached Tinian at the end of June 1945. "After attending some classes [in combat gunnery] we started flying a few missions with just some regular bombs. They sent us out for practice missions against Marcus Island with no opposition and some went to Truk where they had flak. Then we flew our first mission in mid-July against the empire, Kobe with one big bomb. The casing was just like Fat Man, the Nagasaki plutonium bomb. It was a great big round 10,000-pound bomb, strictly a TNT general-purpose bomb. We didn't fly out as a squadron. We went at different times, just one ship to a target. This seemed a little strange to us. One bomb and one plane to a target. On our first mission over Kobe we went back near Osaka on the way out and got a good bit of flak. I never saw a fighter over Japan, but the mission took flak."

On 16 July in the Trinity test at Alamogordo, signals relayed from a control bunker detonated the first nuclear bomb. The senior scientists conducted a betting pool on the explosive yield. The guesses ranged from Edward Teller's extravagant 45,000 tons of TNT down to Oppenheimer's modest 300 tons. Hans Bethe estimated 8,000, closest to the actual figure of roughly 12,500. Convinced the system worked, Groves and company immediately set in motion the events designed to deliver the bombs to the Japanese cities. The target material, a chunk of U-235—the active ingredient for Little Boy—traveled aboard the cruiser USS *Indianapolis*.

Ashworth himself went to a small port at the south end of Tinian to pick up the U-235 from the *Indianapolis* offshore. He commandeered an LCM landing craft for the task and the package was lowered from the cruiser to his boat. "Things progressed satisfactorily until the last moment when either the crew lost control or the LCM was lifted by a wave. The container hit the bottom of the boat with an uncomfortable crash. This was a heavy container and possibly could have gone right through the bottom of the boat. However, it and the boat appeared to have survived." The LCM tied up at a dock and a truck bore the U-235 to the airfield. A few days later, a Japanese sub torpedoed the *Indianapolis* and because, somehow, the Navy did not realize the vessel was missing, only 316 of the more than 850 who abandoned the vessel were rescued.

According to Ashworth, a major fear concerned an aborted takeoff that might result in a runway fire. "Should this occur it was recognized that the powder charge in the

Little Boy bomb could 'cook off' from the heat before the firefighters could put out the fire, resulting in a low-order detonation of the bomb and partial fissioning of the uranium. This kind of accident could contaminate and place out of action the entire north end of the island. There was devised at the naval gun factory in Washington a combination breech block that permitted part of it, just large enough to pass the powder charge into the gun, to be removed after takeoff and the powder charge inserted at that time. The original design of the breech block was too large and heavy to be handled by one man in the bomb bay after takeoff.

"The new design arrived on the island not more than a day or two prior to the upcoming operation [Hiroshima] and Captain Parsons spent many hours in the bomb bay, both in flight and on the ground, familiarizing himself with the task to be done and preparing a final check-off list to be used when the time came, an operation commonly referred to as 'arming the bomb.'

"There had to be the same worry in the case of the B-29 carrying the Fat Man bomb to Nagasaki. However, because of the design of the bomb, there was no way to remove any part of the explosive sphere. Fire in the aircraft could be disastrous as a result of the low-order detonation and partial fissioning that would undoubtedly occur. That danger was accepted and all the rescue and fire-fighting equipment on the island was arrayed along the runway to forestall an explosion in case of fire. In spite of continuing reference to 'arming' the Fat Man, there was no way to do it as was done with Little Boy."

Preparations for the first mission by the nuclear bombers were essentially completed by 1 August, but a small typhoon in the vicinity of Japan shut down operations for several days. The raid was then scheduled for 6 August. "The departure of the *Enola Gay* [named for Paul Tibbets's mother] was a relatively gala affair. There were lights and cameras, sort of a Hollywood preview, with many of the senior officers in the area present. The bomb had been loaded into the aircraft earlier in the afternoon. Captain Parsons had completed his familiarization with the new breech block by which he would 'arm the bomb.' " At 2:45 A.M., Paul Tibbets lifted the nose of the *Enola Gay* and headed north. As Ashworth reported, Parsons, along with Lt. Morris Jeppson, the "weaponeers," the title given to the specialists, armed Little Boy once the *Enola Gay* climbed to 5,000 feet.

Caron recalled, "We knew the big one was coming up but what the big one was we didn't know for sure. We had been thinking in terms of some super TNT explosive. We had heard word of a new British explosive. We were called up outside the old man's office to get our picture taken. We had been playing softball and were kind of raggedy. I had on my Brooklyn Dodgers baseball cap, which was my rabbit's foot. About two nights before [the Hiroshima raid] we had a briefing, all ships involved in this mission, weather ships, and companion ships. There were a lot of scientists with us, civilian personnel, working in some area I never got into. I knew it existed, but it was none of my business. At this briefing we were told we were going to see some pictures. They had some movie film of a test that was just completed, but the projector broke down so they showed some slides. We saw pictures of the test explosion at the Trinity site in Alamogordo. It was just still pictures on slides, but it was just breath-taking. The only way you could think of it was, 'What the hell is this!' Tibbets gave a little talk and told us that's what we'd be taking. As soon as the weather cleared we'd be going.

"Of course we went out that afternoon to look at the bomb

after they had loaded it. It looked screwy to me, with all those antennae hanging out. It wasn't like the big pumpkin shape. It was more cylindrical. This was Little Boy, the first one, the uranium bomb. We found out later that the one that was tested was the plutonium one [Fat Man] at Trinity.

"I had my nice Certo Dollina 35mm camera all loaded. They hustled us to chow and then to the airplane. I left my personal camera loaded with color film lying on my bunk. All during the Hiroshima mission, I worried about it being swiped. As it was, the photo officer, Captain Ossip, gave me a K20 which is like a big Speed Graphic. He gave it to me and I said I didn't want to take it. It was too crowded in that tail. He said, 'Take pictures. Take anything you can. It's all set. Don't touch the lens. Don't touch any speeds. We want you just to take pictures.' I said, 'I don't know if I can even get it in there.' He answered, 'Do the best you can.'

"When we got out to the airplane, it was like a Hollywood movie set. We got out there probably about one o'clock in the morning. It was dark. Floodlights were all over the place, people by the hundreds. I always used to take off in the tail for the weight and balance and also because we had seen some crashes, a couple of ditchings off the island. The reports said the tail gunner always got out. B-29s characteristically broke by the aft-pressure bulkhead, the tail would always end up sticking out of the water last and there's never been a tail gunner lost in ditching. I always took off and landed in the tail.

"This takeoff seemed exceptionally long. I knew every inch of that runway; I had taken off so many times. I thought he was just holding the plane down, because we just came off the end of a cliff and there was the drink down below us. I was a little apprehensive about that extra-long takeoff, using every inch of the runway. Old Tibbets was a wonderful airplane driver! I think I'd fly on a carpet with him. We took off and stayed fairly low until we got to Iwo Jima." When the airplane reached Iwo Jima, a pair of B-29s rendezvoused with Tibbets. One of these ships carried instruments suspended by parachutes that would be released at the moment the *Enola Gay* emptied its bomb bay. These devices would supply information to blast gauges in the B-29. The second Iwo Jima plane held observers, including the *New York Times* correspondent William L. Lawrence, press correspondent for the Manhattan Project. To give the mission a sense of the Allied effort, an RAF pilot flew this plane. Beyond Iwo, the three bombers would start to climb.

Caron recalled, "After takeoff, I'd come out of the tail and I'd sit in the waist until time to pressurize and then I'd go back in the tail because once we were pressurized, you were there, period. A mission would run anywhere from twelve to fifteen hours and I'd be 75 to 80 percent of the time locked in the tail. I'd come back to the waist to stretch my legs. I was sitting in the waist with Bob Shumard, the assistant flight engineer and a qualified engine mechanic, and Joe Stoborik, the radar man. Tibbets came back through the tunnel and stopped to talk with us. Since the two others were relatively new to the crew he sort of addressed himself to me, because he knew me longer. 'Bob, have you figured out what we're doing today?'—his exact words. I said, 'Hell, no, Colonel, with all the security and secrecy we've been living under with this thing, I don't want to get stuck up against a stone wall and shot.'

"He said, 'How're you going to get stuck up against a stone wall and shot? We're on our way. It's too late to do that.' I got to thinking about the speculation amongst ourselves about this new British explosive and said, 'Colonel, is this a chemist's nightmare?' He shook his head a little bit and said, 'Not exactly a chemist's nightmare.' Then all of a sudden a little light lit up and I remembered an incident in the Wendover library about the Columbia University cyclotron. I said, 'Colonel, is this a physicist's nightmare?'

"He gave me a funny look and nodded his head. 'You might call it that.' After a little bit more chatting he said 'I'm going back forward. We're going to be climbing soon.' Just as his leg was sticking out of the tunnel, I reached up and yanked on one foot. He came scampering back down, thinking something was wrong. He asked, 'What's the matter?'

"I said, 'Colonel, are we splitting atoms today?' and he gave me the darndest look and said, 'Yep!' He went forward. He was going to announce it anyway on the intercom. By then I was in the tail and he announced what we were doing. He said, 'We're going to be on a wire recorder. Watch your language. We're going to make this for history, this recording, so watch your language, no cussing, and everybody talk clearly.'

"We had climbed, were pressurized, and came on over Shikoku. We had the word that the primary [target] was clear enough. Hiroshima was clear and that's where we were going. I don't remember exactly when we went on this wire recorder. I was mainly a listener back there, sort of a back-seat driver. I always kept watching. You never could tell, although we never had any opposition as far as fighters.

"I don't remember any extreme apprehension, just the normal. I don't remember [worrying] whether it would work or not, or whether we'd even get away from it. We were told you just don't know. We came over the IP [Initial Point] and we went on the bomb run. Tibbets told us to put our goggles on. We had been given these dense goggles, like welders use, with side pieces completely covering the eyes. I remember looking up at the sun with these goggles on to see how bright it was. At 32,000 to 33,000 feet the sun is pretty bright, but it looked like a dim purple blob through these goggles.

"On the bomb run, we had the two wing ships, one for instrumentation. When the Japanese saw a parachute, they said [the bomb] was dropped by parachute, but that was a canister of instruments dropped by Major [Charles] Sweeney and they were off behind us, maybe five miles behind in a sort of V-formation. We were told there was going to be a fifteen-second tone and at bombs away, the tone would stop. That's when everybody went into this diving turn that we had been practicing. The tone went off, and at bombs away the ship lifted up a little bit and he threw her into the damndest diving turn. I had my seat belt on; I was told to put it on. It was a 160-degree diving turn. I think he redlined the son of a gun. We had practiced and it was mainly a turn to get the biggest slant distance away from the damn thing when it went off. He had just straightened out, I think, when it went off. There was this tremendous flash of light through these goggles and so much brighter than the sun; there was no comparison. I thought, 'Oh, boy!' I understand Tibbets had thrown his goggles off because he couldn't watch his instruments in this turn. But I kept mine on, because I was facing it. Then we took the goggles off and he asked me on the intercom, 'Bob, what do you see? Do you see anything yet?' And I said, 'Outside the flash, Colonel, nothing yet. The tail turret's in the way. I don't see anything yet.' He said, 'Keep your eyes open.'

"About this time, we saw this shock wave but I didn't say anything. I thought, 'What the hell is this!' It hit the airplane. The old man yelled, 'Flak!' Up front, it felt like it was a flak hit. But in the tail, it's so bouncing and jouncing anyway, that I didn't think anything of it. Then the second one came up and this time I called it out. It was a ricochet. The second shock wave was much less severe and I said, 'Here comes another one.' I think Bob Shumard in the waist spotted it, too.

"About that time, [Tibbets] asked me again, 'Do you see anything yet?' I said, 'No, not yet,' and then 'Holy Moses, what a mess!' That's when the mushroom came into view from around the tail. He asked me to describe it. I did to the best of my ability. He had turned a little bit and I asked him to turn a few degrees one way or the other. Then I started shooting pictures. This little turn he had made allowed me to see the city. The mushroom was coming up, right to our level. It was like you see on TV, an interior core of red-hot fire and on the outside this mushroom, black, white, and purplish. What impressed me most beside the mushroom, the most spectacular thing was this turbulent mass of black purplish smoke that was flooded out like liquid mud all over the city and was flooding up into the ravines where the foothills were. Fire started up through it. I gave up counting the fires. You could see them flash up. Maybe they were explosions, maybe they were all fires. Since we knew we were away from it, Tibbets made a turn and we went alongside where everybody could take a look. We didn't hang around too long. We headed on back and the navigator told me, 'Keep you eye on the mushroom and let me know when you lose sight of it. We want to distance measure it.'

"I watched it and actually it didn't disappear over the horizon. But went behind some stratus clouds. I called in and told the navigator and he said, 'That checks out at 365 miles.' On the flight home we were all highly elated. There was that sense of relief. It was earth-shattering, wiping out a city. I don't recall talking about [the people] or thinking about it. To us it was a military target. Bob Lewis claims he said, 'Oh, my God, what have we done?' I don't recall that on the intercom. Maybe he did. I don't recall their saying they hoped it would end the war, but they might have.

"He [Tibbets] called me up and asked me how I was doing and how did I take that turn. I said, 'Hell, Colonel, that was better than a Cyclone ride down at Coney Island, a twenty-five-cent ride.' He said, 'Well, you can pay me when we land.' I said, 'You're going to have to wait until payday. I am broke.' Then I thought, this is really intelligent chatter to put down for history on the wire recorder.

"We landed and there was this reception committee. It seemed like thousands of people out there. We taxied up and piled out of the airplane. There was a lot of brass. Two MPs came up to me with the photo officer and before I could even stretch he wanted his camera to get the films developed. General Spaatz was there, General Davis, the wing commander. General Spaatz pinned the Distinguished Service Cross on Tibbets, standing there in a brace with his pipe hidden in his hand." A debriefing followed and then a celebration. "By the time the crew got to the beer and hot dog party," remembered Caron, "there was no beer left and no hot dogs left." Interviewed by newsmen, Caron, when asked what he thought about the affair, answered, "I am wondering if we are getting into God's territory with this." That question aside, Caesar rendered Silver Stars to Caron and the other participants.

Ashworth remarked that the plan for the assembly of Fat Man envisioned a five-day period to complete the job. But because of predictions of poor weather by meteorologists, the schedule was compressed with only three days of round-the-clock labor allotted for readying Fat Man. "Early in the morning of 9 August, after operations briefings, we gathered on the flight operations line where the aircraft were being preflight checked. There was no fanfare this time, no high-level officials, just us working folks getting ready to go. There were thunderstorms in the area, some rain, and an occasional flash of lightning stabbed through the darkness. Airmen don't like lightning. In many ways our mission seemed somewhat of an anticlimax, but perhaps more exciting than the operation a few days earlier.

"At this point our troubles began. [Charles] Sweeney's aircraft, *The Great Artiste*, named for Capt. Kermit Beahan, the suave bombardier in the crew, still had the yield-recording instruments installed for Hiroshima. It had been decided that the bomb would be loaded in another B-29, *Bock's Car*. In the preflight check, the flight engineer found that the transfer pump in *Bock's Car*, which would move gasoline from the after bomb bay auxiliary tank into the main fuel system to supply the engines, seemed to be inoperative. He reported it would be impossible for us to use the 600 or so gallons of fuel that had been loaded into that tank. We were confronted with our first decision, should the mission proceed with the knowledge that we would be carrying around 600 gallons of unusable fuel."

Ashworth said he wondered whether his responsibilities covered an opinion on the situation, but Sweeney and Tibbets made a decision with which he agreed, that unless something untoward occurred, the round trip could be made with no problem. They also had the option of landing at Iwo, if necessary, to refuel. A second complication involved the now-standard meeting with companion aircraft at Iwo Jima. A storm in the area forced a new rendezvous over a small island near the Japanese coast. The primary target was the city of Kokura.

Ashworth and an Army second lieutenant, Phil Barnes, would serve as the weaponeers for this expedition. Integrated into the various electrical systems of both atomic bombs were power sources, including some "safe separation timers" that started to tick at the moment of bomb release. These disarmed the bomb for fifteen seconds to prevent detonation before the plane could reach safety. Any one of the nine clocks would shut down the system, and at the end of fifteen seconds the bomb would have fallen 10,000 feet. According to Ashworth, his superior, Captain Parsons, demanded a failure rate of only one in ten thousand chances.

At the same time, nine barometric switches were designed to close at an altitude of about 8,000 feet. These triggered fuses that radiated to measure the height desired for the actual explosion. The galaxy of barometric switches prevented any interference from the Japanese who might jam the radiation.

Once aloft and well clear of Tinian, Ashworth replaced green-painted plugs that isolated the arming and firing systems from other electrical components with red ones that readied the firing and fusing systems to activate after the bomb dropped. That procedure went smoothly, but at the rendezvous point, only one of the B-29s showed. Ashworth persuaded Sweeney to wait for forty-five minutes in hopes the second plane would join them. "I told Sweeney that it was particularly important that we have the plane carrying the bomb-yield measuring instruments with us before we proceeded to the primary target. I wasn't worrying much about the plane carrying the observers, but very much wanted to be able to attempt measurement of the bomb yield."

Having loitered about with no sign of the missing B-29, Ashworth said he advised Sweeney they had no choice but to continue with the mission and hope that their one associate carried the technical instruments rather than spectators.

Later Ashworth said he learned that within five minutes after the second plane appeared, Sweeney knew it was the one with the measuring devices, but for some inexplicable reason this vital fact was never relayed to the Navy commander. Meanwhile in *Bock's Car* anxiety built up among the crew. Having heard of the devastation wrought upon Hiroshima, the airmen wondered how ferociously the Japanese might react when they noticed a couple of B-29s circling near their homeland.

Further complicating matters, strict guidelines dictated subsequent action. Said Ashworth, "These missions were under strict orders from Washington that under no circumstances would the bombs be dropped other than by visual bombing, using the Norden Mark XV bombsight. The weaponeer was charged with responsibility for visually certifying that this occurred." Two hours before they finally left the rendezvous point, a weather advisory from a scout B-29 reported Kokura clear and available as the target. It was also clear over Nagasaki, but there appeared to be a chance of a cloud build-up there.

Bock's Car reached the Initial Point, then began its final bombing run. "Captain Beahan [the bombardier] took control of maneuvering the aircraft as it approached the target, based upon the bombing solution being calculated in the Norden bombsight. The target area appeared to be hazy with some smoke in the area. The approach continued, but at the last moment as we neared the drop point, Captain Beahan reported over the plane's intercom, 'No drop.' The smoke and haze had obscured his actual aiming point so that a visual drop could not be made. We were experiencing the situation frequently found when flying at high altitudes that when at the long slant range to the ground it was difficult to see clearly through the natural haze. Then the frustrating part. As the plane reached a position more nearly above the target it became visible through the bombsight telescope, but then too late to solve the bombing problem and release the bomb."

Ashworth suggested a run from a different direction and that surface winds might clear the target area. Sweeney agreed but the visibility did not improve and Beahan again announced, 'No drop.' The Navy commander proposed a third try from still another angle but that failed for the same reason. "Fifty-five minutes of precious fuel had been expended. It was time to think about the secondary target, Nagasaki. There has been considerable criticism of these decisions," said Ashworth, "particularly in view of the fuel situation." He adamantly justified what happened. "Our job was to attack our primary target, Kokura. What might happen after that was incidental to the failure or success of the mission. Should fuel starvation later result in a ditching operation in the sea, so be it."

However, the presence of the B-29 had attracted the notice of those on the ground. Antiaircraft bursts below and behind were spotted by crewmen. More ominously, the officer monitoring Japanese radio frequencies reported conversations on fighter-director circuits that indicated interceptors might be scrambled. The inability to hit Kokura and the potential of an encounter with enemy planes convinced the crew to proceed toward the secondary target, Nagasaki.

The radar recorded the distinctive image of the long bay that led into that city. Ashworth and the others had no doubts they were in line with the new target. But as they drew nearer, the area appeared completely covered by an undercast of clouds. The flight engineer now calculated barely enough fuel to carry the bomb to the nearest friendly airfield on Okinawa. The alternative would be a ditch in the sea with the bomb aboard. On the other hand, it was also clear they could not afford the maneuvering done at Kokura. "We would have one and only one attempt at a successful drop," recalled Ashworth, "and that appeared to be impossible by visual bombsight in view of the clouds beneath us. I informed Sweeney that we would make our approach by radar and if necessary drop the bomb by use of the electronic bomb director, which would be operated by the navigator. The approach continued."

While preparing for such an execution, bombardier Beahan fed information on the position of the plane and continued to adjust his Mark XV telescope along the calculated flight path. The solid cloud coverage became patchier with the ground showing through numerous big holes. Ashworth reported, "Beahan called out, 'I have the target.' He refined the bombing solution generated by the bombsight and it was released automatically by a signal from the bombsight. We ended up actually dropping the bomb visually as he had been directed. He had about twenty seconds to synchronize and release the bomb. When you think about it, under the pressure of the shortage of fuel, picking out an aiming point through a hole in the clouds below, and knowing full well that the success of the mission depended upon this one bomb run, the skill and coolness displayed by Captain Beahan under such stressful circumstances was extraordinary."

Sweeney put *Bock's Car* into the sharp bank turn calculated by the scientists at Los Alamos, to carry the plane the maximum distance from the explosion and shock waves. "About forty-five seconds after release and the time of fall of the bomb," said Ashworth, "we were able to see through the heavy welders goggles a brilliant flash of light. When we were about eight miles away, the detonation, the first shock wave arrived, followed immediately by a second and, to my recollection, a third. The evidence of these shock waves was more one of noise than anything else. I have always characterized it as if someone had struck an empty metal trash can with a baseball bat. There was a minor movement of the plane, no worse than a sharp bump frequently experienced when flying in a commercial aircraft in clear air turbulence.

"After the shock waves had passed, we returned to the vicinity of the explosion, made one turn around the cloud, and because of our fuel situation departed immediately in a long slow glide, engines throttled back to save fuel, for Okinawa, the closest friendly airfield. By this time, the cloud had reached our altitude of about 29,000 feet. There was a tall dark column of smoke and I suppose debris from the target area, topped by a mushroom-shaped cloud, boiling and roiling as it climbed. It looked as if there was flame and fire in the cloud as it swirled around, colored a salmon pink. We learned later that the pink color was from the nitrous oxide generated in the explosion." Some crewmen insisted the mushroom cloud enveloped the plane but Ashworth doubted it. "Had this actually occurred, we would have been in a very dangerous situation and would have received massive amounts of radiation from the cloud as it would be pulled into the aircraft pressurizing system."

Bock's Car barely reached the Yonton air base on Okinawa. "As usual, in the vicinity of a large active airfield," Ashworth reported, "there was a lot of chatter on the landing control radio circuits and Sweeney's request for landing instructions seemed to have been ignored. After all, we were just another aircraft wanting to land. Knowing he was low on fuel and might lose his engines at any time, Sweeney was wisely flying closer than usual to the airport on the downwind leg in order that if this should happen, he might be able to glide into the field without help from his engines. With still no response from the control tower, Sweeney announced over the radio that he was going to land. As is routine in this kind of situation, Sweeney also ordered the copilot to fire a green flare signifying he needed to land immediately. He thought this would get some response, but lacking this, he told the copilot to fire all flares we had aboard, red, green, yellow, and announced, 'This is B-29 on final. I am going to land.'

"The pyrotechnic display indicated that the plane not only had to make an immediate emergency landing, but that we had killed and wounded aboard and needed ambulance assistance on landing. This got their attention and we were met at the end of the runway by fire trucks, rescue equipment, and ambulances." The B-29 appeared to Ashworth as if it would run off the runway end, but the reversible propellers brought the plane to a roaring, safe halt. The two outboard engines shut down from fuel starvation as they taxied to the operations line and an engineer measured their remaining usable fuel at only thirty-five gallons.

On the ground, the staff at the air base, ignorant of the A-bomb mission, treated Ashworth with disdain when he asked to send a message to Tinian. However, the Navy commander gained an audience with Gen. Jimmy Doolittle, who, with the war in Europe over, now bossed operations focused upon Japan. "He asked me to sit down. I spread out on his desk our target maps and proceeded to tell him about the operation and how it had happened. I indicated the point on the map where we were supposed to aim and told him where we were sure that it actually went off and related in some detail why we had apparently missed our target by about a mile and a half. General Doolittle studied the map, asked a couple of questions, and said, 'Son, I am sure that General Spaatz will be much happier that the bomb exploded where it did over the industrial area and not over the city. There will be far fewer casualties. Now I'll help you send your report."

The Soviet Union declared war on Japan two days after Hiroshima and marched into Manchuria. After the second A-bomb demolished Nagasaki, the Supreme War Guidance Council met in Tokyo. While the leading military representatives wanted to continue the war, the civilian leaders proposed to accept surrender terms. Emperor Hirohito, increasingly aware of the devastating effects of the two nuclear weapons used against his country and the threat of more, broke the stalemate. On 15 August, the emperor publicly announced defeat to his people. Prisoners like Richard Carmichael, the downed Doolittle flyers not executed, and those from the Philippines shipped to Korea, Manchuria, and Japan soon became free men.

Peace was now temporarily restored to the world. The United States counted 290,000 military personnel dead on all fronts. Of this number the Army lost 235,000, including 52,000 in the Air Corps. Marine dead added up to nearly 19,000, and the Navy and Merchant Marine KIA totaled about 37,000. About one million earned Purple Hearts for their wounds. The price for land, sea, and in the air went well beyond the costs of all other U.S. wars combined.

20

After Action Reports

THE PERSONAL ACCOUNTS OF THE ENORMOUS NUMBER OF Americans who fought, bled, and died around the globe during World War II are more than a record of what they endured. They reveal much about the essence of war, strengths and weaknesses of our society, and perhaps even touch on the universals of mankind. It was the most democratic of all American wars; there was no $300 surrogate to avoid the draft as in the Civil War; the mobilization far surpassed that of World War I. Korea, as harsh as it was, involved only a fraction of the numbers of World War II, and Vietnam with its exemptions for college students and the ability to flee the country, was overwhelmingly a blue-collar war led by a professional cadre. Events such as the "liberation" of Grenada, the overthrow of Noriega in Panama, and Desert Storm against Iraq, while stirring patriotic fervor, hardly qualified as wars against substantial opposition.

Flagellation of succeeding generations is a popular sport for their forebears, and broadcaster Tom Brokaw, although not of the one that fought World War II, fed that zest for the game with his book *The Greatest Generation* in which he exalted the Americans who fought on land, sea, and in the air. Unlike Brokaw I am a member of that group and I demur. In the company of the veterans, those who actually endured combat, it is difficult not to be awed as they recount their experiences. And the author of *The Greatest Generation* said his inspiration came after visiting the Normandy beaches with people who had been there. But comparisons of generations and their wars is no more valid than the endless blather about whether the 1998 New York Yankees were equal to or better than the 1927 version. Different times make for entirely unique contexts. Geography, history, politics, economics, etc. all changed. Those who shouldered weapons in Korea and Vietnam endured no less hardship than their World War II counterparts and the valor, comradeship, and selflessness as well as the less admirable qualities were no less evident.

Men and women put on uniforms to fight the Germans and Japanese more willingly than in any other American conflict because there was no way to avoid war. In Korea and Vietnam the U.S. was not directly attacked. Under the circumstances one could argue that those who battled in these conflicts were actually more dedicated to the service of their country because there was no imperative for American survival. *The Greatest Generation* also insists that, apparently in contrast to those that followed, the veterans of World War II came home and immediately went to work to create a better America. The author credited them with "an extraordinary generosity of spirit." Those who were demobilized must also be charged with efforts both to preserve white supremacy and to demolish it. They formed the ranks behind the extreme right and left, exploiters like Senator

Joseph McCarthy, and the forces who opposed radicals of any stripe. Along with the millions who either used the GI Bill to further their education or else went to work in private enterprise or the professions, a substantial number belonged to the "52-20 club"—veterans who elected to collect twenty dollars a week for a full year under the same benefit laws. One could cite multiple contradictions within any broad description of that generation, but above all they are the people who bred and raised their successors replete with all of their alleged faults and virtues.

Having said this is in no way a disparagement of what people did during World War II. There is a coterie of academicians that argues war is an unnatural act; a definition that makes all participants social perverts. Reviewing Barbara Ehrenreich's book *Blood Rites: Origins and History of the Passions of War*, Michael Ignatieff summed up, "Wars break out for frivolous reasons; they are sometimes pursued when almost everyone knows they are insane; they drag on when mired in stalemate; and they frequently end with both sides defeated." None of that applies to World War II. One could hardly regard the Allied cause as "frivolous." Both the Third Reich and Imperial Japan predicated their futures on armed conquest. Given their treatment of the people whose countries they occupied it is nonsense to talk about an accommodation. And there were winners as well as losers.

Confrontation with the Japanese militarists and the Third Reich was inevitable. But there was also patriotism, a sense that our way of life was better. Glen Strange, from the 27th Armored Infantry, grievously wounded near the Remagen Bridge, said, "Hitler was a no-good bastard, but he came along at a time when the German people were ripe for a change and needed a leader and this prick had the ability to take over. He had to be stopped, as he was in the process of trying to enslave all of Europe, and what he did to the Jews and to the free people of the countries they captured could not be tolerated in the free world." Undoubtedly there were many who had no ideological commitment or knowledge of world events. Still, there was a zeal that led hundreds of thousands to enlist rather than wait for the draft and then volunteer for the more dangerous duty as Rangers, Marine Raiders, Airborne, flight crews, submarine service.

The America in which these men grew up was marked by the Great Depression. Many of them spoke of hard times, families struggling to survive in a period of massive unemployment, and dust-bowl conditions that wiped out crops and an agricultural economy. Millions desperately seeking a career or to gain an education that might improve chances to earn a living had their options taken away by the obligation to enter the armed forces. Although they flocked to the colors after the Japanese attack on Pearl Harbor, for more than twenty years prevailing opinion held that the country had been inveigled into World War I and military service was not popular. Combined with the traditional American predilection for independence, as opposed to the regimented culture of the armed forces, the task of rapidly converting millions of civilians into a fighting force was not an easy one.

The outsiders, like the British, as well as the enemy, regarded the U.S. forces as lacking in discipline and the resolve to fight effectively. The naysayers were wrong and in fact the streak of independence was one of the great strengths of the American fighting man. As George Ruhlen and George S. Patton Jr. both noted, for the most part this was not a matter of massive armies contending on a grand battlefield but, instead, of a myriad of small-unit actions. While superiors exerted some command and control, in many situations those watchwords of the military text vanished and it fell to groups of men functioning on their own, perhaps without benefit of any officer or even a noncom. Whether they were Marines, paratroopers, infantrymen, naval gunners, or airmen, they built on the training and whatever discipline had been instilled to successfully carry out their missions. And in those cases where coordinated, well-regulated actions were required, aboard ships, on massive air raids, or coordinated attacks on an enemy fleet, the former free-wheeling civilians stuck to the game plan.

At the same time, it would be a mistake to think the war was prosecuted strictly by "citizen-soldiers," who once the fighting ended reverted to civilian life. Professional military people, the graduates of the service academies, some of the reservists, and those who had chosen to make a career in the armed forces, played vital roles. From this segment came both top commanders and the important ranks stretching down to the junior-officer level. Along with MacArthur, Eisenhower, Nimitz, Halsey, Patton, Vandegrift and company, the armed forces succeeded because of younger professionals. West Pointers like paratroop battalion commander Bill Boyle; platoon leader and company commander Carl Ulsaker; Naval Academy alumni like submarine skipper Slade Cutter, and pilot Jimmy Thach; reserve officer converted to regular status, infantry leader George Mabry. They went to war imbued with the motto of "Duty, Honor, Country," and that commitment ought not be discounted.

Under the circumstances World War II stirred the melting pot like no other experience in the history of the country. As navigator for the B-17 *Bad Check*, Jon Schueler, a graduate of the University of Wisconsin and an aspiring writer, said, "My pilot was a Jack Armstrong -type named Billy Southworth. Bill and I hated each other's guts. He was a cocky son of a bitch, the pampered son of the manager of the St. Louis Cards. Our backgrounds and personalities couldn't have been more different, except that we were both prima donnas of kinds." In time, however, they became the best of friends. Their crew also included waist gunner and equally alien personality Bill Fleming, a coal miner's son, and bombardier Milt Coover, a Virginia Military Academy product.

When South Carolinian George Mabry addressed a contingent of draftees from the North at Fort Benning, Georgia, he was disconcerted by their mumbling until one of his sergeants confided, "They can't understand a word you're saying." Heath Carriker, a North Carolina farm boy and Eighth Air Force pilot, remarked, "I felt pleased and happy about being part of what I considered a necessary activity, meeting new people, learning new things, a welcome change from my life to that time. Until then I had never had any contact with Jews, Italians, Polish, or Yankees." Virginia-bred Bob Slaughter, as part of his state's National Guard, said that after the outfit was federalized and added a variety of ethnic backgrounds, "They laughed at the thick-tongued drawl of the mountaineers from Appalachia. And the Southern rednecks had to strain their ears to understand them. When I went on a pass with an Italian boy, he took me to a restaurant where I had spaghetti for the first time in my life." Such encounters were replicated literally hundreds and hundreds of thousands of times. This is not to say that familiarity eliminated prejudice; many felt the sting of bias and the discrimination against blacks remained at a high level.

For all of the homogenization that occurred, war cannot be waged on the basis of democracy. Troops must be led, ships captained, and someone must make the decisions, including those that put someone else's life in jeopardy. However much the propaganda of the times and the legend-makers lionized those at the top, the upper-echelon commanders were not gods but fallible creatures. While hindsight provides a questionable lens through which to view decisions, it cannot be denied that interservice rivalry, differences in combat philosophy, a certain amount of ineptitude born of ignorance, and the political cronyism that permeated much of the National Guard hurt those committed to combat. There was an appalling lack of coordination among the armed services that led to incidents of friendly fire, bombings of American troops by American airmen, lack of support when requested, territorial disputes between armies such as occurred in Sicily. Listening to the eyewitnesses, one may conclude that the Allies muddled their way to victory, overcoming the enemy not by brilliant strokes but by overwhelming them with men, materiel, and resources.

Mistakes in enterprises great and small ordinarily mean loss of money, esteem, advancement. Errors in war are paid in agony and death. All of the U.S. armed services fumbled and stumbled in the development of the tools of war. Intelligence badly underestimated the quality of enemy resources, particularly in regard to Japanese airplanes, their navy and their soldierly qualities. The entire strategic-bombing program began with a horrendous ignorance of the hazards to unaccompanied B-17s and B-24s, entailing a significant delay in the development of fighters. All along the way glitches in design and instruction hampered effectiveness. Untested torpedoes frustrated submariners; the first bazookas were too small and unreliable; as Marine platoon lieutenant Bob Craig discovered, ordnance experts changed the time interval for grenades without informing the troops. In initial encounters with the Germans, American tanks, too light, too weakly armed, and too vulnerable to enemy guns, fought under severe handicaps, and while the medium-weight Shermans shortened the odds, their high silhouette, flammability, and the inability of their guns to match the Panzers weakened U.S. armored units. The superficially tested floating tanks created for the Normandy beaches were another ghastly mistake. While the M1 Garand rifle was the best in the field, the .30- and .50-caliber machine guns were inferior to those of the foe. The German 88 was the best direct-fire artillery piece of World War II, but the proximity fuse, developed by the U.S. after the war began, produced excellent results. The Air Corps, the Navy, and the Marines all flew second-rate planes in the beginning, but by the end of hostilities, with the possible exception of the few jets introduced in Europe, the fliers manned the best in the air.

The believers in the Eureka system that expected to guide paratroopers to their drop zone failed to take into account the navigation problems of transports blundering through the night while carrying pathfinders with the vital equipment. The pilots hauling gliders or troopers often lacked experience in the kind of flying required, and carefully plotted courses were abandoned under severe antiaircraft fire. Similarly, the strategists who placed their faith in the accuracy of high-altitude bombing based their theories on the clear skies of the training areas of the American Southwest and neglected to consider what happened when 88s opened up or fighters attacked.

Beyond the question of manpower and weapons, in war it is not so much a matter of how one has played the game, but whether one has won or lost. War is a very messy business permeated by honest mistakes, inefficiency, foolishness, and wrong-headed obstinacy. Yet, those in command of our fighting men, whatever their faults, led the way to victory even as one may criticize their behavior. The demands of war require a hierarchical military organization, one that functions through automatic responses to orders. Getting an army, company of infantry, a bomber crew or sailors on a submarine to carry out what's necessary requires leadership. This is a subtle quality that goes beyond a matter of silver stars, bars, stripes, a loud voice, the power to discipline and punish, and that is often influenced by who the individual is and by the situation.

At the very top, leadership means something quite different from that which was employed as one moves down the ranks. Dwight Eisenhower never had an opportunity to command in the field, but his handling of the touchy, egotistical, and chauvinistic political and military figures both American and foreign required an extraordinary combination of diplomacy and firmness. By all accounts he was a likeable man, popular with his contemporaries and with genuine ability. He could say no to Bernard Montgomery, coordinate the conflicting ideas for such a massive enterprise as the invasion of Normandy, protect Patton from self-destruction until he could serve a useful purpose, perceive the seriousness of the German penetration in the Ardennes, respond faster apparently than those around him, and restore flagging morale. According to Stephen Ambrose, when the extent of the German breakthrough became apparent, on 19 December he walked into a staff meeting of downcast generals and said, "The present situation is to be regarded as one of opportunity for us and not of disasters. There will be only cheerful faces at this conference table."

He made mistakes. He indulged Winston Churchill's politically motivated insistence on attacking through Italy, anything but a soft underbelly. He kept faith in Mark Clark, whose progress in Italy was questionable. Whatever the merits of the Anzio landings, the Fifth Army never supplied the wherewithal to make it worth the costs in men and equipment. Although Eisenhower reacted swiftly, he, too, underestimated the power of the enemy in December 1944. And the toe-to-toe slugfest that followed, rather than skilled maneuvers to outflank the German armies imperiled by their vulnerable flanks, was hardly the stuff of military brilliance.

In North Africa, George S. Patton directed an effective offense and added to his reputation with victories in Sicily, at St.-Lô, and in the relief of Bastogne. But he then compromised his achievements with a series of less than stellar decisions topped by the ill-fated raid at Hammelburg. He led with a blend of authoritarianism marked by a ferocious temper, an unswerving confidence in himself, tempered by a flair for the dramatic, that gave those of the lowest rank a sense they were part of something special. As Carl Ulsaker saw, Patton knew how to talk in a way that appealed to GIs brutalized by exposure to the miseries of a combat soldier's life. Patton was a mean son of a bitch, but there was a certain pride in being led by such an individual even as the GIs translated one of his nicknames into "Our blood and his guts."

As a human being, Patton, was despicable—a notorious sexual predator, a behind-the-back critic, and a bigot. In his book, *War As I Knew It*, he wrote, "Individually, they [the black 761st Tank Battalion] were good soldiers but I expressed my belief at that time [when the outfit joined his Third Army] and have never found any necessity of changing it, that a colored soldier cannot think fast enough to fight in armor." And after liberating camps like Buchenwald, where he made the local people see the handiwork of their government, he could still write to his wife, "Everyone believes that the displaced person is a human being which he is not, and this applies particularly to the Jews who are lower than animals. . . . Actually, the Germans are the only decent people in Europe." None of this can discount the fact that he did reenergize the American forces in North Africa after their initial defeats; he did boldly sponsor the crucial breakout at St.-Lô; and he did move to the relief of Bastogne and the flattening of the Bulge quicker than anyone thought possible. On the other hand, true strategic coups were never his forte. Patton achieved victory with blunt force, winning at considerable price.

Abe Baum, whom Patton sent on a near-suicidal mission, had mixed feelings about him. "The important thing about Patton was he believed that infantry should support tanks rather than vice versa. He had the foresight to take a stand, lose a lot of personnel in a short period of time, where in the long haul it wouldn't be as noticeable, but you would have even more casualties as the enemy built up its forces. The press ridiculed him as flamboyant and he could put Barnum and Bailey to shame. But he was ideal for the war we fought. He had a feeling for the terrain, he was the most aggressive of all of the generals. If anybody should hate him, it would be me. But I believe he shortened the war. On the other hand, I would not want him as a father."

General Terry Allen led in his own style. His rank of course brought obedience, but his 1st Division and then his 104th Division accomplished their missions without the need for Allen to kick people in the behind, as Patton was so fond of doing. There isn't any real evidence that the 1st Division, while under his leadership reputed to be careless about uniforms and saluting, performed better when Allen was replaced by a stickler for military niceties.

Douglas MacArthur represented still another form of leader at the top. MacArthur recouped from his disastrous decisions in the Philippines with a skillful, strategic island-by-island counterattack marred perhaps only by excess when he returned to the Philippines. Laudable as was liberation of the Filipinos, it was a dubious decision to pursue a cut-off, starving, but still deadly enemy on Mindanao or in the northern sectors of Luzon.

While in World War I MacArthur stayed close to the doughboys, in World War II he functioned at the utmost distance from the common soldier. He demonstrated neither Eisenhower's easy-going style nor the great-man-come-to-earth demeanor exhibited by Patton on selected occasions. Overall he worked well with Nimitz and the Marine generals. MacArthur has been credited with saving many lives by carefully plotting his advances to avoid the head-on confrontations that so often involved the Marines. Some of the brutal battles for the leathernecks were, however, unavoidable, given that the targets were small, fully fortified sites like Tarawa and Iwo Jima. On Leyte, MacArthur's second landing at Ormoc was a master stroke—so good that he replicated it at Inchon, Korea, six years later. However, aside from the mistakes made in the Philippines, MacArthur also could not be faulted for excessive concern for the conquest of territory. That fault in Navy-controlled spheres is most evident with the attack on the unstrategic, valueless island of Peleliu, as well as the continuation of the fighting on Okinawa once the major objectives of a naval base and airfields were secured.

One of the great strengths of top leaders is their removal from the terror and the pain. Although they can be expected to declaim about the sacrifices made by those under fire, generals and admirals, unlike the common fighting men, do not personally have to charge a pillbox or seize the high ground; they rarely witness the evisceration of a close comrade, and have only a distant acquaintance with the stink of death. While Patton became genuinely emotionally distraught upon visiting the wounded, there is not much record of his having agonized over sending these same people to their graves in order to carry out his schemes. Gregory Peck may have broken down when he dispatched the bombers in *Twelve O'Clock High*, but the combat fatigue more often afflicted those who flew the missions rather than those who ordered them.

There were exceptions to the insulation of the senior people from harm's way. Admirals aboard ships enjoyed no more protection from torpedoes, shells, bombs, or kamikazes than their crewmates. They paid in their own blood as well as that of shipmates for their participation, and several flag officers died or were seriously wounded. In the Air Forces, generals flew some missions, taking their chances along with the junior officers and enlisted members of the crews. Again, a number of them perished.

On the tiny beaches of coral atolls, Marine brass was exposed to enemy fire, as were those of the Army at Omaha and Utah Beaches. Indeed, the 4th Division's deputy commander, General Roosevelt, a popular figure, set an example for the troops by his demeanor and his decisive direction after their landing craft put the GIs ashore well away from their appointed site.

There can be little doubt that sharing the danger adds to the strength of a leader. Nowhere is that more apparent than in the airborne forces where the generals either jumped or landed in gliders. They became combat soldiers on the ground until an area could be secured. Into the dark maw of the Normandy night, the 82d Airborne head Matthew Ridgway dropped, a USMA graduate whose trademarks were the hand grenades hanging from his uniform and his .30-06 Springfield rifle. Maxwell Taylor, another West Pointer, made only the second jump of his life as he led the 101st

Airborne. The deputy commander of the 82d Airborne, James Gavin, manned positions in Sicily, Normandy, and Holland. During the Battle of the Bulge, where he entered the battle scene by jeep, he loped about carrying an M1 rifle. Although the weapon may have kept his identity somewhat hidden from snipers looking for VIPs, Gavin in particular was favored by his men. Bill Dunfee, who jumped into combat four times and went into the Ardennes under Gavin, said, "Slim Jim Gavin was respected and loved by every man who served in his command. We of the 505 [Parachute Regiment] were very proud to have served him in his first and last combat missions."

One can argue that a general officer's presence at the front not only adds to morale but in some cases is useful. The German counterparts of the Allies had a habit of personally inspecting the terrain they defended, taking care usually to obscure their rank. The generals who flew bombing missions gained insights into the problems faced and Curtis LeMay's successful innovations in tactics could only have come after he saw firsthand what happened.

It would naturally follow that stress under fire seems to have been almost inversely proportional to rank. Whatever their backgrounds, the Air Force brass all accepted an essential aspect of combat command, a willingness to order men to kill and be killed. They may have been psychologically more prepared for the casualties of war because even in peacetime there was a much higher number of deaths due to aircraft accidents than befell those in the infantry, field artillery, or other outfits. "I won't say you get callous," said Gen. Ira Eaker, "but you get realistic." He remarked to an interviewer of the necessity to be "trained and inured" if one was to carry out his tasks. LeMay said one in his position could not "meditate on the process of death" nor "mope around about the deaths he has caused personally by deed or impersonally in the act of command."

For those caught in the thick of the bloodshed, however, it was a far different matter. As a replacement platoon leader on Okinawa, Si Seibert said his greatest concern had been whether or not he could acquit himself as a leader. He satisfied himself on that score, but was traumatized by the loss of his first GI. "The death of of one of my men, although I was not directly responsible for it, placed a heavy burden on me. I could never, and have never gotten over that feeling." Jon Schueler, the navigator, broke down: "I started to feel guilty, responsible for every death. I was not sleeping, afraid that I'd make errors and cause the death of many."

George Ruhlen remarked, "I sometimes debate whether my decision to establish an observation post removed from infantry support, which did not contribute anything to our advance, yet cost the life of a lieutenant who had served with me for two years, was the right one."

Only after the battalion surgeon informed the regimental commander that he had no 2d Battalion to deploy, were the survivors of the 34th Regiment removed from the battle in the Philippines. Paratrooper Homer Jones identified his company commander as having a kind of heroism that reflected his responsibility and leadership. "Men like Royal Taylor were so intent on what they did, and yet so conscious of the people who were with them. They knew what they were doing and that people might be killed as a consequence. They could feel the weight of these decisions and still carry them out."

Still, it was a sensible policy to keep those responsible for directing a large-size unit away from the fronts where they might be killed or wounded, depriving the organization of its leadership. Brig. Gen. Don. Pratt, deputy commander of the 101st Airborne, died in a glider crash the night of 6 June 1944. General Maurice Rose, Ernest Harmon's chief of staff in North Africa, who took over the 3d Armored Division in Europe, was killed in March 1945 after he drove to the front with the situation still fluid. In Okinawa, artillery fatally wounded the top U.S. commander, Gen. Simon Bolivar Buckner, when he ventured into a danger zone. Losses of this nature could be critical, although in these instances capable replacements were available.

It was another matter for the smaller units, where the grand strategy depended upon specific actions by limited groups of men. Here, where decisions on tactics must be made on the spot, regimental, battalion, and group commanders could be expected to be in the thick of things. Merritt Edson and Tony Walker of the Marine Raiders, Bill Darby of the Rangers, Red Newman of the 24th Division shared the exposure of the grunts.

The mystique Bill Darby aroused in his people undeniably had something to do with his constant presence at the flash points of combat and his force of character in the worst of situations. During the American retreat in Tunisia, Darby addressed his Rangers: "Men, we are the last unit to pull out of this mess! Ahead of us lie 24 miles of flat expanse which must be crossed to reach the next American strong-point at Deria Pass. Behind us and on our flanks are enemy armored columns, looking for straggling units to cut up. We have no tanks to protect us! We have only a few bazookas and a few sticky grenades to fight tanks with. In your hands they will do the trick! Before we start I want you all to know how proud I am to command this unit. You have proved yourself well on all occasions. Onward we stagger; and if the tanks come, may God help the tanks." To some that may have the ring of a football coach's halftime exhortation, but in this instance, Darby would be in the field, facing the same extreme threats as everyone else.

George Mabry as an infantry officer insisted he learned a sound lesson while in the peacetime army. "Never ask anybody to do anything you wouldn't do willingly. Lead by doing." He practiced what he preached, getting off Utah Beach and moving inland during the early days of the invasion of France.

Bill Boyle, the intrepid leader of a parachute battalion said, ". . . the best way to imbue troops with the proper spirit [is]: Let them know you can and will do everything that you ask them to do and the best way to get that across is to let the men see you do it, not just tell it." There was a ferocity to Boyle that was not lost upon his troopers, but fear alone could not have generated the admiration and fondness for him among his troopers.

Along with the exemplars there were also battalion and regimental heads who never ventured beyond a command post and often established that as far from danger as possible. Some GIs saw as little of their regimental leader as of their division general.

Persuading the individual to follow orders is not a matter of a popularity contest. Mabry confessed that he would eavesdrop on soldier conversations during breaks to get an inkling of what his men were thinking. He concluded, "If they said, 'he's a good guy,' he probably wasn't a good noncom or officer and was too lenient or doing something they knew was wrong. If they said, 'he's firm, but a good man,' they'd probably follow him." Mabry learned he was known as "the mean little man, but okay because he was tough but fair."

Only on Omaha Beach did Felix Branham discover praiseworthy quality in his regimental commander, Col.

Charles Canham, who ranged up and down the strand screaming at the GIs to get off the beach. "Canham previously had a BAR shot out of his hand. The bullet went through his right wrist and he wore a makeshift sling. His bodyguard, Private First Class Nami, followed closely behind, keeping the colonel's .45 loaded. Canham would fire a clip and hand the gun back to Nami who would inject another into the weapon. Back in training, we used to call Colonel Canham everything not fit to print. When he took command of the 116th he made life miserable for us. We thought he would be another rear-echelon commander. After seeing him in action, I sure had to eat a lot of crow."

Similarly, it was the 29th Division's assistant commander on that same blood-soaked sand, Gen. Dutch Cota, who apparently shouted "Rangers, lead the way!" And although Frank Buck Dawson claimed he never heard the order, the Ranger lieutenant did respond to the need for someone to lead.

Of tank battalion commander Creighton Abrams, who would eventually become the Army's chief of staff, Abe Baum said, "He was sincere, honest, didn't speak down to people. In eight or ten words he could put more emphasis than someone who spoke for an hour. He led his troops. He didn't have a headquarters out there in his lead tank. Instead he was another gun in the tank."

Marine Richard Wheeler, wounded on Iwo Jima, spoke of his battalion commander, Lt. Col. Chandler Johnson. "He was a rigid disciplinarian and kept us apprehensive about losing his favor. But on Iwo, he quickly began to earn our esteem. He strode about unflinchingly, wearing nothing on his head but a fatigue cap and carrying no gear except a .45-caliber pistol. When he stopped to consult with one of his subordinates, he would often stand erect, gesturing and pointing authoritatively, and making no effort to keep the enemy from learning he was a senior officer.

"In view of the emphasis that combat training places on security it would seem that men like Chandler Johnson and Howard Snyder [the squad leader who did not dig in] must be regarded with disapproval. But their kind are vital to a battlefield effort. It's true that a combat team must be composed mainly of cautious men; wholesale heedlessness under fire would certainly bring the team to disaster. But there is also a need for an audacious minority. It's this minority that set the pace for an attack. If everyone were to dig in deeply and move only when it was really necessary—which is all that duty requires—the team's efforts would lack vigor. There must be a scattering of men who neglect their safety and act with a daring initiative. Most of the tough feats that win the medals are performed by men like this. Though they are called damned fools by many of their more cautious comrades, they are nonetheless greatly admired. They do much for morale, since they seem entirely unafraid, and their cool aggressiveness sets a standard that the cautious, not wishing to be too far outdone, follow to the best of their ability. And that's how objectives are taken and battles are won."

The virtue of leading by doing is not an absolute, even when it comes down to the most junior officers and noncoms. Carl Ulsaker, having gone through extensive combat for five months, developed his own point of view of the question. He recalled interviewing some replacement lieutenants and while he stressed that he expected them to motivate their entire platoons to fight, he put the newcomers through a quick course in what he believed was required. Ulsaker would ask the officer what was the motto of the Infantry School. 'Follow me, sir,' was the inevitable response.

To which Ulsaker replied, "I want you to forget that 'follow me' stuff beginning right now. If you get out in front of your platoon and cry 'Follow me!' you know what your men are going to say? They'll say, 'Go right ahead, Lieutenant,' because they know from experience that the man most likely to get shot in combat is the one in front. Your job is to get the entire platoon to fight; after all twenty or thirty rifles firing at the enemy equates to a hell of a lot more firepower than one officer's carbine. I'm not looking for heroes. I want leaders. I want *pushers*. Your place is behind your men where you can control them; not too far behind but close enough where you can kick someone in the tail if he lags to the rear. Sometimes I think the Army should redefine *leadership* and call it *pushership*." Ulsaker admitted there were some who were not convinced and "would get out in front, wave his arms, shout, 'Follow me, men!' and get shot."

In the Air Corps, John Alison explained, "The squadron commander has to lead. Even if he is not the best pilot in the outfit, he has to lead or else he is not going to have a good outfit. I led every difficult mission we ever flew. I always had more bullet holes in my airplane than anybody else. You can lead by example. You can lead by power. You can do it either way. By my own experience and particularly [for] fighter pilots, it is a hell of a lot better to lead by example."

Still, there is the question of how to generate the responses required in the face of death and destruction. The accepted practice by all military organizations for inculcating the right attitude is through the discipline that begins in training camp. Some officers, notably Patton, belong to the school that believes insistence upon a necktie, polished shoes, shaved faces, and salutes instilled the instinct to automatically obey.

Bill Boyle, who graduated from the U.S. Military Academy, did not exemplify spit and polish. "I had my opinions about discipline, but my emphasis was on combat training, combat reliability, and ability to rely on one another, not spit-shined boots. I was not casual. I trained intensively and expected the same of officers and men." He did not dismiss out of hand such traditions as military courtesy. "Saluting is an exchange of greetings; the subordinate acknowledges the authority of the senior. Grooming in garrison should be neat. Close-order drill is a disciplinary exercise designed to get us in the habit of obeying orders without question. These are necessary, but they must be kept in perspective. One should hardly expect a man to look as if he is going to a dance when he is living out of a knapsack in the field."

The Rangers, fighters that even Patton praised, under Bill Darby and James Rudder, almost entirely eschewed matters of appearance and formal behavior. Paratroop leader William Yarborough described Darby's men at Anzio as looking like "cutthroats . . . the sweepings of the barrooms, stubble beards, any kind of uniform." But Yarborough admitted leadership of the sort exemplified by Darby inspired certain individuals.

There were notable cases, including one cited by Carl Ulsaker, of individuals who during training personified excellent soldierly qualities, but once under fire proved worthless. In fact, frequently soldiers who disdained the strictures on grooming, fractured rules on behavior, and ignored concerns for military courtesy demonstrated uncommon valor, as in the case of Medal of Honor winners Private First Class Harold Moon on Leyte, or Sgt. Maynard "Snuffy" Smith, an Eighth Air Force ball-turret gunner on a B-17 who, after his ship started to burn, extinguished the fire, administered first aid to a wounded tail gunner, and manned the waist guns to fend off predatory FW 190s.

One of the great tests of command is the ability to perform in the most adverse situations. Hank Spicer not only transformed a fumbling fighter group into a high-performance unit, he continued to lead while incarcerated in a prison camp. His behavior in a stalag contrasts sharply with that of Col. Charles Cavender, a West Pointer, who not only surrendered his regiment under questionable circumstances, but also appeared willing to compromise on the issue of Jewish prisoners until others in the camp refused to follow his lead.

In his *New York Review of Books* piece, Ignatieff said, "Killing is so far from being a natural instinct that many soldiers in the First and Second World Wars either didn't fire their weapons at all or fired them over their enemies' heads. This view, angrily denied by some veterans, was first advanced by the U.S. Army historian S. L. A. Marshall in 1947. It has been defended with weighty empirical evidence in *On Killing* [by American military historian David Grossman] a study of firing rates and of the ratios of kills to ammunition. . . ." John McManus reported in his book *Deadly Brotherhood* that Harold Leinbaugh, a company commander in the 84th Infantry Division who wrote a book on his experiences, spoke to many associates and could find few if any who recalled not shooting their weapons. Leinbaugh went on a personal crusade to debunk S. L. A. Marshall and found ample evidence that Marshall never asked questions about whether men fired their weapons. It is dubious that he even conducted some of the interviews upon which he supposedly based his thesis.

It is preposterous to extrapolate from the number of rounds expended how many bullets by individual GIs and leathernecks caused casualties. As anyone who was on the scene can testify, fire discipline was extremely difficult to maintain, although many commanders strove mightily to limit the shooting. Frequently any sound heard or shadow glimpsed during the night provoked volleys of gunfire. The mechanism of the basic infantry weapon, the M1 Garand enabled a man to empty eight bullets in a clip in an astonishingly short time. Furthermore, much of the fighting took place at distances measured in hundreds of yards; and with the enemy concealed in a cave, brush, house, or behind a hedgerow. No one waited until he could see the whites of the eyes before squeezing the trigger, which also explains incidentally much of the friendly fire problem. Under the circumstances in which the bodies of dead enemy were hastily buried, sometimes with mass graves dug by a bulldozer, without benefit of autopsies, it is ridiculous to believe there can have been any accounting of who died from a bullet and who from artillery, mortar rounds, or strafing from the air. That more people, soldiers and civilians, were killed by long-range artillery or air raids than by bullets from the individual soldier is irrelevant; it only makes the case that modern weapons have gone beyond the simple man-with-the-gun.

Based on personal accounts, the willingness to destroy other humans in the war was not affected by class or education. Barely literate Marines and GIs as well as the college bred carried out the necessities of combat. A hard-bitten lawyer-soldier, Dick Thom, said he worried that the infusion of former members of the Army Specialized Training Program would lessen the efficiency of the 96th Infantry Division. "They turned out to be smart kids, quick to learn, good riflemen, good shooters, solid killers, and thoroughly reliable."

Ignatieff's survey of Ehrenreich's book and others delves into the alleged psychological conditioning of religious blessings, training, drilling, parades and martial speeches designed to transform humans from their "normal moral order" into ones able to destroy lives. While all of the pre-combat ritual and instruction may have helped condition the combat soldier, the most compelling influence was the simple imperative, "kill or be killed." During the later years of the war a film with that as its title tried to convince GIs to abandon the scruples of civil society. The testimony of the men on the line time and again is the "them or us" syndrome. It is a question of what is required to survive.

The heat of battle brought on atrocities. It is understandable for a soldier who has just lost his closest friend to gun down the enemy who only runs up the white flag after running out of ammunition. The surprise attack upon Pearl Harbor, the mutilation and murder of prisoners by both the Japanese and Germans, occasioned retaliation. But the savage slaying of prisoners because it was too much trouble to guard them or escort them to the rear speaks of a darker side of men at war. In the case of the Japanese, undoubtedly racism made slaughter easier. The shooting of airmen in parachutes after their plane has been hit was decried throughout the war. But if a pilot would be in a position to return to the war, then how much different would killing him be than murdering a man running away from the battle? For the most part, the act of mercy to an aviator was an offshoot of the kill-or-be-killed principle—if we do this, they will do it to us.

Several eyewitnesses in this book testify to GIs harvesting gold teeth from corpses, looting bodies of valuables, even photographs. In the Air Corps there were those who scavenged in the possessions of shot-down comrades, explaining that the victims would no longer need the items. On more occasions than one wishes to remember, Americans slaughtered those who surrendered or wished to quit.

To be sure, when the action ended, many felt compassion and guilt for the dead. Ranger Bob Edlin remembered emptying his M1 at an enemy soldier. "Afterward I rolled over the man I had shot. I see his face at night, even after almost fifty years. I wondered then and now what happened to the beautiful little boy and girl in the picture that the proud father carried to show his friends." There were numerous similar expressions of remorse from men in all theaters of combat. It was easier for artillerymen and gunners on Navy vessels who did not have to look at the faces of those they killed. Airmen like Cary Salter thought in terms of destroying machines rather than killing people. Only when shot down over Germany did fliers like Jim Goodson and Jim McCubbin become aware of the destruction done by the Air Forces.

Obviously the atomic bomb killed the most people in a single stroke. It is difficult to find a combat veteran, even today, who does not approve of the use of the weapon. Faced with the massive concrete bunker-to-bunker defenses, the availability of thousands of kamikaze planes, and an army of several million that had never deviated from the code of death before surrender, those assigned to invade Japan believe tens of thousands faced death. Infantry sergeant Don Dencker speaks for most when he declared, "God bless the atomic bomb. It probably saved my life."

Arguments against the use of A-bombs revolve around such issues as the extraordinary number killed by only two nuclear explosions at Hiroshima and Nagasaki, 210,000 in the initial blasts and another 130,000 from injuries or radiation effects within five years. Balanced against these losses by those who approved the two attacks are the estimated casualties for an invasion of Japan that run from 46,000 to 1,000,000. While the low figure hardly seems credible in light of the losses at Okinawa, Iwo Jima, and other strongholds, the projections miss the point. Once the body counts rise into the tens of thousands the debate of morality becomes pointless. The issue of whether war could be confined only to the military had been decided with the concept of strategic bombing aimed at destroying the capacity of a nation to fight.

Furthermore, the terrible deaths and disfigurements of the residents in the Japanese cities differed little from those incinerated or suffocated by flamethrowers, disemboweled by shrapnel, decapitated by mortars, who had huge portions of their faces shot away, or lost limbs from mines. Had the bomb not been used, as David Burchinal said, there were plans to firebomb every Japanese city. The incendiary raid on Tokyo killed 85,000 to 100,000, certainly as frightening as the results of the atomic bomb on Nagasaki.

The detonation of Little Boy and Fat Man in fact demonstrate the real nature of a large-scale modern war, the loss of control. The momentum that develops overwhelms the individual, even if he sits in the White House. There was never any genuine doubt that Harry Truman would authorize the use of nuclear weapons. He was the political head of a country facing an unknown amount of death and destruction should the war continue. He could hardly have risked the lives of so many countrymen in order to preserve those of an enemy nation.

Loss of control is what war is about. Bob Slaughter, who saw so many of his childhood friends killed on Omaha Beach, said, "I realized it didn't make any difference whether one was a superior soldier, was more religious, of better character. People were being killed randomly and they could not help themselves." In fact, many of the most repellant events of the war—the atrocities, the use of the nuclear bomb, the looting of bodies, the gamut from manic to depressive behavior—are products of this loss of power to govern one's fate.

Eugene Sledge, who felt "utter and absolute helplessness," said in *With the Old Breed*, "As Peleliu dragged on I feared that if I ever lost control of myself under shellfire my mind would be shattered. To be under heavy shellfire was to me by far the most terrifying of combat experiences. Each time, it left me feeling more forlorn and helpless, more fatalistic and with less confidence that I could escape the dreadful law of averages that inexorably reduced our numbers."

Theirs are common sentiments that lead to the question of why men endure and persevere at war. Writer Paul Fussell, who commanded an infantry company in Europe, attributed the dogged persistence to "inertia." He is at one with Leo Tolstoy, who while describing the Battle of Borodino in *War and Peace*, wrote, "But though towards the end of the battle the men felt all the horror of their actions, though they would have been glad to cease, some unfathomable mysterious force still led them on. . . ." Inertia may be another way of describing loss of control.

For all of the horror and the sorrow, there was also an uplifting feeling that some relished in their war. Clearly it was the best of times for Patton, although since his skin was hardly at peril, his delight is easy to understand. Hamilton Howze similarly appraised the attitude of armored division commander Ernest Harmon. "I never knew anybody of any rank who enjoyed war as much as Ernie Harmon did. His war record was fine. When he had everything in the division fighting he thought the world could give him nothing better. I recall his calling me up and saying, 'By God, I've got everything in the division shooting, including all the tankdozers.' "

Once engaged in the business of war, few lusted for the role of hero. Doolittle Raid pilot William Bower said, "I don't think there was any feeling on anybody's part that they wanted to be the first to bomb Tokyo. They just wanted to do the job and come on home. For years we couldn't understand why people would ask us to come to their town for a reunion. We thought it should have died. Now, as we get older we see that perhaps the reason [lies in] that expression 'can do.' It gave me an association with people that I would never have had."

There were "war lovers." Many line organizations had at least one soldier who seemed to enjoy killing. Others admitted they liked blowing up things. Ben Renton, a lieutenant in the 517th Parachute Regiment, wounded six times, said he "loved" his months in combat. Renton had enjoyed his war so much that he sought to obtain a regular army commission, but his wounds left him physically unfit. His fellow trooper Ludlow Gibbons declared, "Ninety-nine percent of all the excitement I have had in my life took place during the time I spent in combat. I believe it to be the ultimate test. I have never experienced anything close to it, before or since."

Fear triggers an adrenaline rush and others, although less enthusiastic about their experiences, echoed Winston Churchill's comment, to the effect that nothing was more exhilarating than to be shot at and missed. Phil Hannon, taken prisoner during the Battle of the Bulge, recalled "a higher sense of being when under fire." But that is not the same as pleasure. Carmen Capalbo, a scout with the 99th Division, wounded in early December 1944, said, "I saw no exhilaration in anyone. I never heard any person express sentiments remotely resembling those." Frank Barron, a company commander in the 77th Infantry Division, said, "I believe fighting for your country in the infantry in battle is the most purifying experience known to man. These men who trained hard together and fought for extended periods together became so completely unselfish, so absorbed with the welfare of the group that you could believe that their principal concern was for the 'other guy.' I've never wished to die before or since, nor did I wish to die in battle then. But I thought there was a good chance that I would and I thought then there was no better way to die, and no better men to be buried with."

The film *Saving Private Ryan* elicited a few carping remarks from some conservatives who felt the soldiers never voiced any comments on the cause for which they were fighting. In all of the interviews I've done for seven books on World War II I never came across a single individual who recalled foxhole discussions about religion, democracy, the Four Freedoms, the Constitution, or the horrors of totalitarianism. (Nor do they speak of Mom's apple pie, the Brooklyn Dodgers, or similar clichés.) Men under fire think and talk in terms of how to stay alive, whom they've lost, their desires for a warm, dry place and hot food, not abstractions that have nothing to do with their situations. When they pray it is for survival, not in a declaration of faith. While Barron's opening words might be attributed to an idealized recall, the essence of his remarks are close to what most men admit. It was not religion or patriotism that kept them going, but the sense of communion with their fellows.

When Bob Edlin had been treated for his wounds he began a journey to rejoin his old unit. Along the way he saw a Ranger water trailer being filled. "The driver asked me why in hell I was going back. I asked him why he was. We could both just take off over the hill. He thought about it a little and said, 'Hell, the guys up there need this water.' That's why I went back."

Said tanker Dee Paris, "I never saw a man who wasn't frightened. And I've seen cowards. The difference is PRIDE! Two kinds of pride—your personal pride in your conduct and second, you won't want others to see you are a coward."

Bill Boyle noted, "When men live, eat, train, gripe, and suffer together, they stick together. These are men I loved and protected where I could. And when I was wounded, they did the same for me." They refused to "leave him out there." It was the sense of community, the camaraderie that was the single most cited motivation for remaining in the field. A foundation for this closeness lay in the widely accepted reasons for being under fire. There was little or no dissent, in contrast to the succeeding wars. Those engaged in World War II generally spent far more time together. Many units trained for years before they went overseas and unlike Korea and Vietnam, with the exception of aircrews in Europe, there was no "tour" to complete and then return home. Until wounded or killed, for three years, Marines went from island to island and GIs fought from North Africa to the heart of Germany. Sailors prowled the seas from the date "that will live in infamy" until V-J Day, so long as they survived torpedoes, shells, and kamikazes. More than fifty years later, the ties created by shared hardships and danger remain for a huge number of survivors, now banded into alumni organizations with regular reunions, newsletters, and lifetime friendships.

At the same time, it is also true that while World War II drew together individuals from disparate backgrounds and interests, some remained aloof from their fellows and once the common cause ended, so did their association. On the other hand, society's most brutal, murderous activity also witnessed occasions of courage, heroism, and even glory. But the supreme irony is that for all of its evil, perhaps even because of its very nature, the experience generated lifelong bonds among those who fought on land, sea, and in the air.

Roll Call

Adair, Marion. The 4th Infantry Division battalion surgeon resumed his medical practice in Georgia until retirement in 1990.

Alison, John. Air Corps lend-lease consultant, fighter pilot with the Fourteenth Air Force in the China-Burma Theater, an ace, he retired as a major general.

Allen, Brooke. Commander of the 5th Bomb Group at Hickam Field, Hawaii, on 7 December 1941, he supervised training of B-29 crews and retired in 1965 as a major general.

Allen, Terry. Commanding general of the 1st and 104th Infantry Divisions, he is deceased. His only son, who graduated from the U.S. Military Academy, was killed in Vietnam.

Altieri, James. An original Ranger, he has been active in the Rangers Association as well as the World War II Remembrance Society and makes his home in Corona Del Mar, California.

Andrusko, Ed. After thirty-three months of service, earning three Purple Hearts with the 1st Marine Division, he expressed no regrets for his experiences. "I saw our countrymen united against our enemies in a worldwide war. The men in my company were my family and friends, our senior NCOs were our parents. Item Company was my home on land or sea. We protected each other and fought for each other. After the war, I felt I could handle anything in the civilian world and took on all challenges, started college a day after my discharge. We returning veterans had pride in our accomplishments, love for our families, and ambition for our future. We assimilated into the civilian world with ease." After a career in electronics, he lives in Colorado.

Ashe, Walter. The pre-war-Navy sailor sailed on a number of ships in the Pacific theater, was aboard the first vessel to dock in Korea after the fighting began there, and in 1966 retired after thirty years of service. He lives in Asheville, North Carolina.

Ashworth, Frederick. "There's only two guys in the world who have had the experience of essentially being in tactical command of the delivery of an atom bomb in wartime, and I am one of them. You're supposed to get very emotional about it. How did it feel? I didn't feel anything in particular. I guess it is just like so many other experiences. While they are going on, you don't really feel much of anything except that this is a job that has to be done. When you get shot at, you're not scared right then. You are too busy doing what has to be done. You do get scared after it's all over." He retired as a vice admiral and lives in New Mexico.

Austin, Gordon. An Air Corps fighter pilot, hunting deer in the Hawaiian Islands at the time of the Japanese attack, he had graduated from West Point in 1936—"I don't remember choosing anything. My father [an architect and veteran of the Spanish-American War] sent me." He retired as a major general.

Austin, Paul. Following his stint as a company commander and battalion staff officer with the 24th Infantry Division, he worked for a telephone company until retirement. "I was sick to my stomach, of all those who'd been killed or got wounded. But that's the infantry story. You take the mud, the pain, do without food, do without water, and you keep fighting." He lives in Fort Worth.

Barron, Frank Jr. Following his role as a platoon leader and company commander with the 77th Division, he became an executive in the textile industry. He makes his home in Columbia, South Carolina.

Baum, Abe. The leader of the ill-fated task force that bore his name went into the garment industry after the war. He retired to southern California.

Behlmer, Bill. The antitank crewman with the 1st Division received a prosthesis for his amputated right leg and worked in the aircraft industry.

Bernheim, Eli. After combat in the Philippines with the 11th Airborne Division, he worked in the family business before re-entering the service to participate in the Korean War. He retired after more than twenty years to enter business and now lives in Florida.

Biddle, Melvin. The Medal of Honor awardee from the 517th Parachute Regimental Combat Team spent nearly thirty years as an employee of the Veterans Administration in his home state of Indiana.

Bluemel, Clifford. The commander of the 31st Philippine Division in 1941 survived captivity and retired as a major general. He is deceased.

Bolt, Jones E. A P-47 pilot, he recalled the depths of the Great Depression when a man with rags on his feet for shoes asked for a job and his father, a textile manufacturer, had none to offer. "Everybody elected the ROTC [at Clemson University] because we got something like twenty-five cents a day." As a prisoner of war he struggled through the infamous march from StalagLuft III to Moosburg and said, "We found out that Hitler had ordered all of us shot. Goering [Hermann, the Nazi *Luftwaffe* chief] refused to carry out the order." He retired as a major general.

Bouck, Lyle. He became a chiropractor in St. Louis.

Bower, William. The Doolittle Raid pilot who reached China and escaped capture remained in the Air Force until he retired as a colonel.

Boyle, Bill. Commander of the 1st Battalion of the 517th Parachute Regimental Combat Team, he recovered from his wounds in the Ardennes, and served in Korea before retirement. After a few years in security he went back to school, and opened a business in accountancy. "My first company commander after I graduated from West Point told me, 'You take care of the men and they will take care of you.' " He lives in Saratoga Springs, New York.

Buckley, Pete. A glider pilot for D day in Normandy, Market Garden in Holland, and Varsity across the Rhine, he studied commercial photography under the GI Bill. "I came home ten years older than I should have been and I had enough of flying." His home is in Connecticut.

Bulkeley, John D. The 1930 United States Naval Academy graduate awarded a Medal of Honor after he helped MacArthur leave the Philippines aboard a PT boat, later commanded torpedo boats during the Normandy invasion, and then finished the war aboard the cruiser *Houston*, reborn after the original ship was sunk by the Japanese. He died a vice admiral in 1998 after sixty-four years of active duty.

Burchinal, David. A B-29 test pilot and participant in

raids on Japan, he had worked in a factory and been a union leader after graduation from Brown University before the war. He remained in the Air Force, helping develop the Air University curriculum; held staff posts at upper echelons and retired as a general.

Caron, George. The tail gunner on the *Enola Gay* is deceased.

Carlton, Paul. After flying a number of B-29 missions against Japan from China and mining the Singapore Harbor as well as the enemy-controlled portions of the Yangtze River, Carlton piloted pathfinder planes from the Marianas. "We would fly upwind over the target precisely dropping our bombs. Then the follow-on force would come in and bomb on our fire, downwind. The survival rate upwind was kind of atrocious." On one such occasion, the headwind reduced the pathfinder's speed to only eighty knots; ten out of the twelve in the operation went down. The upwind approach was abandoned. He retired as a general after running the Military Airlift Command.

Carmichael, Richard. He was a 1936 graduate of the U.S. Military Academy, after joining the Texas National Guard at age fifteen. Interviewed in 1942 about a number of subjects including morale, he remarked, "The two main topics, except at the dinner table, were bombing and women. I personally believe that if there were some form of controlled prostitution around an Army camp, it would be the best solution . . . it would control the venereal rate and keep the combat crews a hell of a lot happier." He noted that as a prisoner it struck him that the Japanese "were going to fight to the bitter end . . . the military . . . and the populace went along with whatever the military decided. They put us to work digging tunnels, caves actually, inside of hills not far from where our gardens were. We presumed that this was part of their last-ditch defense system." He left the service as a major general.

Carpenter, John. As a 1939 graduate of the USMA, he transferred from the field artillery to USAF, which brought him to the 19th Bomb Group in the Philippines in 1941. After he reached Australia, Carpenter flew missions in the Pacific, and following V-J Day held various staff posts before retiring as a lieutenant general. He lives in North Carolina.

Carter, Norval. The 29th Infantry Division battalion surgeon KIA in Normandy left a widow and two sons. Upon the death of Emma Ferne Lowry Carter in 1995, their son Walter discovered several caches of correspondence between her and his father. Walter Carter researched the experiences of his father and discovered in my book *June 6, 1944: The Voices of D-Day* an excerpt from Frank Wawrynovic's account that mentioned the circumstances of his father's death. Walter Carter wrote to me and very kindly allowed me to make use of portions of the collected letters of Norval Carter.

Chism, John. The medic with the 517th Parachute Regimental Combat Team left the service to attend college, where he earned a reserve commission and went on active duty as a field artillery commander during the Korean War. He remained in the Army until retirement as a colonel.

Cochran, Philip. After he completed his tour as joint leader of the 1st Air Commando unit in the Far East, he trained pilots until the war's end. Physical disabilities forced him to retire in 1947 with the rank of colonel. He provided technical expertise to Hollywood filmmakers before entering business in Pennsylvania. He died in 1979.

Conver, Milt. The bombardier with the 303d Bomb Group coped with respiratory infections that limited his missions with the Eighth Air Force. After V-E Day he left the service, entered business in Ohio. He is deceased.

Creel, Buckner. A platoon leader with the 77th Division on Guam and in the Philippines, he commanded a company on Okinawa. He fought in Korea, where he was wounded, and then in Vietnam before retirement. He lives in Arlington, Virginia.

Cutter, Slade. The former submariner and 1935 USNA graduate retired as a captain and lives in Annapolis.

Darby, William O. After the disaster at Cisterna that destroyed three of his battalions, the founder of the Rangers, who previously refused offers to lead regiments, took over the 179th Regiment of the 45th Division at Anzio. Subsequently named assistant commander of the 10th Mountain Division, he was killed by German artillery fire, two days before the enemy forces in Italy surrendered.

Davison, Michael. A USMC graduate, the former staff officer and battalion commander with the 45th Division earned a graduate degree at Harvard, commanded troops in Vietnam, and headed the army units in Europe before retirement as a general. He lives in Virginia.

Dawson, Frank (Buck). The 5th Ranger Battalion lieutenant who led pinned-down troops off Omaha Beach on D day entered the reserves following V-E Day, but when recalled for the Korean War elected the service as a career, which culminated in 1968 after a tour in Vietnam. He is deceased.

DeHaven, Robert. The USAF ace with fourteen victories retired as a colonel and lives in southern California.

DeLoach, James. The 32d Division company officer chose to enter local government after the war and lives in Columbia, South Carolina.

Duckworth, George. The 2d Infantry Division officer

stayed in uniform, retiring as a colonel, and lives in New Mexico.

Dunfee, Bill. The 82d Airborne trooper worked for a lumber business in Columbus, Ohio, and became a top executive with the organization.

Dunn, Bill. The Air Force fighter pilot began his World War II experience as an infantryman with the Canadian Seaforth Highlanders. After V-J Day he advised in China, Iran, and South America during the 1950s before he put in his papers.

Edlin, Bob. The 2d Ranger Battalion platoon leader in Normandy, the Cotentin Peninsula, and in the grim winter on the German border held the job of a police chief in Indiana before moving to Corpus Christi, Texas, where he operates an antique auction house.

Eller, Ernest. A USNA 1925 graduate and a gunnery officer aboard the *Lexington* at the Battle of Midway, he retired as a captain. He is deceased.

Ellis, Richard. A B-25 pilot in the South Pacific who had been drafted in 1940 before enrolling in flight training, he completed 200 missions. He left the service to practice law, but when called up for Korea he stayed on until retirement as a general.

Emmens, Robert. After the war, the Doolittle Raid pilot who spent two years as a "guest of the Kremlin" served as a military attaché and in intelligence for the Air Force before retirement as a colonel.

Engeman, Len. The 9th Armored Division tank battalion commander who directed the capture of the vital bridge at Remagen remained in the Army until retirement as a colonel. He lives in California.

Erwin, Henry. The Air Corps crewman badly burned by

an incendiary and who received a Medal of Honor is deceased.

Eubank, Eugene. The commander of the B-17 19th Bomb Group in the Philippines on 7 December 1941, he earned Army wings almost thirty years earlier. He recalled that when Boeing produced the first Flying Fortress he and his associates immediately recognized it was far superior to any competitor's wares. However, while the prototype was being tested in 1935 at Wright Field, Ohio, the plane crashed. "We damned near sat down and cried when the first one was wrecked. In those days the manufacturer had to submit an article [a plane] that was tested, evaluated, and the board decided which one was going to win. If it hadn't been for that accident, Boeing would have won the competition and we would have had the B-17 two or three years ahead of what we did." He retired as a major general.

Evans, Bing. An original Ranger who was Darby's sergeant major, he received a commission before being captured at Cisterna. He noted that his experiences as a POW so scarred him that throughout his life he was subject to "black rages." He worked in private industry and now lives in Huntington, Indiana.

Gage, Tom. The Air Corps clerk captured on Bataan acts as a clearinghouse for information about prisoners of war from that period and lives in Tulsa, Oklahoma.

Gangel, Dick. The P-38 pilot came home from the Fifteenth Air Force in Italy to teach other flyers. After his honorable discharge he became an art director, first in advertising and then for *Sports Illustrated.* He lives in Weston, Connecticut, where he creates sculptures.

Gilliam, Tom. As an officer with the 2d Division, he recovered from wounds after a three-month hospital stay in time to participate in the final drives against the Germans.

After the enemy repulsed the unit in a brutal confrontation in the vicinity of Eisenschmitt, Gilliam noted to his superior that for the third time he had wound up the senior company commander in the battalion. He added that the only other officer of that responsibility who was left from their arrival in France on 9 July was home on a forty-five-days leave. Told he was regarded as the best in the division, Gilliam said he replied, " 'Colonel, I am going to be a dead company commander if this keeps up.' We retook the town the next day, but we lost 117 men up there that night. Less than three weeks later I was on orders to return home for a forty-five-day leave. But that three weeks included the second crossing of the Moselle, the closing of the Trier pocket, the crossing of the Rhine at Oppenheim, the capture of Frankfurt am Main, and the memorial service for President Roosevelt aboard ship." He lives in Lakeport, California.

Goode, John. The 36th Division officer shattered by the Rapido River experience is deceased.

Hartman, Tom. The Navy pilot recalled that while a student at Princeton, in his enthusiastic rush to enlist after the college requirements were lowered, his physical exam revealed possible problems with one eye. He was instructed to return for a second test. "A Navy corpsman was to be the examiner. His first question was, 'Are you another college boy?' I thought that I should drop through the floor. Princeton was like the kiss of death in that milieu. But I admitted my status. He said, 'Princeton! That's great.' He told me he had worked as an usher at the Chicago Opera House and the only company passing through that invited the ushers to their cast parties was the Triangle Club [the university's drama group]! He was so excited that he never gave my eye a look and signed my clearance." Hartman returned to his alma mater to complete his education and then taught at Rutgers. He lives in Princeton, New Jersey.

Hayes, Tommy. The Army fighter pilot who fought in both the Pacific and Europe retired as a colonel and lives in Pennsylvania.

Herder, Harry. The 2d Ranger Battalion replacement participated in the liberation of the Buchenwald concentration camp. "We were the last replacements taken into the battalion. Barely in my memory is the first job [that] rumor said we were scheduled to do. They were going to put us, a company at a time, in Piper Cubs and fly us over the Rhine. That was washed out when the Remagen Bridge stood. I remember a ballistic company commander. Being nearsighted made me less than perfect and unfit to be a Ranger. The way that man was mad at me was something else. With him, I did not belong. In 1947 I was accepted in jump school and allowed to be a member of the 82d Airborne for three years and they knew I wore glasses the whole time. Even jumped with them taped on once they found out. The helmet jammed them into my nose on 'opening shock.' They remained in my shirt pocket all the rest of the jumps."

Herder on his third military hitch joined the Navy and served as a corpsman for the Marines in Korea. He lives in Hayward, Wisconsin.

Hill, David (Tex). The former Navy flyer who enlisted in the American Volunteer Group under Gen. Clare Chennault retired as a colonel and is a resident of San Antonio.

Hite, Robert L. The last-minute addition to the Doolittle Raiders, who endured years of captivity, remained in the service after his liberation and worked as an air attaché in North Africa. He retired as a lieutenant colonel.

Hofrichter, Joe. The rifleman from the 24th Division entered a family construction business and makes his home in Port Charlotte, Florida.

Hostetter, Philip. The battalion surgeon with the 24th Division, after mustering out, opened a practice in family medicine and lives in Manhattan, Kansas.

Howze, Hamilton. The 1930 West Point alumnus who spent World War II with armored forces in North Africa and Italy switched to airborne in the 1950s to command the 82d Airborne Division and the Eighteenth Airborne Corps. He retired as a full general in 1965 and died in 1998.

Jackson, Schuyler. The 101st Airborne paratrooper worked in construction until his death in 1995.

Johnson, Fred. The former National Guardsman called up in 1940 and who fought with the 32d Division in the Pacific said, "I approved of what we did in the war then and still do. There was a sense of duty; you were scared, heck yes. But you just did what you thought you had to do. There was pride in not letting the others down. To bug out would make you ashamed. The worst food was in Buna, bully beef, and small rations, two spoons a day. I came home with malaria, having had three separate attacks." After his discharge he became a Superior, Wisconsin, policeman and then was elected sheriff ten times before retirement. He lives in Arizona.

Johnson, Leon. He was in the class of 1926 at the USMA. He led the 44th Bomb Group on the Ploesti raid, where he earned a Medal of Honor and then commanded a bomber wing with the Eighth Air Force in England. He retired in 1961 as a general and died in 1998.

Johnson, Robert. The ground crew sergeant who volunteered for the 4th Armored Division was convicted of a 1971 murder and is serving a life term in North Carolina.

Johnson, Robert. The fighter pilot with the second highest number of planes shot down in Europe worked in the aircraft industry after the war. He died in 1998.

Jones, David M. The Doolittle Raider who parachuted into China then returned to duty was subsequently shot down in a B-26 during a raid on Bizerte. He became a prisoner of war in Germany. Following liberation he held positions in the Pentagon, with NASA, and other research projects. He retired as a major general.

Jones, Harry. The Navy pilot who helped sink the *Yamato* remarked, "I think it was a good idea to drop the atomic bomb because I think the invasion would have killed millions of Japanese. War is hell; stay the hell out of it. We had no business in Vietnam; in my opinion we should stay the hell out of Bosnia. They should have some sort of international police there." He became an FBI agent and now lives in Carlisle, Pennsylvania.

Jones, Homer. After the war ended, the paratroop platoon leader left the service but was recalled for the war in Korea. He remained on active duty until retirement and then taught Spanish in public schools. He lives in Florida.

Kelly, Walter. The Eighth Air Force pilot who flew the first B-17 raid on occupied Europe later flew missions against the Japanese in the Pacific. He continued his career in the Air Force after the end of hostilities and retired as a colonel. He worked in private industry before retiring to a home in Alexandria, Virginia.

Kidwell, Vance. The draftee from Illinois who became a replacement in a supply section of the 2d Armored Division while the outfit was in North Africa was with the outfit when it reached France on D plus 1. He lives in Donnellson, Illinois.

Kitzmann, Erich. The *Suwannee* crewman blown overboard after a Kamikaze explosion worked in aircraft maintenance until he retired to Sedona, Arizona.

Kunz, William J. The former 3d Infantry Division field artillery hand who campaigned through North Africa, Sicily, Italy, Anzio, southern France, and Germany lives in Illinois.

Loiacano, Leonard. An artilleryman, he said, "When the gun was fired it made so much noise that you had to keep your mouth open and if your hands were free you put them in your ears. We would be wet to the skin, cold and in total darkness. Most of the time we got six hours of sleep every other night. One time we went sixty hours without sleep. We were never relieved and always firing for somebody. We dug gun pits and cut down trees [to brace the artillery and cover foxholes] from Normandy to Czechoslovakia." The 105mm howitzer crewman with the 5th Infantry Division had amassed enough points to warrant discharge shortly after V-E Day. "When we were home, the two 'A' bombs were dropped and the war was over. Many years later the bleeding hearts would say what a terrible thing it was to drop the bomb. For all of those people I wish them ten months of combat and then let us hear what they have to say." He makes his home in Yeadon, Pennsylvania.

Lomell, Len (Bud). The Ranger sergeant involved in the destruction of enemy big guns atop Pointe du Hoc on D day received a battlefield commission before being wounded a second time. He studied law under the GI Bill and practiced in New Jersey where he makes his home.

Long, Stanley. The first P-38 pilot to shoot down a Japanese plane in the Aleutians, he remained in the Air Force, retiring as a colonel.

Low, Martin. The fighter pilot, who was at Hickam Field on 7 December 1941 and over the Normandy beaches on 6 June 1944, came home after seventy-five missions in Europe. "I had seen enough of the Army in peacetime to know that it was not for me. I applied to the airlines but they did not think fighter pilots had the right stuff. Because of my experience of war I took up the cause of the United Nations, which I believe is a much more viable method of settling differences." As a civilian he produced commercials for TV and lives in a suburb of New York City.

Lynd, J. Q. The 90th Division platoon leader recovered from his wounds and became a research scientist and teacher at Oklahoma State University in Stillwater, Oklahoma.

Mabry, George L. Jr. The 4th Division officer finally received a regular army commission in 1944 and by the time the war ended he was the second most decorated soldier of the conflict. He subsequently graduated from the Command and General Staff College, the National War College, and held a variety of command, training, and staff positions. He led a 100-man team of officers and civilians to evaluate operations in Vietnam and later served as chief of staff and assistant deputy commanding general for the U.S. Army Forces in Vietnam. In 1975 he retired as a major general and lived in Columbia, South Carolina, until his death in 1990.

McCubbin, James. The fighter pilot now lives in Garberville, California.

Meltessen, Clarence. The 4th Ranger Battalion lieutenant captured at Cisterna survived more than a year in the stalags. He remained on active duty after the war, retiring as a colonel. He has compiled an exhaustive record of what happened to his fellow Rangers and their experiences in the prisoner-of-war camps. He lives in California.

Merrill, Alan. The 2d Battalion Ranger wounded and temporarily captured near Anzio recovered in a Naples hospital. During his recuperation he met a captain who offered to wangle a transfer to the Air Corps, enabling Merrill to serve out his time as a limited-duty, noncombat soldier. Assigned to the 379th Bomb Group, a B-25 outfit, he learned aircraft recognition while assisting in tow-target practice. He even went along on missions that dumped aluminum foil to foul up enemy radar. But when a batch of replacement gunners failed to arrive, Merrill was pressed into service as a tail gunner beginning in October 1944. He flew twenty-four missions, occupying various positions manning a .50-caliber machine gun. Flak ripped into his airplanes on several occasions, killing other members of the crew, and he survived a crash landing in the sea near Corsica. Blackouts, bleeding from his left ear and nose on his last missions grounded him after his twenty-fourth. He waited several months before orders finally sent him home via Casablanca, where he said he visited bordellos supervised by the U.S. Army with military police on duty.

"I went away a frightened boy. I returned a frightened man. The actual battle of enduring a war in the various types of combat that I participated in was not as riveting an experience as the battles my mind fought daily in the ensuing peaceful years. When the actual fighting was done I had to conquer my own personal, mental war of nerves. I found out much later that I had no control over what happened to the unprepared, mindless, loose ends of my young manhood and the residue of the code of killing or being killed. I don't believe I ever really adjusted to this code of the military survivor. Everything I was taught to do to survive was diametrically opposed to a way of life I had been raised to believe in for eighteen years.

"How does one go about 'unlearning' to kill another human being? This unlearning process comes ever so slowly or it never comes at all. It is your own individual struggle.

No one can do it for you. If this cannot be done, then peace of mind eludes you all your days. In my half century, since World War II and with my battles over, I truly believe that war is like a malignant tumor on the face of mankind." He now lives in Florida.

Mott, Hugh. The platoon leader who helped preserve the Remagen Bridge over the Rhine went into politics and in 1949 was elected to the Tennessee State Legislature while remaining active in the National Guard. He retired from the Guard as a major general in 1972.

Mueller, Arndt. The 6th Infantry Division battalion commander attended the Command and General Staff College and eventually joined its faculty. He headed the ROTC program at the University of Miami, earned a law degree, and joined the Florida bar.

Newman, Stan. The P-51 pilot assigned to the Fifteenth Air Force in Italy redeployed to the States after V-E Day in preparation for the finale against Japan. "I changed my mind about a regular air force career, took a reserve commission, and made it back to start my interrupted college at the University of Illinois. I was one of the first vets back and was like a fish out of water. I really missed the Air Corps life, good pay, great airplanes, and wonderful friends. But I eventually adapted." As a reserve officer, however, he was recalled during the Korean War and flew 100 missions in that conflict. During the war in Vietnam he flew cargo missions to Southeast Asia. He retired in 1983 as a major general and lives in Oklahoma.

Northrup, Jay. The replacement officer with the Rangers had been reassigned, but a bout of malaria contracted in Sicily sent him back to the States. After he left the service he entered the field of banking before retirement to Florida.

Odell, Bill. The Eighth Air Force pilot involved in the organization's first raid moved first to North Africa and then the Pacific. After he retired as a colonel he embarked on a career as a writer publishing many novels in the mystery, adventure, and Western genres. He lives in Colorado Springs.

Olson, John E. After liberation from his Philippine prison camp, the 1939 USMA graduate remained in uniform until retirement as a colonel in 1967. He has done extensive research and writing on the Bataan fighting, the Death March, and Philippine guerrilla movements. He lives in Houston, Texas.

Paris, Dee. The 9th Armored Division tank commander retained a reserve commission after the war and made barbershop quartet music his avocation while living in Maryland.

Poston, Tom. The troop carrier pilot chose the life of an actor after being mustered out. He appeared on Broadway, and in numerous roles on radio and then television. He lives in California.

Raaen, John C. Jr. One of the few West Pointers (class of 1943) to volunteer for the Rangers, his jeep accident in France ended World War II for him. In 1951 he earned a master's degree from Johns Hopkins and then held command posts with various units before retirement as a major general. He lives in Florida.

Raila, Frank. The 106th Division soldier taken prisoner in the Ardennes became a radiologist in Mississippi. The emotional outbursts, triggered by his memories of the stalag that disturbed him in the years immediately after the war, subsided.

Rants, Hanford. The wireman with the 24th Infantry Division, which fought in the Pacific theater, used the GI Bill to complete his education at Washington State University, then taught in high school before becoming a principal. He lives in Downey, California.

Robison, Noel (Eugene). As a replacement, he joined the 90th Division in November 1944, where he served as a runner until his frozen feet disabled him during the Battle of the Bulge. He lives in Claremont, California.

Rosson, William. The officer with the 3d Infantry Division, as an honor student in the ROTC program at the University of Oregon in 1940, had obtained a regular army commission. His senior captain instructed a first sergeant, "I want you to make an officer of Lieutenant Rosson." Rosson says, "The training was rather rudimentary and simply wouldn't be accepted today. It was a peacetime oriented affair with more emphasis upon spit and polish, cleanliness of barracks and whatnot rather than combat readiness. I never attended the basic course of the infantry school. I went into the war and learned on the job."

When he visited the Dachau concentration camp after its liberation, he recalled, "I was shaken—so much so that when I left I was literally unable to speak as I drove back to the division. I had never seen such depravity and inhuman treatment." Following his service in Italy and France, Rosson qualified for airborne, was involved in the Vietnam conflict before his retirement in 1975 as a general, and resides in Florida.

Ruhlen, George. The commander of the 3d Field Artillery attached to the 9th Armored Division, a 1932 graduate of the USMA, retired on a disability in 1970 as a major general. He lives in San Antonio.

Salomon, Sid. The Ranger captain who captured Pointe et Raz de la Percée at Omaha Beach entered the paper products field after the war. He makes his home in Pennsylvania.

Salter, Cary. The P-47 and P-51 fighter pilot in the Ninth

Air Force said, "We were shooting down planes but we knew we were killing people, too. I don't know any of our guys who lost sleep over it. We were there to fight a war and the more we killed, the quicker it would be over and the less likely we would be killed." He became a pharmacist, then presided over a wholesale drug firm. Active in the P-40 Warhawk Pilots Association, he resides in Jackson, Mississippi.

Schueler, Jon. The B-17 navigator, invalided home for physical and emotional disabilities, became a well-known painter. His autobiography, *The Sound of Sleat,* was published posthumously in 1999.

Schwarz, Otto. A prisoner of war after the sinking of the USS *Houston*, he endured years of hard labor, beatings, and lack of food in a series of camps. "We were under strict orders that, whenever a Japanese of any rank approached us, the first person seeing him had to shout in good Japanese and call the group to attention. You then all had to properly bow to the person. You had to bow from the hips down with the face tilting up and facing the person. If you deviated from this at all, you very quickly got bashed."

Schwarz recalled that the British captives treated the problem of sanitation far more casually than the Americans and as a consequence suffered a much greater incidence of dysentery. However, they insisted upon maintaining a military mode. "These guys acted as if they were on regimental maneuvers. The British held regular drills—complete uniforms, full field packs—and they would march up and down the hills, and the officers with their little 'dog-chasers,' the little sticks they carried, would be marching alongside of them." The Americans in shorts and ragged garments refused to salute and an intense dislike grew between the two allies.

Shipped to Burma, Schwarz became part of the gangs constructing a railroad much like that described in the film *The Bridge on the River Kwai*. Along with the prisoners, the Japanese conscripted thousands of local people who, said Schwarz, "died like flies. Entire villages, the entire male populations of villages were just wiped out."

Toward the end of the war, while housed in Saigon, Schwarz and three companions escaped and sought refuge in the French quarter of the city, only to be caught up in the Vietnamese effort to oust the French. Jailed by the rebels along with the French, Schwarz convinced his captors that he was an American and was allowed to return to the Japanese prison camp. A U.S. Army officer parachuted in to the camp and officially freed all of the POWs.

"My service in the Navy and World War II were years of great pride and dedication to America. I have been in the presence of men who have cried openly when hearing our National Anthem, which was picked up by a Japanese radio in Saigon. These were the kinds of men I was privileged to serve with. Despite our disadvantage of being ill prepared, outnumbered, and outgunned at the beginning of World War II, and the horrendous ordeal of three and one-half years as Japanese POWs, we never wavered in our loyalty and faith in our country."

In 1948, Schwarz entered the U.S. Postal Service and on retirement in 1980 held a senior management position. He lives in Union, New Jersey.

Shapiro, Alan. After leaving the service, the 87th Division rifleman taught school and now lives in Ridgefield, Connecticut.

Sims, Ed. The paratrooper officer with the 504th Regiment went on inactive reserve after being demobilized, but said, "I returned to active duty because good employment was hard to find and I was more oriented toward military life." He retired as a colonel in 1968, then earned a college degree and held jobs with a title company and, later, as a county probation officer. He lives in New Jersey.

Smith, Robert. The Air Force B-26 pilot in the South Pacific became intelligence director of the Strategic Air Command during the 1950s, where he pioneered in the use of computers for dealing with intelligence. He retired as a lieutenant general.

South, Frank. "The death of FDR [12 April 1945] came as a shock. There was not a dry eye that could be found. I recall leaning against a tree and bawling like an infant." After V-E Day, South's unit became part of Patton's Third Army. For a review before himself and some Soviet officers, Patton ordered clean, pressed uniforms and polished boots, which South considered reasonable. Further instruction to coat helmets with shellac and all arms and vehicles oiled on the surfaces to provide a shine struck the Ranger as foolish because of the prevalence of road dust. "Most of us had long regarded Patton as a bloody popinjay whose exhibitionist streak was witnessed by his dress and pearl-handled revolvers." The medic with the 2d Ranger Battalion used his benefits to study biophysics and physiology. He lives in Maryland.

Southworth, Billy. The B-17 pilot completed his tour in the United Kingdom but was killed on a training flight in 1945.

Stroop, Paul D. A USNA 1926 alumnus, he retired as a vice admiral and died in 1995.

Strange, Glen. The 27th Armored Infantry officer required two years of medical treatment for his wounds before he recovered enough to work in manufacturing. He later became a postmaster in Oklahoma.

Swanson, Wallace. The 101st Airborne company commander worked in the petroleum industry and lives in Alabama.

Taylor, Harold. The 3d Division GI joined the Fort Wayne police department, put in twenty years, and then operated a part-time cabinet-making shop.

Thach, John (Jimmy). The naval aviator says, "Everybody's scared, but it isn't a thing you can let prey on your mind very long because there's always something to do. And you can function just as well, maybe a little better, if you're scared." He retired as a full admiral and died in 1981.

Turner, William (Pappy). The army pilot said, "I did not shoot at anyone in a parachute although I had several chances. I figured he had his problems. Also on the ground he could be captured, some information gained. On one occasion, one of the pilots asked me for permission to strafe the Jap in the parachute. I told him to let his conscience be his guide. He broke off, made a pass at the man, but did not shoot." After the war he worked briefly in private industry before signing on with the New York State Department of Public Works and switched to the Department of Transportation. He now lives in Florida.

Ullom, Madeline. The former army nurse, taken prisoner in the Philippines, now lives in Tucson.

Ulsaker, Carl. The USMA 1942 graduate finished the war with the 95th Division. He collected a master's degree and then taught English at West Point. He retired as a colonel in 1969 and resides in Virginia.

Uzemack, Ed. The 28th Division POW returned to a career as a newspaperman and then entered public relations in Chicago.

Vaccaro, Tony. Born in the United States to Italian émigrés, the 83d Division intelligence specialist had lived in

Italy for much of his childhood and early adolescence where he developed an abiding hatred of the fascist philosophy. After V-E Day he signed on as a photographer for the military newspaper *Stars and Stripes*, and then as a civilian remained in Europe several more years building a reputation for his photographs. Back in the States he worked on staff for *Look* and the short-lived but influential *Flair* before a long successful career as a freelancer. He lives in New York City.

Vogel, Walter. The 1937 enlistee in the Navy started his career in the Asiatic Fleet and served on the ill-fated *Houston* in the first months after the war began. Having survived the sinking of the destroyer *Blue* and other adventures, he was promoted to the rank of chief petty officer and assigned to the destroyer *Hyman* engaged in picket duty off Okinawa. The kamikaze hit on the *Hyman* brought a third Purple Heart to Vogel, but the full extent of his wounds only surfaced several months after V-J Day when he collapsed with ruptured lungs, apparently due to the explosion off Okinawa. He recovered after four months of hospitalization and served on a number of ships including support for the war in Korea. He taught at the USNA as well as other institutions and became a commissioned officer. He weathered an attack of blindness before retirement in 1970. He lives in Tennessee.

Walker, Anthony. The Yale graduate and Marine officer remained in the Corps. "I suppose I decided to stay on because I liked the life, was reasonably successful in the war and had nothing else to do, not being qualified or interested in other professions or business." His three sons all became leathernecks. He makes his home in Rhode Island.

Warneke, Bud. The paratrooper with the 508th Parachute Regimental Combat Team won a battlefield commission and remained in the service until 1964 when he retired and began a TV rental service. He lives in North Carolina.

Warriner, Vic. The glider pilot involved in the D day invasion, and the Market Garden and Varsity operations, completed his education at the University of Michigan and became a real estate developer in Texas. He lives in Fort Worth.

Widoff, Gerald. The interpreter with Merrill's Marauders began a career as a violinist with prominent orchestras before starting a chain of music record stores. His home is in New York City.

Yarborough, William. The USMA Class of 1936 paratrooper officer, following World War II, held top staff positions at home and abroad until his retirement in 1971 as a lieutenant general. He lives in North Carolina.

Bibliography

Adair, Charles. Oral History. Annapolis, Maryland: United States Naval Institute.

Alexander, Irvin. *Memoirs of Internment in the Philippines, 1942–45.* West Point: U.S. Military Academy.

Alison, John R. Oral Histories. Maxwell Field, Alabama: United States Air Force Historical Center, 1943, 1944, 1960, 1977, 1979.

Allen, Brooke E. Oral History. Maxwell Field, Alabama: United States Air Force Historical Center, 1965.

Altieri, James. *The Spearheaders.* Indianapolis: Bobbs-Merrill Company, Inc., 1960.

Ambrose, Stephen E. *Citizen Soldiers.* New York: Simon & Schuster, 1997.

Andrusko, Edward. Unpublished Stories. Denver, Colo.

Archer, Clark, ed. *Paratroopers' Odyssey.* Hudson, Florida: 517th Parachute Regimental Combat Team Association, 1985.

Ashworth, Frederick. Oral History. Annapolis, Maryland: United States Naval Institute.

Austin, Gordon H. Oral History. Maxwell Field, Alabama: United States Air Force Historical Center, 1982.

Benitez, R. C. *Battle Stations Submerged.* Annapolis, Maryland: *Proceedings*, January 1948.

Bidwell, Sheffield. *The Chindit War.* New York: Macmillan Publishing Co., Inc., 1979.

Blair, Clay. *Ridgway's Paratroopers.* Garden City, New York: Dial Press, 1985.

Bluemel, Clifford. Private Papers. West Point: U.S. Military Academy Library.

Blumenson, Martin. *Mark Clark.* New York: Congdon & Weed, 1984.

Bolt, Jones E. Oral History. Maxwell Field, Alabama: United States Air Force Historical Center, 1984.

Bower, William. Oral History. Maxwell Field, Alabama: United States Air Force Historical Center, 1971.

Bradley, Omar. *A Soldier's Story.* New York: Henry Holt and Company, Inc., 1951.

Breuer, William. *Geronimo!* New York: St. Martin's Press, 1989.

Budge, Joseph. Unpublished Memoir. Moraga, California.

Buffington, Herman. Unpublished Memoir. Jefferson, Georgia.

Bunker, Paul D. *The Bunker Diary.* West Point: U.S. Military Academy Library.

Burchinal, David A. Oral History. Maxwell Field, Alabama: United States Air Force Historical Center, 1975.

Byers, Dick. Unpublished Memoir. Mentor-on-the Lake, Ohio.

Carlton, Paul K. Oral History. Maxwell Field, Alabama: United States Air Force Historical Center, 1979.

Carmichael, Richard. Oral Histories. Maxwell Field, Alabama: United States Air Force Historical Center, 1942, 1980.

Caron, George R. Oral History. Maxwell Field, Alabama: United States Air Force Historical Center, 1975.

Carpenter, John W. Oral History. Maxwell Field, Alabama: United States Air Force Historical Center, 1970.

Cass, Bevan, ed. *History of the 6th Marine Division.* Washington, D.C.: Infantry Journal, Inc., 1948.

Chandler, P. R. Oral History. Maxwell Field, Alabama: United States Air Force Historical Center, 1943.

Chernitsky, Dorothy. *Voices from the Foxholes.* Uniontown, Pennsylvania: Dorothy Chernitsky, 1991.

Cochran, Philip. Oral Histories. Maxwell Field, Alabama: United States Air Force Historical Center, 1943, 1975.

Cole, Hugh M. *The Ardennes: The Battle of the Bulge.* Washington, D.C.: Center of Military History, U.S. Army, 1965.

Cox, Luther C. *Always Fighting the Enemy.* Baltimore: Gateway, 1990.

Craig, Robert. Unpublished Memoir. Winter Haven, Florida.

Craven, Wesley Frank, and James Lea Cate. *The Army Air Force in World War II.* Vol. 1: vi. Chicago: U.S. Air Force History Office, University of Chicago Press, 1948.

Crosby, Harry H. *A Wing and a Prayer.* New York: Harper, 1993.

Cutter, Slade. Oral History. Annapolis, Maryland: United States Naval Institute.

Dacus, W. E. and E. Kitzmann. *As We Lived It*—USS *Suwannee (CVE-27).* USS *Suwannee* and its Air Groups, 27, 60, & 40. Reunion Association, 1992.

DeHaven, Robert M. Oral History. Maxwell Field, Alabama: United States Air Force Historical Center, 1977.

Dennison, Robert Lee. Oral History. Annapolis, Maryland: United States Naval Institute.

D'Este, Carlo. *Patton: A Genius for War.* New York: HarperCollins, 1995.

Duckworth, George H. Unpublished memoir. Farmington, New Mexico.

Dunn, William. Oral History. Maxwell Field, Alabama: United States Air Force Historical Center, 1973.

Edlin, Robert. Unpublished Manuscript. Corpus Christi, Texas.

Edmonds, Walter D. *They Fought with What They Had.* Washington, D.C.: Center for Air Force History, 1951.

Eisenhower, David. *Eisenhower at War 1943–45.* New York: Random House, 1986.

Eisenhower, Dwight D. *Crusade in Europe.* Garden City, New York: Doubleday & Company, Inc., 1948.

Eisenhower, John. *The Bitter Woods: The Battle of the Bulge.* New York: G.P. Putnam's Sons, 1969.

Ellington, Paul. Oral History. American Air Power Heritage Museum, Midland, Texas, 1991.

Ellis, John. *Cassino: The Hollow Victory.* New York: McGraw-Hill Book Company, 1984.

Ellis, Richard. Oral History. Maxwell Field, Alabama: United States Air Force Historical Center, 1987.

Emmens, Robert G. Oral History. Maxwell Field, Alabama: United States Air Force Historical Center, 1982.

Eubank, Eugene. Oral Histories. Maxwell Field, Alabama: United States Air Force Historical Center, 1942, 1982.

Fitzgerald, Ed. *A Penny an Inch.* New York: Atheneum, 1985.

Frank, Richard B. *Guadalcanal.* New York: Random House, 1990.

Freeman, Roger A., with Alan Crouchman and Vic Maslen.

The Mighty Eighth War Diary. London: Motorbooks International, 1990.

Gavin, James M. *On to Berlin.* New York: Viking Press, 1978.

Gelb, Norman. *Desperate Venture: The Story of Operation Torch.* New York: William Morrow and Company, 1992.

Gerevas, Larry. Unpublished Memoir. Napa, California.

Golubock, Ralph. *Hello, Pathway: A Bomber Pilot's Memories of Love and War.* Unpublished Manuscript. St. Louis.

Goodson, James. Oral History. American Air Power Heritage Museum, Midland, Texas, 1991.

Grashio, Samuel C., and Bernard Norling. *Return to Freedom.* Spokane, Washington: University Press, 1982

Hagerman, Bart., ed. *U.S. Airborne: 50th Anniversary.* Paducah, Kentucky: Turner Publishing Company, 1990.

Hall, Leonard G. *Brother of the Fox: Company F, 172d Infantry.* Orange, Texas, 1985.

Hallden, Charles. Unpublished Memoir. Madeira Beach, Florida.

Hamilton, Tom. Unpublished Memoir. Santa Barbara, California.

Hammel, Eric. *Guadalcanal: Starvation Island.* New York, Crown, 1987.

———*Munda Trail.* New York: Orion Books, 1989.

Hannon, Philip. Unpublished Memoir. Ellicott City, Maryland.

Hanson, Robert. *Memoirs.* Unpublished manuscript.

Harmon, Ernest. Oral History. Carlisle, Pennsylvania: United States Army History Institute.

Harrington, Jasper. Oral History. Maxwell Field, Alabama: United States Air Force Historical Center, 1981.

Hastings, Max. *Overlord: D-Day and the Battle for Normandy.* New York: Simon & Schuster, 1984.

Hawkins, Ian L. *B-17s Over Berlin.* Washington, D.C.: Brassey's, 1990.

Hechler, Ken. *The Bridge at Remagen.* Missoula, Montana: Pictorial Histories Publishing Company, 1993.

Heinl, Robert Debs Jr. *Soldiers of the Sea.* Annapolis: Naval Institute Press, 1962.

Herder, Harry J. Unpublished Memoir. Hayward, Wisconsin.

Hill, David (Tex). Oral History. Maxwell Field, Alabama: United States Air Force Historical Center, 1977.

Holloway, Bruce K. Oral History. Maxwell Field, Alabama: United States Air Force Historical Center, 1977.

Holloway, James L. III. *Historical Perspective: The Battle of Surigao Strait.* Naval Engineer's Journal, September 1994.

Hostetter, Philip H. *Doctor and Soldier in the South Pacific.* Unpublished Manuscript. Manhattan, Kansas.

Howard, Thomas. *All to This End: The Road to and through the Philippines.* Unpublished Manuscript. St. Charles, Missouri.

Howze, Hamilton. Oral History. Carlisle, Pennsylvania: United States Army Military History Institute.

Hoyt, Edwin P. *Submarines at War.* Briarcliff Manor, New York: Stein and Day, 1983.

Hudson, Ed. *The History of the USS Cabot (CVL-28).* Hickory, North Carolina, 1988.

Jackson, Robert. *War Stories.* Unpublished Memoir. Anacortes, Washington.

Johnson, Robert S. Oral History. American Air Power Heritage Museum, Midland, Texas, 1977.

Kunz, William J. Unpublished Memoir. Rockford, Illinois, 1996.

LaMagna, Sam. *Silent Victory: Fox Company, 169th Regi-*

mental Combat Team, 43d Infantry Division. Unpublished Manuscript. Ocala, Florida.

Leckie, Robert. *Strong Men Armed.* New York: Random House, 1962.

Lee, Ulysses. *The Employment of Negro Troops.* Washington, D.C.: Center of Military History, 1994.

Leinbaugh, Harold P., and John D. Campbell. *The Men of Company K: The Autobiography of a World War II Rifle Company.* New York: William Morrow and Company, 1985.

Lynd, J. Q. *Château de Fontenay: Episode tragique de la libération 1944.* Unpublished Memoir. Stillwater, Oklahoma.

———*Legacy of Valor* [Video Script]. South Hill, Virginia: 90th Division Association.

MacArthur, Douglas. *Reminiscences.* New York: McGraw-Hill Book Company, 1964.

MacDonald, Charles. *A Time for Trumpets.* New York: William Morrow and Company, 1985.

———*Company Commander.* New York: Bantam, 1987.

———*The Mighty Endeavor: American Armed Forces in the European Theater in World War II.* New York: Oxford University Press, 1969.

McClintock, D. H. Narrative. Washington, D.C.: U.S. Naval Historical Center, 1945.

McClure, John. Oral History. American Air Power Heritage Museum, Midland, Texas, 1991.

McCubbin, James. Unpublished Memoirs. Garberville, California.

McManus, John. *The Deadly Brotherhood.* Novato, California: Presidio Press, 1998.

Mack, William. Oral History. Annapolis, Maryland: United States Naval Institute.

Manchester, William. *American Caesar.* Boston: Little, Brown & Company, 1978.

Martin, Harry. Unpublished Memoir. Mt. Arlington, New Jersey

Merillat, Herbert C. *Guadalcanal Remembered.* New York: Dodd, Mead & Company, 1982.

Milkovics, Lewis. *The Devils Have Landed.* Longwood, Florida: Creative Printing and Publishing, 1993.

Miller, Thomas G. Jr. *The Cactus Air Force.* New York: Harper & Row, 1969.

Mills, James. Unpublished Memoir. Vandalia, Ohio.

Moore, Ellis O. *Notes on Leaving Okinawa.* Pelham, New York: Privately Published, 1988.

Morison, Samuel Eliot. *The Battle of the Atlantic.* Boston: Little, Brown & Company, 1984.

———*Coral Sea, Midway and Submarine Actions.* Boston: Little, Brown & Company, 1984.

———*The Struggle for Guadalcanal.* Boston: Little, Brown & Company, 1949.

———*The Rising Sun in the Pacific.* Boston: Little, Brown & Company, 1961.

Morton, Louis. *The Fall of the Philippines, U.S. Army in World War II.* Washington, D.C.: Center of Military History, U.S. Army, 1953.

Muehrcke, Robert, ed. *Orchids in the Mud.* Chicago: Privately Published, 1985.

Mueller, Arndt. *Hill 400: The Destiny and the Agony.* Monograph.

Murphy, Robert. *Diplomat among Warriors.* Garden City, New York: Doubleday & Company, Inc. 1964.

Murray, S. S. Oral History. Annapolis, Maryland: United States Naval Institute.

Old, Archie Jr. Oral History. Maxwell Field, Alabama: Historical Research Center, Air University, 1982.

Olson, John E. assisted by Frank O. Anders. *Anywhere, Anytime: The History of the 57th Infantry (PS).* Houston: John Olson, 1991.

———*O'Donnell: The Andersonville of the Pacific.* Houston: John Olson, 1985.

Patton, George. *War As I Knew It.* Boston: Houghton Mifflin, 1947.

Philos, C. D., and Ernie Hayhow. *1987 History of the 83d Infantry Division.* Hillsdale, Michigan: Ferguson Communications, 1986.

Potter, E. B. *Bull Halsey.* Annapolis, Maryland: United States Naval Institute, 1985.

Potts, Ramsay. Oral History. United States Air Force Historical Center, Maxwell Field, Alabama, 1960.

Prange, Gordon W. *Dec. 7 1941.* New York: McGraw-Hill Book Company, 1988.

Pyle, Ernie. *At Dawn We Slept.* New York: McGraw-Hill Book Company, 1981.

———*Here Is Your War.* New York: Henry Holt and Company, 1943.

———*Brave Men.* New York: Henry Holt and Company, 1944.

———*Last Chapter.* New York: Henry Holt and Company, 1946.

Rants, Hanford. *My Memories of World War II.* Unpublished Manuscript. Downey, California.

Rodman, Gage. Unpublished Memoir. Hurricane, Utah.

Rooney, Andy. *My War.* New York: Random House, 1996.

Rosson, William. Oral History. Carlisle, Pennsylvania: United States Army Military History Institute.

Ryan, Cornelius. *A Bridge Too Far.* New York: Simon & Schuster, 1974.

Salomon, Sidney. *2d Ranger Infantry Battalion.* Doylestown, Pennsylvania: Birchwood Books, 1991.

Samson, Jack. *Chennault.* New York: Doubleday & Company, Inc., 1987.

Schueler, Jon. *The Sound of Sleat.* Unpublished Manuscript.

Schultz, Duane. *The Maverick War*. New York: St. Martin's Press, 1987.

———*The Doolittle Raid.* New York: St. Martin's Press, 1988.

Schwarz, Otto. Unpublished Memoir.

Seibert, Donald A. Unpublished Memoir. Fort Belvoir, Virginia.

Shapiro, Alan. Unpublished Memoir. Ridgefield, Connecticut.

Sherrod, Robert. *Tarawa: The Story of a Battle*. New York: Duell, Sloan and Pearce, 1944.

Sledge, E. B. *With the Old Breed.* Novato, California: Presidio Press, 1981.

Smith, John F. *Hellcats Over the Philippine Deep.* Manhattan, Kansas: Sunflower Press, 1995.

Smith, Robert. Oral History. Maxwell Field, Alabama: United States Air Force Historical Center, 1983.

Spector, Ronald. *Eagle Against the Sun: The American War with Japan.* New York: Free Press, 1985.

Stroop, Paul. Oral History. Annapolis, Maryland: United States Naval Institute.

Svihra, Albert. Transcripts of letters to his family and Diary. West Point: U.S. Military Academy Library.

Teeples, Robert. *Jackson County Veterans,* Vol. II. Black River Falls, Wisconsin, 1986.

Thach, John (Jimmy). Oral History. Annapolis, Maryland: United States Naval Institute.

Tregaskis, Richard. *Guadalcanal Diary.* New York: Random House, 1943.

Ullom, Madeline. Memoir. Washington, D.C.: U.S. Army Center for Military History.

Van der Vat, Dan. *The Pacific Campaign.* New York: Simon & Schuster, 1991.

Walker, Anthony, ed., *Memorial to the Men of C/P Company, 4th Marine Raider Battalion.* Middletown, Rhode Island, 1994.

Ward, Norvell. Oral History. Annapolis, Maryland: United States Naval Institute.

White, W. L. *They Knew They Were Expendable.* New York: Harcourt Brace and Company, 1942.

Index